Hearing Vocation Differently

Hearing Vocation Differently

Meaning, Purpose, and Identity in the Multi-Faith Academy

Edited by

DAVID S. CUNNINGHAM

OXFORD
UNIVERSITY PRESS

OXFORD
UNIVERSITY PRESS

Oxford University Press is a department of the University of Oxford. It furthers the University's objective of excellence in research, scholarship, and education by publishing worldwide. Oxford is a registered trade mark of Oxford University Press in the UK and certain other countries.

Published in the United States of America by Oxford University Press
198 Madison Avenue, New York, NY 10016, United States of America.

Library of Congress Cataloging-in-Publication Data
Names: Cunningham, David S., 1961– author.
Title: Hearing vocation differently : meaning, purpose,
and identity in the multi-faith academy / edited by David S. Cunningham.
Description: New York, NY, United States of America : Oxford University Press, [2018] |
Includes bibliographical references and index. Identifiers:
LCCN 2018016556 (print) | LCCN 2018038610 (ebook) |
ISBN 9780190888688 (updf) | ISBN 9780190888695 (epub) |
ISBN 9780190888701 (online content) | ISBN 9780190888671 (cloth)
Subjects: LCSH: Vocation. Classification: LCC BL629 (ebook) |
LCC BL629 .C86 2018 (print) | DDC 204/.4—dc23
LC record available at https://lccn.loc.gov/2018016556

3 5 7 9 8 6 4 2

Printed by Sheridan Books, Inc., United States of America

Dedicated, with gratitude, to

Shirley J. Roels

Founding director of the
Network for Vocation in Undergraduate Education

Longstanding supporter of its Scholarly Resources Project

Tireless advocate for new voices in the conversation

Force of nature

Contents

Foreword

OVER THE PAST half century, higher education has witnessed a number of remarkable transformations. The number of students enrolled in college has increased dramatically, as has the diversity of that group: what was once primarily a destination for upper- and upper-middle-class white males has gradually opened its doors to people of all genders, races, and socioeconomic backgrounds. Equally significant has been the increasing religious diversity of higher education. Many church-related colleges have seen declines in the number of students who identify with the institution's founding denomination; more US students are identifying with a world religion other than Christianity; and an increasingly large percentage of college-age students identify themselves as "seekers," as "spiritual but not religious," or as not identifying with any faith tradition whatsoever.

These changes are occurring at a time when undergraduate students are experiencing two sets of pressures that often seem in tension with one another. On the one hand, they are regularly reminded, through a wide variety of cultural channels, that their college experience should prepare them for gainful entry into the labor market. They choose majors based on employability, sign up for internships, struggle to hone their résumés, and fret about their job prospects. On the other hand—and perhaps partly because of the decline in their institutions' religious affiliations—they are deeply interested in questions about the meaning of life, the purpose of their existence, and the contours of their own identity.

These developments have many colleges and universities in a quandary. Because students are less clearly tied to traditional religious communities, they (and their parents) often assume that their undergraduate experience will fill the gap: that college will provide for the moral, emotional, and even spiritual development that were once the mainstay of traditional religion. But not all colleges and universities are well prepared to offer this kind of guidance. Public universities are constrained by residual concerns about separation of church and state, while the assumptions about intellectual pursuits at some private and public universities tend to cast affective and spiritual matters in a negative light.

Thus, it is perhaps not surprising that smaller private liberal arts colleges and universities are increasingly attractive to today's prospective college students. Here, a young person can expect to be asked to face some of those "big questions" of meaning, purpose, and identity that their peers at other kinds of institutions may be able to avoid. Students will still be prepared for the job market, but not in a way that ignores their other concerns. They will be allowed, or more likely encouraged, to consider questions of faith and doubt, of virtue and vice.

Perhaps this is why some of these same institutions have found the language of *vocation* and *calling* to offer an effective approach to these issues. Students who participate in programs of vocational reflection and discernment remain aware of the practical demands of their futures; in fact, many people continue to associate the language of vocation with paid employment, so vocational discernment often begins with "figuring out what I'll be when I grow up." Increasingly, students view vocation to include how they will live with meaning and purpose, as well as what they will do for a living. Reflection on one's vocation leads to questions about what it means to live a good, productive, and fulfilling human life.

Two decades ago, Indianapolis-based Lilly Endowment Inc. through its Programs for the Theological Exploration of Vocation (PTEV) recognized, in a way that now seems remarkably prescient, that the language of vocation and calling could help to integrate some of the diverse concerns described here—particularly within undergraduate education. This language has theological roots, so it can be particularly useful in the context of church-related institutions; but it has implications for anyone concerned about larger questions of meaning and purpose. It has quickly become part of the wider intellectual landscape, increasingly resonant in secular institutions as well. The word *vocation* can help educators build bridges across some of the divisions among students: differing religious beliefs and philosophical perspectives, contrary political commitments and conflicting allegiances, and even the (often radically) opposed methodologies and assumptions of various academic disciplines and applied fields.

This volume provides a concrete instance of this bridge-building. Thirteen scholars—working from widely varying religious traditions, philosophical perspectives, and academic fields—have entered into a fascinating conversation with one another, working within and around the long history of the language of vocation. Together, they demonstrate that, far from being the unique property of a particular religious tradition, this language opens a wide range of concerns in higher education. These include not only the large questions of meaning, purpose, and identity but also broad theoretical issues such as difference, pluralism, and attentiveness—as well as many practical matters: attending to student and faculty recruitment, addressing the levels of stress and anxiety among today's undergraduates, and developing ways of integrating curricular and co-curricular programming. When this book is placed alongside the two volumes that preceded it, something quite remarkable emerges: a group of 37 scholars have provided a solid academic foundation for the theory and practice of vocational reflection and discernment.

These books have been produced through the Scholarly Resources Project, an initiative of the Council of Independent Colleges' (CIC) Network for Vocation in Undergraduate Education (NetVUE). This is a nationwide consortium of more than 225 colleges and universities that, for the past decade, have been sharing ideas, resources, and effective practices for vocational exploration among students. The CIC administers NetVUE's diverse initiatives, including conferences, seminars, a wide range of grant programs, and other services, with the continuing generous support of the Lilly Endowment. NetVUE's founding director, Shirley Roels, has provided leadership throughout the work of this project, working closely with David Cunningham, professor of religion at Hope College, who served as the editor of all three books in this series. In September 2017, Dr. Roels retired as director of NetVUE. A smooth leadership transition was assured by the fact that she was succeeded in this role by Professor Cunningham, who completed the editorial work on this volume as he began his duties as director of NetVUE. I want to express my appreciation to these two leaders, as well as to NetVUE program coordinator Lynne Spoelhof and to Harold V. Hartley III, CIC senior vice president, who provides oversight for the entire NetVUE initiative.

I am especially grateful to Lilly Endowment Inc. for its generous funding, and particularly to Christopher L. Coble, vice president for religion at Lilly, for his support and counsel. All of us who have witnessed the success of programs for vocational reflection and discernment owe a special debt of gratitude to Craig Dykstra, former vice president for religion at Lilly, who together with Dr. Coble provided the vision for the PTEV program and for CIC's subsequent establishment of NetVUE and related endeavors. Aided by program officers Jessicah Duckworth and Chanon Ross, the Endowment continues to strengthen its vocational initiatives in a variety of venues.

In order for American higher education to address the challenges of a culture that is increasingly diverse in almost every respect (including in matters of religious belief and worldview), a wider range of practices, perspectives, and resources is needed. The reflections and proposals contained in this volume represent a genuine contribution to that effort. This book will be of great value to administrators, faculty members, and staff who are engaged in helping students reflect on their callings in the contemporary multi-faith academy.

Richard H. Ekman
President
Council of Independent Colleges

Preface

THIS BOOK WAS developed and produced under the aegis of the Scholarly Resources Project of the Network for Vocation in Undergraduate Education (NetVUE). It follows two previous volumes, also published by Oxford: *At This Time and In This Place: Vocation and Higher Education* (2016), and *Vocation across the Academy: A New Vocabulary for Higher Education* (2017). Taken as a set, these three books provide an initial foray into the scholarship of *vocation* and *calling* as an important element of higher education, both in theory and in practice. When the project began, its stated goal was to deepen and enrich the work of vocational reflection and discernment among undergraduate students, and to do so by engaging these students' teachers, mentors, advisers, and other professionals in guiding and encouraging undergraduates in this important enterprise. We believe that the project has accomplished this goal, and indeed, has exceeded our expectations in this regard.

The first two books aimed to set out a broad, general account of vocation and calling; to consider the pedagogical work necessary to make it a part of the undergraduate experience (and indeed, to describe vocation as itself a kind of pedagogy); and to examine how vocational reflection and discernment relate to the work of the diverse range of academic disciplines and applied fields. This third volume charts a course that might be considered both more specific and more general: it focuses quite narrowly on the question of whether the language of vocation is tenable in the increasingly multi-faith context of higher education, and—by answering this question with an (at least provisional) affirmative—it broadens the scope of this language as potentially useful for *all* undergraduate students. Even though vocation has long been recognized as stretching beyond the bounds of its original theological (and indeed, specifically Christian) context, this language is still avoided by some faculty and administrators, who assume it to be insufficiently secular for the academic context. To whatever extent this assumption still holds sway in some circles, the arguments set forth in this book will make it increasingly difficult to maintain. Vocation and calling can no longer be seen as narrowly sectarian concerns.

Of course, this language does have Christian roots, and it continues to be used in very specifically theological ways, in those contexts where such usage is appropriate. Those colleges and universities that emphasize their mission as Christian institutions, as well as Christian faculty and students in secular settings, can continue to draw on the particularities of vocation's theological history, as well as its biblical and doctrinal resonances. But other faith traditions have found vocation to be useful as well; in addition, agnostic and atheistic thinkers have discovered in it a useful conversation partner. We are increasingly aware that a person of any faith, as well as one whose life is guided by a strictly secular philosophical perspective, can still have a calling. Moreover, as the essays in this volume make clear, vocation and calling are closely related to a number of other matters that are of great concern to undergraduate students, their parents, and their teachers: matters such as the meaning of life, one's larger purpose in the world, and the process of coming to terms with one's own identity. And in turn, this terminology billows out into other circles of language: allegiance, attention, difference, fluidity, multiplicity, pluralism, responsibility, and receptivity—as well as renunciation and commitment, uncertainty and assurance, frustration and anger, and hope and love. These are matters that concern us all, regardless of our religious or philosophical perspectives and worldviews; and they lie close to the heart of any form of undergraduate education that is truly worthy of the name.

The authors whose work appears in the following pages spent a year thinking about these matters: reading, talking, and writing about them—and wrestling with them. They did so with an extraordinary degree of passion and commitment, recognizing the importance of these concerns and aware that their own traditions and perspectives had a great deal of wisdom to contribute to our understanding of such matters. They plumbed the depth of those perspectives and considered how they interacted with other views, some of which were very different from their own. They allowed their views to be examined, prodded, questioned, and challenged by one another. Yet in spite of their wide-ranging diversity on every issue under the sun (and a few issues beyond the sun), they produced a volume with a clear and coherent thesis: that the language of vocation and calling addresses some of the most critical concerns in higher education today. The authors' dedication to this work is rooted in their own vocations; these are many and varied (and rarely linear or obvious; for more on this, be sure to read the "Vocations of the Contributors" section that follows). But they all share at least one calling, and that is to be teachers and learners: of (and from) their students, of (and from) other scholars in their respective fields, and of (and from) one another.

Hence, even more than was the case for the two volumes that preceded it, this is truly a coauthored work. Every chapter bears the marks of the book's other contributors, as will be clear from the many common bibliographical citations, the numerous cross-references, and the responses that follow each chapter. These authors were also in conversation, directly or indirectly, with many of the contributors to the two previous volumes of this project; thus, the three books together form a deeply interwoven conversation. Indeed, this conversation is ongoing, and will continue—supported by a range of NetVUE initiatives: a large biennial conference, smaller regional and topical gatherings, faculty seminars, and an active online community, including a blog (http://www.vocationmatters.org), where many of the authors from all three volumes have further developed and extended their essays, or branched into completely new areas of conversation.

On behalf of the authors, I want to convey our thanks to those who helped make this project possible. First, we are grateful to Lilly Endowment Inc., and particularly to Craig Dykstra, Chris Coble, and Jessicah Duckworth, who have underwritten these conversations (not only financially, but with a great deal of moral, spiritual, and intellectual support as well). Second, we appreciate the work of the Council of Independent Colleges, which has taken up the challenge of bringing the language of vocation into higher education—and particularly to Rich Ekman and Hal Hartley, who have given close attention to vocation-related projects. Finally, we offer thanks to Shelly Arnold, office manager for the CrossRoads Project at Hope College, who served as the administrative assistant for the project. As Shelly transitioned to other duties at the college, support for completing this third final volume was provided by the NetVUE program coordinator, Lynne Spoelhof.

And it is to Lynne that I, as the volume's editor, owe my own particular words of gratitude. During the past year, when the director of NetVUE announced her retirement and I was granted the enormous privilege of succeeding her, Lynne provided an anchor of continuity. The chapters of this book were largely written when the transition occurred, but my editorial responsibilities were far from complete; moreover, I was trying to take on a job that—as we were all fairly convinced—only Shirley Roels could do. I would never have been able to carry out this work had it not been for a program coordinator who organized my life, triaged my commitments, explained to me how everything works, and—whenever too many people were "embellishin' my elegance and eloquence"—expertly knocked me right off my pedestal. Thank you, Lynne: best of guides and best of graces.

My family has always been unfailingly supportive of my work, even when it has taken me away from them more than I would have liked. To my loving wife, Marlies; to my fabulous children, Nick and Lee; and to my dear parents, Don and Patsy Cunningham, I can only say "thanks, and thanks, and ever thanks." Last summer, my parents were able to celebrate their seventieth wedding anniversary; a few months later, just as this book was being sent off to the publisher, my mom passed away. She was a gifted teacher who loved art, literature, and life; I am deeply grateful for the sparks of joy that she lit in me. With apologies to Billy Collins, I'd like to think of this book as one more lanyard for her.

Thanks also to my colleagues at Hope College, who helped make space for my work on the NetVUE Scholarly Resources Project from the very start, and who have been gracious and supportive in my transition to directing NetVUE. Special thanks to former and current presidents John Knapp and Dennis Voskuill for their willingness to "lend" me to this work for a season. Finally, thanks to everyone at Oxford University Press, particularly to Cynthia Read (who believed in this project from day one), and to her assistant Drew Anderla and the team of copy editors, production assistants, and designers: you have produced three truly beautiful books.

This volume is dedicated to Shirley Roels, the founding director of the Network for Vocation in Undergraduate Education. Under her leadership, NetVUE has grown beyond all expectations; its programs and resources are helping to underwrite the work of vocational exploration and discernment at over 225 colleges and universities across the country. Shirley always took a personal interest in the development of these books, regularly attending the gatherings of scholars and providing additional resources whenever they were needed. Her energetic attention to detail kept the work moving ahead, while her trust in the process allowed the authors (and the editor) the freedom to do their best work. On the occasion of her retirement, all of us at NetVUE and CIC want to express our gratitude for her work—and to wish her Godspeed.

David S. Cunningham
Professor of Religion, Hope College
Director of NetVUE, Council of Independent Colleges

Vocations of the Contributors

Florence D. Amamoto wanted to teach since she was in the first grade, but the insecurities of a female Asian-American first-generation college student led to a somewhat circuitous path. Being in college during the Vietnam War—and during the rise of the Black Power and women's movements—shaped how she teaches American literature and how she thinks about the purposes of higher education. The four years she spent helping with biological research (and birdwatching) widened her world, as she prepared to head off to graduate school. Helping a professor with a survey of the educational use of the Southern California deserts reminded her that there are many things one can do with an English major! She feels lucky to have spent her career at an institution that has supported her interest in vocation, diversity, higher education, and religion. On the cusp of retirement, she knows she will miss the students but is looking forward to doing more reading, traveling, English country dancing . . . and further vocational exploration.

When **Jacqueline A. Bussie** was little and people asked her what she wanted to be when she grew up, she always answered "authoress." The thought of becoming a princess made her gag, while becoming an author(ess) gave her goosebumps. As a first-generation college graduate and the first woman in her family to go to college, Jacqueline never dreamed of becoming a professor, let alone a theologian or director of an interfaith center; but, blessedly, she's discovered that those vocations give her goosebumps too. Today, Jacqueline is the award-winning author of three books: *The Laugher of the Oppressed* (2007), *Outlaw Christian: Finding Authentic Faith by Breaking the* "Rules" (2016), and *Love Without Limits: Jesus' Radical Vision for Love with No Exceptions* (2018). As professor of religion, co-chair of interfaith studies, and director of the Forum on Faith and Life at Concordia College–Moorhead, she is amazed and grateful that every day she actually gets paid to do what she loves most: (1) interact with incredible students, (2) write, and (3) try to make the world a more compassionate place.

Jeffrey Carlson went to college right out of high school and bombed out. A commuter with a sick father at home, he would divide his time between helping at home and staying out too late after working at a restaurant. He often arrived late for his first morning class, took a nap in the car, and then, later that afternoon, was awoken, chastised, and drummed out of his vehicle by his best friend. When he quit that university after one term, he went from office to office, collecting signatures; he remembers that no one asked him why he was withdrawing. He tried again the next fall at another school, where things went better. Later, when he was a faculty member at that second school (DePaul University), he found himself deeply involved in the reinvention of the general education program. Soon enough, he was hooked on the "why at all" questions of higher education, later becoming a department chair and then associate dean at DePaul, and then a dean and interim provost at Dominican University. He now lives by twin mantras: "Ask why" and "Get out of the car."

Growing up in a small city on the plains, **David S. Cunningham**'s idea of "interreligious encounter" was having some friends who were Lutherans and others who were Methodists; his most radical act was dating a Catholic in high school. Things changed at Northwestern University, where a few students wore turbans, some fellow dorm residents had no pictures in their rooms, and, on one day in October, his workaholic debate partner suddenly did no work at all. David was fortunate to have professors (and an envelope-pushing university chaplain) who helped him think of his own faith in non-exclusivist terms; still, his eventual academic specialization (in Christian theology and ethics, at Cambridge and then at Duke) meant that he learned less about other traditions than he would have liked. Fortunately, the last five years have provided him with many interfaith encounters, particularly through his friendships with the authors of this volume. His own ongoing process of vocational discernment led him to Hope College and to the directorship of NetVUE, where he is learning to navigate the most challenging interfaith endeavor of all: being taught how to do his job by the NetVUE program coordinator (a Calvinist!).

Rahuldeep Gill was still a minor when he was dropped off—from a sedan and a minivan—at the University of Rochester by his mom, dad, two sisters, and grandfather. They left him to pursue his pre-med track as expected, but medical school was no longer on the agenda when he left five years later (hey, it takes some of us longer, okay? and I earned an extra certificate!). Instead, he chose to pursue a prescription-free doctorate on the Santa Barbara coast. He was born in Chandigarh (Punjab, India) and raised in Cambridge and Billerica (Massachusetts). He now plays rec league basketball (badly) in the Western San Fernando Valley of Los Angeles (California), where he teaches at California

Lutheran University and lives with his family (including a new puppy named Z-Bo that his wife let him adopt).

Katherine (Trina) Janiec Jones was 11 years old when she started reading two books at about the same time. She had often heard people say that she should read the Bible, so she sat down on the sofa and started on page one, but soon started skipping around. She did find the Psalms to be interesting, so she made an appointment with an Episcopal priest to ask some questions. She was miffed when she received a dismissive verbal pat on the head, rather than the deep exploration of hermeneutics that she wanted (though at the time, she didn't really know what the word meant). The second book was Pearl Buck's *Mandala*. She hasn't read this book in over 30 years and doesn't remember the plot, but she does remember it as the beginning of her lifelong fascination with India. After Davidson College (more confusing and interesting books) and the University of Chicago Divinity School (where she finally learned about hermeneutics), she now helps students at Wofford College to realize that it's okay not to understand texts at first glance. Her current plans involve re-reading *Mandala* to see what her adult self thinks of it.

Rachel S. Mikva was raised with the benign illusion that she could be anything she wanted when she grew up. Although born with many privileges and blessed with loving, supportive parents, it wasn't quite true: alas, becoming a ballerina wasn't in the cards. At age seven, she briefly entertained becoming a nun (after watching a film with a wonderful vestal heroine), until she learned all that was involved. In junior high, an English teacher thought she might become the first female president, but after the 2016 election, she was glad she didn't try that. Rachel was a designer and production manager in the theater before becoming a rabbi—a progression that makes more sense than one might think; theater and ritual both have the capacity to transform our perspective through the power of sacred drama. Eventually, believing that a rabbi is above all a teacher, and remembering that the people who made the biggest impact in her life (outside of family) were her teachers, she became a professor. She currently teaches at Chicago Theological Seminary, where she serves as the Rabbi Herman Schaalman Chair in Jewish Studies and Senior Faculty Fellow at the InterReligious Institute. Not a ballerina, but it keeps her on her toes.

Younus Y. Mirza started college thinking he was going to be a lawyer and make a lot of money. He envisioned a future of tailored suits and power lunches, rather than nights of endless grading. However, the next year 9/11 occurred—and suddenly he was intensely aware of American misconceptions of Islam and of the disconnect between the United States and the Muslim world. He embarked on a course of study in Arabic, international relations, and the Middle East; he also lived in the tiny Gulf State of Qatar for two years, studying and teaching Arabic. But he got homesick and returned to complete his PhD in Arabic and Islamic studies at Georgetown. He then traveled to the deep south of Mississippi for a postdoctoral fellowship at Millsaps College, where he learned that Muslims were not the only ones who cared about scripture. He soon developed a strong interest in the relationship between the Bible and the Qur'an and their common stories and figures. The following year Younus moved to his current position at Allegheny College, where he teaches college students who are searching for their callings and trying to better understand the world that we share.

Many meet **Anantanand Rambachan** for the first time in his role as a medical examiner—visiting crime scenes, meticulously examining evidence, and engaging in intense discussions with his team of investigators. He is admired for his ability to remove a shoe and put on a wading boot while standing on one foot. He teaches his associates never to see corpses, "but complete human beings that don't exist any longer in this particular time and place." Or is this perhaps all an allegory for the life of a scholar of religion? After all, he studies people who have passed on, collects evidence meticulously, reads between the lines, formulates reasonable conclusions, and argues about these with his academic gang. (He also has occasionally read manuscripts in advanced stages of decay.) His training as a scholarly examiner took him to a Hindu monastic ashram in India, the University of Leeds, and, since 1985, St. Olaf College. Vocation is a new subject for his reflection but, like every challenging case, he sees it as a wonderful opportunity to think anew and to learn in deep dialogue, this time with the NetVUE team. He never had so many tasty (and lengthy) meals as a medical examiner!

Tracy Wenger Sadd grew up in Lancaster County, Pennsylvania, where her primary memories are of a Christ-centered, hospitable, service-oriented community, whose ministers and teachers always wanted her to button her coat in winter and stop asking so many questions. Believing that everyone has many possible callings in both work and life, Tracy has traveled to more than 40 countries, has wondered what life would be like if she had been born in another place and time, and hopes to live long enough to see time travel become a reality (yes, she likes science fiction). She knows she could have been happy pursuing a PhD in psychology, being a lawyer, running a large-scale ranch, or consulting in the nonprofit sector. Her latent vocational dream is to live in a house in Maine overlooking the ocean and to write books; yet everyone who knows her would say that, within ten minutes, she would be out and about, looking for a new adventure. She said she would never return to Lancaster County; and yet, here she is—teaching and doing ministry, at Elizabethtown College.

Blessed with a short attention span, **Matthew R. Sayers** has been a serial hobbyist as long as he can remember (baking, writing, carpentry, quilting, woodworking, camping, and painting, among other distractions). In college, he mastered the art of moving on, meandering from engineering to computer science to philosophy to religious studies to Asian studies. His capacity for being distracted by new shiny objects was channeled into an interdisciplinary approach to various . . . ooh, sociology! . . . Oh yes, theodicy *is* an interesting problem. . . . Oh look, Sanskrit! After 32 years in school, from pre-school through two community colleges and three state universities (each at least twice as large as the previous one), he found a position as a religion professor at Lebanon Valley College; only then did he grow up and figure out what he wanted to be (besides entertained). He brought with him the privilege to ignore the world outside the scope of his own interests; but ironically, at this small, isolated institution, he learned to look beyond a wealth of entertaining distractions. He now works to channel his creative urges and eclectic interests toward helping students see the world beyond their own assumptions and perspectives. He is trying to be a teacher.

As the oldest son and middle child of a psychiatrist, and grandson of a psychologist, **Noah J. Silverman** missed his calling to go into mental health professionally, but has amply contributed to the profession as a patient. Growing up near the campus of the University of Chicago, where both his parents worked, he further unconsciously rebelled against the life choices of his parents by becoming a thespian; his portrayal of Barnaby in his high school's production of *The Matchmaker* is still quoted by his mother to this day. Sensing too much parental acceptance, upon graduation he traveled to Israel/Palestine, where he serendipitously discovered what would become his long-lasting vocation in interfaith engagement (for a far more detailed account of this episode, see Noah's chapter in this volume). Ultimately resigning himself to the wisdom of his progenitors, both immediate and ancestral, he embraced his academic and Jewish identities and pursued undergraduate and graduate degrees in religious studies. Along the way, he encountered and joined Interfaith Youth Core (IFYC), where he has had the blessing of working the bulk of his professional career, most recently as the senior director of learning and partnerships. His parents have (mostly) forgiven him for his erstwhile transgressions, while he is slowly learning to do the same for his own son.

Homayra Ziad is a writer, dreamer, scholar-activist, and mother. She was raised within Islamic spiritual traditions, with a love of God grounded in music and verse. Her vocation lay on the crossroads of spirituality and poetry, but she tried for years to ignore it. Instead, she applied herself with great stubbornness (and a shocking lack of interest) to a number of other "practical" disciplines, including economics and international relations. At some point in her mid-20s, when the writing was clearly on the wall, she found the courage to study religion full time. As a God-seeker and activist, she hoped to "find herself" in graduate school; but while her doctorate from Yale was fodder for the intellect, it was not as productive for her creative soul. Still, she taught Islamic studies at a liberal arts college for six years. Looking back, she was indeed "finding herself" at every step; as her spiritual journey unfolded, she was drawn to the affective work of building interreligious communities. Homayra has also led the integration of the study of Islam and engagement with Muslim communities at one of the oldest freestanding interfaith organizations in the country. More recently, as a mother raising Muslim children, she has rediscovered her creative soul. She is returning to the crossroads of spirituality and poetry that once nourished her, creating resources for artful living that spring from Islamic traditions.

Introduction

Hearing and Being Heard

RETHINKING VOCATION IN THE MULTI-FAITH ACADEMY

David S. Cunningham

MANY COLLEGES AND universities have been making use of the language of *vocation* and *calling* as a way of helping students think about larger issues of meaning and purpose, about the shape of their worldviews, and about the future direction of their lives. Most of the contributors to this volume have been deeply involved in programs that focus on vocational reflection and discernment, and are convinced of the benefits of this work. The 13 authors are committed to a wide variety of religious faiths and philosophical perspectives; yet in the midst of this diversity, they all agree that their own institutions and organizations—as well as others that have employed the language of vocation (or hope to do so)—should be engaged in the work of *hearing vocation differently*. If the concepts of vocation and calling are to have a genuine place in higher education in the modern era, they will need to be rethought and reheard, and perhaps even rewritten, in ways that make them accessible and amenable across a wide range of perspectives.

This brief introduction seeks to explain why we are making this claim. It begins with a description of the significant ways that higher education has expanded and become more diverse over the past century, with particular attention to its (more recent) growth in religious diversity. A second section introduces the language of *vocation* and *calling*, explaining why it has attained something of a foothold in higher education over the past two decades. A third section turns to the lurking tension between the first two sections: the fact that a concept with historically Christian roots has become prominent in an era in which the academy is becoming more deeply marked by its multi-faith character. This tension requires us to undertake the project that this book describes. A final section outlines the chapters of the book; it comprises four parts, in which we employ four different perspectives to explore the meaning, significance, and implications of this project.

The expansion and diversification of higher education

Once upon a time—not all that long ago, really—only a small segment of the US population had access to, or interest in, higher education. "Going to college" marked a person as genuinely out of the ordinary; in the typical secondary school setting, the majority of young people had already determined the future course of their lives (or had it determined for them). The contours of those lives would depend mostly on family circumstances, longstanding assumptions and expectations, and the availability of jobs and other roles in the towns or neighborhoods where they were born and raised. The small minority of high school graduates who went to college were those from whom big things were expected; they would become the doctors, lawyers, bankers, and other professionals who, if their hometowns were lucky, would return and provide professional and civic leadership into the future. Nor were the goals of higher education limited to career preparation; the young man who went off to college (and it remained a majority-male path until quite recently) was expected to come back as a more mature, well-rounded, responsible person. College was a relatively uncommon path, chosen by (or expected of) a small percentage of young people, while everyone else stayed at home and took up various trades or domestic roles.

After the end of World War II, a number of factors dramatically increased the percentage of high school graduates who went to college. More people were able to afford college, as a result of the GI bill and significant increases in real wages. More professions began to expect at least some college education; primary and secondary teaching, for example, which had until that point usually been open to any high school graduate, now demanded a certain number of college credit hours (and that number increased over time until, in most states, a bachelor's degree was a minimum requirement). A few additional professions opened to women, and more women began attending college (though this shift was quite slow and gradual). At the beginning of the 1950s, about 15 percent of US citizens went to college; by the end of the decade, the figure was 24 percent, and at the end of the next decade, 35 percent.[1] Today, well over half of high school graduates go to college, and the majority of those graduate: the number of 23-year-olds who hold bachelor's degrees rose from around 5 percent just before World War II to upward of 30 percent in the 1990s.[2] Of course, even today, the composition of the college-bound population remains out of phase with the demographics of the population at large; I will return to this point shortly.

With this considerable expansion of undergraduate education have come corresponding changes in expectations about what it means to "head off to college." In the immediate postwar era, undergraduate education continued to be seen as a means of creating a new generation of adults who were not only well educated but also well-rounded and responsible—increasing the number of professionals and potential community leaders, and providing a deeper and broader basis for civic life in a democracy. College students themselves reflected this optimism, with large majorities of undergraduates indicating that "finding a philosophy of life" (and similarly worded expectations) formed an essential part of the college experience. But as colleges continued to grow and as various economic and political forces created more complex job markets, these expectations shifted. Today, most students list—as their primary reason for going to college—the desire to find better or higher-paying employment.[3] This goal ranks still higher among parents of college students.

And yet, the old expectations remain. The goal of "finding a philosophy of life" still appears among the hopes that young people express about their own college experience, and graduates are still expected (by parents, employers, and society in general) to be more well-rounded, mature individuals. In fact, given that an ever-increasing percentage of high school graduates go on to college, this latter expectation has become stronger and more general; college is now the place where kids are expected to become adults.[4] These expectations are even more firmly in place for students who attend private institutions, as well as their parents. Private

---

1. Thomas D. Snyder, ed., *120 Years of American Education: A Statistical Portrait* (Washington, DC: National Center for Education Statistics, 1993), https://nces.ed.gov/pubs93/93442.pdf (accessed July 12, 2017).

2. Snyder, ed., *120 Years*.

3. The percentage of students listing this as a concern reached an all-time high of 87.9 percent in 2012. It has since declined, but only slightly (to 84.8 percent). See Kevin Eagan et al., *The American Freshman: National Norms* (Los Angeles: Higher Education Research Institute, UCLA, 2016), 7–8.

4. A great deal of literature has developed on this topic, reaching back at least to the work of Jeffrey Jensen Arnett, *Emerging Adulthood: The Winding Road from the Late Teens Through the Twenties* (New York: Oxford University Press, 2004).

liberal arts colleges and research universities are widely seen as having the potential not only to improve one's job prospects, but also to shape thoughtful, broadly educated, civic-minded leaders for the future. Even among those who express significant doubts about whether college achieves its aims, graduating from college remains an important goal—for themselves and for their children.[5]

Of course, the massive expansion of higher education over the past 75 years means that college has become a very different place. When college-bound populations were smaller, the institutions they attended were much more homogenous; the typical student was white, male, upper class (or at least upper-middle class), and Christian (most likely an adherent of a Protestant denomination). With the founding of more Roman Catholic institutions, this last category shifted considerably; and although at first this tended to segregate Christians into two groups, recent trends have brought Protestant and Catholic undergraduates into regular contact with one another. As college became more accessible for women, racial minorities, and students from a wider variety of family income brackets, college students have become far more likely to encounter people different from themselves: people whose race, gender, and social class (and, increasingly, sexual orientation and gender identity) differ from one's own. Undergraduates also become aware that these differences often lead people to see the world in ways that may be hard for others to grasp. If young people have not already encountered difference in their lives, they will certainly do so in college.

Yet one aspect of diversity and difference remains more complicated than the rest: the role of religion. Many US colleges and universities were founded with specifically Christian charters, and many of the oldest among them originally understood their primary mission to provide for an educated clergy. In the late nineteenth century, as has been well documented, some of these institutions began to move in a more secular direction; but at the same time, many other schools were founded with an even more specifically Christian (and often denominational) focus. As a result, through a good part of the twentieth century, higher education tended to bifurcate into two distinct approaches. The first group, which included many larger private universities and most public ones, expected students' religious and spiritual needs to be met through co-curricular programming, while the academic program took a more sociological or anthropological approach to the study of religion. The second group, which included a smaller (but very energetic) cadre of liberal arts colleges and denominational universities, sought to address theological questions within the curriculum, as well as through

5. Even at its lowest ebb (in 2012), this goal was still embraced as "very important" by more than two-thirds of incoming college students; in 2016, the figure had risen to 75.6 percent of incoming students. Eagan et al., *American Freshman*, 8.

campus activities and student development programs. The former group tended to have more religiously diverse populations, but tended to draw a distinction between the academic study of religion and the extracurricular spaces for nurturing students' spiritual lives; the latter group sought to integrate these matters into the curriculum, but tended to have much more religiously homogenous populations.[6]

Because of the predominance of Christianity as the religious perspective of so many students and faculty members during this era, colleges and universities tended to adopt a great many Christian perspectives and assumptions as part of their culture—regardless of the degree to which the institution was committed to a specifically Christian mission. Even those institutions that severed ties with their founding denominations tended to remain residually Christian. As a result, Christians who work at and attend these institutions participate, to a greater or lesser degree, in a kind of *Christian privilege*. This term parallels the term *white privilege*, popularized by an article with that title by Peggy McIntosh.[7] Her point was that, without directly intending it or sometimes even being aware of it, those in the majority culture are automatically granted a degree of privilege. In the case of white privilege, for example, McIntosh points out that in white-majority cultures, a white person's actions are rarely attributed to his or her race. If one is late to a meeting or decides not to participate in some social activity, few people will say, "Oh, that's because she's white." People of other races do experience such judgments, as unfair as they might be. They are not accorded the privilege of allowing their race to remain "invisible."

Christians at majority-Christian institutions experience a similar kind of privilege. The academic calendar often makes way for Christian holidays and weekly worship services, whereas people of other faiths must often decide whether to attend their religious services or to attend class. The symbols and trappings of Christianity may be scattered around campus such that they are seen by everyone, every day; but such attention is rarely paid to religious symbols of minority faiths. Of course, at a college or university that understands itself as explicitly and avowedly Christian, this makes sense. But these same markers of privilege are often still present, even at institutions that have severed all formal ties to the Christian faith

---

6. Space prevented us from addressing, in this volume, the complexities of how this entire process has been affected by the complexities of immigration into the United States, and the role of immigration policy in shaping it. This is clearly an area where further research and writing are needed.

7. Peggy McIntosh, "White Privilege: Unpacking the Invisible Knapsack," *Peace and Freedom Magazine* 49, no. 4 (July/August 1989): 10–12. A number of authors have considered how "Christian privilege" might operate in parallel ways; see, for example, Caryn D. Riswold, "Teaching the College Nones: Christian Privilege and the Religion Professor," *Teaching Theology and Religion* 18, no. 2 (April 2015): 133–48.

or to a specific denomination. And even Christian institutions are sometimes unaware of how thoroughly the symbols, practices, and assumptions of their faith confront those of other traditions on a daily basis.

At the same time, an increasing number of students are coming to college without having been formed in a single religious tradition. Many describe themselves as belonging to a variety of faith traditions, while others may identify with a particular tradition but reject any alignment with its institutions. A growing percentage of students do not identify with any religious tradition. Much attention has lately been paid to this phenomenon, often referred to as "the rise of the nones"—a reference to the fact that, in answering a typical survey question on religious affiliation, these students would check the box marked "none." In this book, however, we have avoided using this terminology; we believe that it often amalgamates, in unhelpful ways, several distinct groups. Indeed, it highlights the ongoing failure of language to determine, with any degree of clarity, exactly what constitutes a "religion."[8] For example, some students might strongly identify with a perspective that is not usually classified as a religion (such as atheism or secular humanism); others might not identify with any worldview *in particular* but still describe themselves as "seekers" or "spiritual but not religious." Hence, we have tended to avoid trying to determine or to specify whether a particular worldview is "religious" or otherwise. We have instead sought to cast the net widely; many authors use the term *lifestance*,[9] while others speak of "worldviews" or "religious beliefs and philosophical perspectives." In all these cases, we are trying to use terminology that can make space for viewpoints that are not usually, or not always, classified as *religious*.

In some ways, those students who check the box marked "none" have forced many institutions of higher education to think more carefully about how they define, deploy, and construct the entire concept of religious belief. Many "secular" institutions are coming to a more complete realization that, all over the world, worldviews and lifestances (whether described as "religious" or not) make a great deal of difference in all aspects of many people's lives. In departments of psychology, sociology, and political science—not to mention literature, history, and languages—scholars seem increasingly aware that these worldviews simply cannot be written off or ignored. On the other side, a great many institutions that

8. Many scholars note the difficulty of defining this term but continue to use it as though its meaning and reference were clear. For a helpful typology and analysis of these uses, see chapter 1 of William T. Cavanaugh, *The Myth of Religious Violence: Secular Ideology and the Roots of Modern Conflict* (New York: Oxford University Press, 2009).

9. For a definition and brief discussion of this term, see Rachel Mikva's comments at the beginning of chapter 1 in this volume.

were founded as denominational entities have witnessed significant increases in the diversity of their faculty and student body, such that it is now rare to find an institution where a significant majority of either group are adherents of the school's founding denomination. Regardless of what might have been intended or desired by an institution's founders, administrators, faculty, and other constituencies over the decades, a significant majority of US colleges and universities are becoming part of *the multi-faith academy*.

Beyond job training: meaning, purpose, vocation

Partly because of the increasing diversity of higher education, but for a number of other reasons as well, it has become more important than ever to question the (still very popular) assumption that the primary purpose of college is simply to prepare students to take on a particular job. This misconception is driven in part by economic analysis, political rhetoric, and governmental data collection, all of which seems determined to reduce the entire college experience to the first-year salary of its graduates. In spite of this effort, however, prospective students and parents continue to demonstrate a great deal of interest in practically all aspects of undergraduate life. Even though incoming undergraduates still rank future job prospects as their greatest concern, they also recognize that their emotional well-being, their social lives, and their overall assessment of these four years will be deeply affected by their choice of college or university. Many parents continue to hope that their children will emerge from college with an increased sense of responsibility, some notion of what makes for good character, and a degree of maturity that will allow them to enter into independent life as an adult. If such forms of personal development don't take place in college, then the experience will not have met expectations—regardless of the graduate's first-year salary.

Colleges and universities have therefore continued to struggle with the question of how to provide undergraduates with the kinds of "value added" elements that students and parents have come to expect. They have employed a wide range of approaches in an effort to redirect their students' attention away from a singular, instrumental focus on the job market—helping them see that concerns about employment and career can coexist with, and even be clarified by, close attention to larger questions about the meaning and purpose of life. Some colleges have assigned common readings that encourage all students to grapple with these larger questions;[10] others have developed broader and deeper advising

10. See, for example, Florence Amamoto's description of a capstone course in chapter 10 of this volume. See also the description of the core curriculum at Dominican University in Cynthia Wells, "Finding the Center as Things Fly Apart: Vocation and the Common Good,"

and mentoring programs, designed to lead students on a path of self-discovery.[11] Some have returned to the classics with Great Books programs, while others have required greater exposure to writers from a variety of racial, ethnic, and religious backgrounds. Many have encouraged students to think about their future happiness, not in the sense of a temporary feeling of elation, but closer to Aristotle's word *eudaimonia* in his claim that "all human beings seek happiness": something much deeper and longer-lasting, a fulfilled and fulfilling life. Still others have employed terms such as *flourishing* and *liberation* to describe the kind of formation that colleges and universities hope their students will experience during their undergraduate years.[12]

In the midst of all this language, a new word has arrived on the scene—or rather, a very old word, re-purposed for the present day. This word, *vocation*, derives from the Latin verb *vocare*, which means "to call." One's vocation is one's calling in life—not simply what one "wants" to do or "is expected" to do, but that toward which one is drawn, and which (it is hoped) will provide one's life with meaning, purpose, and a sense of genuine fulfillment. The word once had a fairly narrow range of reference, focusing on a call to the religious life of a priest, monk, or nun; in the Reformation era, however, it expanded to the claim that all human beings are called by God into particular stations of life—whether in the home, the workplace, the civic order, the church, or some combination of these.[13] While this had positive effects (in that it suggested divine validation of all states of life), it also had the negative effect of suggesting that one's lot in life, no matter how wretched, was an outworking of God's will—which implied, in turn, that one should be satisfied with it. Hence, while this expanded sense of vocation certainly had its virtues, it could easily be employed to reinforce the status quo[14]—and this was only magnified by the pressures of industrialization, with the result

in *At This Time and In This Place: Vocation and Higher Education*, ed. David S. Cunningham (New York: Oxford University Press, 2016), 47–71; here, 66–68.

11. See, for example, Sharon Daloz Parks, *Big Questions, Worthy Dreams: Mentoring Emerging Adults in Their Search for Meaning, Purpose, and Faith*, rev. ed. (San Francisco: Jossey-Bass, 2011).

12. See, for example, Lisa Tessman, *Burdened Virtues: Virtue Ethics for Liberatory Struggles* (New York: Oxford University Press, 2005).

13. Martin Luther is, of course, a key figure in this shift. For an exploration of some of his insights, see Kathryn A. Kleinhans, "Places of Responsibility: Educating for Multiple Callings in Multiple Communities," in Cunningham, ed., *At This Time*, 99–121; here, 102–7.

14. I have elsewhere referred to this as the "core danger" of using the language of vocation and calling. David S. Cunningham, "Time and Place: Why Vocation Is Crucial to Undergraduate Education Today," Introduction to *At This Time*, 1–19; here, 8. I agree with Douglas J. Schuurman's description that this is an "abuse" of the concept of vocation; nevertheless, the danger remains. Schuurman offers some responses to this and other misuses of the language of

that *vocation* eventually came to be seen as a synonym for work. Indeed, during most of the twentieth century, "vocational education" was usually equated with learning a trade. But we are in the midst of a revival of sorts: a harkening back to the roots of the term in the verb "to call," which has in turn been drawn into conversation with some of the other language mentioned here (meaning and purpose, big questions, fulfillment, flourishing). The result is that vocation is among us once again: the "once and future language" of higher education.[15]

The recent renewed success of this language is due in part to certain of its qualities, which I have described elsewhere as capacious, dynamic, and elastic.[16] It is *capacious*, in the sense that vocation creates a very big tent: it can house a variety of pedagogical commitments, theological perspectives, and cultural assumptions. It is one of those terms, increasingly difficult to find, which has not already been captured by a particular school of thought, or ecclesial community, or political perspective. This language is *dynamic*, in that it recognizes the ever-changing nature of our search for meaning, our big questions, and our accounts of fulfilling and flourishing lives. None of these questions will look the same for a person in 5 or 15 or 50 years, and the language of vocation encourages us to consider the changing nature of our callings throughout life. And it is *elastic*, because vocation is a malleable term that can be molded to fit a variety of institutional contexts, from the specifically theological to the intensely secular, from large universities to small colleges, and across a wide range of academic disciplines and applied fields.

Of course, a word can become so capacious and so dynamic and so elastic that it means nothing at all. But over the last 20 years, a great many colleges and universities have employed this language, or something very much like it, in ways that have given it specific contours that are appropriate for their own (diverse and complex) contexts. These programs have taken a great many forms, from curricular initiatives (common readings, specific courses that focus on vocation, courses on the disciplinary major as a "calling") to internship and shadowing programs in particular professions, and from programs housed in various offices of an

---

vocation in *Vocation: Discerning Our Callings in Life* (Grand Rapids, MI: Eerdmans, 2004), especially chapter 4.

15. Further discussion of this point, as well as the terms used in the following paragraph, may be found in David S. Cunningham, "Language that Works: Vocation and the Complexity of Higher Education," in *Vocation across the Academy: A New Vocabulary for Higher Education*, ed. David S. Cunningham (New York: Oxford University Press, 2017), 1–18; here, 7–14.

16. I will return later to the question of whether these descriptions are still applicable to a concept of vocation that is "heard differently" in a multi-faith environment, but these three qualities help explain why some advocates believe that the language may be able to adjust to new environments.

institution's student development division (themed residence halls, retreats for athletic teams, alumni panel discussions) to initiatives focusing on spiritual life (opportunities for guided meditation, seminars on faith and learning, the study of sacred texts). Some programs, such as community engagement projects or a campus-wide weekend retreat, have drawn on resources from all divisions of a college (academic and otherwise). For the most part, these programs have been quite successful in helping students to think about larger questions of meaning and purpose, about their future direction in life, and about the fit (or lack thereof) between their own talents and gifts and the ways they expect to engage in economic, domestic, and civic life.[17]

In short, the language of vocation and calling has made a significant impact on higher education in the United States—particularly at liberal arts colleges, but also at a number of large private universities. More and more institutions are drawing on this language to help students grapple with large questions of meaning and to articulate a vision of their own purpose in life. But at this point, many readers will have noticed a problem.

An exclusively Christian concept?

The first two sections of this introduction have argued, first, that contemporary higher education has become increasingly diverse, including with respect to religion; and second, that many institutions are making ever greater use of a concept that runs deep in the soil of a specific theological tradition. We have already seen that this language once specified a call to the religious life as a priest, monk, or nun. But of course, its roots run deeper still into Christianity: Jesus *called* disciples, and they in turn called others; early Christians were reminded "to lead a life worthy of the calling to which you have been called" (Eph. 4:1). Indeed, the Christian name for its gathered community, "the church" (*ekklēsia*), referred to those who had been "called out" from the world, drawn by God into a different kind of communal relationship with one another. Deeply embedded in all these usages was the notion that God calls or summons human beings into a particular form of life, and that the discerning hearer should listen for and respond to that call. The later Latin word *vocatio* was simply a more circumscribed and more specific reference to a claim that had been in place from the beginning

17. For more detail on successful programs of vocational discernment, see the two book-length evaluations of the Lilly-funded Programs for the Theological Exploration of Vocation: Tim Clydesdale, *The Purposeful Graduate: Why Colleges Must Talk to Students about Vocation* (Chicago: University of Chicago Press, 2015), and William M. Sullivan, *Liberal Learning as a Quest for Purpose* (New York: Oxford University Press, 2016).

of the Christian faith: God calls, and people respond. Even when the term was widened to include secular vocations in the economic, domestic, and civil sphere, these too were understood as a divine summons into certain forms of life.

Needless to say, the Christian roots of the language of *calling* and *vocation* would seem to raise serious questions about its ability to function well in multi-faith contexts. If one's vocation is narrowly defined as the human response to the specific call of God, and if *God* is understood in specifically Christian terms, why would a follower of another faith tradition or philosophical perspective be the least bit interested in having a "vocation"? Even among adherents of those theistic traditions that offer certain parallel accounts of the relationship between God (or the Gods) and the world, the language of vocation would seem to be deeply troubling; its dominant Christian overtones are not easily muted. Add to this the cultural and political hegemony of Christianity in the West (and its more-than-occasional alliances, across the centuries, with the violent structures of the empire and the state), and most of the world's population would seem to have good reason to be highly suspicious of yet another Christian concept being foisted upon them—even (or perhaps especially) one that is advertised as being "good and good for you."

The concern is an urgent one in the present cultural moment, since—as already observed—the language of vocation and calling is being increasingly adopted in higher education (particularly at undergraduate liberal arts institutions). Some of these institutions are specifically Christian, and in some of these cases described here, the concerns might not be so strongly felt (though perhaps they should be; I will return to this point shortly). But in undergraduate settings in which the student body is more religiously diverse—and that means a substantial majority of institutions today, including many that self-identify as connected in some way to the Christian faith—the problem has become more salient. Can those students who do not profess the Christian faith be expected to participate in programs that are geared toward vocational exploration and discernment? Does *vocation* remain, in essence, a Christian concept?

Concerns of this sort have prompted this volume. As I suggested at the beginning of this introduction, the phrase *hearing vocation differently* is meant to remind us that, if the language of vocation and calling is to have a genuine place in the multi-faith academy, it will need to be rethought, reheard, and rewritten—making it accessible and amenable to a wider range of students (and not only those who have absorbed the language of vocation as part of their own religious heritage). This is not to say that Christian students cannot continue to understand its elements in specifically Christian ways. But it does mean that, at least in most instances, the concept will need to be employed more flexibly and thoughtfully, so that it will be useful for *all* undergraduates at an institution, rather than only for those who identify with one particular religious tradition.

This, in turn, raises questions for Christians and for institutions that understand themselves as having a calling of their own[18]—a calling that may include cultivating the Christian faith in their students. Will these institutions create descriptions and programs that accent the specifically Christian origins of vocation, such that it will have meaning primarily in specifically Christian contexts? Or will they too engage in a process of "hearing vocation differently," of "rewriting" the literature on vocation and calling, such that it can play a role beyond the confines of the Christian faith as traditionally defined?

Today, many historically Christian institutions find themselves thinking in increasingly multi-faith terms. As already noted, college and university students across the country identify with an increasingly diverse range of lifestances. A great many institutions of higher education, including those with specifically Christian foundations, are admitting significant numbers of Jewish, Muslim, Hindu, Sikh, and Buddhist students, as well as a great many who understand themselves as fitting into more than one category of religious belief (or who do not identify with any such belief). In addition, institutions are finding that their surrounding communities are increasingly diverse (ethnically, religiously, and in every other way); those who live in these communities are often looking to their local colleges and universities as they seek to further their education. Many of these institutions are church-related colleges and universities, and some of these take their faith commitments quite seriously; many of them have been deeply engaged in the work of vocational reflection and discernment on their campuses. Since many institutions are seeking to attract and to welcome more non-Christian students (or hope to do so), and since many believe that their vocational discernment programs truly have something to offer, they will need to find ways of presenting these programs in ways that can be heard and received by those whose deepest commitments are not specifically Christian. This, in turn, will create a more inviting environment for all students—regardless of their religious or philosophical perspective.

This work has additional implications that go well beyond the goals of making colleges more open and welcoming to a diverse student body and raising vocational questions among a wider audience. Deeper attention to the increasingly multi-faith character of our culture can make an enormous difference for the future of civil discourse. At a time of intense polarization, when many people seem

18. See David S. Cunningham, "Colleges Have Callings, Too: Vocational Reflection at the Institutional Level," in Cunningham, ed., *Vocation across the Academy*, 249–71.

more eager than ever to retreat into tribal enclaves and to lash out at anything that seems "other," our society is in desperate need of institutions and structures that will bring us into generous and responsible conversation with one another. Higher education should be playing a pre-eminent role in this effort; too often, however, it seems to have lacked a wide enough range of categories for doing so. Perhaps the language of vocation and calling can have a positive impact in this regard, particularly when it is attentive to the many forms of diversity (including religious diversity) that are part and parcel of contemporary American culture.

Hearing others—and hearing one another

This book was written over the course of a year, during which time its contributors met three times for four days at a time. We explored common readings, exchanged ideas, argued, agreed, and occasionally agreed to disagree. We wrote chapters, read one another's work, provided feedback, revised our work, and sought to create a book that would address a wide range of issues concerning the role of vocation and calling in the multi-faith environment of contemporary higher education. We claim and practice a wide variety of religious traditions, philosophical positions, and lifestances; nevertheless, from the outset, we agreed that we would not attempt to describe or "translate" vocation into the idiom of each particular tradition.[19] Instead, recognizing that all traditions, religious and secular, have resources for (and questions about) the meaning and purpose of life, the authors have focused on a shared set of questions that accompany the work of rethinking, rehearing, and rewriting vocation. They have reflected on these questions from the perspective of their own traditions, their institutional positions, and their academic specializations. These reflections demonstrate the rich insights that can come to light if we are willing to take the risk of hearing vocation differently.

The first part of the book is called "Reframing Vocation: Creating Spaces for New Ways of Hearing." Its first chapter offers a detailed description of the many ways that college students encounter difference, and how this shapes their understanding of their future direction in life. This chapter emphasizes the communal and reciprocal aspects of reflection and discernment on our callings, drawing especially on Jewish traditions in sacred texts and in modern thought. It also

19. This work has been done elsewhere; see John C. Haughey, ed., *Revisiting the Idea of Vocation: Theological Explorations* (Washington, DC: Catholic University of America Press, 2004), and Kathleen A. Cahalan and Douglas J. Schuurman, eds., *Calling in Today's World: Voices from Eight Faith Perspectives* (Grand Rapids, MI: Eerdmans, 2016). Some of the contributors to each of these volumes raise questions about whether it is possible to translate the Christian concept of vocation into the thought-world and practices of other traditions.

includes a description of an encounter with difference from the author's own experience, which made for a significant change in her vocational journey. As noted earlier, this chapter also introduces the term *lifestance*, which is used by a number of contributors to account for a wide range of perspectives without necessarily assuming that these will always be connected with "religion." Chapter 2 bears out this latter concern, noting that many undergraduates find themselves drawn to more than one lifestance. Indeed, the concept of "multiple religious belonging" may describe a very common circumstance: we often find ourselves drawn to, and sometimes overwhelmed by, an eclectic blend of beliefs and practices. As the author observes, certain parallels may be drawn between these experiences and the broader experience of adolescent women, who find themselves pulled in many directions by the demands of contemporary culture. Rather than assuming that such experiences result from confusion or indifference, we can choose to meet these perspectives where they are, and to consider how this quest for meaning might positively shape vocational reflection and discernment. The final chapter in Part one turns to a reality that every human being faces: the prospect of death. By bringing this reality to the forefront, we find ourselves considering our callings in a different way; they begin to take on greater depth, and we are encouraged to consider the *quality* of our vocations, rather than simply being satisfied that we have found one. All three chapters draw on the resources of a variety of traditions (including Judaism, Buddhism, Christianity, and Sikhism) to provide a sense of the larger context within which vocational reflection takes place.

Part two is titled "Releasing Expectations: Overcoming Misleading Assumptions about Vocation." In each chapter, the author draws on the insights of a particular tradition to call into question certain longstanding prejudices about vocational reflection and discernment. One such misleading assumption is that vocational discernment should direct us toward a clear and definitive path, but chapter 4 suggests that the work of finding our callings will necessarily be accompanied by doubt and uncertainty. Moreover, rather than thinking of this as an obstacle, we should see the ambiguous and shadowy nature of our callings as a positive feature. Many stories from various religious traditions remind us that even the most deeply committed and vocationally focused individuals have experienced doubt about their own callings and uncertainty about the course of their lives—a point that this chapter illustrates using the story of Joseph in the Qur'an. Chapter 5 offers an alternative account of the Christian understanding of vocation, suggesting that vocational discernment is best understood not as obedience to God's call, but as a disposition of "gracious reception." The cultivation of this disposition plays an important role in the Christian theological and liturgical traditions, and it has important implications for thinking about vocational discernment in a multi-faith context. It also marks the ministry of Jesus, including his encounters with difference. A more receptive disposition can help us make better use of the offers of advice and constructive criticism that may come from outside our own perspective. Then, in chapter 6, we turn to a question that arises for many people at some point in their lives: namely, whether we might sometimes be called to renounce a vocation—to turn away from our callings—because of some moral, relational, or religious demand. This chapter draws on elements of the Hindu tradition to suggest an alternative: renunciation *within* vocation. It may be possible to separate ourselves from attachment to certain of the fruits of our labors without renouncing the work itself; and this may in turn have a number of additional benefits for the ways that we carry out other aspects of vocational reflection and discernment. The three chapters in Part two thus seek to release us from the expectation that vocational discernment requires certainty, obedience, and undifferentiated commitment.

We then turn, in Part three, to "Restor(y)ing Our Lives: Narrative as a Vocational Catalyst." These three chapters draw on a wide range of narrative frameworks (including Jewish, Muslim, Hindu, and secular accounts) in order to raise a series of questions about how our lives are shaped by and through the stories that we tell. Chapter 7 examines our allegiances to a variety of communities (including communities devoted to differing faith traditions), exploring how we narrate the tensions and conflicts among these allegiances. How do we go about resolving such conflicts, and how is our vocational judgment affected by these encounters? The author suggests that we should not seek to dissolve the tensions too quickly, since our allegiances typically spring from genuine commitments to communities that we hold dear. Nevertheless, a commitment to an interfaith perspective may give us new insights, encouraging us to tell the stories of our lives and of our vocational reflections in ways that acknowledge not only our various commitments but also the potential tensions among them. Chapter 8 continues the theme, examining how narratives shape our perceptions of our selves, and how the future directions of our lives emerge from the ways that we construct and tell our own stories. Indeed, these stories are woven together and interconnect in ways that are best described using the word *myth*: we are always engaged in a process of myth-making as we explore the contours of our lives. This language, suggests the author, may help us to reshape the concept of vocation in a way that clarifies matters of agency and puts the past into a proper relationship with the future. Part three concludes with a chapter focusing on two important practices that are essential to the work of shaping the stories of our lives: the cultivation of *attentiveness* and of *humor*. College students who are committed to a particular religious tradition face not only the usual distractions and demands that all undergraduates face, but also cultural, social, and institutional pressures to "perform" their beliefs in a certain way. If students are to narrate their own lives in ways that make space for these complexities, they will need to engage in certain kinds of spiritual practices to re-center themselves and to tell their stories in their own voices. By cultivating the practice of attentiveness, and by allowing their encounters to be graced by a lightness of perspective and a dose of humor, students may be able to navigate their undergraduate years in ways that allow them both to *restore* and to *re-story* their lives, even in the face of cultural demands that make this work so difficult.

Our final section is called "Reimagining Our Campuses: The Practice(s) of Hearing Vocation Differently." All four of its chapters examine practical questions that arise within the work of vocational reflection and discernment in a multi-faith environment. We begin in chapter 10 with a consideration of what it means for a person from one religious tradition (in this case, Buddhism) to work at an institution committed to a different tradition (Christianity). In what ways can the individual and the institution make space for each other, and what might transpire as a result? After presenting her own story of negotiating these issues, the author describes the advantages that can arise from this situation in the vocationally significant areas of academic advising and teaching in general education courses. Chapter 11 examines the myriad challenges that must be faced by academic institutions as they broaden their focus from a single religious perspective to a multi-faith approach. Academic discourse about religion is too often divorced from the actual experiences of real human beings, but careful attention to such experiences is essential in the undergraduate environment. This chapter tells the story of one institution that underwent a significant transition, from its original focus on one faith tradition (and indeed a single denomination within that tradition) to become a genuinely multi-faith environment—for its students and for its faculty and staff. The author also suggests that such a transition can go hand in hand with efforts to make sure that multiple traditions and lifestances are given voice in the classroom. This theme continues in chapter 12, which argues that the shape and style of classroom teaching makes a tremendous difference in the work of bringing vocational reflection into a multi-faith environment. The author draws on insights from a variety of fields to provide specific guidance about how the geography and atmosphere of the classroom can create a positive space for vocational reflection discernment across a variety of lifestances. The second half of the chapter offers a number of specific pedagogical exercises to accomplish this work, along with a discussion of how student engagement in this project might be appropriately evaluated. Our final chapter broadens the discussion to describe the student academic experience as a whole; it explores the ways that a multi-faith environment can inspire and encourage students and teachers to enter into deeper conversations with one another. It can help to focus attention on ultimate questions: What gives life meaning? What counts as a truly good life? How will my own understanding of these questions be reshaped by my encounter with people who hold different beliefs and engage in different practices? How do I understand my own identity in light of these questions? This chapter calls for educators to allow themselves to be shaped by the responsibility, and the joy, of empowering students to participate in an ongoing interreligious conversation about what makes for a good life.

The book concludes with a short epilogue that seeks to summarize and draw out the implications of our reflections. But the collective nature of our effort is reflected in another way as well: we have each written a brief response to another contributor's essay. At the end of each chapter, readers will find a short reflection by one of the book's other authors, noting a particular theme or issue that she or he found especially meaningful, resonant, or attention-getting. By offering these reflections, we hope to model and to participate in the kind of appreciative response that one hopes might mark all genuine encounters with difference.

The 13 contributors to this volume are united in their conviction that questions of meaning, purpose, and identity—which have traditionally played a role in undergraduate education—demand even more attention today. We also believe that good progress toward this goal can be, and has been, made by programs that encourage vocational reflection and discernment. But we also believe that, due to the origins of this language in a particular religious tradition, it needs to be *heard differently* in order to be truly heard in the contemporary context—a context in which students enter college with an ever wider variety of lifestances. This volume seeks to offer some interesting and worthy examples of how this work might be accomplished; we hope that others will join us in this project.

PART ONE

Reframing Vocation

Creating Spaces for New Ways of Hearing

The project of this book is described using an auditory metaphor: "hearing vocation differently." But all language, words, and sounds are heard within a particular context; they are heard according to the space within which they are produced. So a project that urges us to "hear differently" must also be attentive to the spaces within which such hearing takes place. This need animates the first three chapters of the book.

As noted in the introduction to this volume, an increasing number of colleges and universities are urging their students to undertake the work of vocational reflection and discernment. The spaces within which this occurs—the contexts for this work—vary widely from one institution to another. Indeed, few colleges have had the luxury of being able to shape, intentionally, the spaces in which conversations about calling can take place. Most have felt fortunate to make use of whatever locations might be available—optional retreats, residence hall conversations, perhaps a module in a first-year seminar course—to introduce the language and the practices of vocational reflection to undergraduate students.

On the other hand, because of the increasing attention being paid to vocation, colleges now have an opportunity to become more intentional in creating and maintaining appropriate and productive settings for cultivating practices of reflection and discernment. In addition, given the increasing diversity within undergraduate education, more attention will need to be paid to the language used to frame the process of discernment, and to the settings within which it occurs. Indeed, the success or failure of projects for vocational reflection will likely depend on an institution's ability to structure this work in ways that resonate with its increasingly diverse student body.

The following three chapters offer important insights for this project of "reframing vocation." Specifically, they argue that the space within which vocational discernment occurs should be marked by encounters with *difference*, by an acceptance of *multiplicity*, and by an emphasis on *quality*. This is not to suggest that current programs of vocational reflection and discernment are not marked by these characteristics; rather, the argument of these chapters is that institutions can strengthen their work in this area, and make it more accessible to a wider range of students, by becoming more intentional in addressing these concerns. In the increasingly multi-faith context of undergraduate education, these kinds of questions seem to demand attention:

- Are academic institutions providing opportunities for vocational reflection that allow students to encounter difference, in various forms? Are students being exposed to assumptions, expectations, and processes of discernment that are different from their own (sometimes radically so)?
- As they enter college, students may well be exposed to a more diverse range of writers, thinkers, and artists than they had previously encountered. But is this same diversity present when they are asked to reflect on their callings? Are they made aware of the resources of less familiar traditions for examining the meaning and purpose of their own lives?
- When students bring religious and philosophical perspectives to the process of vocational reflection, are they too quickly and easily assigned to predetermined categories? Do the traditional "check boxes," which tend to list the names of various "world religions" (plus a box marked "none"), actually reflect the lived experiences of undergraduate students?
- Do educators give adequate attention to the degree to which students may feel shamed, marginalized, or subjected to being "called out," simply because of the particularities of their outlook on life, whether or not that outlook is labeled "religious"?
- Does vocational reflection sometimes become a largely instrumental process, in which the primary goal is for students to declare a major or to find a career that suits them? Does the pressure to "make a decision" sometimes eclipse the need for vocational discernment to bear the marks of depth and quality?
- Are students adequately encouraged to think of their callings in the broadest possible terms—as something that will affect the entire shape of their lives, as well as the wider world within which they carry out their vocations? Are they given adequate opportunities to reflect on the finite nature of earthly human life, such that their own processes of vocational discernment can be seen, not just as a choice to be made in the present, but as an essential part of shaping a life well lived?

These questions, and many others like them, are explored in the chapters that follow. All three authors help us to examine the space within which we hear, and respond to, our various callings in life. By constructing a frame in which vocational reflection is characterized by difference, multiplicity, and quality, they demonstrate how the language of vocation can help college students to reflect more deeply on issues of meaning, purpose, and identity.

1

The Change a Difference Makes

FORMATION OF SELF IN THE ENCOUNTER WITH DIVERSITY

Rachel S. Mikva

FOR MANY UNDERGRADUATE students, time spent in college or university is their first or most intense encounter with difference. They may meet people of diverse races, classes, religions or lifestances,[1] sexual orientations, and gender identities (beyond the binaries to which many are accustomed); they are also likely to encounter a host of new ideas, as well as critical tools for thinking about them. The experience can be extremely challenging. "Research has shown that social diversity in a group can cause discomfort, rougher interactions, a lack of trust, greater perceived interpersonal conflict, lower communication, less cohesion, more concern about disrespect, and other problems. So what is the upside?"[2] Indeed, given this list of potential complications, why do colleges and universities often actively encourage such encounters?

1. Harry Stopes-Roe uses "lifestance" to enlarge religious discourse to include nonreligious perspectives without identifying such orientations by what they are *not*. He defines the term as "the style and content of an individual's or a community's relationship with that which is of ultimate importance; the presuppositions and commitments of this, and the consequences for living which flow from it" ("Humanism as a Life Stance," *New Humanist* 103, no. 2 [October 1988]: 21). Recent expansion of "interreligious" studies to include secular humanism, multiple religious belonging, "spiritual but not religious," and other lifestances presses for inclusive language.

2. Katherine W. Phillips, "How Diversity Makes Us Smarter," *Scientific American*, October 1, 2014, https://www.scientificamerican.com/article/how-diversity-makes-us-smarter (accessed February 23, 2017).

Decades of research demonstrate how diversity makes us more innovative, diligent, and successful.[3] In the context of higher education, diversity's most emphasized value may be how it prepares students to thrive in and contribute to the flourishing of a multicultural world.[4] When General Motors filed an *amicus* brief on behalf of the University of Michigan to defend the school's affirmative action admission policies, for example, it argued that

> diversity in academic institutions is essential to teaching students the human relations and analytic skills they need to succeed and lead in the work environments of the twenty-first century. These skills include the abilities to work well with colleagues and subordinates from diverse backgrounds; to view issues from multiple perspectives; and to anticipate and respond with sensitivity to the cultural differences of highly diverse customers, colleagues, employees, and global business partners.[5]

Essential well beyond the world of business, constructive relationships across difference are considered fundamental to the functioning of democracy: "Community and democratic citizenship are strengthened when undergraduates understand and experience social connections with those outside of their often parochial 'autobiographies,' and when they experience the way their lives are necessarily shaped by others."[6]

---

3. See, for example, Sheen S. Levine and David Stark, "Diversity Makes You Brighter," *New York Times*, December 9, 2015, based on their research "Ethnic Diversity Deflates Price Bubbles," *Proceedings of the National Academy of Sciences* 111, no. 52 (2014): 18524–18529; Katherine Phillips, Katie A. Liljenquist, and Margaret A. Neale, "Is the Pain Worth the Gain?," *Personality and Social Psychology Bulletin* 35 (2009): 336–50; M. J. Chang, "Does Diversity Matter? The Educational Impact of a Racially Diverse Undergraduate Population," *Journal of College Student Development* 40 (1999): 377–95.

4. See Patricia Gurin et al., "Diversity and Higher Education: Theory and Impact on Educational Outcomes," *Harvard Educational Review* 72 (2002): 330–66. Much of the social science research cited in this chapter can be discovered through the citations in Gurin's article. See also "Benefits and Challenges of Diversity in Academic Settings," https://wiseli.engr.wisc.edu/docs/Benefits_Challenges.pdf (accessed February 23, 2017). Several studies of the Higher Education Research Institute and Center of Inquiry at Wabash College also investigate the value of diverse learning contexts: https://heri.ucla.edu/publications; http://www.liberalarts.wabash.edu/study-research.

5. Grutter v. Bollinger, 137 F. Supp. 2d 821 (E.D. Mich. 2001), Brief of General Motors Corporation as *amicus curiae* in support of appellants, p. 2, https://diversity.umich.edu/admissions/legal/gru_amicus/gru_gm.html (accessed February 23, 2017).

6. Richard Guarasci and Grant Cornwell, *Democratic Education in an Age of Difference* (San Francisco: Jossey–Bass, 1997), xiii. On an interpersonal level, the focus on diversity is not a cure for systemic social ills; Ellen Berrey argues that it may actually *tame* the demand for racial

In this chapter, I argue that engagement with difference is also a vital catalyst for addressing questions of meaning, direction, and purpose—what might be described, in classical Christian language, as *vocation*. I do not come to this reflection as a Christian, however, but as a Jew—and I present not a Jewish theory of vocation, but the experience of one Reform Ashkenazi/Sephardi Jewish woman making her way in the world. This experience is drawn into full expression through a particular spiritual tradition and encounters with diversity.

The concept of vocation employed here is not a discovery of what to "do" with one's life, but rather intimations of how to live it out most fully in *lo cotidiano*—the stuff of our daily reality. This term, borrowed from *mujerista* thought, constructs theory around the many quotidian details of our lives.[7] In the rabbinic imagination, we are each imbued with *yetzer tov* and *yetzer hara* (asymmetrically framed as "a good inclination" and "the evil inclination"); we choose between them in every moment in order to walk the path of a meaningful life. Whatever I, as a Jew, might make of the historically Christian investigation of vocation, it is never once and for all; the journey of becoming is ongoing and involves all aspects of my being.

Recent scholarship on vocation has similarly broadened the discernment process to explore what kind of person one aspires to be, with a recognition that this "calling" is shaped by countless small decisions made every day over the course of a lifetime.[8] It has also come to acknowledge the importance of the dialogical, to explore how we discover our path through relationship.[9] I hope to extend this discourse by emphasizing that *encounters with difference* are essential to the dialogue. The key inquiry becomes: How should I live my life, and how does my engagement with diversity help me to answer that question?

Exploring various dimensions of this thesis, I begin with a brief reflection on the way "difference" operates in human psychology and society; paradoxically, it appears to be a catalyst both for conflict and for personal growth. The chapter then investigates Jewish text and tradition to unpack these complex dynamics, ultimately asserting a mutually formative process that is key to answering

---

justice, diverting our attention from the core issues of civil rights and empowerment (*The Enigma of Diversity: The Language of Race and the Limits of Racial Justice* [Chicago: University of Chicago Press, 2015]).

7. For a discussion of this Latina theology and the role that *lo cotidiano* plays, see Ada Maria Isasi-Diaz, *Mujerista Theology* (Maryknoll, NY: Orbis Books, 1996), 67–73.

8. See, for example, Jerry Organ, "Of Doing and Being: Broadening Our Understanding of Vocation," in *Vocation across the Academy: A New Vocabulary for Higher Education*, ed. David S. Cunningham (New York: Oxford University Press, 2017), 225–43.

9. See the contribution of David S. Cunningham in chapter 5 of this volume.

the question. Drawing on theoretical and experiential learning, I connect these insights back to the context of higher education, and conclude with a personal reflection on interreligious teaching that hopefully illuminates this perspective on vocation.

The nature of difference

As noted earlier, diversity is not easy for humans to navigate. Difference should not be viewed as evidence of inequality; nevertheless, we frequently judge distinctions among human beings in negative ways. Research in social identity theory has demonstrated that group membership, even if arbitrarily assigned, is sufficient to catalyze favoritism among members of the group and discrimination against those outside.[10] Society generally fabricates its Others, "selecting, isolating and emphasizing an aspect of another people's life and making it stand for their difference."[11] Moreover, the construction of these identities is bound up with power.[12] Those who have the power to define set those who are different as the Other—their (somehow less worthy) counterpart. "Thus abnormality is the other of the norm, deviation the other of law-abiding, illness the other of health, barbarity the other of civilization, animal the other of the human, woman the other of man."[13] The latter element in each pair defines the former, but also depends on it for its self-assertion.

Power dynamics aside, the idea that self and other are mutually constituted is not inherently problematic; in fact, it can bring us back to my thesis regarding vocation: to figure out who I am, I must encounter and understand who I am not. If "a 'theory of the other' is but another way of establishing a 'theory of the self,' "[14] then a more robust engagement with diversity necessarily requires a deeper dive into discernment. Indeed, a substantive encounter with difference is likely a prerequisite for finding one's true vocation.

10. Henri Tajfel and John Turner, "An Integrative Theory of Intergroup Conflict," in *The Social Psychology of Intergroup Relations*, ed. William G. Austin and Stephen Worchel (Monterey, CA: Brooks/Cole, 1979), 33–47.

11. William Scott Green, "Otherness within: Towards a Theory of Difference in Rabbinic Judaism," in *To See Ourselves as Others See Us*, ed. Jacob Neusner and Ernest Frerichs (Chico, CA: Scholars Press, 1985), 50.

12. Edward Said, *Orientalism* (New York: Vintage Books, 1979), 332.

13. Zygmunt Bauman, *Modernity and Ambivalence* (Malden, MA: Polity Press, 1991), 15.

14. Jonathan Z. Smith, *Relating Religion* (Chicago: University of Chicago Press, 2004), 275.

The vocational value of encountering difference can be underscored by psychosocial studies such as those of Jean Piaget, who demonstrated that a person's intellectual and moral development depends on the capacity to understand ideas and feelings of others ("perspective taking").[15] Similarly, Rose Coser established that experiences of diversity (which she calls "complex social structures") lead to a stronger sense of individuality and a deeper understanding of one's place in the world.[16] These disciplinary insights resonate powerfully with student development goals in higher education.

In analyzing the way religious communities set themselves apart, Jonathan Z. Smith observes that "meaning is made possible by difference.... Relations are discovered and reconstituted through projects of differentiation."[17] He follows a train of thought in anthropology, invoking Claude Lévi-Strauss to establish the confrontation of difference as the essence of thought. More simply, consider how Sesame Street uses the sorting song, "One of these things is not like the others..." to teach basic cognitive skills. Difference is how we learn.

It is within scripture and tradition that I discover the richest insights into the complex role that difference plays in the human psyche and society. For example, the fact that our minds are hard-wired to identify difference is poetically illuminated by the biblical creation narrative that envisions God fashioning the universe through distinction of night from day, seas from land, waters above and waters below (Gen. 1). We understand the nature of something—it "comes to be" in our minds—by separating it from what it is not.

Encounter with difference in Jewish text and tradition

Within modern Jewish thought, a number of authors bring to light the positive, even redemptive dimensions of difference; they also affirm the coformative nature of encounter. Many readers are familiar with the basic premise of Martin Buber's *I and Thou*, appreciating his insistence that we can engage with others—not only human beings, but all of creation—in ways that transcend utilitarian

15. Jean Piaget, *The Moral Judgment of the Child* (New York: Simon and Schuster, 1965). See also Lawrence Kurdek, "Perspective Taking as the Cognitive Basis of Children's Moral Development: A Review of the Literature," *Merrill-Palmer Quarterly of Behavior and Development* 24, no. 1 (January 1978): 3–28.

16. Rose Laub Coser, "The Complexity of Roles as a Seedbed of Individual Autonomy," in *The Idea of Social Structure*, ed. Lewis A. Coser (New York: Harcourt Brace Jovanovich, 1975), 85–102.

17. Smith, *Relating Religion*, 246.

experience and objectification (what he calls an "I–It" relationship). We must seek out the fullness of one another's being, each one the subject rather than an object of the other in our meeting ("I–Thou"). Less well known is Buber's assertion that we become our complete, actualized selves *only through* such I–Thou relationships: "[A person] becomes an I through a You. What confronts us comes and vanishes, relational events take shape and scatter, and through these changes crystallizes, more and more each time, the consciousness of the constant partner, the I-consciousness." To Buber, "all actual life is encounter."[18]

In Joseph Soloveitchik's reading of the second creation narrative in Genesis, he discerns that we are existentially hungry for this kind of meeting. "It is not good for *adam* to be alone" (Gen 2:18; the Hebrew word refers simply to a human being, not a male named Adam). In order to fully realize the quest for redemption, says Soloveitchik, this being "must initiate action leading to the discovery of a companion."[19] To become fully human requires relationship and even sacrifice, as the second person is fashioned from the side of the first. College students often experience this struggle to discover companions in profound ways, having left home and family to recreate themselves anew.

Emmanuel Levinas sets such encounter as the foundation of ethics, and establishes difference as its key. He maintains that the claim of the Other upon us has priority, in importance and chronologically, to our own being; it is how we *come into* being. Playing with the Hebrew construct *hineni*, meaning "here I am," he points out that the "I" is found in the suffix. To Levinas, this suggests that "I" do not really exist until I present myself in response to your claim upon me. My responsibility is triggered by the mere existence of the other person, he insists, challenging the tendency to found our social contract on reciprocity and the premise of sameness. While human beings often have much in common, Levinas cautions that the world as we know it will always identify someone as outside that circle of concern. Further, if I merely absorb the otherness of a person into some similarity to self, some embodiment of society or a larger sense of "the human," I have erased that person's essential particularity. Ultimately, God is revealed in otherness rather than sameness; the Holy Other is realized in meeting the face of difference.[20]

---

18. Martin Buber, *I and Thou*, trans. Walter Kaufmann (Edinburgh: T. & T. Clark, 1970), 80, 62. A common alternative translation of this last phrase (*Alles wirkliche Leben ist Begegnung* in the original German) reads: All real living is meeting.

19. Joseph Soloveitchik, *The Lonely Man of Faith* (1965. New York: Doubleday, 1992), 36–37.

20. Emmanuel Levinas, *Otherwise Than Being or Beyond Essence*, trans. Alphonso Lingis (Dordrecht: Kluwer Academic Publishers, 1981), 114, 142–43, 152, 185, 199.

What gives rise to this emphasis in modern Jewish thought? One response might be theological: Judaism's covenantal tradition binds me in sacred relationship to God, to Torah, to the people of Israel, and to all creation. These relationships are rooted in a life of *mitzvah* (pl. *mitzvot*). *Mitzvah* is appropriately translated as "commandment," yet the Hasidic masters taught something profound when they reimagined its etymology; they connected it to an Aramaic term with the same root that means attachment, companionship, joining together.[21] *Mitzvot* are the actions that form the glue of our relationships—constructing and shaping both self and other.

In a captivating little book that deliberately mistranslates Hebrew words in order to get at something deeper, Lawrence Kushner tells us that *mitzvah* means "response."[22] By responding to the claims made on me—whether I identify their source as a Divine commander, family tradition, Jewish peoplehood, or a universal social contract—I deepen my relationship with the "one" who calls. I also deepen understanding of my place in the world. As with Buber and Levinas, living in response-ability is the key action of self-realization.[23]

The rabbis paint a mental image: every person carries a single letter of Torah, and each is an essential part of the Divine plan for creation. The possibilities generated in meeting one another offer a potentially unlimited range of outcomes; certain formations and connections among these letters start to "make sense." Because our individual letters bear little significance on their own, we need others to fashion meaning. We become the collective fulfillment of our destinies.[24]

In addition to such theological foundations, history surely plays a role in the formation of Jewish thought. The co-constitutive quality of self and other was

---

21. The Aramaic term appears multiple times in the Babylonian Talmud, presenting this range of meaning, e.g., BM 28a, Ber 6b, Suk 52a, BB 80a. Hasidic interpretations can be traced to the Baal Shem Tov, as cited in *Degel Machaneh Ephraim*. See also Abraham Joshua Heschel, *God in Search of Man* (New York: Farrar, Straus and Giroux, 1976), 287. Classical rabbinic understanding of *mitzvot* as commandments included many identified as responsibilities of one person to another (*mitzvot bein adam l'chavero*).

22. Lawrence Kushner, *The Book of Words* (Woodstock, VT: Jewish Lights, 1993), 91–94.

23. See Florence Amamoto's discussion in chapter 10 of this volume; see also Margaret E. Mohrmann, "'Vocation Is Responsibility': Broader Scope, Deeper Discernment," in Cunningham, ed., *Vocation across the Academy*, 21–43.

24. *Zohar Hadash Shir haShirim 74d, Migaleh Amukot 186*. These medieval texts identify the people of Israel as the bearers of Torah's letters, since the Jewish covenant is an effort to embody its teachings. I take the liberty of applying the notion to a broader conception of the collective human enterprise.

evident as Jews became the consummate "Other" in Western culture; Christianity took shape over against its constructed image of Judaism.[25] Continuing hostility and pressure on Jews to assimilate into dominant cultures yielded a complicated range of attitudes toward non-Jews, but it also highlighted the existential value of diversity in human history. Jonathan Sacks speaks of the "dignity of difference," and identifies Judaism as a tradition of resistance to the imposition of a single truth on a plural world. He rightly traces this commitment back to the Hebrew Bible and its critique of empire. In particular, he reads the story of the Tower of Babel (Gen. 11:1–9) as a rejection of the imperial monoculture of the builders. Western culture tends to privilege universal truths, and we have been accustomed to reading Babel's story of confused languages and dispersed peoples as a punishment rather than a correction, or as an etiology of cultural diffusion and conflict. The building of the imperial tower, however—with its unitary worldview and objective—runs counter to the natural (even desired) proliferation of languages, cultures, and peoples described in the preceding chapter of Genesis.[26]

At the same time, the fundamental common ground of humanity is established at our creation—each one in the "image of God" (Gen 1:26)—and this remains the anchor of our solidarity. Similarity and difference are not opposites; they are necessary corollaries. In fact, the Hebrew Bible presents a complex understanding of humans' multifarious relationship with difference. My interpretations of the text are neither comprehensive nor inevitable, but I till this inexhaustibly rich soil of Torah to cultivate its multitude of possible meanings.

Biblical sources

Given that the Hebrew Bible was redacted in Babylonia after the destruction of the Temple and forced dispersion of the people in 586 BCE, it should not surprise us that this text sometimes displays the fear of difference that frequently plagues us. The exiles' deep anxiety that Israelite identity might be swallowed up by the dominant culture gives polemical force to the imprecations against the Canaanites in Deuteronomy 7, and to other passages that depict them in disturbingly negative fashion. We continually divide the world into "us and them";

25. See Miriam Taylor, *Anti-Judaism and Early Christian Identity: A Critique of the Scholarly Consensus* (Leiden: Brill, 1994); Jeremy Cohen, *Living Letters of the Law: Ideas of the Jew in Medieval Christianity* (Berkeley: University of California Press, 1999).

26. Sacks, *The Dignity of Difference* (London: Bloomsbury Academic, 2003), 50–66.

even though prophetic voices warn against the chauvinism and parochialism that often result, the text sometimes slips into these easy tropes.[27]

Such vulnerabilities are evident in our own context as well. American exceptionalism fosters a sense of superiority, and a latent nationalism threatens to transform "we're number one" rhetoric into "we're the only ones who matter" policies. Some people imagine that outsiders are dangerous: they commit crimes, they take our jobs, they corrupt our culture. Some individuals claim that the nation needs to be taken back from people whom they perceive to be "other." We sometimes see difference as danger.

Yet the Hebrew Bible also problematizes these human tendencies. The character of Jonah cannot muster an iota of compassion for the people and animals of Nineveh, capital of the Assyrian empire. Essentialized and stripped of individual identity, they represent only the enormous harm inflicted by the empire on his nation. Although we are surely meant to understand his terror when he intuits that God sends him to warn the enemy so they may repent and be forgiven, the text clearly criticizes him for this human failing. The final chapter of the book portrays God orchestrating events so that Jonah sees how his own welfare is bound up with a plant that gave him shade. "You cared about the plant, which you did not work for and which you did not grow, which appeared overnight and perished overnight. Should not I care about Nineveh, that great city, in which there are more than 120,000 people who do not yet know their right hand from their left, and numerous animals?" (Jonah 4:10–11). They are no longer faceless; the "other" is rehumanized.

The Hebrew Bible insists that we recognize the perils of our tendency toward "othering." In the Book of Esther, Haman convinces King Ahasuerus to order the annihilation of the Jews with this simple argument: "There is a certain people, scattered and dispersed among the other peoples in all the provinces of your realm; their laws are different from those of other people and they do not obey the king's laws. It is not in the king's interest to tolerate them" (Esther 3:8).[28] In Exodus 1, the Israelites are enslaved as Egyptian leadership easily persuades the population that their neighbors suddenly pose a threat; there are too many

27. Prophetic passages that warn against chauvinism include Amos 9:7: "Children of Israel, are you not just like the Ethiopians to Me, declares YHWH. Did I not bring Israel up from the land of Egypt, but also the Philistines from Caphtor and the Arameans from Kir?" Deutero-Isaiah insists that foreigners and eunuchs are equally part of the people as a result of their faithfulness to the teachings of Torah (Isa. 56). Yet the Hebrew Bible also portrays the figure of Ezra as objecting to intermarriage because it mixes the "holy seed" of Israel (9:2).

28. Haman also offers to pay 10,000 talents of silver into the royal treasury if the king agrees to order that the Jews be destroyed.

of these foreigners and they might become a fifth column. As readers, we identify with the Israelites' suffering and their dread; we ache for the humanity that is stolen from them. As citizens of the modern world, we shudder as we recognize continuing marginalization of those seen to be "not like us." Immigrants, Muslims, the formerly incarcerated—it is so easy to demonize their differences as justification for stripping people of their freedoms. Students acquire tools for *analyzing* systems of power, privilege, and oppression, but it is much harder to dismantle them.

The Hebrew Bible's most repeated instruction involves the stranger: "You shall not oppress a stranger, for you know the heart of the stranger, having yourselves been strangers in the land of Egypt" (Exod. 23:9), "Love the stranger as yourself" (Lev. 19:34)—and similarly over thirty times throughout the sacred text. I am powerfully struck by the idea of empathy as a commandment. Jonathan Sacks writes,

> To be a Jew is to be a stranger. It is hard to avoid the conclusion that this is why Abraham is commanded to leave land, home and father's house; why, long before Joseph was born, Abraham was already told that his descendants would be "strangers in a land not their own"; why Moses had to suffer personal exile before assuming leadership of the people; why the Israelites underwent persecution before inheriting their own land; and why the Torah is so insistent that this experience—the retelling of the story on Pesach, along with the never-forgotten taste of the bread of affliction and the bitter herbs of slavery—should become a permanent part of their collective memory.[29]

By itself, however, empathy is not sufficient: Torah is explicit and emphatic about protecting those on the margins (e.g., Exod. 22:20–26, Deut. 24:17–22) with concrete deeds to support and sustain them. There are gleaning privileges (Lev. 19), forgiveness of debts in the sabbatical year (Deut. 15), and redistribution of wealth in the jubilee (Lev. 25). With action and reflection, these experiences—continually retold and rehearsed—shape us. The command that we love the stranger as ourselves whispers that our self-discovery and self-fulfillment are bound up in relationship with those who are different.

In the emergence of Wisdom literature, the Hebrew Bible also records an inevitable shift toward a multicultural world, as the older tribal culture of ancient

29. Jonathan Sacks, "*Mishpatim* 5768—Loving the Stranger," February 2, 2008, http://www.rabbisacks.org/covenant-conversation-5768-mishpatim-loving-the-stranger/ (accessed February 27, 2017).

Israel adjusted to a bigger, more complicated universe. Encounters with difference led to profound interrogation of accepted truths, as illustrated in the Books of Job and Ecclesiastes. In another text of this genre, the Book of Proverbs, Wisdom travels everywhere just to make our acquaintance:

> It is Wisdom calling,
> Understanding raising her voice.
> She takes her stand at the topmost heights,
> By the wayside, at the crossroads,
> Near the gates at the city entrance;
> At the entryways, she shouts,
> "O men, I call to you;
> My cry is to all humanity." (Prov. 8:1–4)

Wisdom is presented in female form, rather forward in making herself available to anyone who might come by. Her promiscuity is not disparaged; it is essential to cultivate the courage to embrace new ideas—ideas the Israelites encountered through cultural difference. Timeless strumpet that she is, Wisdom-woman is still out hustling on the streets. In our pluralistic context, in our global society—*our* bigger, more complicated world—her fullness is discovered only in the teeming masses of "all humanity" as we meet at the crossroads. Self-realization is achieved at the gateway of the strange, wide world.

The biblical characters of Esther, Daniel, and Ruth all find their direction in confronting otherness. Although each story is unique, Esther and Daniel both discover their power and purpose by standing up for their own distinctive identities despite tremendous personal risk. Likely a message from the redactors to the diaspora Jews of their own age, the narratives show how individuals might be liberated by embracing their differences.[30]

In the Book of Ruth, the recently widowed title character leaves the familiarity of Moab, where she belongs. Her relationship with her Israelite mother-in-law, Naomi, has provided a new sense of identity: "Your people shall be my people, and your God my God" (Ruth 1:16). Accompanying Naomi on her return to Bethlehem, in a land where Ruth is a stranger, she also finds her "vocation." She is supported by Israelite society's laws protecting the poor and the stranger; ultimately, she helps to redeem the family's land, heal Naomi from her consuming

30. Audre Lorde called the acknowledgment of difference an act of self-love. As a self-described black lesbian mother warrior poet, she realized that she could discover her true identity only if she let go of universal categories, truths, and expectations. Cited in AnaLouise Keating, *Women Reading Women Writing* (Philadelphia: Temple University Press, 1996), 31.

emptiness, and build a future for herself and her adopted people. Revealed at the end to be the great-grandmother of King David, Ruth's bold actions to find her path are presented also as the catalyst that establishes the anointed royal house of Israel.

Jacob similarly distills his core identity through his own meeting with difference, as he emerges limping but renamed in the dawn after wrestling with a divine being. He is now called *Yisrael* (Israel), God-wrestler, in the wake of his transformative encounter with the angelic Other (Gen. 32). In fact, it is possible to see the entire People of Israel as formed through their experience in the crucible of Egypt (delineated in Hebrew as *mitzrayim*, "narrow straits"); they go down as seventy souls merely seeking to survive, but emerge as a great nation with covenantal purpose (Deut. 10:22, 26:5).

Perhaps the most radical insight of the Hebrew Bible is the mutual self-actualization of God and humanity in relationship with each other. There could be no more absolute Other than God; nevertheless, in the unfolding of creation and covenant, both God and people evolve—luring each other to respond and to become. "You shall be My people, and I shall be your God" (Exod. 6:7; similarly, Lev. 26:12, Jer. 30:22). Process theologians of diverse faiths have explored this dynamic of simultaneous, mutual formation, described earlier as "coformation." Among them, Catherine Keller notes how it holds true in the interpersonal realm as well:

> It is precisely the dynamism of our interdependence, by which we constantly influence each other—flow into each other—that keeps us in process. "We influence each other by entering into each other." If the world is an open-ended process of interactions, it is because we may exercise choice in the way we influence each other's becomings and the way we shape our own becoming out of the manifold of influences.[31]

Keller highlights the importance of a "robust relationalism" to effect the blessings of pluralism.

---

31. Catherine Keller, *On the Mystery: Discerning Divinity in Process* (Minneapolis: Fortress Press, 2007), 22. The internal quotation is from John B. Cobb Jr. and David Ray Griffin, *Process Theology: An Introductory Exposition* (Louisville: Westminster John Knox Press, 1976), 23. For Jewish explorations of process theology, see *Jewish Theology and Process Thought*, ed. Sandra Lubarsky (Albany: State University of New York Press, 1996); Bradley Shavit Artson, "*Baderekh:* On the Way—A Presentation of Process Theology," *Conservative Judaism* 62, nos. 1–2 (Fall–Winter 2010): 3–35; Toba Spitzer, "Why We Need Process Theology," *CCAR Journal* 59, no. 2 (Winter 2012): 84–95.

As we turn to explore the nature of coformation in higher education,[32] we should not lose sight of the Hebrew Bible's special interest in the encounter with substantive difference—among individuals, between peoples, and with the most Holy Other. Its manifold insights into the pitfalls and possibilities help us to see how navigating these rocky shoals is a fundamental journey of human existence.

Coformation in higher education

The idea of coformation grows from consciousness of our intersubjectivity. Replacing the myth of the fully autonomous self, we recognize how shared meaning-making is essential in shaping our ideas and relations. It reflects the teaching philosophy of Paulo Freire: "The thinking Subject cannot think alone. In the act of thinking about the object s/he cannot think without the co-participation of another Subject. . . . *It is the 'we think' which establishes the 'I think' and not the contrary.*"[33] Through encounters with diversity, students are challenged to become more conscious of their own particularity and more adept at narrating their journey within it, with perspective to view their identities from outside as well as from within.

To examine how engagement with difference enhances students' sense of meaning and purpose, it can be helpful to focus on a particular type of difference, even though we meet each other in the multitude of our attachments. Here, I continue to use a religious lens, sharing a few examples that make use of theoretical analysis and anecdotal evidence; still, many of the insights apply to other types of difference as well.

---

32. Coformation theory has been applied in therapeutic settings and sociological analysis; see, for example, Bette Katsekas, "Holistic Interpersonal Mindfulness: Activities and Application of Coformation Theory," *Journal of Clinical Activities, Assignments and Handouts in Psychotherapy Practice* 2, no. 3 (2002): 1–12; Gaston Pineau, "Autoformation et coformation," in *Autoformation et lien social*, ed. Séraphin Alava (Toulouse: Éditions universitaires du Sud, 2000). Jennifer Peace utilizes the term in interreligious engagement: "Coformation through Interreligious Learning," *Colloquy* 20, no. 1 (Fall 2011): 24–26. See also my case study on coformation in a seminary context in Part 2 of Rachel Mikva, "Reflections in the Waves," in *Experiments in Empathy for Our Time: Critical Reflection on Interreligious Learning*, ed. Najeeba Syeed (Leiden: Brill, forthcoming).

33. Paulo Freire, *Education for Critical Consciousness*, trans. Myra Bergman Ramos (1974. London: Continuum, 2005), 124, emphasis added. Freire speaks of intersubjectivity and intercommunication as the "primordial characteristic" of our cultural and historical world (123). For more on the relevance of Freire's work for vocation, see Caryn Riswold, "A Pedagogy of Humanization," in *At This Time and In This Place: Vocation and Higher Education*, ed. David S. Cunningham (New York: Oxford University Press, 2016), 72–95, as well as Jeff R. Brown, "Unplugging the GPS: Rethinking Undergraduate Professional Degree Programs," in Cunningham, ed., *Vocation across the Academy*, 204–24; here, 214–16.

Student life in theory

Scholars have long identified the illumination that can shine through encounter with diverse religious traditions. Comparative theologian Francis Clooney, for instance, finds that his study of Hinduism deepens his Catholic commitments. He embraces the invitation to be transformed by the life and literature of other faiths—appreciating how the Hindu divine name of *Narayana* enriches his own articulation of God's manifest qualities, and how Hindu goddess worship helps him understand what it means to engender God as male *or* female, causing the hymns to Mary in his own tradition to resound in new ways.[34]

Of course, people and traditions should not be reduced to what they can teach us about ourselves. Moreover, coformative self-discovery cannot be accomplished only through engagement with ideas. Substantive transformation happens in relationship, with actual people and their messy, not-exactly-textbook, lived religion.

Students often arrive on campus with a minimal understanding of their own religious heritage. Christian Smith and Melinda Lundquist Denton describe teenagers' most common spiritual perspective as "moralistic therapeutic deism"—a sense that God creates and orders the world, and that God wants them to be good and to be happy, but is not particularly involved in their lives (except when they need God to solve a problem).[35] James Fowler delineates six stages of faith development, noting that many young adults move from a synthetic-conventional perspective (Stage 3) to an individuative-reflective one (Stage 4) during their college years (ages 18–22). In this growth, they develop a capacity to question their assumptions, interrogate dissonance, and shift from dependency on authority to interdependent engagement with a variety of other people—ultimately taking greater ownership of their journey.[36] Critically oriented coursework can challenge an immature spiritual formation, as does the general process of maturation. Yet this process is powerfully advanced through relationships with people of diverse lifestance perspectives, prodding students to question matters they had never stopped to consider, to learn more about their

34. Francis X. Clooney, *Comparative Theology* (Malden, MA: John Wiley & Sons, 2010).

35. Christian Smith and Melinda Lundquist Denton, *Soul Searching: The Religious and Spiritual Lives of American Teenagers* (New York: Oxford University Press, 2005), 164–65.

36. James Fowler, *Stages of Faith: The Psychology of Human Development and the Quest for Meaning* (San Francisco: HarperSanFrancisco, 1981), 151–83. See also Paul V. Sorrentino, "What Do College Students Want? A Student-Centered Approach to Multifaith Involvement," *Journal of Ecumenical Studies* 45, no. 1 (Winter 2010): 79–96, as well as the reflections of Matthew R. Sayers in chapter 8 of this volume.

own traditions (and possibly about others'), and to develop a more sophisticated sense of their purpose and place.[37]

Student life in practice

These processes do not unfold automatically in contexts of diversity. As noted previously, people have complex responses to encountering difference. To reap the benefits of constructive coformation, we must carefully till the soil, plant seeds of transformative conversation, and tend the shoots that grow. Not every effort takes root, but each nurtures the field of interfaith engagement.

In my own work with students, we cultivate relationships of meaning in which differences in lifestance are part of the glue that binds us. My Christian students are wary of the anti-Jewish polemic in the New Testament, for example, not simply because they were taught about it in class, but because I invite them to picture me sitting in their congregations. They grapple with Christian privilege because we construct an encounter that strips off the cloak of normativity; they see how privilege impacts their peers. Non-Muslims become personally invested in the fight against Islamophobia because they are in real relationship with Muslim classmates and communities, learning to be allies instead of saviors. As the coformative relationships grow, students develop the requisite resilience to work for social change because their commitments are not merely intellectual. Their own religious identity is bound up with an allegiance to pluralism—an energetic engagement with diversity and a commitment to seek understanding across lines of difference.[38]

Students of diverse lifestances begin to grasp the complex politics of representation, because they know people who do not fit in tidy boxes—interspiritual, spiritual but not religious, seekers—and they see how religious identity is dynamic rather than static. They come to know people who were not historically invited into interreligious spaces, like secular humanists and independent Catholics, and it presses them to think about who "owns" various traditions.[39] Students bring their collection of individual identities into relationship, examining the very

37. For discussion of interactional diversity's impact on student development, see Ernest T. Pascarella and Charles Blaich, "Lessons from the Wabash National Study of Liberal Arts Education," *Change: The Magazine of Higher Learning* 45, no. 2 (March 2013): 6–15.

38. These elements are borrowed from Diana Eck's working definition of religious pluralism, http://www.pluralism.org/what-is-pluralism (accessed March 20, 2017).

39. See the comments of Trina Jones in chapter 2 of this volume. "Independent Catholics" refer to individuals and denominations who identify as Catholic but do not recognize the ultimate authority of the Vatican in Catholic life.

specific intersections of race and class and gender and sexuality, and learning to become accountable to one another.[40]

Are these matters of vocation? Yes, if we take seriously the significance of coformation. Our relationships are central to our becoming. Especially as young adults, the borders of our being are porous and dynamic. Students come to know other ways of being and experience their identities not only as boundaries but also as meeting places. As the Qur'an reminds us, "Humanity! We created you from a male and female, and made you into peoples and tribes, so that you might come to know each other" (49:13). Through this process of mutual acquaintance, students recognize how their beliefs take shape in a complex, intersubjective world.

Coformation unfolds in sharing personal stories, as well as grappling together with the challenges and opportunities of higher education. The process asks students to be vulnerable to one another—to trust that the tensions will yield new insights, and that the journey together will enable them to live more fully into their commitments and to fulfill more deeply their human potential. They catalyze change in each other, making room for growth and even reinvention of self. "The lived experience of on-the-ground, co-inhabited cultural diversity" sustains a dynamic, global social context that is "always-in-the-making."[41]

Students learn to cultivate the fertile common ground among different lifestances. They may discover so much shared beauty that they become tempted to focus all their energies there, building bridges of understanding. But a "lowest common denominator" engagement between and among people who "orient around religion differently"[42] flattens the richness of traditions and dulls the growing edges of encounter. We should be willing to excavate our disagreements *and* cultivate our commonalities. While differences can be celebrated as expressions of the vital, vibrant diversity of human life, they can also occasionally lead to conflict; consequently, students should also learn to make space for difficult conversations. Coming to terms with irreducible difference yields, not a debate about conflicting truths, but a dialogical necessity.[43] This challenging terrain strengthens the sinews of students' lifestance formation.

---

40. For unpacking of these complexities, see Rachel Mikva, "Six Issues That Complicate Interreligious Studies and Engagement," in *Interreligious/Interfaith Studies: Defining a New Field*, ed. Eboo Patel, Jennifer Howe Peace, and Noah J. Silverman (Boston: Beacon Press, 2018), 124–36.

41. Cinthya Martinez, "The East," in *Fleshing the Spirit: Spirituality and Activism in Chicana, Latina and Indigenous Women's Lives*, ed. Elisa Faco and Irene Lara (Tucson: University of Arizona Press, 2014), 27.

42. Interfaith Youth Core uses this phrasing to talk about religious difference; see Eboo Patel, *Interfaith Leadership: A Primer* (Boston: Beacon Press, 2016), 37.

43. Matthew R. Sayers helpfully pointed out that difference *does* sometimes lead to debate. Recognizing the tension generated by competing truths, one rabbinic text advises that we make

My story: encounter with difference as *vocation*

How did I come to be doing this work? This essay maintains that engagement with difference advances our thinking about how we should live our lives—not that it necessarily presents a vocational path or calling in the classic sense of the term. On occasion, however, it may happen:

I was standing before the congregation on Rosh Hashanah as we came to the communal confession—a litany of all the ways in which we as human beings continue to miss the mark. It is customary to take your fist and softly strike your chest as you begin each phrase, "*Al chet shechatanu l'fanecha*—For the sin which we have sinned against You. . . ." Never violent, this ancient breast beating still strikes some as odd in our day. I was taught to think of it as a knocking at our hearts, like a gentle rap at the door, asking the heart to open.

Who was knocking at the door of my heart on that day—one week after the attacks of September 11, 2001? Members of my New York congregation, certainly, some of whom lost friends as the World Trade Center buildings collapsed. My city, traumatized by the suddenly empty sky, etched by immeasurable sorrow. My nation, shuddering in its vulnerability, despite vast military might and oceans of protection. More insistently, however, I felt the knocking of those made instantly "other" by association: Muslims.

So began a journey of interfaith leadership, in which encounter with difference became my vocation. It started slowly. I convened a multi-faith service of mourning. Several leaders declined to read the excerpt I had chosen from the Qur'an; they thought it offensive to quote a sacred book that had also inspired the terrorist attacks. They must have forgotten how the Bible has similarly inspired great goodness and also "justified" violence. Perhaps they were unaware that right-wing extremism is responsible for the greatest percentage of terrorist incidents in the United States.[44]

---

our heart of many rooms in order to grasp contradictory ideas (*t. Sotah* 7:12). It does not intend the modern pluralism that we might hear in such a phrase; yet it clearly claims that diverse opinions derive from God, giving Divine authorization to polysemy. Its pluralism embraces an intellectual culture in which there were multiple schools of thought and positive value in teaching the controversy. For more on this point, see the comments of Noah Silverman in chapter 7 of this volume.

44. The Center for American Progress collated information on terrorist threats between 1995 and 2011: https://thinkprogress.org/chart-17-years-after-oklahoma-city-bombing-right-wing-extremism-is-significant-domestic-terror-805653857c40#.6zh5ahnvo (accessed March 24, 2017). When Christians suggest that the New Testament is free of passages that invoke violence, I cite a text such as Luke 19:27, the concluding sentence in one of Jesus's parables: "But as for these enemies of mine, who did not want me to reign over them, bring them here and slaughter them before me."

With no organized Muslim community in our area, we had no partners to present a different face of the faith. So I began to teach my congregation about Islam. (I had to learn something first.) Still, my world felt too small. Eventually, I left the congregational rabbinate, earned a doctorate with a focus on comparative exegesis, and began teaching at a primarily Protestant seminary.

It was there I met André LaCocque, a Christian scholar of Hebrew Bible, who was the first real interreligious leader at Chicago Theological Seminary. Over 30 years ago, André started the Center for Jewish, Christian, and Islamic Studies. He argued that one cannot understand Christianity without understanding its roots in Judaism; Jesus, after all, was a Jew.[45] When he first explained this to me as his primary motivation, I was troubled. Such study runs the risk of being interested only in pre-Christian Judaism—Judaism as a dead faith, not the living, breathing, vibrant faith of Jews today.

Then André told me the story of interreligious engagement in which he was transformed. In Belgium during the Shoah, his parents risked everything to hide a Jewish family. André spent the war pretending the child was his cousin. When André became a parent, he and his wife sent their children to Jewish day school, even though they initially faced as much suspicion and hostility as did Jewish kids who wound up in Catholic schools. André believed that, in order to know oneself, one needs to know the heart of the stranger—indeed, to *be* the stranger, to be transformed by the life and faith of the other.

I am not quite that bold, but I nonetheless came to realize that much of what I understood about myself, I too had learned through difference. My minority status as a Jew, for instance, made me committed to lifting up marginalized voices and emphasizing the profound multivocality within my own tradition. *Tikkun olam*, which posits a collective task of repairing the world so that it better resembles what an omnibenevolent God may have had in mind, became foundational for me, particularly once I "met" the fight for civil rights. Deep learning in other lifestances enhances my appreciation of Judaism and adorns my spiritual journey with special luminance. While I have long been able to articulate categories of my social location and recognize the tremendous advantages of my

45. Although the point was once considered mildly subversive, Chicago Theological Seminary professors of New Testament have been teaching the texts through a Jewish prism for many years. They present Jesus as an observant Jew, and the literary assaults on the Pharisees as an internal Jewish polemic with the closest "competition." They recognize the Jesus movement as an emerging particularity, alongside other expressions of Judaism—all struggling to maintain their identity over against the universalist imperial engine of the Greco-Roman world (even as they were also significantly impacted by it). These insights help to defuse some of the anti-Judaism that stained Christian teaching in history.

white, cis-gendered, upper-middle-class, and heterosexual identities, I understand their implications and their intersectionality fully only through encounters with difference. This process of discernment is not about mastering theories of multiculturalism; it is about coming to know who I am and how I should live my life.

Ultimately, I am required to decenter myself; otherwise, the meeting of persons from different perspectives, as described throughout this chapter, can become merely an instrumental means to improve my self-understanding. Again, people should not be reduced to what they can teach us about ourselves. In the encounter with diversity, the formation of self means learning to live in ways that are responsible and accountable to others.

I decided to relaunch André's Center for Jewish, Christian, and Islamic Studies; to work with the seminary leadership to make our school a fertile and inviting place for individuals of diverse lifestances; and to think about what it means to be, and to train, interreligious leaders. The drive to live in response-ability to difference, and to work toward the repair of the universe, can become a catalyst for the discernment of meaning, direction, and purpose.

My vocation is in need of you.

Response

Homayra Ziad

The search for commonality is a natural step in the art of relationship. Yet I am grateful to Rachel for reminding us that genuine growth takes place in the encounter with difference. Her chapter teaches us that when we approach boundaries as meeting places rather than as breaking points, we become far more significant interlocutors for one another. I may know that you and I build our systems of meaning on different sets of assumptions; yet not only do I see you as a complex human being, I also witness that your sources of wisdom have the capacity to enrich and challenge my own convictions. This encounter requires hard work, individually and in community, as well as the discovery of resources within our traditions that inspire us to commit and to recommit.

As we see far too often, the mere presence of diversity does not necessarily bring about a productive encounter with difference. We may celebrate diversity in theory, but society often conflates difference and discord. In moments of doubt,

I take seriously the Qur'an's celebration of diversity as a gift from God that should be acknowledged and engaged:

> Among God's wonders is the creation of the heavens and earth, and the diversity of your tongues and colors. There truly are signs in this for those who know. (Rum, 30:22)
> People, we created you all from a single man and a single woman and made you into nations and tribes so that you might come to know one another. (al Hujurat, 49:13)

The call in these verses is to *know* one another. The word does not indicate a superficial encounter, or even a well-intentioned book-knowledge. It is a heart-deep knowledge borne of engagement—as Diana Eck names it, an encounter of commitments.

Here, the virtue of humility becomes critical. Humility creates the vulnerability that allows for this encounter. The Qur'an reminds me of this in the ubiquitous phrase *Allahu Akbar* ("God is greater") and in *wa fawqa kulli dhi 'ilmin 'alim* ("Above every knower is one who knows more": Yusuf, 12:76). Can we learn, as the Qur'an asks elsewhere, to challenge one another "in the most beautiful of ways" (an-Nahl, 16:125), with humility and with a willingness to be transformed? Can I learn to honor our difference in such a way that your joys and troubles become mine? And can we engage these dispositions in ways that help us create the pluralist democracy to which we all aspire?

2

Reviving Sheila

LISTENING TO THE CALL OF MULTIPLE RELIGIOUS BELONGING

Katherine (Trina) Janiec Jones

WHAT MIGHT THE language of *vocation* and *calling* mean for those who identify with multiple religious traditions? We have become increasingly aware of the tension between an individual's dynamic, multi-layered concept of self, on the one hand, and the seemingly static, reified nature of various identity groups, on the other. This tension has led many people (including a great many undergraduate students) to describe their own identities in multiple ways—some of which may seem, at least to outside observers, to be mutually exclusive. In an era of multiple identities and multiple belonging, what does it mean to think critically about the meaning and purpose of one's life? Can the language of *calling* and *vocation* play a role in such an environment?

If we are engaged in the project of "hearing vocation differently" (as the title of this volume suggests), we must also cultivate the discipline, forbearance, and openheartedness required to *listen* differently. The process of thinking about vocation in a multi-religious context can be hermeneutically challenging, in that the very idea of "vocation" evolved within a Christian framework of meaning. Can a concept associated with one religious tradition become operative in other traditions? *Should* it do so? At a minimum, we need to remain alert to the fact that how we choose to listen to others might determine the boundaries of our efforts, perhaps excluding some potential conversation partners. Nevertheless, if a cross-religious conversation is undertaken in an invitational way, it can be productive rather than alienating.[1]

1. For more on this point, see the comments of David S. Cunningham in the introduction to this volume, particularly the section titled "An exclusively Christian concept?"

Unfortunately, any conversation about religious identity has the potential to create shame or defensiveness among some interlocutors, due in large part to their fear of censure. This fear may be even more pervasive among women, due to the already-existing cultural pressures for them to act in particular ways, or to perform "femininity" according to cultural scripts that are ever shifting (and potentially marginalizing or silencing). As they are growing up, many young girls receive the message that their primary calling is to be "properly female" (whatever that might mean), and that their personal, individual vocation takes a secondary role to their socially prescribed (and proscribed) vocation as women.

In this chapter, I explore the challenges faced by those who don't behave according to norms, or who don't fit neatly into the parameters of already-established groups. I will introduce the problem by offering some personal reflections on my own experience of these challenges and their potentially silencing effects. I then turn to Mary Pipher's book *Reviving Ophelia*,[2] in which she describes the identity pressures adolescent girls face as they enter the rocky waters of womanhood. I want to suggest that some of Pipher's observations also apply, with particular force and across ages and genders,[3] to those whose identity formation is characterized by multiple religious belonging— or by other kinds of religious belonging that do not fit established categories. I then turn to a passage in the 1985 book *Habits of the Heart* concerning a woman named Sheila, who describes herself as living in the "spaces between" clearly defined religious traditions. Many readers of *Habits* responded to Sheila's sense of her own religiosity in ways that could charitably be characterized as less than positive. I will argue that, rather than stemming from a solipsistic self-regard or a lack of commitment to community, Sheila's self-described "do it yourself" religious identity might have been rooted in the desire to protect herself against dominant cultural demands concerning gender and religious affiliation.

By examining vocation with attention to identity formation and multiple religious belonging,[4] we will discover new factors that demand consideration. For

2. Mary Pipher, *Reviving Ophelia: Saving the Selves of Adolescent Girls* (New York: Penguin Group, 1994).

3. Conversations about gender run the risk of describing sex and gender in essentializing or normative ways. The feminist movement has raised questions about whether these conversations have adequately addressed the lived experience of nonwhite, non-upper- to middle-class women. For more on this topic, see Janell Hobson, ed., *Are All the Women Still White? Rethinking Race, Expanding Feminisms* (Albany: State University of New York Press, 2016) and Louise Michele Newman, *White Women's Rights: The Racial Origins of Feminism in the United States* (New York: Oxford University Press, 1999).

4. Rather than attempting a definition of "multiple religious belonging," I will focus on the dispositional qualities salutary to fostering a conversation about vocation with those who

those who might not feel entirely at home within any particular culturally defined religious or philosophical tradition, conversations about vocation are likely to be fraught with confusion or hesitancy. This issue will be magnified when employing an understanding of vocation that is indexed to a specific religious framework. How might a person talk about her vocation, about what she feels called to do with her life, if others question the legitimacy of the identity she currently inhabits? If we hope to hear vocation differently—and to hear voices that might be speaking in unfamiliar languages with new syntactical combinations—we must be sure to create spaces where those voices are likely to have the courage, will, and energy to speak.

If I don't know your language, Can you still hear my voice?

Many of us have had the experience of being in an environment where we don't speak the local language very well. This sense of inarticulacy might spring from a literal language difference (a French speaker in a predominantly English-speaking country) or from differences in cultural or behavioral "languages" (a Christian attending her friend's *bat mitzvah*, or someone with no interest in sports attending a football game). When we find ourselves in such situations, we might simply try to keep quiet; but we could still find ourselves labeled as outsiders—or even end up in genuine peril. Similarly, students sometimes hesitate to raise their hands in class, lest they say something "wrong" and appear silly or stupid to their peers. Students of color might find the tacit cultural terrain of a predominantly white college or university to be challenging to manage; they may hesitate to draw attention to themselves in public spaces (including classrooms).

I experienced this self-protective urge when I first entered graduate school. I remember sitting inconspicuously in my classes, trying not to draw undue attention to myself, while I worked furiously to figure out what in the world everyone else was talking about. I felt like I was swimming in a sea of disciplinary jargon,

---

might feel that they belong multiply with regard to religion. Two scholars who have written extensively about the category itself are Paul F. Knitter and Catherine Cornille. See also Rachel A. Heath, "Lessons in Multifaith Chaplaincy and Feminist Thought: Making Room for Multiple Religious Belonging in Interfaith Practice," *Journal of Interreligious Studies* 20 (March 2017): 71–79, http://irstudies.org/journal/lessons-in-multifaith-chaplaincy-and-feminist-thought-making-room-for-multiple-religious-belonging-in-interfaith-praxis-by-rachel-a-heath/ (accessed January 24, 2018) and Douglas Jacobsen and Rhonda Hustedt Jacobsen, *No Longer Invisible: Religion in University Education* (New York: Oxford University Press, 2012), 26–45.

trying to parse out messages and meanings when no one had given me a key to the code. It seemed that everyone else had read books that I hadn't read, knew things that I didn't know, and understood how they were supposed to frame their comments so as to invoke approving nods from professors. Like many people in graduate school, I felt a bit like a fraud; I was sure that, somewhere along the line, people would realize they had made a mistake by letting me in. The safest thing to do, then, was to just keep quiet, to stay alert, to listen hard, and to figure out how to play along. I kept my mouth shut a lot of the time.

Graduate school was a competitive environment, and I'm sure my fellow students felt insecure as well. We were being trained to think critically, to construct good arguments, and to find the weaknesses in the arguments of others. Being able to critique someone else's claims aggressively was often taken as a sign of one's intellectual acumen; proving one's worthiness often took the form of listening to another's statement only for the purpose of identifying its weaknesses. This demonstrated one's legitimacy as a member of the in-group; it also built up fortresses against one's own self-inflicted sense of fraudulence.

This tendency—trying to prove one's own worthiness by critiquing others—frequently arises in religious circles. Many people experience a competitive, anxiety-fueled desire to prove that their own tradition is right and others are wrong, or to assert that their own ways of embodying a religious tradition are the best ways. Indeed, some hear others' claims to religious identity as a direct challenge to their own. If I were to claim to be a Christian, for example, other members of that group might expect me to "prove my case"—to corroborate my claim to legitimate belonging. This in turn might make me hesitant to claim my own identity publicly, especially if I experience resonances with more than one religious tradition. In such circumstances, silence might seem the best way to avoid conversational obstacles and arguments.

Asam Ahmad describes this kind of discourse—noninvitational and listening only to find matters of critique—in an article on "call-out culture." He defines this term as "the tendency among progressives, radicals, activists, and community organizers to publicly name instances or patterns of oppressive behavior and language use by others."[5] Ahmad's argument is not that such statements shouldn't be addressed; clearly, one should not let one's interlocutor marinate in statements

5. Asam Ahmad, "What Makes Call-Out Culture So Toxic," *Films for Action*, March 4, 2015, http://www.filmsforaction.org/articles/a-note-on-callout-culture/ (accessed May 29, 2017). Originally published as "A Note on Call-Out Culture," *Briarpatch Magazine*, March 2, 2015, https://briarpatchmagazine.com/articles/view/a-note-on-call-out-culture (accessed March 7, 2018).

of racism or sexism. Rather, Ahmad points to the *performative* (and often very public) nature of the call-out:

> Especially in online venues like Twitter and Facebook, calling someone out isn't just a private interaction between two individuals: it's a public performance where people can demonstrate their wit or how pure their politics are. Indeed, sometimes it can feel like the performance itself is more significant than the content of the call-out.[6]

Ahmad then observes the tendency, among those calling others out, to lose track of their target's humanity:

> In the context of call-out culture, it is easy to forget that the individual we are calling out is a human being, and that different human beings in different social locations will be receptive to different strategies for learning and growing. For instance, most call-outs I have witnessed immediately render anyone who has committed a perceived wrong as an outsider to the community. One action becomes a reason to pass judgment on someone's entire being.[7]

Of course, call-out culture is not limited to "progressives, radicals, activists, and community organizers"; it is prevalent in more conservative circles as well.

One paradox of call-out culture (and the exhaustion and anxiety it can foster) is that it folds back in on itself: by naming call-out culture as being problematic, one runs the risk of being heard as implying that one *shouldn't* declare that certain things are wrong. But even if one finds the right balance of naming injustice and avoiding shaming others, one can still experience a kind of spiritual exhaustion, as a result of always being in the rhetorical line of fire. The prevalence of call-out culture can thereby make those in marginalized groups feel even more hesitant to speak out for what they feel is right. For those who are accustomed to having to qualify their statements, to explain what they mean (and then explain again) for the benefit of those in less marginalized groups, it can be exhausting to know that any such statement requires that they gird their loins and prepare themselves for attack. For example, Palca Shibale describes the exhaustion of having to explain racism over and over again.[8] She also quotes Toni Morrison's description of the

---

6. Ahmad, "Call-Out Culture."

7. Ahmad, "Call-Out Culture."

8. See Palca Shibale, "Why I Am Tired of Explaining Racism to People," *Seattle Times*, June 20, 2016, https://www.seattletimes.com/seattle-news/why-im-tired-of-explaining-racism-to-people/ (accessed March 7, 2018).

"depleting" nature of this process: "It keeps you from doing your work. It keeps you explaining, over and over again, your reason for being."[9] Thus, even those who have the courage and will to speak, and who avoid shaming or humiliating others in the process, will still have to negotiate the depletion of their energy and spirit.

How, then, does this all relate to multiple religious belonging? A person who understands herself as belonging to multiple identity groups, religious or otherwise, might well have the courage and the will to speak. Nevertheless, maintaining the energy to remain in conversation with those who might not understand the language she is speaking is even harder in the context of rapid-response call-out culture. Those who feel that they belong to more than one religious group—or, perhaps, that no institutionally recognized religious group accurately reflects their own deepest selves—might well be expected, as Morrison was, to explain their reason for being. In such circumstances, it can be easy to retreat into oneself—into a self-protective interiority.

In the next two sections of this chapter, I will examine two instances in which people have retreated into silence when others seemed unable (or perhaps unwilling) to hear their voices, or have responded to those voices with disapprobation, censure, or mockery. The common thread among them is the subjects' cultural liminality: they do not fit neatly into others' categories.

Selfhood and the performance of identity

Psychologist Mary Pipher wrote about her experiences working with young women in her 1994 book *Reviving Ophelia: Saving the Selves of Adolescent Girls*. In her introduction, she explains that she had been struck by the prevalence of common themes among the sufferings of her young clients. Many had eating disorders; many were withdrawn; some were self-mutilators or had even attempted suicide. Many had suffered sexual abuse. While she accepted the fact that these problems were not new, she felt that the characteristics of suffering among adolescent women were different in the 1990s than those she remembered from her own adolescence:

> Girls today are much more oppressed. They are coming of age in a more dangerous, sexualized, and media-saturated culture. They face incredible

9. Portland State University, "Black Studies Center public dialogue. Pt. 2," *Special Collections: Oregon Public Speakers* 90 (1975), http://pdxscholar.library.pdx.edu/orspeakers/90 (accessed March 7, 2018), audiorecording.

> pressures to be beautiful and sophisticated, which in junior high means using chemicals and being sexual. As they navigate a more dangerous world, girls are less protected. As I looked at the culture girls enter as they come of age, I was struck by what a girl-poisoning culture it was.[10]

These "girl poisoning" elements arise from conflicting social scripts about what it means to be a woman (and what it means to be "feminine") in the broader culture. For example, as their bodies begin to change, girls begin to realize the extent to which they are valued (and policed) on the basis of their bodies—or, more specifically, on what their bodies look like and what they can do in terms of sexuality and reproduction. There is great pressure for girls to be sexual—but not *too* sexual, lest they be labeled as promiscuous. They are pressured to display their beauty, but not to do so with enough competence that they might be seen as growing up too fast, being too womanly, or inadvertently inviting actual sexual activity. They are told to be pretty, but also to be strong; to take care of themselves, but also to be caregivers for others.

For each of these endeavors, there is a ready audience of watchful critics, sitting on the sidelines, prepared to evaluate how well the young woman has fulfilled each of these inchoate demands, many of which seem to be mutually contradictory. It should therefore not surprise us that adolescent young women—those who, just years before, might have been fearless experimenters with life and lovers of learning—suddenly retreat into a shell of interiority. They often seek to keep quiet and stay out of the way, particularly when inhabiting spaces that no longer feel safe or inviting.

Pipher describes the adolescent phase of life as a "social developmental Bermuda triangle" into which girls can very easily disappear. Their "IQ scores drop and their math and science scores plummet. They lose their resiliency and optimism and become less curious and inclined to take risks. They lose their assertive, energetic and 'tomboyish' personalities and become more deferential, self-critical and depressed. They report great unhappiness with their own bodies."[11] Pipher's "Ophelia" refers, of course, to the character in Shakespeare's *Hamlet*, whom we meet at the point when she is just entering the phase of life described here. It seems that she has had a positive relationship with Hamlet in the past, but now she finds herself caught in the mounting tensions among the king, her father Polonius, and Hamlet himself, whose apparent mental imbalance (whether real or affected) is projected onto Ophelia. She is made to question her

10. Pipher, *Reviving Ophelia*, 12.

11. Pipher, *Reviving Ophelia*, 19.

own judgment, even about Hamlet's level of interest in her ("Indeed, my lord, you made believe so": III, 1). She is forced to absorb the anger and intrigue among the three male characters. Pipher suggests that Ophelia therefore serves as a useful allusion for

> the destructive forces that affect young women. As a girl, Ophelia is happy and free, but with adolescence she loses herself. When she falls in love with Hamlet, she lives only for his approval. She has no inner direction; rather she struggles to meet the demands of Hamlet and her father. Her value is determined utterly by their approval. Ophelia is torn apart by her efforts to please.

Eventually, Ophelia goes mad; in the wake of her sorrow and struggle, she drowns herself.

Pipher asserts that adolescence is when girls' perception changes: it grows sharper, or perhaps just begins to pick up on different stimuli. Girls begin to see the ways in which power, and perhaps even safety, arise not from their own autonomy, but from performing according to culturally sanctioned scripts about what a woman should be. Further, they begin to realize that the very scripts themselves often directly contradict one another. Thus, "adolescent girls experience a conflict between their autonomous selves and their need to be feminine, between their status as human beings *and their vocation as females*."[12]

Reviving Ophelia was written in 1994. Pipher admitted that, while some of the circumstances that she described had worsened since her own adolescence, others had improved. However, since her book was published, some things have certainly gotten worse. For example, the entry of social media onto the scene and the ubiquity of easy online access have increased the variety of venues in which young women can be critiqued (or "called out"); these developments have also exacerbated the speed with which the critiques can be leveled.[13] Of course, young women are not the only people to go through tumultuous changes as they grow up. However, Pipher's description of girls' "vocation as females" is suggestive and revelatory; she is pointing to something fundamental in a young person's search for meaning, purpose, and identity. "Calmness is replaced by anxiety. Their way of thinking is changing. Far below the surface they are struggling with the

12. Pipher, *Reviving Ophelia*, 21–22, emphasis added.

13. Sarah Marsh, "Girls and Social Media: 'You Are Expected to Live Up to an Impossible Standard,'" *The Guardian,* August 22, 2017, https://www.theguardian.com/society/2017/aug/23/girls-and-social-media-you-are-expected-to-live-up-to-an-impossible-standard (accessed March 7, 2018).

most basic of human questions: What is my place in the universe, what is my meaning?"[14]

This question of meaning, of wondering where one ultimately belongs, returns us to the issues of religion and vocation. What implications might Pipher's findings have for young people's thinking about vocation in a multi-religious context? Or, even more so, in a context where they are experiencing *themselves* as multiple: as being under multiple demands, as having multiple (and competing) desires, and as having dreams that nudge them in multiple directions? In this sense, Pipher's argument applies more broadly to all aspects of identity formation—including religious and theological development, at both the individual and the communal level.

Consider, for example, the groups known demographically as "nones." As noted in the introduction to this volume, this category is fairly amorphous, sometimes including not only those with no religious affiliation but also those who identify as "spiritual but not religious" (SBNR) or as "seekers." As Linda Mercadante notes, these individuals still often "think theologically," even though they eschew self-identification with institutionalized religious communities.[15] Theology, she asserts, has to do with the existential questions that human beings ponder, "such as: 'Why are we here?' 'For what can we hope?' 'Why do we suffer? 'How can we thrive?' 'Is death the end?'"[16] Mercadante's interviews with self-identified" "nones" or "SBNRs" suggest that theological and religious questions do not vanish just because someone does not identify with a specific religious group.

The same applies to those who think of themselves as belonging to multiple religious groups. If theological questions are not limited to the issues of a particular community, but are instead understood as involving a broad range of existential concerns, we can begin to think of Pipher's observations in a different light. The challenges faced by Pipher's "Ophelias" begin to resemble the identity formation challenges of those who hear resonance in more than one religious tradition.

By thinking about these groups together, we bring to light the ways in which we often impede each other's vocational development—and our own—through social norming. As noted previously, this process of norming lies at the root of "call-out culture," which often involves shaming, mockery, or other dehumanizing

---

14. Pipher, *Reviving Ophelia*, 22–23.

15. Linda A. Mercadante, *Belief without Borders: Inside the Minds of the Spiritual but not Religious* (New York: Oxford University Press, 2014), 227.

16. Mercadante, *Belief*, 228.

actions. But Mercadante's analysis helps us to see two further points. First, even those who do not use typical or traditional theological language may well still have a range of significant theological concerns. Second, many of those who disassociate themselves from "theology" or "religion" are often objecting to a very specific kind of theological or religious language—language that is primarily understood as rigid, punitive, limiting, shame-inducing, judgmental, and/or deeply exclusionary.[17]

All of this suggests how well Pipher's findings might apply to these groups. The defensive silence about many things of deep import, and the reflexive and improvisational performances of different cultural scripts (offered in an effort to please multiple audiences simultaneously)—these youthful tendencies, as Pipher notes, never entirely go away. And, as we are increasingly aware, these kinds of social pressures and psychological effects are not restricted to one side of a binary understanding of gender.[18]

Indeed, anyone who is seen as "not fitting" into particular social norms and cultural categories can, to use Pipher's metaphor of Shakespeare's Ophelia, lose their ability to breathe. Ophelia's death could have been avoided if someone had only been willing to revive her. Similarly, in the face of the hurricanes of adolescence, of multiple religious belonging, or of other ways that people might fail to "fit" into cultural norms, people often lose their breath, their voices, and their animating energy; they too need to be "revived." Perhaps they need to regain consciousness—consciousness of themselves as important beings who have worth, whose stories matter, even if they don't speak comfortably through predetermined scripts. Perhaps they simply need friendship and an open and loving ear to listen, as they find themselves identifying with more than one group—and, as a result, feel liminal, hidden, unseen, or lost. Perhaps, like patients in need of the constancy of an alert and responsive nurse, they need someone to administer the life-giving air of listening presence, of compassion, and of nonjudgmental forbearance so that they can regain strength and energy.

Perhaps it should not surprise us that many people, perceiving the absence of anyone who would be willing and able to "revive" them, might well prefer to retreat into themselves and to avoid talking about their interior lives in public. This is especially likely if their interior lives (and specifically, in this case, their religious

17. Mercadante, *Belief*, 236.

18. For one account of the relationship between multiple religious belonging and nonbinary accounts of gender, see Michelle Voss Roberts, "Queering Multiple Religious Belonging," *Feminist Studies in Religion*, November 15, 2016, http://www.fsrinc.org/queering-multiple-religious-belonging/ (accessed March 7, 2018).

identities) do not fit into preapproved, easily identifiable categories. In the next section, I explore one example of such a "retreat."

Sheila

In their 1985 book, Robert Bellah and his coauthors express serious concern about the "privatization" of American religion.[19] The reasons for their concern are manifold, complex, and interesting. They observe that religious institutions had served as one of the primary vehicles through which societal cohesion could be attained (and maintained) for the sake of the common good. They worry that, with the influence of these institutions now eroding, other social structures will become more fragile—perhaps endangering that commitment to the common good.

In chapter 9 of *Habits*, the reader briefly meets Sheila, who serves as one example of this privatization. She is described in the book as follows:

> One person we interviewed has actually named her religion (she calls it her "faith") after herself. This suggests the logical possibility of over 220 million American religions, one for each of us. Sheila Larson is a young nurse who has received a good deal of therapy and who describes her faith as "Sheilaism." "I believe in God. I'm not a religious fanatic. I can't remember the last time I went to church. My faith has carried me a long way. It's Sheilaism. Just my own little voice." Sheila's faith has some tenets beyond belief in God, though not many. In defining "my own Sheilaism," she said: "it's just try to love yourself and be gentle with yourself. You know, I guess, take care of each other. I think He would want us to take care of each other." Like many others, Sheila would be willing to endorse few more specific injunctions.[20]

Because Sheila had individualized her religion and privatized her religiosity, and because she was unmoored from any religious institution or community, she represented the antithesis of what the authors felt could best serve the common good—at least with respect to religious institutions. She is treated as an archetype of complete privatization; in the authors' judgment, she had cut herself off from deep, meaningful, and sustainable relationships with others, bound by

---

19. Robert Bellah et al., *Habits of the Heart: Individualism and Commitment in American Life* (Berkeley: University of California Press, 1985), 220, 224, 234.

20. Bellah et al., *Habits*, 220–21.

commitments of mutual care. Readers also tended to interpret Sheila as an example of a peculiarly American emotional immaturity, marked by shifting norms, narcissistic primary concern for self (at the expense of community), and a nearly solipsistic isolation.

Later in the same section, the authors mention Martin Marty's conception of "the public church" as an entity that developed in response to shifting conceptions of both Protestant and Catholic authority in contemporary culture.[21] In so doing, they articulate what they see as the need for "public responsibility rather than individual or group withdrawal" in American cultural life, lest the broader culture be left "without the leavening of a creative intellectual focus," replaced by a "quasi-therapeutic blandness."[22] In short, they describe a withdrawal into individualized religious interiority in negative terms; it leaves people unmoored and alone. As a result of these concerns, then, Sheila is seen as the paradigm of radical religious individualism—a person who is not stepping forward toward public responsibility, and who lacks the support and guidance that a community of like-minded travelers might provide.

Even though Sheila takes up a miniscule amount of space in the book, she seems to have hit a nerve with many readers of *Habits of the Heart*, as evidenced by the following excerpt from a 1986 lecture by the book's lead author, Robert Bellah:

> To get the conversation started this evening I thought I would talk a little bit about some of the findings of *Habits of the Heart,* about religion, and particularly about the tendency in America in the direction of religious privatism. Early in chapter nine, which is the chapter on religion in *Habits*, we describe someone whose real name we don't use but who has become sufficiently paradigmatic that as I go around the country I find people talking about this before I have a chance to say anything.[23]

Why did Sheila "become paradigmatic"? What kind of nerve did she hit among readers?

We learn very little about the deeper context of Sheila's life—only that she has been in therapy and that she works as a nurse. One cannot help but wonder why the authors felt it important to choose, from everything that might have been said

21. Bellah et al., *Habits*, 239.

22. Bellah et al., *Habits*, 238.

23. Robert Bellah, "Habits of the Heart: Implications for Religion," Lecture at St. Mark's Catholic Church, Isla Vista, CA, February 21, 1986, http://www.robertbellah.com/lectures_5.htm, (accessed December 5, 2016).

about her life, to tell the reader that Sheila had "received a good deal of therapy." Might they have wanted to sow doubts about her stability, suggesting that she was so misguided and rootless that she herself could tell she needed help—and in response, had sought out the help of a therapist? Alternatively, might it have been the case that she was not particularly forthright in describing the details of her own commitments, of her own spiritual life, because of prior experiences of harsh critique from her conversation partners? Might Sheila have been an adult version of the adolescent Ophelias described by Mary Pipher?

Despite the lack of additional biographical information, it seems reasonable to suppose that Sheila's interior life and her interaction with the broader communities of which she was a part were more complicated and nuanced than her rendering in the book suggests. It is particularly interesting and suggestive, for example, that Sheila worked as a nurse. Nursing is a life-giving profession—one that many nurses describe as a *vocation.* The nurse's call is to provide healing, care, and sustenance; in some cases, especially for those who work with the terminally ill, its goals include providing a sense of dignity and wholeness to patients as their bodies begin to wear out. Those who are ill frequently find that their own senses of themselves become threatened and begin to disappear as their bodies begin to change, and as they find that they are no longer able to do the things that they were once able to do. Nurses provide succor; they offer day-to-day, on-the-ground support to those who are sick and suffering. They cleanse the bodies of the sick and help to ease their pain; in many cases, they provide life-sustaining oxygen and medicines to patients who are losing their strength, who are losing their ability to breathe. Nurses maintain, and often revive, those who are facing their own kinds of existential hurricanes.

Being present for another person, and listening well enough to respond to who that person is from moment to moment, requires a great deal of strength and love. I see nothing weak or timid in Sheila's assertion that her guiding principle—call it her *vocation*—was to "just try to love yourself and be gentle with yourself" and to "take care of each other." In fact, this language implies a brave expression of a willingness to take up a very challenging calling: to be present to others with responsive love. Sheila might have had trouble filling out a census survey about her religious identification, but she certainly seemed to have a sense of what she had been called to do.

Perhaps this provides us with a clue as to what it might mean to "revive" Sheila—and by extension, many others like her. It is not that her life or her perspective needs to change, but that *we* need to think about her anew. Rather than serving as an example of someone who can be written off—or who seems to threaten the integrity of religious communities because she doesn't identify with one—perhaps she can help us learn *to listen differently*.

Ophelia, Sheila, and me

Ophelia and Sheila are not representative of all women, nor are women the only people who find their breath being taken away. Nevertheless, by paying better attention to the Ophelias and Sheilas of the world, and to the assumptions that we make about them, we can better find our way into our increasingly multi-faith context. These figures remind us that religious pluralism—both within cultures and within each individual person—is sure to become an even more pressing challenge to our interactions with one another.

In the context of higher education in particular, this emerging context has important implications for all of us—students and teachers alike—who are seeking to discern our vocations as we make our way through the hurricanes of life. We would be wise to broaden our understanding of what it means to "belong" to a religious group, or to any group for that matter, and to think about the fact that the need to belong (or the pressure to belong) can take a real toll on those trying to forge a different path. While Sheila didn't feel that she belonged to any particular religious tradition, she clearly thought about ultimate questions—about what she should do and who she should be[24]—and about her relationships with others. Her guiding voice was her own, and while the tenets of her religiosity might not seem very specific, a generous reading could cast her understanding of her own vocation as being oriented toward taking care of the people whom she met, in all of the particularity of their stations in life at that moment—regardless of their circumstances.

Both Sheila and Ophelia serve as useful examples to consider in light of the "call-out culture" described in the first section of this chapter. Sheila's description of her own religion as "Sheilaism" was called out—mocked and critiqued—by many who read *Habits*, even though the book itself was published long before the advent of social media. Sheila's malleable sense of religious identity was called out as being less than optimal and not really even properly religious. What kind of chilling effect, then, might people's denunciation of Sheila have had on others who felt similarly about their own religious identity?

Sheila, I think, serves as a sort of Rorschach test. Readers see in her (or project onto her) their own sense of what a religious community *should* look like—as well as their own, perhaps painful, experiences and memories of feeling "othered"

24. This phrase, often cited as an explication of two of the most important concerns of vocational discernment, appears as the subtitle of Mark Schwehn and Dorothy Bass, eds., *Leading Lives That Matter: What We Should Do and Who We Should Be* (Grand Rapids, MI: Eerdmans, 2006). See also Jerry Organ, "Of Doing and Being: Broadening Our Understanding of Vocation," in *Vocation across the Academy: A New Vocabulary for Higher Education*, ed. David S. Cunningham (New York: Oxford University Press, 2017), 225–43.

by a group to which they thought they belonged (or toward which they had at least performed the gestures of belonging[25]). Perhaps Sheila is reviled by some because she gives voice to the deep, dark secret that many of us harbor: we aren't entirely sure who we are with regard to our religious selves and our religious belonging. We might not even be sure what "belonging" actually *means*, so we make it up from day to day, trying to respond to things as best we can—hoping all the while that no one outs us as frauds, as "other than," as "not quite good enough," as somehow less than "pure."

When I was discussing an early draft of this chapter with a group of colleagues, I was surprised by the degree to which Sheila still evoked spirited—almost visceral—response and discussion. One comment in particular sticks in my memory from that discussion. "Why," one colleague asked rhetorically, "do we hate her so much?" I didn't say anything out loud, but in my own mind, I thought, "Well, I don't hate her. I think I kind of *am* her." Interestingly, over the next few hours, a few people approached me individually and told me that they didn't hate Sheila at all—that they actually felt a great deal of empathy for her. Indeed, they told me that, in her story, they heard resonances of their own interior multiple belonging—their own religious or spiritual fluidity.

How do I see myself in Sheila? Even though I was raised within a Christian framework, I still think I often don't know what "being a Christian" really means. My ideas on the matter have shifted throughout my life, even from day to day and from moment to moment; but in some ways, I have always lived in the spaces between various religious identities. When I was growing up, my mother, who was raised as a Southern Baptist but later became an Episcopalian, took me and my sister to church with her, while my father attended services at the Catholic church in town. This didn't (and still doesn't) seem odd to me; we all come from backgrounds in which multiple rivers lead into the spillway of our own identity. I certainly never thought of my mother as "the former Baptist Episcopalian who happens to be my mother," or of my father as "my Catholic father." They were just Mom and Dad, in their own particularity. I tried to interact with them in the way that Asad Ahmad describes as the one for which we should strive: "to engage with them as people with complicated stories and histories."[26]

And this is certainly the way I want people to engage with me. Here, I intentionally use the word *engage* to imply a way of interacting with people from moment to moment, seeing (or at least trying to see) our conversation partners

25. For some helpful comments of the "performance" of one's religious identity, see Homayra Ziad's comments in chapter 9 of this volume.

26. Ahmad, "Call-Out Culture."

as whole, complicated people with multiple stories.[27] The details of these stories become more or less important at different points in time, depending on context. However, I know how difficult it is to see one aspect of a person's identity and not assume that this element exhausts, or even determines, the entirety of that person's being. As a result, I am often not readily forthcoming about my own religious identity. I worry that my conversation partner will essentialize me on the basis of this one aspect of who I am—or assume that one facet of my life represents my entire being.

I have vocationally relevant reasons for not talking too readily about my own religious identity (at least not until a certain amount of trust has been established). First of all, my job—and I do see it as my vocation, as my calling—involves teaching undergraduate students about religion. College students are often in liminal phases of their own development, questioning who they are and who they want to be. For pedagogical reasons, I try not to make my own identity into the lens through which we approach our discussions. Part of my vocation as a teacher involves my being a listener, a sounding board; hence, it is of the utmost importance to me that I foster an atmosphere in which students feel that they can pursue questions with their own whole, complex selves.

Second—and this reason is related, but perhaps less noble—I find it very frustrating when people learn about one aspect of who I am, or about my past, and assume that they then can predict what I will think about things, or how I will respond. Perhaps some of this springs from my cultural "training" as a woman: I have often been the "only woman" in various groups, and have therefore been at least somewhat aware of how the gendering process impacts how my words are heard and how my actions are interpreted. Perhaps some of my reticence springs from the fact that I speak with an accent (I was born and raised in the southern United States)—and that, at least in academic circles, this accent has not historically been immediately associated with towering intelligence.[28]

27. In the context of religious pluralism and multiple religious belonging (or religious hybridity), I am influenced by the distinction Diana Eck makes in "What Is Pluralism?" between *pluralism* and *tolerance* (http://pluralism.org/what-is-pluralism/). I see *engagement* as differing from *tolerance* in that the latter suggests a somewhat grudging willingness to share the same space with another, no matter how distasteful or even abhorrent one might find that person to be. *Engagement* suggests a greater effort to talk to, be with, or *see* and *hear* (and not just tolerate) the other person—employing a hermeneutic of open-heartedness, giving the person the benefit of the doubt, and of assuming that person's value.

28. A recent editorial emphasizes the point: Adam Kirk Edgerton, "What's Wrong With Being From the South? Just Ask an Academic in the North," *Chronicle of Higher Education* 64, no. 36 (June 22, 2018): A52, https://www.chronicle.com/article/What-s-Wrong-With-Being-From/243510 (accessed July 10, 2018).

Perhaps it is a combination of my being audibly Southern and having been raised as a Christian that leads me toward a desire to avoid being stereotyped within the two-dimensional confines of a particular way of being religious, or of being Christian. In addition, the mere thought of constantly having to provide caveats, or to "prove" that I am not two-dimensional (or "properly" female, or academic, or Christian)—all of this has simply made me tired.

On a deeper level, I believe that my vocation as a human being is to be as present, responsive, and awake as I can be, for all people I meet—whatever their own cultural identities might be. I know that the way I present myself (or am presented) to others—the way in which I am present to them—will impact the interactions I am likely to have. Perhaps some parts of my identity will not seem very inviting to others, because of stereotypes they have arrived at on the basis of their own prior experiences—stereotypes they might not even realize are operational and being projected onto me.[29] If I want to be able to listen differently, then, I must be mindful of fostering an atmosphere in which my conversation partners feel safe enough to speak. Like Sheila, I know that sometimes I can be a Rorschach test, simply because of the way I look and how I sound.

My concern arises, in part, from my sense that, upon hearing that I am a Christian, others will find (in themselves) some sort of deep need to make sure that I am "doing it right." They might think that I need to "be Christian" in a particular way for my own good, or they might want to make sure that I am not impugning the integrity of the group by not being Christian in "the right way." But of course, there is more than one right way to be "properly" Christian. In any case, I know that I cannot be loving to others if I am mired in self-hatred, so I consider it vital to try to love myself and be gentle with myself, as Sheila says. Like Sheila, I also think that the most important thing is to "take care of each other," and that God "would want us to take care of each other."[30] And "taking care of each other" manifests itself in different ways.

As a graduate student, I studied Indian Buddhist philosophy. My dissertation focused on one Gupta-period Indian Buddhist thinker's ideas about the nature of the soul, or the self, with a comparison to one contemporary British Christian philosopher's ideas about the same. Rather than trying to prove who was right and who was wrong, I found myself trying primarily to *hear* their arguments attentively, and to present them as well as I could—while finding ways in which

---

29. In particular, my being white might make people put up certain defenses before we have begun to engage with one another.

30. Bellah et al., *Habits*, 221.

their thoughts might mutually enrich each other. I have found that the spirit in which I wrote my dissertation has spread into much of the work I do now, which focuses on interfaith engagement.

As I have grown older, I have realized that my thinking about the important matters in life has been as heavily influenced by my study of Buddhism as by anything else: as much as carrying and bearing a child, as much as falling in love, as much as sitting by the bedside and watching loved ones die. Buddhist and Christian metaphors and frameworks have merged, stirred together, and swirled like a kaleidoscope of meaning in me, and have shed vital and important lights on my existence—refracting, with each new day, new shades of understanding (and a renewed, humbled sense of how much I don't know). Through this experience, I have realized, in a way that goes far beyond an academic, intellectual understanding, that fluidity marks the identity not just of religious traditions, but of religious *persons* as well—and I am one such person.

So, as I have become more and more involved with interfaith dialogue and the issues surrounding engagement with religious pluralism in the public sphere, I have wondered about my "mixed identity." Many models of interfaith engagement presuppose that the participants are each beginning from a clearly defined, perhaps monochromatic, identity location. If productive dialogue requires that each participant have a clearly delineated theological-spiritual "home" at the outset, where does that leave me? Do I have to "fake it," feigning my own assuredness of a clear location that will make sense to other people, in order to participate? Do I have to perform a certain religious identity before I can even enter into the conversation? Would it be best to just keep my mouth shut, be quiet, and watch—lest I be outed as not really being "ready to play"?

I know that if I were to profess in any way to "being" Buddhist, of "belonging" to Buddhism, that claim would, in all likelihood, be heard as something that I don't necessarily mean. I do not engage in its usual practices and I haven't taken any vows; moreover, I am quite aware of the dangers of cultural appropriation. Nevertheless, as I watched both of my parents descend into dementia in their final years, and as I struggled to understand who they were becoming so that I could best respond to their needs, Buddhist metaphors and heuristics helped me cope and to remain present to them in ways that defy simple description. At the same time, I also realized that by reciting familiar Christian prayers to my parents—language that they knew and remembered—I was able to provide them (and myself) a great deal of succor. As I sat and held my mother's hand as she took her final breath, I knew that I was present to her, and that she knew I was there; my group affiliation didn't matter to her one bit. My own multiple belonging, my ability to think through a variety of metaphors from different religious traditions, allowed me to listen to her in ways that might not have otherwise been possible. And I knew that, even though disease had altered her mind in ways I couldn't possibly comprehend, she was listening. She could hear that I was there, and that—even in that moment, in the midst of my own multiple religious belonging—I was still trying to live into my own vocation.

Response

David S. Cunningham

I found Trina's essay convicting in a number of ways. For one thing, *Habits of the Heart* was published while I was in graduate school, and I was one of those people who responded to Sheila in ways that were "less than positive," as Trina so mildly puts it. In fact, I skipped right over the identification of her as a nurse (a profession about which I should have cared deeply) and reduced her to a cipher for the worst forms of American religious individualism—what Christian Smith and Melinda Lundquist Denton would later describe as "moralistic therapeutic deism." While I still have concerns about highly individualistic accounts of religious belief, Trina has helped me to recognize the need to see beyond the category—and to consider the *person* whose life has given her this perspective.

Trina's chapter also reinforced the notion (emphasized by many authors in this volume) that all traditions are always a complex amalgam, built from slices and segments of many different traditions, and constantly evolving. When college students self-identify as adhering to multiple religious traditions, they are simply enacting, in a more particular and accelerated form, the kinds of evolution through which all traditions eventually pass.

I fully understand this way of seeing things, but I still harbor some concerns about it—and they are concerns for Sheila herself, and for all those who find themselves actively constructing their faith perspective from a variety of traditions. Specifically, I worry that, for those who fully embrace "multiple religious belonging," it can become increasingly difficult to find fellow travelers along the way. While I realize that religious belief need not always be a broadly communal affair, I also think that a highly individualized account of belief is ultimately very lonely. I could never be a renunciant (see chapter 6), nor would I be satisfied to dwell primarily in myths of my own construction (see chapter 8). So I continue to identify as a Christian, even though that may sometimes mean accepting aspects of Christianity about which I have serious doubts—or not adopting some highly admirable element of another lifestance, if it seems in deep conflict with Christian belief. I do this, not because I think that there is anything wrong with multiple religious belonging, but because my desire for communion with more-or-less like-minded individuals seems to overpower my desire to put the pieces together as I might like to do. Still, Trina's discussion of these issues has helped me better appreciate those whose inclinations are the opposite. And since some of those individuals are likely to be our students, I want them to receive the same degree of validation and support as do those whose perspective is closer to my own.

3

The Call of Death and the Depth of Our Callings

THE QUALITY OF VOCATIONAL DISCERNMENT

Rahuldeep Gill

GERMAN THEOLOGIAN DIETRICH Bonhoeffer, martyr in the struggle against Nazism, argues that we have allowed quantity to overtake quality in many aspects of our lives. He urges us to recall and make prominent those elements of our lives that call us to go deeper, to replace mere accumulation and quantity with a dedication to nobility and quality:

> Nobility arises from and exists by sacrifice, courage, and a clear sense of duty to oneself and society, by expecting due regard for itself as a matter of course; and it shows an equally natural regard for others.... We need all along the line to recover the lost sense of quality and a social order based on quality. Quality is the greatest enemy of any kind of mass-levelling. Socially it means . . . pleasure in private life as well as courage to enter public life. Culturally it means a return from the newspaper and the radio to the book, from feverish activity to unhurried leisure, from dispersion to concentration, from sensationalism to reflection, from virtuosity to art, from snobbery to modesty, from extravagance to moderation. Quantities are competitive, qualities are complementary.[1]

1. Dietrich Bonhoeffer, "After Ten Years: A Reckoning Made at New Year 1943," in *Letters and Papers from Prison*, enlarged ed., ed. and trans. Eberhard Bethge (New York: Touchstone Books, 1997), 13. My attention to this has been part of my work at a Lutheran institution,

In addition, Bonheoffer believes that our investment in quality must go beyond the comfort of the private realm of piety: "Here and there people flee from public altercation into the sanctuary of private virtuousness. But those who do this must shut their mouths and their eyes to the injustice around them."[2] He urges us not to retreat, but to seek "civil courage," which Bonhoeffer himself pushed to its limit in trying to kill Adolph Hitler. In fact, it may be a necessary aspect of "quality"—and of imbuing all our work with quality—that we are prepared to put our lives on the line when that is demanded of us. Bonhoeffer takes his inspiration from Jesus's suffering on the cross, ultimately concluding that it is possible to "still love life" *and at the same time* to seek out "a death freely and voluntarily accepted."[3]

Others have recognized that in order to endow our work with genuine quality, we must face the real possibility of death. In Memphis, Tennessee, the night before he was assassinated, the Reverend Dr. Martin Luther King Jr. ended his final speech with these words:

> Like anybody, I would like to live a long life. Longevity has its place. But I'm not concerned about that now. I just want to do God's will. And He's allowed me to go up to the mountain. And I've looked over. And I've seen the Promised Land. I may not get there with you. But I want you to know tonight, that we, as a people, will get to the promised land! And so I'm happy, tonight. I'm not worried about anything. I'm not fearing any man! Mine eyes have seen the glory of the coming of the Lord.[4]

Dr. King recognized that his work could only reach its true depth and its potential impact when he faced the possibility of death without worry and without fear.

How might we achieve this attitude toward death, such that our own work—including the work of vocational exploration and discernment—can be imbued with the quality and the depth that it deserves? This chapter seeks to address this question from a Sikh perspective. It foregrounds the radical understanding of the call of death upon our lives, as well as the Sikh challenge to be ever ready to receive that call. The chapter interweaves my translations of Sikh scriptural

---

but has also developed through my friendship and professional relationship with scholars like Jacqueline Bussie, whose work also appears in this volume.

2. Bonhoeffer, "After Ten Years," 5 (translation slightly altered).

3. Bonhoeffer, "After Ten Years," 16.

4. Martin Luther King Jr., "I See the Promised Land (1968)," in Martin Luther King Jr., James M. Washington, and Coretta Scott King, *I Have a Dream: Writings and Speeches That Changed the World* (New York: HarperOne, 1992), 203.

poetry with my own experiences, frustrations, and hopes about what it means to be called. It posits that the depth, and therefore the quality, of our vocational reflection and discernment—as well as the quality and depth of our *response* to that calling—hinges on our ability to address the call of death.

Death calls us all: a Sikh perspective

What does it mean to strive for the good while bound up in systems that oppress us and our neighbors? A meditation on death's call is made essential by our knowledge of the damaged nature of the world: a world tinged by death. I am heartbroken that some of my fellow Sikhs' love for baby boys has driven them to create, through selective-sex abortions, one of the most imbalanced sex ratios in the world (in, for example, the Sikh-majority state of Punjab in India). More broadly: What does it mean to live a good life when images of war-torn Aleppo and Damascus greet us in newspapers at the breakfast table? I pay taxes to a government that (as of the time of writing) gives medicine to the poor domestically yet uses drones to strike children internationally; more civilians have now died in drone strikes in the Afghanistan/Pakistan region than died on 9/11. Sadly, the comparison is an apt one, since the 9/11 attacks undergirded the case for American military involvement in those areas, as well as in Iraq. This is not even to mention a host of other issues, from the ways that US farm subsidies cripple international farmers to the working conditions of the factories where our T-shirts are made.

Despite our growing awareness of these sad realities, traumatic scenes continue to play out the world over. How might we strive to live a *good* life in a damaged world? If we are complicit (at some level) in one another's oppression, on what moral ground can we stand, such that we can write and speak about—and to hope for—living a life to which we are called? With what privilege are we able to ask such a question? As a first step in considering how we might escape the oppression of these existential conundrums, I turn to the Sikh tradition's foundational sources. These sources help us remember that the questions raised here are as inescapable as death itself, and that only in confronting them can we expect to discern, and to follow, our vocations. In brief: vocation is the heroic act of defying the impending horizon of death by committing oneself to a meaningful life.

Making death visible: historical roots

In the South Asian culture out of which Sikhism emerges, death is a public event. Walking through a city, or driving past a village, one may be hit with wafts of smoke from a funeral pyre. Funeral processions are often public, and loudly so. Perhaps the public nature of death in that culture inspires greater discussion of dying. But how do college students respond to the idea of death in a culture where dying is sanitized, removed from view, intentionally hidden? If we hope to address this question, we need to pursue the world's many answers—and questions—about death.

Sikhs' perspectives on these matters are deeply influenced by their tradition's history, which involves a series of direct encounters with death. In his memoirs, Jahangir, the emperor of India, reflects on his decision to execute the fifth Sikh Guru in 1606: "I ordered that he be brought to my presence. I gave over his homes and houses and children to [my minister], confiscated his goods and ordered him to be capitally punished." Jahangir was irked by reports that the Sikh Guru, fourth in succession after the founder Guru Nanak, had given shelter and favor to one of Jahangir's rivals for the Mughal throne.

Up until that point, the Sikh community had been in existence for about a century; it had grown from a small farming commune to an intergenerational religious tradition the reach of which spanned thousands of miles. For all we know, Jahangir—the "world conqueror," king of kings, and head of perhaps the world's greatest empire—brought down the decision to kill the Guru with the flick of a wrist, quickly moving on to the dozens of other imperial decisions for the day (to say nothing of his love for his wine and his wives). But for members of the bourgeoning Sikh community, the execution of its fifth founding figure was the most traumatic event they had had to face in their short history. In 1606, Sikhs came face to face not only with the death of their leader, but with the potential extinction of the community itself.

And so it is quite remarkable that, in this context of trauma, Sikh literature of the time elevated the concept of *parupkārī*, literally "other-helping." Seventeenth-century Sikh poetry says that, for Sikhs to overcome their deepest tragedy and bring light to their darkest days, they needed to think about others, and to act on others' behalf. They needed to be like an orchard of banyan trees in a world burning with the heat of intercultural conflicts.

Although the fifth Guru's execution was once seen as the greatest tragedy in Sikh history, it certainly wouldn't be the last. Several times over the centuries, Sikhs across the world have had to lean on their resilient tradition. The radical vision of overcoming tragedy through benevolence is at the core of Sikh thought. And even though the feeding of thousands every day at Sikh *langar*s (community kitchens) makes evident the Sikh commitment to social justice, the link between benevolence and tragedy is perhaps less apparent in contemporary Sikh practice.[5] Still, it is deeply embedded in the tradition's founding history—whether in the general terms described here or in the writings of its founder.

5. For more see Rahuldeep S. Gill, *Drinking From Love's Cup: Surrender and Sacrifice in the Vārs of Bhai Gurdas Bhalla* (New York: Oxford University Press, 2017).

The heritage of Guru Nanak

The Sikh readiness for death emerges out of the ethics rooted in the compositions of Nanak (1469–1539), whom Sikhs view as the founder of their faith. Nanak was a contemporary of Martin Luther; the views of these two religious actors evolved on separate continents. Nanak was a son of Punjab, a region which sits at the crossroads between Central Asia and South Asia—an extensive, verdant riverbed fertile enough to make it the "breadbasket" of multiple civilizations. Guru Nanak, as he is commonly known, founded the Sikh tradition; his poetry, full of introspection and wonder concerning the divine ways, forms the basis of Sikh scripture. Sikhs revere his compositions (as well as those of his successors) as divinely inspired revelation, around which they build their lives. These writings untangle the complexities of living a genuinely good life in the midst of a world that is lost in delusion, egotism, and selfish pursuits.

For Guru Nanak, the most profound call—that universal call that we will all hear in our lives—is the call of death. Our own capacity for selfishness means that we are complicit in the harm we do to others when we follow our lower, baser, selfish natures. Attunement to the divine nature of reality is the solution to this problem. Ultimately we will all leave this broken world through our own deaths; but until then, how are we to face the world? For Guru Nanak, the answer to that question is a life of enlightened participation in the world—not apathy, not complicity, not escapism. That is why, if we are to prepare ourselves for living a "good life" (however that may be defined), we must also address the question of what it means to die well.

In a poem of confession about his own enticement by the superficial world, Nanak writes of himself as a scavenger:

> My companions are a dog
> and two bitches
> Who rise early
> and bark.
> Falsehood is my knife,
> I feast on the carrion of theft,
> Having taken the ways
> of a huntsmen, O Creator![6]

Inserting myself in place of the confessing persona here, I am struck that all that I can feast on, in this life, is carrion (*murdār*)—meat that I myself have not

6. *Guru Granth Sahib* (hereafter GG), 24. There are now several websites for the original text and translations of the 1430-standardized-page scripture of the Sikhs, such as http://www.KhojGurbani.org.

hunted, flesh that I wander upon and that lies before me. And even that I have come upon dishonestly, through theft (*muṭhā*). This speaks to me as an American who benefits from devastating imbalances in the global power structure. It speaks to me as an immigrant whose parents brought him here to enjoy a life in which the slanted power structure allows abundant fruit to roll down to us. I do not live in a fair world, and many times over I am the beneficiary of that unfairness—even if I am not myself the hunter for flesh. I exist as part of a world that feasts on death and calls it life.

Guru Nanak's call

Before receiving God's call to preach a new song of human dignity and divine justice, Guru Nanak describes himself as a "minstrel out of work" whom the Lord employed.[7] We learn about Guru Nanak's "call" from God in the earliest source for Nanak's life, written about 40 years after his death.[8] This source depicts a young Nanak having just found a prestigious job in a town, and having traveled from his village to work in a nobleman's storefront. In the middle of this success, Nanak is suddenly summoned to the divine presence and comes face to face with God. Divine messengers are then sent to bring him back from the divine presence to the world. He is returned mute and profoundly transformed; his only words when he returns are "There is no Hindu, there is no Muslim."[9]

Historically speaking, we know that Guru Nanak was raised as the son of a revenue official, and that his family's intention was that he become a revenue official as well. He was trained in the language of the government—in record keeping, and in mathematics for the calculation of taxable agricultural yields. During his lifetime, the government itself proved to be unstable scaffolding for reality; after a series of violent military confrontations, the Lodi dynasty was crushed and its treasures taken over by the Mughal conqueror Babur. In a reflection on the capture of India by Babur, Nanak gives concrete form to his self-description of a "minstrel out of work." He offers what appears to be a postapocalyptic view of a once-vibrant place, recently decimated by invasion—events that he lived through himself:

> Where are those homes, gates, pavilions and mansions?
> Where are the beautiful inns now?

---

7. GG, 150.

8. This is the late sixteenth-century *Puratan Janam Sakhi*. Rattan Singh Jaggi and Gursharan Kaur Jaggi, eds., *Purātan Janamsākhī: Adhiain Ate Sampādana* (Patiala: Gurmat Prakashana, 2010).

9. Jaggi and Jaggi, *Purātan Janamsākhī*, 131.

Where are those luxurious beds and enchanting women
  whose glance stole sleep away?
Where is the enjoyment of betel[10] in the harems?
  Like shadows, they are gone.
Many have found ruin for the sake of such bounty,
  and many have been led astray.
It can't be amassed without misdeeds,
  and it departs not with us at death.
Whoever that One wants to lead astray
  is first left bereft of goodness.[11]

I hope that most of the readers of this volume will not have to face such scenes of devastation in their lives. Nevertheless, every year, undergraduate students are launched into worlds where others dwell, where such events have taken place in recent history (and continue to haunt us in our present moment). In such tumultuous times, not only do we need to think through and decipher our "callings"; we also need to acknowledge the ephemeral nature of the world into which we are called, as well as the fragility of life itself. Because these circumstances mark both Guru Nanak's context and our own, it will be helpful to consider his metaphors and his poetry in greater detail.

Exploring the insights of a minstrel

In an era of shifting political landscapes and great social change, why might the son of a high-caste revenue official have called himself a "minstrel"? The term (*ḍhāḍī*) describes someone sufficiently bound to a tradition to be inspired by it, but who is also free to innovate, perform, create, and improvise; in fact, the tradition's performative contexts would demand this. Important research on modern Sikh *ḍhāḍī*s argues that, given the contexts in which these singers lived, their unique position allowed them simultaneously to uphold the system of domination enjoyed by the powerful and to subvert it.[12]

Nanak on the nature of work

After heeding God's call, and having found a deeper purpose after being "a minstrel out of work," Guru Nanak set off on a series of travels to spread the

10. Betel leaves are prepared and chewed in South Asia as a cultural practice.

11. GG, 417–18.

12. Michael Nijhawan, *Dhadi Darbar: Religion, Violence, and the Performance of Sikh History* (New Delhi: Oxford University Press, 2006).

message of God and sing of his experiences, seeking to glorify God through his compositions. After several trips encompassing years of his life, he settled back down in the Punjab and founded Kartarpur, a new religious community. Its focus was on farming; it was located strategically off the military road, but on route to several sites of pilgrimage.

We know from early accounts that Guru Nanak participated in the farm labor at Kartarpur, and in his compositions he often writes about ethics in farming terms:

> Your heart is the plow, your actions are the farming.
> Modesty is the water, and your body is the field
> Sow the Renown (*nām*),[13] level it with contentment,
> and maintain poverty (*garībī*) as your protective fence.[14]

For Nanak, the guise of poverty protects us from the outside influence that could interfere with the cultivation of our personal identities. Poverty's permeable wall sifts out the dangerous elements from our work of cultivation. Insofar as we are dedicated to living a life of poverty and humility (another connotation of *garībī*), we maintain the possibility that our spiritual work will yield fruits. Guru Nanak states that benevolence flows naturally from knowledge and from reflection on that knowledge[15]; this in turn becomes the content of the scriptural revelation, as well as the experience of living a life in response to it. But that life cannot be lived without reflection on action, in addition to reflection on divine knowledge.

Guru Nanak does not write about "working hard"—only working honestly, so that one can give. He discusses this in the context of religious leadership:

> Those without wisdom sing songs,
> Hungry Mullahs are at home in mosques,
> Good-for-nothings pierce their ears,
> Another drops his station to become a hermit.
> If someone calls himself a "gurū" or "pīr"

---

13. *Nām* is often translated as God's "name"; I translate it as God's "Renown." Although they are cognates, "name" does not capture the connotations of *nām*, which include an entity's reputation, eminence, and prominence. The divine *nām* constitutes one of the most profound concepts in Sikh thought, a spiritual force reverberating in the universe and in the life force of beings.

14. GG, 595.

15. GG, 356.

But begs, do not ever bow down to him!
But the one who eats from his own labor [*ghāl khāe*] and gives
from his hands, Nanak, knows the way.[16]

Indeed, it would be arrogant to focus only on what we can do with our human hands, in the face of the divine's abilities:

Why do you take pride in the created?
The One who gives bestows by hand.
Whatever the One gives, or doesn't:
the created have no say about it.[17]

So the command to follow only those who work hard (*ghāl khāe*) is more about self-reliance and honesty than an attempt to enshrine hard work as a virtue in and of itself. The superior alternative is reliance on the divine—and directing our work toward the divine.

Guru Nanak does respect a particular kind of toil and effort: that required by the spiritual path. Here there are no shortcuts, but the journey will result in the soul's exaltation in God's presence:

Those who have focused on the Renown,
having toiled at the work,
Will find their faces radiant,
says Nanak,
and liberate many with them.[18]

Elsewhere he uses *dhandhā* as a word for work:

Praise to the Creator! True Lord!
Who has put me to this work (*dhandhe lāeā*)
[in order to remind you that]
When the hourglass empties,
our dear being will be hauled away.
The dear being will be hauled away when
the summons comes, and kin are left bewailing.

16. GG, 1245.

17. GG, 25.

18. GG, 8.

The body and soul are pulled apart when
our days run out, mother.
We receive what we have recorded
as we have spent our days, thus
Praise to the Creator, The True Lord,
who has put the world to work.[19]

For Nanak, the Divine Being beholds creation with great joy, having set it to work:

You created this world
and set each to work (*dhandhā*).
You behold your power,
You roll the dice, My Dear.[20]

Dhandhā could mean either *work* or *distraction*. One might interpret this confluence by suggesting that, while God has indeed set the universe to work, the works of the universe are themselves a distraction for those who forget the Creator behind the creation.

How are work and death related? Martyrs bear witness to something greater than themselves by dying for their "callings," their work. We need not force the question all the way to our own martyrdom. But still, in the face of these realities and knowing about the martyrs' quests, we must ask: what kind of life will we live, and what calls will we answer?

God's sacred work created the world. Perhaps our work can be sacred if it emerges from the heart's yearning for the cosmic knowledge of the ongoing expansion of the created order—a created order that is a result of God's first fiat that something "be" rather than not be. Sacred work is actually *union with* that creation.[21]

19. GG, 578. At the opening of this long composition, the customary invocation of praise is followed immediately by death talk. This is exactly what the "laments" or "elegies" are about from the perspective of a folk form: the ways that family members mourn the dead. Here the idea is quickly laid out that the suddenness, the uncontrollability of death is part of the way of the world as designed by the divine.

20. GG, 71.

21. For further perspectives on the relationship between work and creation, see Christine M. Fletcher, "Laboring in the Garden: Vocation and the Realities of Work," in *Vocation across the Academy: A New Vocabulary for Higher Education*, ed. David S. Cunningham (New York: Oxford University Press, 2017), 183–203.

Work is creativity that taps into the creativity of the creation as it expands. Work is creation bound in time:

> Having created, the One is merged with creation;
> Only by considering time is one a servant.[22]

God is the Being who is the cause of creation, but who is also fully immersed in it as an effect. God is potter and pot, spider and web. The human predicament is our need to find the traces back to union with the divine source; this requires active work, spiritual work. We toil toward union with the divine, and work in community toward greater community.

The Sikh fascination with how we must live in the world leads me to the belief that there really is no Sikh theological tradition removed from the Sikh ethical tradition. That is, it hardly matters in Sikh *life* what God is like; God is gracious, mysterious, and ineffable, unknowable in its totality. Yet God is also just and caring; thus, what matters is what *we do* in this life. The question, then, is not what God is like, but rather: what are *we* like? Or rather, what *ought* we to be like?

Nanak on death, the cosmos, and love

This death-tinged world is impermanent (or "false," *kūṛ*), as opposed to the divine essence which is everlasting (or "true," *sachiār*). The very first stanza of the Guru Granth Sahib, the revered scripture that is our divine teacher, lays this out:

> So then how can I get to Reality (*sachiārā)*?
> How do I break this wall of deceit (*kūṛai*)?
> Nanak says:
> heeding the order (*hukam*),
> in the One's way,
> as is written for me.[23]

The word translated as "order"—*hukam*—refers to the divine command and order that runs the universe we inhabit. Many spiritual traditions teach that our forgetfulness about the broader universe—our tendency to get lost in our own egocentrism—is the cause of great suffering. This suffering is not ours alone; it

22. GG, 83.

23. GG, 1. While some may be tempted to read the "order" in a deterministic way, I would caution against it. —Even as it "determines," the order is dynamic, not static; moreover, God's will remains beyond total human comprehension.

also includes that which we inflict on others, as well as the suffering that we too often tolerate in the world. A core duality in Sikh life is that between the aforementioned *hukam*, on the one hand, and on the other, *haumai*—the "me me" of our selfish natures. This duality is introduced in the very next stanza:

> From the order (*hukam*) came the expanse,
>   though the order cannot be said.
> From the order came all life,
>   and from the order all Renown.
> The order determines high and low.
>   Written for us in the order: pain or peace.
> Some find blessings by the order
>   And by it some ever wander.
> All exists within this order,
>   nothing can exist outside it.
> Nanak says:
>   selfishness (*haumai*) cannot nag
>   those who heed to the order.[24]

To neglect the divine order is to fall into the trap of our selfish natures and our base impulses. Guru Nanak offers us shelter under the divine mark, or Renown, which is reverberating throughout the universe.[25] God's Renown is the promise of redemption and absorption in the unimaginably massive cosmic drama that plays out by divine grace, as divine grace. Without constantly practicing the deeper reality underpinning the phenomenal world, we are subject to forgetting divine glory and falling for attractions of the world:

> Baba! The allure of creation
> blinds us to forget the Renown.
> We lose both here and hereafter.[26]

In Sikh thought, "here and hereafter" can refer both to the relationship of this world to the afterlife, and to the opportunity for divine encounter that the present moment avails (which may be lost if it is neglected).

---

24. GG, 1.

25. See footnote 13 on the translation of *nām* as "Renown."

26. Literally "this and that"; *this* refers to the illusory and impermanent world (*māiā*), *that* to *nām*; GG 15.

In his poetry, Nanak writes about the call of death[27] as if it were a wedding invitation:

> The day of my wedding is set!
> So let us pour out oil in libation:
> Give me your blessings, friends!
> That I may meet my Sovereign Beloved.
> The invitation has been sent house to house,
> The calls (*sadṛe*) go out every day.
> Let us remember the One who summons us,
> Nanak: the day draws near.[28]

Our soul is a bride who must wake up to the reality of her impending "wedding" day:

> Why don't you hear, fair one,
>   this news with your ears?
> You'll have to go to your in-laws',
>   you can't stay at your parents'.[29]

But our indolent inability to imagine anything beyond our familiar, daily routine leads us to forget that we will not bring anything with us in our travels to the next world. Nanak writes that when the grave calls us, we leave our life as it is, with our meals on the table and all of our wardrobes left behind (*rahiā pīṇā khāṇā*, 24). Elsewhere Nanak narrates the events of a funeral:

> Born into this birth-and-death world,
>   we spend this life consuming.
> But where we are to go and learn what we have done,

27. GG, 1327. The "call" of death is a recurring theme in Guru Nanak's thought. Death's call is more real than attachments we hold on to; when death calls us, we can make no delay nor maintain our grip on this world. Linguist Christopher Shackle says that *shabad* ("word; sound; communication," especially as "the Word, communicated by the Satiguru") comes from the Sanskrit *sabda* but can be compared to *saddu,* which connotes a "call, cry, summons; invitation to wedding." Christopher Shackle, *A Guru Nanak Glossary* (London: SOAS, University of London, 1981).

28. GG, 15. For a feminist treatment of Sikh scripture that portrays the bride imagery in positive terms of liberation, see Nikky-Guninder Kaur Singh, *The Feminine Principle in the Sikh Vision of the Transcendent* (Cambridge: Cambridge University Press, 1993).

29. GG, 23.

no one can accompany.
All the weepers at the funeral are left
tending to trivium.[30]

These "trivial matters," which the funeral goers are left to tend, literally mean "tying bundles of grass" (*bannahi piṇḍ parāli*), which probably refers to funerary rites.

Guru Nanak teaches not only that life is a preparation for death, but also that we must live as though we are, in part, dead. The part of us that must be strangled is that part that justifies our money-making and accumulation, which thereby is exposed as a mere excuse to enjoy fleeting pleasures on the way to death. We know that there is no amount of success that we can procure that will mean anything in the face of eternity. Not only that: there is no amount of success that we can achieve that will fulfill our human need for more. Guru Nanak writes:

Were I to create palaces of pearls inlaid with jewels
and enjoy coating their walls with musk, saffron, sandal, and
scented wood.
But, no.
Lest I forgot you
and Your Renown found no place in my heart.

Without the Lord, my life goes to waste.
Having asked my guide: there is no other place.

Were I to inlay the ground with diamonds and my bed with rubies,
where an alluring enchantress indulged me in pleasure.
But, no.
Lest I forgot You
and Your Renown found no place in my heart.

Were I to become an adept commanding tricks of magic,
and could appear and disappear, demanding the world's devotion.
But, no.
Lest I forgot You
and Your Renown found no place in my heart.

30. GG, 15.

> Were I to become a sultan commanding armies from my throne,
> issuing orders, leveling taxes.
> But all this is nothing, Nanak.
> Lest I forgot you
> and Your Renown found no place in my heart.[31]

So long as we ignore the certainty of death and lose ourselves in the tasks of money-making, power-grabbing, stuff-accumulating, and other selfish ends, we lose sight of the divine plan. "Keep your eyes on the prize, and hold on" was a line from a great American folk song that took on a liberationist meaning in the struggle for civil rights. Like activists working to free a once-enslaved people, we are called to bring our "head on our palm," as Nanak demands for any of those who want to "play the game of love":

> If you wish to play the game of love with me,
> Then come to my street with your head on your palm!
> Come now, place your foot on this path.
> Give your head and pay no heed![32]

Love for the divine empties out into death, and empties us of our fear of death.

Courage in the face of death

At the beginning of this chapter, I described Bonhoeffer's call for us to focus on matters of quality and depth, rather than of quantity and immediacy. This requires us to overcome our fascination with the superficialities (such as wealth, time, and possessions) that have become our limitations, and to focus instead on attending to others. One can trace this "change in focus" in the lives of Bonhoeffer and King; a similar shift is invoked in the Sikh tradition, both in its historical traditions and in Guru Nanak's life and writings. All these thinkers help us to understand that all our work is a form of commitment to others. Service to others is the answer to our selfishness; it converts quantities into qualities.

Vocational reflection and discernment that follows the path of Nanak, Bonheoffer, and King demands this kind of commitment to others. It prepares us to respond rightly to the systems and structures that render us complicit in oppression and sin. In order to undertake this kind of augmented vocational

---

31. GG, 14.

32. GG, 1412.

discernment, however, we need to be attentive to the call of death, and to follow the path to which it calls us. When a focus on death allows us to live with greater depth, courage emerges as an alternative to fear. It may be simple, but it is certainly not easy.

In many traditions, deep and thoughtful preparation for death is strongly associated with courage; this is the only way to stare death in the face and to extract a meaningful life out of the mouth of the beast. This notion is expressed clearly in the thought of the great teacher Cornel West, for whom *courage* is a favorite word. For West, courage describes a virtue that enables us to look beyond the daily considerations of a milquetoast life for something greater than ourselves. Borrowing from Rabbi Abraham Joshua Heschel, West reminds us that the opposite of courage is not cowardice, but indifference. Courage is not about fitting in and going with the grain; courage is about belonging to a cause greater than oneself. Belonging to such a cause, or creating spaces for it, is a much greater task than merely "fitting in" with the world as it is.

Courage may or may not be contagious, but indifference certainly is—and our culture is often more inclined to the latter than to the former. Facing the call of death courageously is not something the Sikh tradition invented, and humanity is heir to a diverse array of wisdom traditions that have much to offer us in the ways of meditations on death. I have argued elsewhere that the Sikh literary tradition borrows tropes for fearlessness in the face of death from Shi'a Islam and from the mystical Muslims known as Sufis. Islam's tropes are related to those of Christian and Jewish traditions (for example, the notion of consuming wine in preparation for death, enacted in the Christian Eucharist and in the Jewish Passover celebration). The roots of this broad, wide-ranging tradition—of courage in the face of surrender and sacrifice—run deep in the world's religions. According to a scholar of Punjabi Sufism,

> The ultimate goal of [the mystical] journey is to lose one's identity within the greater identity of God, or to attain spiritual death before physical death. The quest for death before dying is based on a saying attributed to the Prophet [Muhammad]: "Die before you die!"[33]

For many Sufis, the death anniversaries of their masters are celebrated; the celebrations (*'urs*) are styled as weddings, occasions that mark the soul's union with the divine. The same connotation for death is celebrated by Guru Nanak

---

33. Jamal Elias, trans., *Death before Dying: the Sufi Poems of Sultan Bahu [d. 1691]* (Berkeley: University of California Press, 1998), 3.

as a bride's nuptial union with her (divine) husband.[34] These traditions are not advocating a passive acceptance of death, but rather rising up and actively accepting it—even preparing for it. If we are passive, we are not only unable to rise up and meet the challenge of death; we are also unable to enjoy the bliss of union with the divine.

Thus, from a Sikh perspective, the development of an ethic arises from our response to the certainty of death's call. The threat of death continuously impinges upon our decisions in life. Guru Nanak's response to death is to come to terms with its inescapability. Addressing it is the only hope for freedom, allowing for our liberation (*muktī*, or *moksha*) from the cycle of birth and death that constitutes the causes and effects of the universe's history. Perhaps in confronting the certainty of death's call, we can think more critically about our ability to live lives that are more deeply marked by true freedom.

Death, then, is not something to be denied or ignored. Rather, its certainty gives us a challenge to rise to, and a life to celebrate. Voices of wisdom call us to reframe our default orientation, which is to respond to death by shrinking from it (or by working harder, drinking more, or spending our way out of its clutches). We are inspired to face death, and to live in its wake, with a spiritually motivated abandon—without fear of it, but with deep and constant concern for our response to the challenges before us. At the moment of death we are going to be asked, Nanak says, just what we did with our hands. We will have to prove our sanction:

> Burn your grasping,
> rub it into ink and
> make fine paper of your intellect.
>
> Turn your love into a pen
> and ask your guide
> how to write with your heart.
>
> Pen the One's name,
> inscribe your praise,
> write that the Transcendent has no end.
>
> Baba! Learn the way to write so that
> when you are asked, you can prove your sanction.[35]

34. GG, 580.

35. GG, 16.

Work is therefore not just one's job; work is one's "occupation" in a larger sense—an occupation with God's greatness:

> Deep understanding is the way,
> I ride horses with golden reins.
> Virtues get me to gallop with quiver,
> arrows, a bow, and blade.
> Appearing honorably before You is my lance,
> Your grace is my occupation.[36]

This work is never done.

My own calling—and the calls of depth and death

At the moment, I am working on a translation of Nanak's poetry. The Western study of Sikhism is so behind the times that one cannot walk into a bookstore and buy a translation of ideas of the founder of the world's fifth largest religion. The situation is not much better online; there is no good translation available. Part of my vocation right now is to change that; as I do, I am learning a great deal about what it means to be called.

As someone who has the ability to do this work, to speak on behalf of his community, and to write academic works, I also have a *responsibility* to do these things. I have a responsibility to my students because of the career I chose. As a scholar of Sikh literature, I know that my work itself brings a singular kind of joy. Sharing it with my children, and perhaps sharing it with students and the world's English-speaking readers, provides me with great hope. It is certainly a joy to share the thoughts of a too-little-known sixteenth-century poet, who birthed a major world religion, and who saw life as a preparation for death. In facing such work fearlessly, we are given the opportunity to carry it out authentically, and our readers and listeners are given the opportunity for an authentic response. This is the fearlessness with which we must enter both the interfaith encounter *and* our civic work for a better world.

Possibility is a beautiful thing, but infinite possibility is a dreadful burden. Viewing the horizon of our own finitude in death puts some dreadful limits on our possibility, but it also lifts the burden of having to be more than a finite being. Possibilities are what led us to this moment, but we are so caught in the net of the moment that we forget what lies in front of us: not the trap of limitations, but the whole great blue sea—if we will only choose to shrink ourselves small enough

36. GG, 16.

to get out of the holes of the net, and then to expand ourselves to the size of the ocean. In that case, the life to which we are called is not the product of curses but of care: care taken to produce outcomes from infinite possibility.

Death's certainty recapitulates the inescapability of responsibility. Limits are real. Faced with the unavoidability of our limited life, our choices include the possibility of chasing away the discomfort with comfort. In a recent address, Barbara Brown Taylor described her own vocation as one of "avoiding comfort"[37]; here, I am arguing for a similar course. To make death visible, and to face it directly, does indeed push past the comfort of an unreflective life. In the religious perspectives that Guru Nanak would have known, the typical response was one of celibate asceticism—seeking out one's own liberation from the cycle of birth and death (*jogīs*). Nanak responded differently; for him, a life of family commitments—while seeking liberation—was a way of responding to the inescapability of limitations:

> They wouldn't call death vile
> if they knew the way to die:
>
> Serve your Almighty Master
> and the road to the hereafter
> is easy.
>
> Enjoy the pleasures of the easy road,
> and find glory hereafter,
>
> Enter with your offering, merging with truth,
> and your honor will be accounted.
>
> The house will be yours,
> you will please the Master,
> Who will dip you in Love.
>
> They wouldn't call death vile
> if they knew this way to die![38]

Each of us, like Nanak, is a minstrel—a troubadour seeking meaningful work. Each of us can be the hero of an epic story we narrate with choices we make, and

37. Barbara Brown Taylor, "Renewing the Theology of Vocation," plenary panel at the 2017 NetVUE Conference, Charlotte, NC, March 25, 2017.

38. GG, 579.

sing in harmony or in discord with those around us.[39] Each of our own stories will come to an end; that end may or may not be happy, but none can doubt its certainty. Will we tell our stories privately, or live them out publicly? How will our stories be woven into the larger story of the human family—the tribes we sought to unite, and the conflicts we sought to quell?

In chapter 4 of this volume, Younus Mirza observes that some things only make sense after we have lived through various events and connected the dots. For some well-known individuals, this process of "connecting" is undertaken by biographers, poets, and painters. But Nanak's challenge is that, even if we are not regal enough to have our exploits sung posthumously, we can still be our own bards, our own minstrels, writing the ballads of heroism that we face in confronting the most gruesome and mighty monster of them all: death. This requires a willingness to do the right thing, and to stick with it in spite of the challenges. In doing so, we will likely be faced (as Mirza suggests) with a great deal of uncertainty and doubt; we will be faced with the certainty of death, and our mortality will drive our morality. Let us not choose a morality unthinkingly or unreflectively; and let us not allow the world to choose that morality for us. Guru Nanak reorients us to a deeper reality—that is, God's reality. But God's reality is also the human reality, which is bounded by birth and death.

Earlier, I mentioned Nanak's claim that no one can accompany us along the path that death demands for the soul; it abandons the "weepers at the funeral." But he also believes that holiness is truly found in community:

> If I found a million ideas, having mingled
>   with a million people,
> But without holy company, I remain unsatiated. . . .[40]

And:

> In the heart is a priceless jewel:
>   God's Renown brings dignity,
> the company of the holy delivers God,
>   and by the guide we remain immersed.
> When the self is gone, peace is found,
>   like when waters merge.[41]

---

39. For more on the stories we narrate about ourselves, see the remarks of Matthew R. Sayers in chapter 8 of this volume.

40. GG, 20.

41. GG, 22.

The better the quality of people with whom we spend our time, the better we will be. The ultimate peace of uniting with God comes from praising the divine in a community of those who praise.[42] For the pious, mere company with the holy is as efficacious as making pilgrimage.[43] It is a moment of divine grace that brings us to the company of true seekers.[44] In the context of community, we can serve the world—and through our service, we find our place in God's court, hereafter:

> Words have pierced my body,
> I find peace when I live to serve,
> though the world is caught in its cycle.
>
> If we live to serve in this world,
> then we find a seat at the court, and go
> with our arms swinging, O Nanak![45]

Elsewhere Nanak writes that in the company of God's servants we find the far shore of transcendence.[46] The soul that attains God liberates not only herself but also her entire community.[47]

Called to death, yet striving for liberation

Liberation and transcendence are themes in many of the world's religions. Buddhist leader Thich Nhat Hanh says, "No mud, no lotus." The lotus is the beautiful effect that transcends the mud out of which it grows. Christians speak of resurrection. For Sikhs, to be "liberated" means to be free from the fear of death. And perhaps this is where the Sikh ethos can teach us about courage: something needs to die (among educators, among students, and within all our communities) so that something new can take its place. The current ways we imagine the world might need to die for a new, better world to be possible.

At the outset of this chapter, I quoted Martin Luther King Jr.'s description of the risk-laden nature of his life. In fact, part of the preparation for direct action is

42. GG, 1041.

43. GG, 597.

44. GG, 412.

45. GG, 25.

46. GG, 1344.

47. GG, 352.

a spiritual practice called "self purification," which was a process of reflection and recommitting to the cause while part of a learning community. In reflecting on his organizing activities in Birmingham, Alabama, Dr. King writes:

> We had no alternative except to prepare for direct action, whereby we would present our very bodies as a means of laying our case before the conscience of the local and the national community. Mindful of the difficulties involved, we decided to undertake a process of self purification. We began a series of workshops on nonviolence, and we repeatedly asked ourselves: "Are you able to accept blows without retaliating?" "Are you able to endure the ordeal of jail?"[48]

This process was fundamental to preparation for the radical activism that was the catalyst of the heroic civil rights movement.

Our finitude, as well as the finitude of those who deserve justice, requires us to pursue these activities— and urgently. Dr. King reflects on the notion of waiting for justice:

> For years now I have heard the word "Wait!" It rings in the ear of every Negro with piercing familiarity. This "Wait" has almost always meant "Never." We must come to see, with one of our distinguished jurists, that "justice too long delayed is justice denied." We have waited for more than 340 years for our constitutional and God given rights.[49]

Dr. King often spoke about the urgency of pursuing justice, as in his 1963 speech at the March on Washington for Jobs and Freedom:

> We have also come to this hallowed spot to remind America of the fierce urgency of Now. This is no time to engage in the luxury of cooling off or to take the tranquilizing drug of gradualism. Now is the time to make real the promises of democracy. Now is the time to rise from the dark and desolate valley of segregation to the sunlit path of racial justice. Now is the time to lift our nation from the quicksands of racial injustice to the solid rock of brotherhood. Now is the time to make justice a reality for all of

48. Martin Luther King Jr., "Letter from a Birmingham Jail (1963)," in King, Washington, and King, *I Have a Dream*, 83–100.

49. King, "Letter from a Birmingham Jail," 87–88.

> God's children. It would be fatal for the nation to overlook the urgency of the moment.[50]

A life of meaning—the response to a profound call—is best pursued with a fierce urgency. It also requires this kind of reflexive, self-oriented praxis within a community. College classrooms—as well as coffee shops, chapels, and residence halls—are spaces that are primed for reflection on our finitude. Doing so will push us away from the market forces at work in only training future workers for the labor force. Depriving students of the opportunity to do more would be an act of negligence and malpractice.

I think the college environment is an appropriate context to reflect on the questions of the boundaries of our own comfort. Are we comfortable only in our corners? Or does this world and this work require more of us? Does it require an extreme discomfort? Does it require us to ask what we would put on the line? We have a great responsibility to find our courage during these monumental days in human history, when the processes of extinction can commence in many forms: nuclear, digital, by means of the ice caps turning to liquid. In this age of climate change, genocide, and endangered species, do we have the courage to ask, "What does it mean to live on the edge of extinction?"

To the staff and faculty reading this chapter, I want to say that my tradition encourages us to help students be "communitied." They need to be loved.[51] They need to be shown what a "blessed community" can look like. The role of the educator is to love the apathy out of them, to love the prejudice out of them. To get to those students, educators will need to deepen our capacity for love. This will take great courage; still, we can rely on one another. For Guru Nanak, only in the encounter with others (who are also pursuing the divine, or the good, in their own ways) can our pursuits be meritorious; community with holy seekers is necessary. Sikhs, as a community, are brought together by memories and the religious practices by which those memories are invoked. We can also be brought together by hopes, which are imaginations of God's memory. And our human hands are responsible for ensuring the dignity of one another as that dignity expands. Sikhs are a people, as evidenced by our martyrs (beginning with the Gurus themselves), who don't just stand up for themselves. We stand for others first.

To the students reading this chapter, I want to say that this requires great courage on the part of your teachers—including the courage to get beyond their

---

50. Martin Luther King Jr., "I Have a Dream (1963)," in King, Washington, and King, *I Have a Dream*, 103.

51. For more on this point, see the comments of Jeffrey Carlson in chapter 13 of this volume.

own prejudices about you. Hold them to a higher standard and inspire them to fulfill their vocation more fully. We learn from you; your education is our own. That makes our jobs worthwhile. Yet at the same time, I do not wish to put more pressure on those students who are already scheduling the protests and the programs. If you are in this group, we need to give you our love and compassion; we need to help you find resilience and self-care. But the students who are not showing up to the programs are the ones who need love more than ever. They may not be engaged because they have fully bought into the existing structures, or because they are video gaming in their dorm rooms, or because they are working multiple jobs to pay for college (or to feed a family). These students need love from their teachers more than ever. And yet, they are not the ones who draw the most immediate attention from educators who focus on matters of vocation and calling. It is always easier to love those who present themselves more directly.

Teachers and students alike will be in a better position to face and to respond to the reality of our own impending deaths if we draw on wisdom from diverse religious, spiritual, and philosophical traditions. Perhaps in sharing our mortality, or at least our diverse views on it, we can learn to live better lives together, and heal our damaged world together. If we hope to work together, we will certainly need to know one another.

This is why I am sometimes taken aback when the interfaith encounter is met with trepidation by some Christian brothers and sisters—whose faith begins with the Spirit's indomitability and its triumph over death. There are, by some counts, over 2 billion Christians in the world, compared to perhaps 25 million Sikhs. What the majority seems to be bemoaning here is the threat of the diminishment of quantitative dominance. God is said to have freed them, through Christ on the cross, from anxiety about eternal life. Does not living a life of some quality, then, dare them to take some greater risk?

How can educators garner the courage to explain to their discerning students the noble truths of this existence? As these students discern their vocations, are we fully honest with them about the fact that even the pursuit of a good life faces down the horizon toward a finality that cannot be seen or known? Of course not. This would not be judged a good pep talk to give to a 20year-old, or a 40-year-old returning student. And yet, life *is* short. Death *is* certain. A college education *does* beget privilege in our society, even to those who have had to struggle to get it—even to those who are crippled by the cost of trying to afford it. What kinds of students are we launching into the world, and what are the risks of arming them with nothing other than unquestioned privilege?

If we hope to answer these questions authentically today, we will need to distance ourselves from our desire to be simply comfortable—most of all by ignoring the deeply uncomfortable questions about our own finitude. In reading the writings and biographies of King and Bonhoeffer, I can see that the Sikh ethic of preparation for death is not a particular abstraction for a particular context, but part of the human language of love, justice, and fulfillment of life. I believe Sikhs, like all the world's faithful, (as well as those who profess no faith), need to perform benevolence (*parupkārī*) by working toward interreligious harmony through caring for others.

Benevolence helps us overcome the trauma of death because benevolence is itself rooted in a confrontation with death. A Sikh response to vocation comes in confronting death's call; this call is, after all, inescapable, as is our complicity in the birth-and-death trauma of the world. The vocation of benevolence is a commitment to the practice of changing the world and bringing the divine reality closer. Martyrs like Bonhoeffer, King, and Guru Arjan testify to the notion that, even though we are complicit in one another's oppression, we are also one another's hope for liberation. Guru Nanak's response to the call of death is to engage in the work of the heart and face the future boldly. If we can all do this, we can work together for a better world—while we still have time.

Response

Rachel S. Mikva

The call of death might seem a strange message in Jewish tradition; in Deuteronomy 30:19, the prophet Moses charges the people as follows: "I have put before you today life and death, blessing and curse. Choose life."

Yet on Yom Kippur, by some measures the holiest day of the year, we rehearse our own death. We do not eat or drink. By abstaining from sexual relations and by not wearing leather shoes, we resist physical desires for intimacy and comfort. The instruction not to wash or anoint (i.e., perfume) our bodies evokes the stench of death, albeit in mild form. Liturgy for the day is laden with consciousness of our own mortality. These practices are designed, just as Rahuldeep suggests about Sikh tradition, to inspire and illuminate how we should live our lives.

Like most things in Jewish life, the attitude toward death is dialectical. Yes, our annual rehearsal readies us in some fashion. Community responsibility for preparing a body for burial and other traditions surrounding death make it natural and familiar. Yet it is precisely the fear of death that helps to energize the changes we want to make in our lives—before it is too late. Fear of death is a foundation for learning not to treat anyone's life cheaply.

Judaism cultivates a deep investment in this world—not in order to pursue the false path against which Rahuldeep cautions (the "money-making, power-grabbing, stuff-accumulating" approach), but precisely in order to dismantle the systems of oppression that keep him up at night. We rejoice in the manifold blessings of our lives, for they represent the "prize" due to all creation and we must recognize their immeasurable value.

To Rahuldeep's powerful challenge—interrogating the moral ground on which we try to stand when speaking about the good life—I acknowledge that the celebration of life within a broken world may indeed entail some complicity in one another's oppression. From my tradition, I respond with the modest, provisional, and (of course) dialectical teaching of Rabbi Tarfon: you are not obligated to complete the work, but neither are you free to desist from it (*Pirkei Avot 2:16*).

PART TWO

Releasing Expectations

Overcoming Misleading Assumptions about Vocation

Because the language of vocation and calling has been in circulation for many centuries, it has accumulated a diverse array of meanings and connotations. As noted in the introduction to this volume, the word *vocatio* was once associated fairly narrowly with a call to holy orders; in another era, vocation became practically synonymous with one's job. For some, a "calling" is a clear and definitive sign from God, which must be obeyed; for others, it is a reminder to pay attention to whatever provides happiness, and to "follow your bliss." Given the wide range of associations with the words *vocation* and *calling*, we should not be surprised that this language is employed in myriad ways—and that those who employ it often differ in the meanings they assign to it.

Given this elasticity of meaning, it can be difficult to speak of "better" and "worse" uses of the terminology, or to describe—as this second part of the book attempts to do—how certain assumptions about vocation might be inaccurate, or at least misleading. Nevertheless, from the perspective of the authors who have contributed to this volume, such assessments are necessary in order to develop an account of vocation and calling that can be useful and salutary in the contemporary context of undergraduate education. Given the increasingly diverse nature of that context, the contributors to this book have sought to avoid a too narrowly conceived account of vocation, which might well exclude certain perspectives. But at the same time, a number of these authors believe that certain common assumptions about vocation may prevent it from achieving its full potential as a constructive and relevant approach within higher education today.

In this section, a number of misleading assumptions about vocation will be explored. For example:

- Vocational discernment is often portrayed as an experience of great clarity, in which people come to know for certain what they are meant to do with their lives. But many "call stories" suggest the opposite: the call itself is often unclear; it engenders a good deal of doubt and uncertainty; and it may remain opaque for much of a person's life.
- Similarly, the response to a call is sometimes portrayed as instantaneous; the words that are spoken, whether by a divine or human source, seem to bring about an immediate response on the part of the person being called. Frequently, however, vocational discernment is a long, complicated process, experienced in fits and starts; one's ability to make a definitive commitment only arrives, if it arrives at all, when a person can look back on a series of experiences and discern some pattern of meaning and direction.
- When a person experiences a call—particularly if that call is believed to originate from a divine source—the proper response would seem to be absolute obedience. But it may be that the true importance of such experiences is their potential for helping us cultivate a stance of openness to, and acceptance of, the voices of others—rather than merely obeying a command.
- A call is often assumed to adhere closely to the structures of one's own religious or philosophical tradition. The origins of this assumption are likely to be found in the older meaning of *vocatio* as a call to the religious life; by responding to such a call, one declared a deeper acceptance of the claims of one's own faith. But our vocations sometimes raise questions about the commonly received accounts of our own traditions; indeed, they may call us to reshape and reform those accounts, even as we continue to describe ourselves as faithful adherents of our traditions.
- Embracing one's vocation can seem to be an all-or-nothing affair. Embedded in the language of "accepting one's calling" is the implication that one must give one's life over to it entirely—or, if other obligations make that impossible, that one must reject it entirely. But our callings are typically more nuanced; pursuing them need not require binding ourselves to those elements that we cannot carry out in good conscience—even elements that might be considered an essential aspect of our callings.
- The modern American enthusiasm for practicality and productivity can lead us to assume that the purpose of one's vocation is to bring about a particular set of results. But this can distort the entire nature of one's calling, making it a mere means to an end. Perhaps the "point" of following one's vocation is *the act of following*—rather than whatever might be achieved by it. Being true to

one's calling may require detaching oneself from the fruits of one's actions, focusing instead on the action itself.

Each of the three chapters in this section employs the language, literature, and texts of each author's particular tradition (Islam, Christianity, and Hinduism, respectively). In doing so, the authors raise questions about some of the characterizations of vocation and calling that are typically operative today—both within each author's own tradition and in the culture at large.

Although these chapters name certain "misleading assumptions," they do not seek to draw a tight border around the definition of vocation. Rather, the elasticity of the concept allows us to foreground certain claims, while other assumptions may need to be questioned or marginalized. In offering their critiques of certain "absolute" accounts of vocation, these three authors encourage us to consider a more accessible, flexible, and nuanced understanding of the concept. Our hope is that, when these features are emphasized, undergraduate students may come to see that vocational discernment need not be an anxiety-producing venture or a threat to their best-laid plans; instead, it can become an ally in their ongoing quest for meaning, purpose, and identity.

4

Doubt as an Integral Part of Calling

THE QUR'ANIC STORY OF JOSEPH

Younus Y. Mirza

IN HIS 2005 Stanford commencement address, Steve Jobs reflected upon his life: his birth and adoption, his early firing from Apple and his marriage, and then his scare with death after being diagnosed with cancer.[1] The first part of the speech was dedicated to "connecting the dots" through his early life and college experience. Jobs relates how his birth mother wanted to give him up for adoption, but felt strongly that he should be taken care of by college graduates. Everything was set for him to be adopted by a lawyer and his wife, but they backed out at the last minute, wanting a girl. His future parents then received a call: "We have an unexpected baby boy; do you want him?" They did, but Jobs's birth mother refused to sign the final papers after she learned that his mother-to-be never graduated from college and that the father had never finished high school. She only relented after they promised that Jobs would someday go to college.

Seventeen years later, Jobs chose to go to Reed College, but his working-class parents struggled to pay the tuition; after six months, he decided to drop out. He was scared at the time, but contended that it was the best decision he ever made. As he noted, "The minute I dropped out I could stop taking the required classes that didn't interest me, and begin dropping in on the ones that looked interesting." Jobs stayed another 18 months at Reed, taking classes that he enjoyed.

---

1. Steve Jobs, "Steve Jobs' 2005 Stanford Commencement Address," Stanford University, http://news.stanford.edu/2005/06/14/jobs-061505/ (accessed November 30, 2016). Further quotations from the address are from the same webpage. For commentary on other vocation-related aspects of Jobs's commencement speech, see David Fuentes, "To Whom Do I Sing, and Why?," in *Vocation across the Academy: A New Vocabulary for Higher Education*, ed. David S. Cunningham (New York: Oxford University Press, 2017), 111–32; here, 112.

For instance, Reed was known for having the best calligraphy instruction in the country; Jobs decided to benefit from that program. He encountered various beautiful fonts and learned the rules of typography. Jobs did not see any practical application of taking the course at the time, but when he began to design the personal computer ten years later, he designed the fonts into the Macintosh. As he explained, "If I had never dropped out, I would have never dropped in on this calligraphy class, and personal computers might not have the wonderful typography that they do." While he did not see it at the time, Jobs's decision to take the course provided him with a remarkable return. As he reflected, "Of course it was impossible to connect the dots looking forward when I was in college. But it was very, very clear looking backward ten years later." Jobs concluded the first part of his speech by stressing the importance of "connecting the dots"—a rule that he has always tried to live by:

> Again, you can't connect the dots looking forward; you can only connect them looking backward. So you have to trust that the dots will somehow connect in your future. You have to trust in something—your gut, destiny, life, karma, whatever. This approach has never let me down, and it has made all the difference in my life.

Jobs's comments here address the anxieties of many college students. They often fear taking the courses that interest them, simply because they don't see any clear career path attached to these courses. In economically challenging times and with the rising cost of higher education, students feel tremendous pressure to choose a major that will have immediate financial benefits; they have difficulty justifying "fun" courses to themselves and to their parents. Taking an interesting course in college can be exhilarating, but it can also produce anxiety. Will the cost, time, and effort put into the class be worth it?[2]

While I would not advocate dropping out of college, Jobs's perspective resonates with me as a college professor—particularly as I advise students who are in the midst of their vocational journeys. Some students are clueless as to their choice of major and career, but still feel tremendous pressure from parents and others to make the "right" choice. Other students come in with a very fixed idea of who they are and what they want to become, making them hesitant to

---

2. As Richard H. Ekman notes, "Economic pressures prompt students—and, even more so, their parents—to wonder about their job prospects after graduation. Politicians and other opinion leaders have questioned the utility of a broad liberal arts education in favor of more narrow technical fields, some even proposing penalties on educating students in so-called 'dead-end' fields such as philosophy and anthropology." Foreword to Cunningham, ed., *Vocation across the Academy*, ix.

hear callings to other potential ways of life. In my experience, the most successful students are the ones who are able to do what Jobs did: they follow their passions and interests, while remaining mindful of the importance of being gainfully employed. They participate in the "dynamic" nature of vocational discernment, in that they are open to hearing multiple callings and are adaptable to the circumstances in which they find themselves. They are also willing to change majors and careers if circumstances so dictate.[3] The most successful students are able to "connect the dots" in that they are able to look back at the sum of their experiences, create a compelling narrative, and produce something meaningful for themselves and those around them.

In this chapter, I will build upon Jobs's claim that "connecting the dots" can only be done in retrospect, which suggests in turn that uncertainty and doubt are essential parts of the process of vocational discernment. Calling should not be seen as always clear and direct, but as something that gradually unfolds; it is more like a journey or a quest. In fact, a great many religious and intellectual traditions suggest that clarity about one's direction in life may take some time to appear.

Here, I will explore how the idea manifests itself within Islam, and specifically in the qur'anic story of Joseph. This story, which has themes and plots rooted in other religious traditions as well, can help us to recognize the deep interconnections of people of different faiths and ideological backgrounds, all of whom face uncertainty in considering and finding their callings. In addition, the story of Joseph may open us to a deeper exploration of Islam as a source for reflection on vocation and calling. Many of the ideas explored here are also found elsewhere in the Qur'an—particularly with respect to righteous figures who, although they face many obstacles, are able to persevere through their moral character and faith in God. Throughout the Qur'an, these figures are frequently unsure of their path, worried, or frightened; they may even doubt their divine instructions. However, matters gradually become clear and the dots are eventually connected. This implies that Islam, as represented through its most authoritative scripture, can help us recognize that doubt and uncertainty are central features in the work of vocational reflection and discernment.[4]

---

3. In explaining the "dynamic" nature of vocation, David S. Cunningham observes, "Students are often told that, across their future lives, they can expect to have not just a number of different jobs, but even a number of wholly different careers. Some of the fields they will enter will fade away during their lifetimes; late in life, they may well embark on careers that do not yet exist. Hence, vocational reflection and discernment . . . is an ongoing, lifelong endeavor." "Language that Works: Vocation and the Complexity of Higher Education," Introduction to Cunningham, ed., *Vocation across the Academy*, 1–18; here, 11.

4. Doubt has always played an important role in the history of Islamic law. As Intisar Rabb explains, "Instead of rejecting doubt, medieval Muslim scholars largely embraced it. In fact,

Vocation as a quest

The terms *vocation* and *calling* primarily grow out of the Christian tradition and have historically been tied to a religious framework. As Urban C. von Wahlde observes, "The notion of 'vocation' is born of the conviction that one's life task can be chosen and lived out in some sort of response to a divine invitation."[5] Here, vocation is related to God's call, which leads us to take a particular path through life—one that arises from a "conviction" or a sense of certainty. People are selected to act in a particular way and guided by God in that direction. For many Christians, Jesus can be understood as a model for vocation—both in responding to his own calling and in the various ways that he called others. This Christian view sometimes takes on a "grand narrative" quality, which may lead some to "develop a strong belief that there can be only *one* particular vocational path and that it must be discovered and pursued regardless of any signs to the contrary."[6] Influenced by this "grand narrative" approach, people may come to believe that only one clear and direct calling will guide them for the rest of their lives.

More recently, scholars have challenged the notion of calling as being understood only as a direct and definitively recognizable call from God. For example, David S. Cunningham contends that by "recognizing the degree of mystery that will always be a part of vocation, we might help to counter the tendency to understand it as a fixed and stable reality—or as something that will always provide certainty."[7] Rather than seeing vocation as clear and straightforward, Cunningham introduces the possibility that calling can be fluid and can allow for surprising changes. As he further explains, "Our process of discerning our vocation is a lifelong journey, in which the purpose of each step along the way is to prepare us for

---

these scholars—the expert jurists who articulated the main contours and rules of Islam's legal system—held doubt so closely that it came to be at the heart of Islamic criminal law"; *Doubt in Islamic Law: A History of Legal Maxims, Interpretation, and Islamic Criminal Law* (New York: Cambridge University Press, 2014), 1.

5. Urban C. von Wahlde, "'My food is to do the will of the one who sent me' (John 4:34): Jesus as Model of Vocation in the Gospels of John," in *Revisiting the Idea of Vocation: Theological Explorations*, ed. John C. Haughey (Washington, DC: Catholic University of America Press, 2004), 53–76; here, 53.

6. Celia Deane-Drummond, "The Art and Science of Vocation: Wisdom and Conscience as Companions on a Way," in Cunningham, ed., *Vocation across the Academy*, 156–77; here, 162. Deane-Drummond notes that this approach "may lead to anxiety and to unnecessary restrictions on vocational exploration and discernment."

7. "'Who's There?': The Dramatic Role of the 'Caller' in Vocational Discernment," in *At This Time and In This Place: Vocation and Higher Education*, ed. David S. Cunningham (New York: Oxford University Press, 2016), 143–64; here, 156.

the next."[8] One should not necessarily see vocation as a single evident event, but rather as a process that unfolds throughout one's life.

But even if a Christian account of vocation is not wedded to the "grand narrative" approach, it does not always neatly fit within other religious traditions. Marcia Hermansen provides a helpful survey of how vocation has been understood within Islam, but nonetheless contends that "one must be cautious about forcing theologically simplified identifications across traditions."[9] Even though the Arabic equivalent of the word *call* is present in the Qur'an, it does not always have the same connotations that it may within Christianity. Similarly, Edward Breuer delineates his reservations about participating in a project in which he was asked to consider vocation from a Jewish perspective. He prefaces his comments with these words of caution:

> My initial reaction to this project, in fact, was one of incomprehension, tinged with a touch of exasperation: incomprehension because the notion of vocation does not appear to be significantly operative in Jewish teachings, and exasperation because the very question thereby appeared to ask one religious tradition to speak—conceptually, if not literally—in the language of another.[10]

Breuer here expresses something that is probably felt by observers from a wide range of traditions: a concern about trying to fit his own tradition into a Christian framework, and about asking that tradition to speak to a concept that originates within Christianity.

Nevertheless, by understanding vocation as a "process," it may come to be seen as relevant across a wider range of traditions. As Darby Ray notes, in contrast to the language of "achievement," that of "discernment" suggests "an ongoing process that takes time and courage. It is an attempt to see things as they really are—to discern the truth of the matter—while also opening oneself to new possible truths."[11] Instead of having a single, divinely ordained "calling" that leads to a definite career, students can be encouraged to explore their talents and capacities,

8. Cunningham, "Who's There?," 156.

9. Marcia Hermansen, "Islamic Concepts of Vocation," in Haughey, ed., *Revisiting the Idea of Vocation*, 77–96; here, 78.

10. Edward Breuer, "Vocation and Call as Communal Imperatives: Some Reflections on Judaism," in Haughey, ed., *Revisiting the Idea of Vocation*, 41–52; here, 41.

11. Darby Ray, "Self, World, and the Space Between: Community Engagement as Vocational Discernment," in Cunningham, ed., *At This Time*, 301–20; here, 313.

and gradually to discover their passions. Similarly, Paul Wadell puts forward the metaphor of vocation as a journey—or, more accurately, a *quest*—the meaning of which "can only gradually be fathomed as we experience it."[12] If they are willing to understand vocation as a quest, students "do not need to be clear about their futures in order to begin thinking and living vocationally; they can still embrace and enter into their core vocation of responding to the appeal of the good."[13] Hence, even those who are unsure of their calling can still live a life of goodness that can add up to a magnanimous way of life. Later, Wadell adds that this journey or quest will inevitably be filled with challenges. "To say yes to a calling—to follow one's vocation—is to enter a journey that may be immensely promising, but will unquestionably involve moments of doubt and uncertainty, periods of disillusionment and darkness, and times of hardship, suffering, and perhaps considerable loss."[14] Such is the nature of a quest.

In the remainder of this chapter, I hope to build upon the associations of vocation with notions such as *mystery, uncertainty*, and *quest*. In particular, I explore the story of Joseph in order to highlight the qur'anic concept of doubt and uncertainty as part of calling. I will also note how this story represents the larger themes that are found throughout the Qur'an and within Islam in general, as well as its stress on the importance of family and reconciliation as part of a successful vocational journey.

Scholarly accounts of the story of Joseph

The secondary literature on the qur'anic story of Joseph has generally focused on how the story compares with the versions in the Hebrew Bible and Christian Old Testament. Early literature often viewed the qur'anic story as a derivative and relatively unoriginal retelling of the biblical one. In more recent times, scholars have argued that while the qur'anic version draws on biblical characters and story lines, it has its own purpose in emphasizing faith and piety.[15] In contrast to

---

12. Paul Wadell, "An Itinerary of Hope: Called to a Magnanimous Way of Life," in Cunningham, ed., *At This Time*, 193–215; here, 202.

13. Wadell, "Itinerary of Hope," 202.

14. Wadell, "Itinerary of Hope," 207.

15. Marilyn Waldman, "New Approaches to 'Biblical' Materials in the Qur'an," *The Muslim World* 75, no. 1 (January 1985): 1–16; M. A. S. Abdel Haleem, "The Story of Joseph in the Qur'an and the Old Testament," *Islam and Christian–Muslim Relations* 1, no. 2 (1990): 171–91; Ayaz Afsar, "Plot Motifs in Joseph/Yūsuf Story: A Comparative Study of Biblical and Qur'ānic Narrative," *Islamic Studies* 45, no. 2 (Summer 2006): 167–89; and Marc Bernstein, "The Story of Our Master Joseph: The Spiritual or the Righteous," in *Judaism and Islam: Boundaries,*

the biblical story (which is part of the larger history of the people of Israel), the qur'anic chapter is more connected to the life of Muhammad and his early prophetic message. A number of scholars have further examined the literary aspects of the story, including its use of dramatic dialogue, irony, and human emotion.[16] These scholars analyze how the story is structured, as well as its various characters and how they interact and communicate.[17] A final group of writers has examined the symbolism and typology of the chapter, noting (for example) how Joseph's shirt continues to play important roles throughout the story (it appears when his brothers betray him, when Potiphar's wife tries to seduce him, and when Jacob's eyesight is restored).[18] However, there has been no work that focuses explicitly on the story's relevance to discussions of vocation, nor to its presentation of a paradigm of how one might live a fulfilled and fulfilling life.

Muslim tradition holds that the story of Joseph was revealed in the latter part of the Meccan phase of Muhammad's preaching.[19] This phase is marked

---

Communications, and Interaction: Essays in Honor of William M. Brinner, ed. Benjamin H. Hary, John L. Hayes, and Fred Astren (Leiden; Boston: Brill, 2000), 157–67. Bernstein also speaks about how the Islamic story of Joseph may have influenced later Jewish renditions of it.

16. Mustansir Mir, "The Qur'anic Story of Joseph: Plot, Themes, and Characters," *The Muslim World* 76, no. 1 (January 1986): 1–15; Mustansir Mir, "Irony in the Qur'an: A Study of the Story of Joseph," in *Literary Structures of Religious Meaning in the Qur'ān*, ed. Issa J. Boullata (Richmond, Surrey: Curzon, 2000), 173–87; Anthony H. Johns, "Joseph in the Qur'ān: Dramatic Dialogue, Human Emotion and Prophetic Wisdom," *Islamochristiana* 76, no. 1 (1981): 29–55; Anthony H. Johns, "The Qur'anic Presentation of the Joseph Story," in *Approaches to the Qur'ān*, ed. G. R. Hawting and Abdul-Kader A. Shareef (London; New York: Routledge, 1993), 37–70; Gary Rendsburg, "Literary Structures in the Qur'anic and Biblical Stories of Joseph," *The Muslim World* 78 (April 1988): 118–20; and James Winston Morris, "Dramatizing the Sura of Joseph: An Introduction to the Islamic Humanities," *Journal of Turkish Studies* 18 (1994): 201–24.

17. For works that discuss the structure of the chapter see Angelika Neuwirth, "Zur Struktur der Yūsuf-Sure," in *Studien aus Arabistik und Semitistik: Anton Spitaler zum siebzigsten Geburtstag von seinen Schülern überreicht*, ed. Werner Diem and Stefan Wild (Wiesbaden: Harrassowitz, 1980), 123–52.

18. F. V. Greifenhage, "The qamīṣ in 'Sūrat Yūsuf': A Prolegomenon to the Material Culture of Garments in the Formative Islamic Period," *Journal of Qur'anic Studies* 11, no. 2 (October 2009): 72–92, and Todd Lawson, "Typological Figuration and the Meaning of 'Spiritual': The Qur'anic Story of Joseph," *Journal of the American Oriental Society* 132, no. 2 (April–June 2012): 221–44. Lawson provides a helpful review of the secondary literature written on the story and provides insightful Shi'ī readings of the Prophet.

19. For more on how the chapter represents this later Meccan phase (and Muhammad's prophetic mission in general), see Johns, "Qur'anic Presentation," as well as M. S. Stern, "Muhammad and Joseph: A Study of Koranic Narrative," *Journal of Near Eastern Studies* 44, no. 3 (July 1985): 193–204. Noting the similarities between Muhammad's mission and the story of Joseph, Stern comments: "How fitting this parallel must have seemed to Muhammad. His

by a small fledgling community that is facing persecution and struggling to survive. Muhammad is frequently slandered by his clansmen, who reject his claim to prophecy and the call to worship one God. The later Meccan phase was especially difficult, as Muhammad was beginning to lose hope in his tribesman; in addition, his wife and strongest supporter, Khadijah, passed away.

Recent scholarship further confirms that the chapter reflects a particularly challenging and desperate time. For example, the Qur'an scholar Walid Saleh argues that it fits within a transitional period where Muhammad had been preaching to his clansmen for years but only a handful had converted; he was searching for other options.[20] However, the later Islamic tradition would eventually overlook or even reread sections of this chapter that deal with these desperate circumstances—based on the eventual success of Islam and the Islamic empire. As Saleh explains, "The cataclysmic success of the early Islamic state has resulted in our failure to see this despair as a major topic in the Qur'an: the giving up on humanity, the deeply felt conviction that those who were receptive to the message had already converted, whereas those who had not would never do so."[21] The Muslim tradition has largely read the story of Joseph as triumphalist; he becomes the head of the storehouse, is reunited with his family, and is favored by God. However, like Saleh, I believe that the Islamic tradition has largely overlooked certain verses within the chapter that speak to its central theme of despair and hopelessness. In particular, the final verses of the chapter are frequently ignored or entirely reread.[22]

people resented him because they thought that he sought superiority over them for his own personal ends. Would they not understand that he was asserting himself only because God had thrust a special role on him for their salvation? God had caused Joseph to ascend to power to provide food in famine. Muhammad had been sent to provide his people with the wherewithal to face judgment. Their sin was brought on by ignorance; the messenger must not cease to combat that ignorance. Meanwhile he must fear God and be patient" (200).

20. Walid Saleh, "End of Hope: Suras 10–15, Despair and a Way Out of Mecca," in *Qur'ānic Studies Today*, ed. Angelika Neuwirth and Michael A. Sells (New York: Routledge, 2016), 105–23.

21. Saleh, "End of Hope," 107.

22. The theme of triumphalism is evident in the secondary literature which emphasizes the eventual success of Joseph and the prophets in general. For instance, M. A. S. Abdel Haleem states in his article on the chapter of Joseph that verses 103–11 "are a general comment on the Prophet's call and the unbelievers' response, confirming that a good future lies ahead for prophets—a lesson to be learned from their stories in the Qur'an" ("Story of Joseph," 172). Later on, at the end of the article, Haleem concludes explaining how "God has supported young Joseph when his brothers plotted against him" (189). Haleem then quotes Joseph's final soliloquy in verse 102 where he realizes the meaning of his dream that he had as a young child and praises God for giving him authority and reconciling with his brothers. Haleem then skips over verses 103 to 110 and ends his article with the beginning of verse 111, "a moral for men of understanding." Thus, Haleem does not put much weight on these final verses or reads them

In what follows, I will present an alternative reading of the story of Joseph—one in which despair and uncertainty play a central role.[23]

Joseph: a story of desperation

The account of Joseph seems to acknowledge the grim period in which Muhammad found himself. It begins by addressing the Prophet: "We tell you the best of stories in revealing this Qur'an to you. Before this you were one of those who knew nothing about them." To provide comfort to Muhammad, the Qur'an states that it is informing him of a previous story of a prophet who faced similar trials and tribulations. The Qur'an then launches immediately into the story.

Joseph's early trials

As the story begins, Joseph approaches his father, Jacob, with uncertainties about a dream that he had: "Father, I dreamed of eleven stars and the sun and the moon: I saw them all bow down before me" (12:4). Jacob does not provide an interpretation of the dream, but rather advises Joseph not to tell his envious brothers, who may try to harm him.[24]

---

as part of a "good future" that God will provide to the prophets. The verses do not fit neatly within a triumphalist narrative in which Joseph, Muhammad, and the prophets always succeed. Similarly, the *Study Qur'an*, which is quickly becoming one of the important English commentaries on the Qur'an, skips over the final verses in its brief summary of the chapter, stating only, "By the end of the tale, Joseph's parents and brothers come to Egypt to stay with him (v. 99), and the dream he had at the beginning of the story is fulfilled (v. 100)." There is no mention of the final verses which return back to Muhammad and discuss the prophets and desperation; *The Study Quran: A New translation and Commentary*, ed. Seyyed Hossein Nasr, Caner K. Dagli, Maria Massi Dakake, Joseph E. B. Lumbard, and Mohammed Rustom (New York: Harper One, 2015), 589.

23. For a work that rethinks the role doubt plays within the Christian tradition, see Jacqueline Bussie, *Outlaw Christian: Finding Authentic Faith by Breaking the "Rules"* (Nashville, TN: Thomas Nelson, 2016).

24. Joseph's dream here is similar to other qur'anic stories in which the prophets are unsure about the meaning of a dream. For example, in the famous story of the sacrifice, Abraham has a vision in which he is slaughtering his son. Abraham is seemingly confounded to the point that he asks his son regarding the dream's interpretation: "My son, I have seen myself sacrificing you in a dream. What do you think?" (37:102). The son does not seem to fully understand the dream either, but responds by declaring, "Father, do as you are commanded and, God willing, you will find me steadfast" (37:102). Similarly, Muhammad has a dream in which he is entering Mecca and performing the rites of Hajj. As the divine voice of the Qur'an states, "God has truly fulfilled His Messenger's vision: 'God willing, you will most certainly enter the Sacred Mosque in safety, shaven-headed or with cropped hair, without fear!" (48:27). However, Muslim tradition records that when Muhammad and his followers returned to Mecca to perform the rites,

As Jacob forewarned, Joseph's brothers become jealous of him to the point that they plot to get rid of him. One of them contends that they should kill Joseph, while a more merciful one suggests that they should throw him in a well, where a caravan may pick him up. They then approach their father, asking for his permission to take Joseph out to play. Put in a difficult position, Jacob does not directly voice his concern that the brothers will harm Joseph; instead, he expresses his worry that when they are not paying attention, a wolf may come and devour his son. Nonetheless, Jacob finally relents and the brothers take Joseph away—and indeed, they do eventually throw him into a well. In the pit of the well, God inspires Joseph by declaring to him, "'You will tell them of all this [at a time] when they do not realize [who you are]!'" (12:15). Of course, it is unclear (both to Joseph and to the reader of the story) how such an event could ever occur.

The brothers then return to their father with Joseph's bloodstained shirt, claiming that—as their father warned—he was eaten by a wolf. A group of caravans move by the well and discover Joseph; the drivers make plans to sell him into slavery. The Qur'an states that, not knowing Joseph's true value, the caravan drivers sell Joseph for a few pieces of silver to a well-off family whose members think that they can adopt him as a son. The divine voice of the Qur'an interjects here and states, "In this way We established Joseph in that land and later taught him how to interpret dreams: God always prevails in His purpose, though most people do not realize it" (12:21). Once again, however, it is unclear how God has "established" (*tamkīn*) Joseph in the land when he is only a slave at this point in the narrative.

When Joseph grows up, the mistress of the house tries to seduce him; he responds that his master has been good to him and attempts to escape by running to the door. However, she leaps at him and tears his shirt from behind. As they reach the door, they encounter the master, who asks what is happening. The mistress claims that Joseph attempted to seduce her, while Joseph declares his innocence. A member of the household suggests that if the shirt is torn from the front then Joseph was guilty, but if it was torn from the back then he was innocent. After the shirt is inspected and found to have been torn from behind, Joseph is exonerated. However, the city's male elite feel it is better for them to imprison Joseph for a certain period of time.

---

they were prevented by the native tribes from entering the city. Some of Muhammad's followers began to doubt the veracity of the dream to the point that Muhammad responds by asking, "Did I say the dream would occur this year?" The tradition records that after the signing of a treaty with the Meccan tribes, Muhammad and his followers had to return to Medina, but that they were able to come to Mecca again the following year and perform the rites. These examples suggest that, while the various qur'anic dreams represent revelation, their precise meaning and import are not always entirely clear.

While in prison, two men approach Joseph with dreams that they have had, noting that they see him as righteous and knowledgeable. The first explains that he dreamed that he was pressing grapes, while the other states that he had bread on his head and the birds were eating from it. Joseph explains that one of the prisoners will serve the king wine, while the other will be crucified and the birds will peck at his head. Joseph asks the future servant to mention him to the king, but the servant forgets to do so—leaving Joseph in prison yet longer.

The king himself then has a dream in which he sees seven fat cows being eaten by seven lean ones, as well as seven good ears of corn and seven others that are withered. He asks his advisers about the dream, but they admit that they do not have the expertise to interpret it. However, the prisoner who had been freed remembers Joseph, who is then asked about the meaning of the dream. He responds that there will be a plentiful harvest for seven consecutive years and that the kingdom should store food during this period. Afterward will come seven years of hardship, during which time they will have to depend on their savings.

Hearing the interpretation of the dream, the king asks for Joseph to be brought to him, but Joseph refuses, demanding that his name be cleared. The mistress admits that it was she, not Joseph, who was guilty of the crime, and that he is an honest man. Upon his release, Joseph requests that he be put in charge of the storehouses—the very ones that will save the harvest for the impending drought. His request is granted, and the divine voice of the chapter then reiterates that it is God who settled Joseph in the land and that God has mercy upon those who do good and are conscious of him. From being thrown into a well to becoming a slave and then being put into prison, Joseph has now entered into a new phase of his life: that of a manager and minister.

The brothers seek help

As the drought begins, Joseph's brothers come to the storehouses asking for food. Joseph recognizes them, but they do not realize that they are speaking to their brother. After giving them some food, Joseph says that, if they want more corn, they must bring their younger brother. (He is referred to as Benjamin in the Bible and in the Islamic exegetical tradition, but his name is not mentioned in the text of the Qur'an.) The brothers return home and plead with their father, ironically employing the same phrase that they used when asking to take Joseph: "we shall guard him carefully" (*wa inna lahu la-ḥāfiẓūn*) (12:63). Jacob then asks the natural question: "Am I to entrust him to you as I did his brother before?" (12:64). The brothers persist, and Jacob eventually relents, but he makes his sons pledge that they will bring Benjamin back.

When the brothers come for a second time, Joseph draws Benjamin close to him and reveals himself to him. Joseph then places a cup within the bag of Benjamin, framing him as a thief so that he will be forced to return. When the cup is found, his brothers are stunned; they blurt out, "If he is a thief then his brother was a thief before him" (12:77), referring to Joseph. Joseph is enraged, but still does not reveal himself to the rest of his brothers. They begin to plead with Joseph, stating that their father is an old man and that he should take one of the other brothers in Benjamin's place. Joseph, however, denies their request, explaining that it would be unjust to take anyone else in the place of the thief.

This scene is remarkable in that it presents the episode of Joseph's childhood in reverse. Joseph tricks his brothers by taking Benjamin, just as they tricked their father by taking him. The difference, in contrast, is that Joseph wished for the good of his brother, while his other brothers had wished Joseph harm. It is as if Joseph's actions here are what he would have wanted his brothers to do with him.

When the brothers lose hope in persuading Joseph, they withdraw to confer with one another. The eldest asks his fellow brothers, "Do you not remember that your father took a solemn pledge from you in the name of God and before that you failed in your duty with regard to Joseph?" (12:80). The eldest refuses to go back home with them until his father permits him to do so. When the rest of the brothers return home and explain to their father what has happened, Jacob does not believe them. It is as if they have "cried wolf" too many times.[25] Jacob states that they have done wrong, but declares that he will be patient and that God may bring all of them back to him. Nonetheless, Jacob's grief intensifies to the point that he becomes blind.[26] The brothers worry about their father, fearing that his health will decline further and that he may even die. Jacob responds that he pleads his grief and sorrow before God, and that they should not despair of God's mercy.[27]

The story then reaches its climax when the brothers return to Joseph for the third time. In this instance, they do not have any merchandise to barter; they must resort to asking Joseph for charity. In a moment of weakness, Joseph reveals himself: "Do you now realize what you did to Joseph and his brother when you were ignorant?" (12:89). The brothers, startled, begin to put the various pieces

25. Mir, "Irony," 181.

26. The qur'anic expression literally says that "His eyes went white" (12:84).

27. Thus, Jacob goes through a number of transitions throughout his lifetime. For more on the idea of hearing different callings throughout one's life, see Catherine Fobes, "Calling over the Life Course," in Cunningham, ed., *Vocation across the Academy*, 91–110. See also Kathleen A. Cahalan and Bonnie J. Miller-McLemore, *Calling All Years Good: Christian Vocation throughout Life's Seasons* (Grand Rapids, MI: Eerdmans, 2017).

together: "Could it be that you are Joseph?" He responds, "I am Joseph and this is my brother. God has been gracious to us: God does not deny anyone who is mindful of God and steadfast in adversity, the rewards of those who do good" (12:90).

Outcomes of the story

Joseph's response to his brothers provides us with one of its most important lessons of the story. The events of Joseph's life were not of his choosing: being thrown into a well, sold into slavery, put into jail, and called upon to serve the king. For much of his life, Joseph seemed to be acted upon, rather than acting. Nonetheless, he explains that throughout his life he maintained a strong core that allowed him, eventually, to succeed; we might well describe this core as a commitment to a life of virtue.[28] While Joseph was not always in control of the events of his life, he continued to be committed to a moral struggle that allowed him ultimately to discern and define his vocation.[29]

Moreover, Joseph is not simply preaching to his brothers; he is sharing a principle that he implemented in his own lifetime. As a government minister and head of the storehouse, he is a model of how to live a life of virtue. As Wadell explains, people "are far more likely to recognize the beauty of the good and to appreciate the delight and joy that inhere in lives of virtue and integrity when they not only hear someone talk about it, but when they see it enacted in another person's life."[30] Here Joseph embodies the righteousness, patience, and perseverance that allow him not only to be a good person but also to outpace his peers.

Despite the positions now being reversed (in that Joseph is the one in power and his brothers are in a position of weakness), Joseph does not seek revenge. Instead, he declares, "You will hear no reproaches today. May God forgive you: He is the Most Merciful of the merciful" (12:92). Joseph forgives his

---

28. As Paul Wadell observes ("Itinerary of Hope," 201), "Since many callings demand something new of us, it may take time to live into them fully, hence we need the virtue of patience to work through frustrations and difficulties in order to achieve important goals. . . . It would be difficult to guide students in thinking about their callings without also teaching them about the importance of the virtues for both discovering and living into those callings."

29. As Mir further explains ("Qur'anic Story of Joseph," 10), "Every individual must go through a series of trials. But success or failure in these trials is not predetermined in the sense that a good character will necessarily succeed, while an evil character will necessarily fail. Success or failure in a moral struggle is the result of independent choices made and executed during the struggle itself."

30. Wadell continues: "Overcoming these obstacles requires courage, along with patience, perseverance, and hope—and perhaps even a certain boldness of spirit" ("Itinerary of Hope," 203).

brothers, invoking the mercy of God; he also asks his brother to take his shirt and lay it over Jacob's eyes, which will restore his sight. Joseph then commands them to bring his whole family back to Egypt.

From Joseph's words, it is evident that he has never forgotten about his parents; he continues to remember them and is concerned about their well-being. Joseph's calling was never directed to him alone; it also included his family and their collective welfare. As his parents enter into Egypt, Joseph welcomes them and then raises them on his throne. This symbolic gesture demonstrates his appreciation to them in providing the moral and spiritual foundation that allowed him to succeed. It is as though the parents are among the kings of Egypt, because their child has reached such a stature. His family then bows down in respect to Joseph, which he realizes was the fulfillment of the dream that he had when he was a child. His soliloquy to his father reflects on his life, his family, and God:

> Father, this is the fulfillment of that dream I had long ago. My Lord has made it come true and has been gracious to me—He released me from prison and He brought you here from the desert—after Satan sowed discord between me and my brothers. My Lord is most subtle in achieving what He will; He is the All Knowing, the Truly Wise. My Lord! You have given me authority; You have taught me something about the interpretation of dreams; Creator of the heavens and the earth, You are my protector in this world and in the Hereafter. Let me die in true devotion to You. Join me with the righteous. (12:100–101)

Joseph, who throughout his entire life has been interpreting the dreams of others, is finally able to understand his own. The most difficult moments of his life now make sense—from being in prison to finding himself in opposition to his brothers. He is able to "connect the dots" and find meaning in the most challenging times in his life.

Even though the story of Joseph ends here, the chapter itself continues with the divine voice speaking to Muhammad:[31] "All the messengers We sent before you were men to whom We made revelations, men chosen from the people of

31. This return back to Muhammad is significant because it demonstrates the importance of the story in the life of the Prophet. As Lawson explains ("Typological Figuration," 238), "The story of Joseph has a special place in Islam and in the Qur'an. It may be offered that while Abraham and/or Moses have frequently been considered the ideal exemplar for Muḥammadan prophecy, a study of the shirt of Joseph suggests that this qamīṣ may have also served as a veil for another possibility. It is actually Joseph who represents a truer type—or at least a more complete type—for the Prophet, whether among Sunni exegetes or Shiʿī. In this amplitude of Qurʾanic detail and narrative there is rhetorical power."

their towns" (12:109). Just as the account began, it ends by emphasizing that Muhammad is not alone; he is part of a longer line of figures who have called their people to monotheism. The chapter then concludes by discussing messengers as a group; here, the theme of uncertainty which eventually turns into despair becomes paramount. "When the messengers lost all hope and thought that they had been lied to, Our help came to them: We saved whomever We pleased, but Our punishment will not be turned away from guilty people" (12:110).[32]

In the various studies of the story of Joseph, these final verses are often overlooked; indeed, they were considered problematic to many Muslim exegetes, who had trouble with the idea that the messengers could doubt God's promise.[33] Several exegetes even tried to read the verse differently, contending it was the messenger's *followers* who lost hope in God's promise, rather than the prophets themselves.[34] Regardless, the verse demonstrates that uncertainty and despair were essential parts of the prophetic mission: in this moment of doubt, God's support came and the people were saved. Significantly, the verse uses the same root of the word for *despair* (*ya's*) that Jacob uses when preaching to his sons. Jacob had commanded his sons not to "despair in the mercy of God" (12:87), since despair is a sign of disbelief.[35] In fact, verbs that derive from the root word *despair* (*ya's*) only appear 10 times in the Qur'an, 4 of which are found in the story of Joseph. It is as if this account is an antidote for those who are in a state of desperation or despair.

Implications for vocational reflection and discernment

The story of Joseph contributes to our understanding of vocation, particularly in terms of understanding our calling and its relationship to the callings of others.

32. Regarding these verses, Saleh ("End of Hope," 115) says, "Indeed, prophets have by then actually come to believe that they have been given the lie (*wa-ẓannū annahum qad kudhdhibū*). The doubting prophet is now nearly a fixture in these suras, weak of heart, tight of chest, full of despair, eager to compromise, and wishing for the very thing that God is not willing to grant—the conversion of humanity or at least vindication through miracles."

33. Saleh ("End of Hope," 117) explains that "The use of the verb 'despair' in this verse was a problematic issue for the later Islamic exegetical tradition because a believer never despairs."

34. However, early interpretations of this verse maintain that it was the messengers themselves who started to believe that God lied to them. This interpretation is captured in the translation of Anthony H. Johns, "Until even [these] messengers [almost] despaired, and imagined they had been deceived. But then our help came to them, and those whom We willed were saved. Our anger cannot be turned aside from evil-doers"; Johns, "Qur'anic Presentation," 55.

35. Johns makes this point as well; Johns, "Qur'anic Presentation," 36.

First, Joseph's vocational journey was a quest, in that it took years to manifest itself and to be realized. Although Joseph was "called" in his childhood, the calling was not entirely clear and did not become manifest until much later in his life. Thus, Joseph's calling was not a single event but rather a "lifelong journey, in which the purpose of each step along the way is to prepare us for the next."[36] The various moral tests that Joseph faced during his life, whether as a slave or in jail, allowed him to be a successful manager—in which he is not only gainfully employed but also in a position where he could help the general population and eventually his own family.

This first point leads to the second: Joseph's call was never simply about himself, but also about his family and the people who were closest to him. In his soliloquy, Joseph explains the various ways that he has found success; he feels that he has been blessed in his life. It is interesting to note that Joseph does not mention his job, nor the material possessions that he acquired. And even though he does state that God has given him "authority," he seems more concerned with the fact that he has been released from hardship and reunited with his family. While Joseph is certainly living a much more comfortable life than he did as prisoner or slave, his real success is that he has reconciled with his brothers and reconnected with his parents. Thus, the story of Joseph makes us rethink the vocational journey as more than an individualistic, materialistic enterprise. For Joseph, "success" involved more than his work and "career"; it also meant offering service to, and maintaining meaningful relationships with, those who were the closest to him. As we discern our vocations, "our lives will be linked to the lives of others, and the work that we do will be in their service."[37]

Third, this analysis sheds light on the danger of triumphalism, which can lead us to ignore the most difficult, uncertain, and challenging parts of our lives. The various commentaries frequently overlook the verses regarding despair and emphasize the eventual success of Joseph. However, Muslim tradition and modern scholarship are consistent in recognizing that this chapter originates from a time when Muhammad did not feel that he was succeeding in his prophetic career. We often fall into the trap of triumphalism in interacting with students who themselves don't always feel successful, particularly when they are just beginning their vocational journeys. Colleges often present models of success to students, whether it be through their course material, the professors who teach them, or the staff members with whom they interact. Students find themselves surrounded

36. Cunningham, "Who's There?" 156.

37. David S. Cunningham, "Vocabularies of Vocation: Language for a Complex Educational Landscape," epilogue to Cunningham, ed., *Vocation across the Academy*, 315–24; here, 322.

by people who seem to be successful, confident, and self-assured. However, what if the student is beset with despair, feeling hopeless, or suffering from depression? The story of Joseph reminds us that despair and hopelessness are essential parts of the vocational journey; they should not be ignored or looked down upon, but rather embraced. In my experience, students often want to hear more about failure, doubt, and despair—and not just about achievement and success.

Finally, the story points out that, in spite of the various obstacles that Joseph faces, he never succumbs to cynicism or to a loss of moral authority. Joseph maintains his moral compass and spiritual strength throughout his life, even when he finds himself in the most difficult circumstances. As Wadell states, even those who are doubtful and uncertain "can still embrace and enter into their core vocation of responding to the appeal of the good."[38] Put differently: doubt, uncertainty, and despair are not a license to act wrongly, whether for oneself or on behalf of others. Rather, these are necessary components of a vocational quest; they help us understand our callings and unlock the mysteries of our lives.[39]

Response

Jacqueline A. Bussie

I read Younus's chapter with great fascination and appreciation. I learned a great deal from his interpretation of the qur'anic story of Joseph. Indeed, as is often the case for those who engage in interfaith dialogue and collaboration, reading this essay and engaging in subsequent conversations with its author have deepened and nourished my own faith. As a Christian and a theologian, I have long struggled to reconcile doubt, despair, and uncertainty with a life of faith in God. My mother suffered from a debilitating terminal illness for 17 years; while I was her caregiver, I felt myself plagued with doubt and hopelessness. Other Christians often made me feel ashamed for those feelings, condemning despair and doubt as forms of faithlessness, blasphemy, and sin. I, however, hold a contrary view, based on the example of Jesus; when he is dying on the cross, he cries out, "My God, my God, why have you forsaken me?" (Matthew 27:46). Jesus's

38. Wadell, "Itinerary of Hope," 202.

39. I would like to thank my students Sarah Shapley and Logan Welch for their help with the literature review and helping me think through the theoretical and practical aspects of vocation. Their work was supported through the Andrew W. Mellon Collaborative Undergraduate Research in the Humanities grant to Allegheny College. I would also like to dedicate this essay to my wife, Rehenuma Asmi, for our various conversations about doubt and uncertainty.

words signify that doubt is not a sin, but an integral aspect of a faith that is alive and authentic. Unfortunately, however, as I argue in my recent book *Outlaw Christian*, Christians often neglect Jesus's cry of dereliction, and allow a shallow triumphalism to swallow its profound message.

I discovered striking parallels within this chapter. Within Islam too, theological triumphalism leads many exegetes to condemn despair and overlook the doubt exhibited by the prophets, including Joseph. But Younus, a practicing Muslim, reinterprets the text and retrieves doubt as essential. His conclusion liberates all of us who struggle with doubt: "The story of Joseph reminds us that despair and hopelessness are essential parts of the vocational journey; they should not be ignored or looked down upon, but rather embraced." When we as educators share our doubts and failures with our students, it sets them free to face and share theirs—and thus to embark on journeys of healing rather than shame.

5

Gracious Reception

A CHRISTIAN CASE FOR HEARING VOCATION DIFFERENTLY

David S. Cunningham

IN THE INTRODUCTION to this volume, as well as in a number of its chapters, various authors have expressed concern about the deeply Christian roots of the concepts of vocation and calling. They have suggested that, if this notion is to function successfully in a multi-faith environment, its advocates will need to be attentive to the specific features of its history, as well as its continuing identification with a particular faith tradition. Still, although the language of vocation will always carry with it certain Christian overtones, most of the contributors believe that it is a concept worth keeping—and one that can continue to be useful in the increasingly multi-faith environment of higher education. For this to occur, however, the concept will need to be rethought and reimagined in the contemporary context. This conviction led to our formulation of the book's title: *Hearing Vocation Differently*.

As the book's editor, I very much agree with this perspective; however, any significant reformulation of a longstanding theological concept necessarily raises the traditional problem of continuity and change.[1] Like many faiths and philosophical perspectives, Christianity has undergone tremendous changes throughout its history; yet most of its adherents would want to claim that it remains, and should remain, the "same" faith that was practiced by Jesus's first

1. For an excellent discussion of this problem, as well as an explication of how it has been addressed by Christian theologians such as Newman and Blondel, see Nicholas Lash, *Change in Focus: A Study of Doctrinal Change and Continuity* (London: Sheed and Ward, 1973).

followers. Indeed, as many have observed, the word *vocation* itself marks a significant instance of continuity and change; this word has shifted significantly, in its range and applications, over time.[2] This shift has demanded theological description and explication in the past, and this need continues today. Among the questions facing us: What are the core meanings of the language of vocation? Can these be preserved in light of the effort to "hear" such language in a different key? What should be the Christian theological response to such an effort? And, perhaps most appealingly from my perspective: Might Christians themselves have something to learn, about their own understanding of this concept, from those who stand in other traditions and who have encouraged us to hear vocation differently?

In this chapter, I hope to make the case that the Christian theological tradition itself lends support to the claim that the concept of vocation can function well across a wide range of lifestances.[3] I recognize, of course, that some may prefer to employ an understanding of vocation that retains its distinctive Christian contours. Nevertheless, I am also aware that a great many others—including many who would self-identify as Christians—are actively searching to broaden their range of conversation partners about vocational issues. I want to address both audiences by observing that certain Christian theological claims encourage us to rethink the concepts of vocation and calling in ways that make them accessible to all people—regardless of their degree of adherence to, practice of, or agreement with the Christian faith.

The chapter has three major sections. First, I outline what I take to be one of the most important insights of vocational thinking: attention to perspectives that come from *outside* or *beyond* one's immediate influence. I draw on a poem by Rainer Maria Rilke that encourages us to think about the empowering, bridge-building, and world-creating significance of that which comes to us from outside ourselves. In the second section, I argue that a Christian account of vocation should attend closely to one of that faith tradition's most significant claims: that it advocates the embodiment of a commitment to *gracious reception*. I want to suggest that, contrary to some accounts, accepting one's calling is not primarily about sheer obedience to God. Rather, it involves allowing the perspectives of other human beings (and, through them, the perspective of God) to resonate in,

2. This shift is described briefly in the introduction to this volume. I offer a more complete account in "Time and Place: Why Vocation is Essential in Undergraduate Education Today," in *At This Time and In This Place: Vocation and Higher Education*, ed. David S. Cunningham (New York: Oxford University Press, 2016), 1–19.

3. For a definition and description of this term, see Rachel Mikva's comments in chapter 1 of this volume.

and exercise some degree of control over, one's life. In a final section, I suggest that the appeal to "hear vocation differently" is itself a kind of calling—one that may well help Christians live more fully into their own theological commitments.[4] I illustrate this claim with three vignettes from the life of Jesus, each of which shows him encountering difference in a mode of gracious reception. The overall argument of the chapter is that, when Christians learn to think about vocation in ways that recognize its significance for those who do not share their own faith convictions, they will not only be increasing their range of conversation partners on the subject; they will also be more fully embracing the theological claims of their own faith.

Learning to play catch

I begin with one of the chief contributions of "vocational thinking": that it encourages us to think about our future directions in life in terms that transcend our own desires and abilities. For decades, undergraduate institutions have encouraged students to think about what they want to do with their lives; indeed, they have often done so in grand terms, using words like *meaning* and *purpose* and *significance*. But the language of vocation and calling explicitly encourages active listening and attention—not just to one's own needs and desires, but to the perspective of those who see us from beyond our own perspective.

In this respect, the move into vocational thinking parallels the early stages of the lives of athletes, artists, and artisans, who—up until a certain point—have only dreamed and worked and practiced on their own. When they come into the company of other people who also practice their particular sport or art or craft, everything changes. Teachers, coaches, trainers, fellow members of the team or troupe or guild, and even the spectators who cheer them on: all change the dynamic of our participation in a particular endeavor, requiring us to see things from their point of view as well as our own. In fact, some of these enterprises actually demand the participation of others in order to be what they truly are; team sports need teammates, most plays require a cast and crew, and the studios of artists and artisans eventually fill up with pupils, patrons, and enthusiasts.

This feature of many human activities—the importance of the participation of more than one person—also marks the practice of vocational reflection and

4. For further thoughts on the ways that interfaith conversations can strengthen one's own faith commitments, see the reflections of Noah Silverman, Florence Amamoto, and Jacqueline Bussie in chapters 7, 10, and 11 of this volume, respectively.

discernment. We can, in some sense, undertake this work on our own (even though, as with even the most individualized sports and crafts, we typically rely heavily on others to teach us what to do, and to indicate whether we're doing it well). But we are likely to become better at it, and to enjoy it more, if we engage in it with others. This is why, as I have argued elsewhere,[5] vocational reflection and discernment can be usefully compared to *playing catch*. Of course, a person can throw a ball up into the air and catch it, or throw it into some kind of machine that returns it; but the best games of catch are those in which one's partners are fully empowered agents. By bringing their own experience, ability, and perspective to the activity, these co-players complement our own abilities, show us new possibilities, and make us better practitioners of our particular art or craft or sport. In addition, the whole endeavor becomes more interesting, since other people have their own ways of doing things. They may occasionally throw a curve ball; this will probably annoy us at first, but eventually we may learn to appreciate it. This explains why we often seek out experts, or at least people with more experience than ourselves, to be our partners in these activities—whether this involves a simple game of catch, a deep participation in a sport or an artistic endeavor, or a lifelong commitment to vocational reflection.

Rilke's insights

I first began thinking about the relationship between vocational discernment and playing catch when I happened upon this excerpt from a poem, originally written in German:

> Catch only what you yourself have thrown,
> It's all just skill and meaningless gain;
> But when you're suddenly the catcher of a ball
> Thrown by an eternal partner,
> To you, to your center, with accuracy and skill,
> In one of those arcs of the great bridge-building of God—
> Only then does the ability to catch become a power:
> Not yours. That of a world.

5. See my September 2016 post on the NetVUE Scholarly Resources blog at http://www.vocationmatters.org/2016/09/15/finding-your-calling-and-playing-catch/ (accessed January 4, 2017).

The original source of these lines is an untitled poem by Rainer Maria Rilke.[6] It serves as the epigraph of an important work of twentieth-century philosophy: Hans-Georg Gadamer's 1960 treatise on the interpretation of texts, titled *Wahrheit und Methode* (*Truth and Method*).[7] Gadamer's chief metaphor was that of the "fusion of horizons," in which the horizon of the reader was drawn into contact with the horizon of the text itself. By giving both these elements equal emphasis, he raised questions about the postmodern tendency toward putting the reader in absolute control of the process of interpretation, which he (like Rilke) might have described as "catching only what you yourself have thrown." Gadamer argued that texts, like their readers, have a certain degree of autonomy, not only because of the indelible nature of the word on the page, but also because of their *Wirkungsgeschichte*, their "effective-history" or "history of their effects"—that is, the ways that the texts have shaped real events in the world, as well as the history of their various interpretations over time. Particularly in the case of an older text, the process of interpretation is like catching a ball thrown by an eternal partner—since such texts have already accumulated a history of interpretation, and have often had a significant effect on the world, long before we encountered them. Interpreting them gives us the power to enter into their world, or perhaps to create a world of our own.[8]

Both Gadamer and Rilke thus remind us of the importance of what is external to us—that which is beyond us and which comes to us from the outside. This is an important lesson, because we are often uncertain how our own perspective relates to those of others. We tend to assume either that everyone's perspective should be identical (as in the "objectivity" that is typically attributed to the natural sciences), or that everyone's perspective is different and that there is no way to evaluate which ones might be better or worse (as in the "subjectivity" that is often attributed to the arts and humanities). In the midst of this polarization, Gadamer was one of a handful of thinkers[9] who recognized that neither of these accounts

---

6. Written on January 31, 1922. German text in Rainer Maria Rilke, *Gedichte 1910 bis 1926*, vol. 2 of *Werke: Kommentierte Ausgabe in vier Bänden*, ed. Manfred Engel (Frankfurt am Main: Insel, 1996), my translation.

7. Hans-Georg Gadamer, *Truth and Method*, trans. Joel G. Weinsheimer and Donald G. Marshall (New York: Crossroad, 1989).

8. As I will make clear later in the chapter, I am here prescinding from the question of whether the primary agency is that of the "thrower" or the "catcher" (or whether it is perhaps shared by both). I am open to the possibility that the "world" that is created in this process may be a largely human creation, as is suggested by Matthew R. Sayers in chapter 8 of this volume.

9. Others include Jürgen Habermas, Hannah Arendt, and Richard Rorty; for an excellent study of these three figures, along with Gadamer, see Richard J. Bernstein, *Beyond Objectivism and Relativism* (Oxford: Basil Blackwell, 1983).

adequately characterizes how we gain knowledge, and who tried to develop an alternative approach. Gadamer's quotation of Rilke is meant to remind us that *both* the subject *and* the object are of extraordinary importance.

Implications for the undergraduate setting

As abstract as this description may sound, it actually reflects the circumstances in which many undergraduate students find themselves. In the face of a culture that tells them they can "grow up to be anything they want," they are blocked by one obstacle after another. They are told to think for themselves and to make their own choices, but they often lack the resources to do so.[10] Their internal compasses have been preprogrammed by inherited assumptions, simplistic advice, and messages carefully tailored to their inclinations by Big Data. Is it any wonder that they sometimes long for a clear and definitive directive—perhaps by means of a forceful actor (whether cultural, theological, or political)—who will resolve all these tensions by please just telling them what to do?

Since some of these young people have chosen to spend four years of their lives in academic institutions where they will be encouraged and challenged to wrestle with these questions, those who serve those institutions as educators have an extraordinary responsibility, and opportunity, to offer them an alternative to two equally deleterious mindsets. The first of these is the temptation to assume that no one else can possibly have one's best interests at heart, so one should simply go it alone; the second is the temptation to declare that it's all just too overwhelming and to hand everything over to the will of another—be it a well-meaning parent, a charismatic friend, or a xenophobic demagogue. Part of the educator's job is to help students to consider the role of external (as well as internal) sources of guidance and motivation in their lives.[11] Students also need help prioritizing these sources, identifying the most benevolent and constructive ones, and reflecting on what they might learn from them. And, particularly for those students who are accustomed to thinking in theological terms, educators have an opportunity to help them consider God's role in the various external and

10. See William T. Cavanaugh, "Actually, You Can't Do Anything You Want (And It's a Good Thing, Too)," in Cunningham, ed., *At This Time*, 25–46.

11. I do not mean to suggest a clear distinction between internal and external motivations. All external motivations must be internalized, to some extent, if they are to move the will; conversely, all internal motivations have their roots in some external influence. The distinction is a heuristic, meant to describe motivations that have been more actively internalized (so that we begin to name them as "our own"), as opposed to those that we identify, first and foremost, as a way that our lives are influenced by some other person, idea, or system.

internal motivations that they experience, as well as in the guidance that they receive from others.

I believe that Rilke has something to say to faculty and staff in higher education as they consider how to carry out this charge. College is never a solitary intellectual enterprise; students do not wander through their undergraduate years as though no one else were there, constantly catching only whatever they themselves have thrown. On the other hand, it would be better if they didn't catch just *any* object, and certainly not *every* object, that is thrown their way. Ideally, they might take into consideration the nature of their partners in this business—the abilities, expertise, and character of those with whom they are playing this highly consequential game of catch.

Identifying the players in the game

In this respect, the original German version of Rilke's poem is important, at least in the case of one particular line: the one that speaks of an "eternal partner." The German word that I have translated as "partner" is *Mit-Spielerin*, literally a "with-player," someone who plays the game along with you; we might translate it as "teammate," except that Rilke hyphenates the word (it wouldn't ordinarily be hyphenated in German). We could do the same—team-*hyphen*-mate—in order to put greater accent on the word *mate*. This might suggest one's partner in a stronger sense: perhaps one's best friend who just happens to be on the team, or even one's soulmate.

In addition, this is not a *Spieler*, but a *Spielerin*, which is the female form, so this eternal team-and-soul-mate is female—and this in an era in which most readers would have assumed that any truly worthy partner would necessarily be male. Such references were common in German Romanticism, which used them to emphasize the depths of difference.[12] Perhaps in our own era, we might allow this reference to remind us that *any* voice might be that of an eternal partner—whether it be masculine, feminine, or someone who transcends gender binaries.[13] Speaking to us from over a century ago, Rilke might be a vehicle for unsettling our (often heavily gendered) assumptions about the "eternal

12. This trope pre-dates Rilke, of course; consider the *ewige Weibliche* that closes part II of Goethe's *Faust* and the *Tochter aus Elysium* of Schiller's *Ode to Joy*. But gender has been used as a marker of difference for the entire history of letters; I will provide some examples from the biblical text in the last section of this chapter.

13. This third possibility is something that students are often teaching their teachers to consider, against considerable resistance. I would guess that many educators, upon first hearing a young person intentionally refer to a friend as "they," jumped right out of their grammatical skin.

co-player" who has so accurately and skillfully thrown something right to us, to our very center.

In any case, the arc of that throw—the path taken by something sent our way by someone who really knows how to send it—can seem to many people to be divinely ordained, or at least divinely inspired. This, in turn, leads to a consideration of the multi-faith context in which vocational reflection increasingly takes place. This work can and should make room for all students: not only those who would describe all good forms of guidance as coming directly "from the great bridge-building of [a very particularly defined] God," but also those who do not find themselves drawn toward divine sources for guidance. Consideration of vocational questions can provide college students (and their teachers) with excellent opportunities to plumb the depths of one's heart, and mind, and soul, and strength.

Indeed, for many people, these questions carry a degree of ultimacy. They include: How should we understand the relative agencies of the caller and the called? Should we focus our attention on specific calls (to forms of work, domestic life, communities, and civic life), or on the broader call shared by all people (to service, to renunciation, to attentiveness, to death)? Is there a divinity that shapes our ends, or is vocational discernment essentially an activity among human beings? These questions, and many others of great significance, are taken up in many of the chapters in this volume.

Yet I also want to argue that, however we resolve these important questions, we can still identify a central core of meaning in the language of vocation: the notion that our lives are not determined simply by acts of our own will, but that we are always in the business of *receiving*—attending to the motivations and the forms of guidance that come to us as a gift.

Gracious reception

If vocational discernment is made possible by our ability to receive a gift, and given the Christian roots of the language of vocation, it will be worth exploring what the Christian theological tradition has to say about giving and receiving. For some, the emphasis will automatically fall on the identity of the "giver" of the gift: the claim that that call comes from God. Yet in many biblical narratives (and much of Christian history), the call to a particular vocation is often heard through another individual. This often leads to a great deal of wrestling and doubt in the mind of the one who is called—seeking to determine whether the call should be treated as divinely sanctioned, as given from God. In many cases, the hearer is presented with no definitive evidence one way or the other. This forestalls any shortcut through process of vocational discernment; one cannot answer all the relevant questions simply by saying that "God called me and that settles it." Even those who are initially wholly convinced as to the divine origin of their callings often find themselves, somewhere along the way, in doubt about this feeling of assurance.[14]

Hence, rather than focusing on God as the "caller," I want to suggest that Christian theology's most important contribution to the understanding of vocation is closely related to the element that I explored in the first section of this chapter: the notion that the call comes from beyond ourselves, and that we are asked to make a place for it in our lives. We are called to a stance of *gracious reception*, in which we learn that giving and receiving gifts are among the most important, and the most complex, acts that human beings can perform. These complexities face both the givers and the receivers of gifts, and are reinforced by cultural assumptions, religious beliefs, and perhaps the sheer nature of human existence.[15]

The difficulties of giving

Consider, first, the giving of a gift.[16] Even the most selfless givers know that, by giving generously, the recipients of their gift will come to feel a certain kind of obligation; they will want to return the gift. This is one of the things we love about the giving of gifts; it is contagious. But this is also one of its paradoxes, because this imposed sense of obligation ends up making the gift into something more like an *exchange*. We begin to assume that everything has a price, and that everything that is given creates an expectation of return. If we give a present, we may well expect a present of similar significance in return, when the time comes; and even if we don't expect one, we are aware that the recipient is likely to feel a strong sense of obligation to give one. In fact, we sometimes hesitate to give gifts at all—or we limit the significance of the gifts that we give—not so much out of selfishness or a lack of generosity, but because we feel a certain anxiety that others will feel beholden to us.

---

14. For an excellent discussion of the role of doubt and uncertainty in responding to one's calling, see the work of Younus Mirza in chapter 4 of this volume.

15. The material in the following two subsections is revised from chapter 9 of David S. Cunningham, *Christian Ethics: The End of the Law* (London: Routledge, 2007), 199–204.

16. The modern literature here is vast, beginning with Marcel Mauss's 1925 *Essai sur le don* (Paris: Presses Universitaires de France, 2012) and proceeding up into postmodern philosophy and theology. See, inter alia, Jacques Derrida, *The Gift of Death*, trans. David Wills (Chicago: University of Chicago Press, 1996); John Milbank, "Can a Gift Be Given? Prolegomena to a Future Trinitarian Metaphysic," *Modern Theology* 11, no. 1 (January 1995): 119–61; and Sarah Coakley, "'Why Gift? Gift, Gender, and Trinitarian Relations in Milbank and Tanner," *Scottish Journal of Theology* 16 (2008): 224–35.

Common meals can reflect this same paradoxical relationship: we invite others for a meal just for the pleasure of it, but find them asking what they can bring. If we invite someone several times in a row without receiving a reciprocal invitation in return, we assume that something may be wrong with the relationship, or else we receive an embarrassed explanation as to why such an invitation has not been forthcoming. Fortunately, however, the exchange model has not completely infected the enterprise of common meals: within families and among some friends, a particular host can take on the work of offering the gift of a meal together without any expectation of exchange or return. Some may do so out of duty or under compulsion, but for most, the gift of a good meal is a genuine pleasure to give. It is a way that we offer our very selves to one another.

The Christian tradition builds on this idea of the meal as pure gift, through its practice of the Eucharist[17] (also known as Holy Communion, or the Lord's Supper). In this ritual, bread and wine are offered to God and blessed; they are then further understood as a gift given back—by God and through Christ—to those who participate. This food is freely offered, but its significance is greater than its ability to nourish us physically; it finds its source in Jesus's description of his own last meal with his disciples as a gift, not so much of his time and energy in preparing the meal, but as a gift of his own self: his *body*. In the face of his imminent death, Jesus describes the bread and wine that his friends are about to eat as his own body and blood.[18] He is, quite literally, giving up his own body so that his followers may become his body in the world.

In the Eucharist, therefore, Jesus becomes the model of bodily giving; he gives his time, his resources, and indeed his very life for the sake of others. From his actions, Christians are encouraged to learn to take up a similar posture of giving. Needless to say, participation in this ritual cannot always fully counteract the aforementioned cultural obstacles to giving; here, I only want to suggest that Christianity offers some resources for pushing back against the dominant cultural tendencies. More significant, for my argument here, is that the Christian practice of the Eucharist is also meant to be a lesson in how to *receive*.

---

17. The understanding of the Eucharist varies significantly among Christian denominations. The account I give here will probably resonate most with Christians from the Roman Catholic, Eastern Orthodox, Anglican, and (most) Lutheran denominations., Still, other Christian denominations also trace this practice back to Jesus's last meal with his disciples—and understand it as, in some sense, a gift from God to those who participate in the ritual.

18. This is one of the points where emphases among denominations will vary, but most Christians have felt the need to reckon with Jesus's words in the biblical text, including (with respect to the bread at the Last Supper) that "This is my body" (Matt. 26:26; Mark 14:22; Luke 22:19), as well as his claim that "I am the bread of life" (John 6:35).

The difficulties of receiving

If giving is difficult in our culture, receiving may be harder still. The giver of a gift experiences the same burdens concerning exchange and reciprocity, but the receiver of a gift experiences all these difficulties and more. In addition to feeling obligated by a sense of exchange, the receiver is in the socially less acceptable position of being in need, of lacking something that another person must supply. In the contemporary context, in which "fending for oneself" and "pulling oneself up by one's bootstraps" are taken for granted as actions to be approved and emulated, the acceptance of a gift implies an inability or unwillingness to do these things; it is an admission of dependence on others. Children are allowed to assume this perspective, but adults (by and large) are not. Perhaps this is why the sheer pleasure of participating in a meal or attending a party, so evident in the faces of children, can sometimes evaporate among adults: we are all calculating how much this might have cost, and the degree to which we feel obligated to find a way to go about repaying it.

At its best, however, a common meal can provide a space where some of these concerns can, at least temporarily, be set aside—where the focus can be on the grace of receiving another's gift. In my own experience, this can be a difficult lesson to learn: the meal provided to me by a parent or a relative or a friend seems to be something to which I should contribute, actively, in all its stages: purchase of ingredients, preparation of the food, setting the table, cleaning up afterward. But I can sometimes get so caught up in my felt need to "give back" (sometimes even before the gift has been given to me!) that I don't actually allow the giver *to be a giver*. In order to allow space for others to give, we need to be able to receive: graciously, thankfully, and without moving immediately to the exchange-oriented question of how much the gift cost and how to repay it.

While Christians are certainly called to imitate Jesus's act of giving, they are also called—more directly and obviously, in the way that the Eucharist takes place—to be gracious receivers of Jesus's gift to them. Implicit in this idea is the claim that God gives freely, abundantly, and without counting the cost. For those who understand themselves as receiving this gift, the act of reception becomes a way of testifying to their own dependence on God's provision, and a way of expressing their trust that they will continue to be sustained by this divine act of giving.

Giving and receiving in mutual relationship

These two practices—of giving and receiving—are obviously dependent on one another: human beings are able to give only because they have first received gifts from others (including life, nourishment, nurture, and sustenance). At the same time, their continued ability to receive is strengthened by the experience of giving to others: they learn the importance of being able to give a good gift, and to give it freely. They also learn how engaging in this practice, and doing so repeatedly, can help develop the habit of giving—such that they engage in it without entering into a cost-benefit analysis of its features. They may likewise come to understand the importance of gracious reception as something that makes it possible for them to cultivate the practice of giving.

If Christians have learned this lesson well, then it should also pervade their understanding of vocational discernment. The words that we hear from teachers and mentors, the advice that we are offered about our choices, the guidance that we are given about our future direction in life: these are all gifts, given to us without expectation of return. Those who have learned to adopt a stance of *gracious reception* may be better able to receive calls that come from beyond their own immediate perspectives and perceptions—and perhaps to offer such calls as well, if they have the opportunity to serve as mentors and advisers to others.

Vocation amidst difference: the example of Jesus

The previous two sections make two basic claims: first, that vocational discernment focuses primarily on the perspective of those outside ourselves; and second, that Christianity can and should cultivate an attitude of gracious reception, which encourages a willingness to hear and receive what others have to offer us. While these two claims can help to shape Christianity's own development of a theology of vocation, they also have important implications for thinking about vocation in a multi-faith context. In this section, I will explore three elements of this call to a stance of gracious reception: first, an openness to those who engage in unfamiliar practices; second, an attitude of reserve in the face of those who break rules that we may have considered inviolable; and third, a willingness to learn from those outside our own faith traditions. I will illustrate each of these elements with a vignette from the life of Jesus, in which he experiences, and adopts a stance of receptivity toward, three encounters with difference.

Receptivity to unfamiliar practices

Many people find themselves uncomfortable in their first encounters with other lifestances, given that they are likely to encounter unfamiliar practices: rituals, accessories, words, music, and all manner of actions in daily life. All of these may well be different from those to which one has become accustomed. Jesus encounters one such unfamiliar practice—unfamiliar, at least, to some of his followers—shortly before his death:

> Six days before the Passover Jesus came to Bethany, the home of Lazarus, whom he had raised from the dead. There they gave a dinner for him. Martha served, and Lazarus was one of those at the table with him. Mary took a pound of costly perfume made of pure nard, anointed Jesus's feet, and wiped them with her hair. The house was filled with the fragrance of the perfume. But Judas Iscariot, one of his disciples (the one who was about to betray him), said, "Why was this perfume not sold for three hundred denarii and the money given to the poor?" . . . Jesus said, "Leave her alone. She bought it so that she might keep it for the day of my burial." (John 12:1–7)

We know that, in this era, hospitality to guests was a common practice, and this would have included the washing of feet; but the use of costly perfume was apparently an extravagance, or so it seemed to at least one of Jesus's followers. Judas's critique seems to be directed both at Jesus, who accepted this ritual welcome, and at Mary, who performed it. Jesus's rebuke demonstrates his own receptivity to a practice that others might criticize.

Of course, we too rarely encounter such unfamiliar practices, because we too rarely find ourselves in a situation in which we are likely to do so. Among the many opportunities afforded by undergraduate education, it places students in circumstances in which they are likely to encounter genuine difference.[19] In our contemporary multi-faith context, colleges are being called to create more opportunities for this kind of encounter, and to help their students become more open and receptive to unfamiliar practices. This does not mean that all such practices are good, nor that they should be adopted by all. Note that in this story, Jesus does not counsel all the disciples to follow Mary's practice, nor does he even render a judgment as to whether it is a "good" practice. He simply offers an interpretation of what she has done, and does so in such a way that his own followers will accept its significance.

In the undergraduate context, we can draw out a further implication of these reflections: namely, the importance of avoiding barriers to the exchange of good ideas and good works among those whose practices differ markedly from one

19. On the importance of this point, see the comments of Rachel Mikva in chapter 1 of this volume.

another. For those institutions that have developed successful programs of vocational exploration and discernment, this means giving careful consideration to whether these programs are accessible to everyone. Do these programs take place on days and times that collide with the practices of particular faith traditions, thus rendering them inaccessible to those who practice those traditions? Is the language used in connection with these programs—how they are advertised, undertaken, and reviewed, including the illustrations and examples they use—something that can be heard and understood by those whose practices differ markedly from those who developed the language? Do these programs provide space for people from a wide variety of lifestances to bring their own practices with them, such that their traditions, too, can become an integral part of the work of reflection and discernment? These and related questions need careful attention if we hope to develop a stance of receptivity with respect to vocational reflection and discernment in a multi-faith context.

Receptivity to those who break the rules

Every faith tradition and lifestance has certain rules, written and unwritten, that shape those who participate in or follow that tradition. Some of these rules are typically seen as more important than others; but in any case, how we react to those who break the rules—even the rules of our own traditions—will partially determine how we will engage with people from other traditions. This is not to say that the rules should be done away with; indeed, in most faith traditions and lifestances, rules often play an important role in creating community identity and solidarity. But they are also likely to be broken.

In Jesus's own milieu, the prohibition against adultery was certainly among the most definitive and clear-cut rules. So the men who brought a woman before Jesus probably felt fairly confident about the outcome when

> they said to him, "Teacher, this woman was caught in the very act of committing adultery. Now in the law Moses commanded us to stone such women. Now what do you say?" They said this to test him, so that they might have some charge to bring against him. Jesus bent down and wrote with his finger on the ground. When they kept on questioning him, he straightened up and said to them, "Let anyone among you who is without sin be the first to throw a stone at her." And once again he bent down and wrote on the ground. When they heard it, they went away, one by one, beginning with the elders; and Jesus was left alone with the woman standing before him. Jesus straightened up and said to her, "Woman, where are they? Has no one condemned you?" She said, "No one, sir." And Jesus

> said, "Neither do I condemn you. Go your way, and from now on do not sin again." (John 8:3–11)

Most of the commentary on this passage stresses the unstrained quality of mercy that Jesus demonstrates in refusing to condemn the woman (though this is usually followed by an explanation of why this action does not thereby countenance adultery). Admittedly, Jesus's attitude toward the law is an important element of the story, very much in keeping with his views as recorded elsewhere in the New Testament.[20] But I am even more interested in the way that this passage demonstrates the speed at which Jesus responds—or, better, the *slowness* with which he responds.

Whenever we are met with someone who has broken the rules, our tendency is to pass judgment quickly. If we agree with the rule, we are likely to condemn; if we think the rule is nonsense, we are likely to acquit (or even to celebrate). When we react in this way, the rule (and the violation of it) become primarily about *us*—as those who are rendering judgment—rather than about the person who has broken the rule, or about the views of those who are outraged by (or sympathetic to) this action. Jesus, faced with something that might seem like a dilemma (the demands of the law versus the positive assessment of mercy, both important elements of his own Jewish tradition), does not act quickly. He pauses, delays his response, writes on the ground. We are not told what he wrote, and it does not seem to matter; what does matter is that, twice in the story, he takes some time before responding.

This pause, I want to suggest, has implications for vocational discernment. Throughout our lives, we will encounter people who break the rules, who engage the world in unfamiliar ways, who do things differently than we would do them. When faced with such circumstances, will we react automatically in whatever way we have been trained? Will we decide that the "other" is evil, or a sinner, or just plain wrong? Or will we take time to think about *why* we are inclined to react as we do, to look inward, to think about the various influences that have made a particular conclusion seem so obvious or automatic? When we encounter difference, and especially a different perspective on "the rules," it can be all too easy to forget the great variety of our own commitments and allegiances that might

20. Briefly stated, Jesus does not condemn the law or seek to set it aside, but rather emphasizes that it applies to thoughts as well as to actions, which means that most people are in violation of it most of the time. See his comments on murder, adultery, divorce, responding to evil, and swearing oaths (Matt. 5:21–48). Paul claims that "Christ is the end of the law" (Romans 10:4), using the Greek word *telos*, which means "end" in two senses: not only an endpoint, but also a purpose or goal.

conceivably pull us in different directions. We need to take a moment, at least, to think about how these commitments have made us who we are. In short, we need to think about the shape of the life to which we are called.

I cannot say whether Jesus went through a moment of "vocational discernment" as he wrote on the ground, but he certainly responded in a way that neither dismissed the importance of the law nor failed to show mercy. He recognized the range of allegiances in his own life and in the lives of his questioners, and perhaps in the life of the accused woman as well, and he responded in a way that did justice to them all. We may not be endowed with Jesus's range of knowledge and observational acumen, but we can still take a few moments for discernment. In his short book on the 9/11 attacks, Rowan Williams concludes his own reflections with this story, suggesting that, in such cases, we should all be willing to do some "writing in the dust." When we do so, we provide ourselves with a bit of time—"long enough," he says, "for some of our own demons to walk away."[21]

Our multi-faith encounters often present us with people who don't follow the rules as we have learned them—or who follow other rules that are foreign to us. While we may eventually feel the need to make judgments about these differences, our first reaction should be to pause, and do some of our own "writing in the dust." There may well be good reasons for the rules, as there may be for some of those of our own traditions; and there may be good reasons to ignore them, critique them, or break them. And this goes not just for the rules and laws of a particular religious tradition, but also for those of nation-states and other authorities that may seem—at least to people who adhere to some lifestances—to be either in keeping with, or directly opposed to, the rules of their own perspective. (Rules and laws about gender and sexuality come immediately to mind, in our present context; they are heavily contested and aligned, in complicated ways, among various national governments, faith traditions, and philosophical perspectives.)

Again, the undergraduate milieu provides a very useful space in which to cultivate the practice of pausing before passing judgment, such that it becomes a habit that marks our encounters with one another. As has been noted, the college years provide a substantial period of time, and a "free and ordered space," within which new perspectives can be encountered, considered, and evaluated.[22] The time and space of undergraduate education allows us to remove, at least temporarily, the pressures that create the "rush to judgment" that besets our culture

21. Rowan Williams, *Writing in the Dust* (Grand Rapids, MI: Eerdmans, 2002), 85.

22. This notion is referenced specifically in Cunningham, "Time and Place," 5, and alluded to throughout that volume (Cunningham, ed., *At This Time*).

generally, particularly when encountering those whose thoughts and beliefs are significantly different from our own. When students develop the habit of pausing before coming to a conclusion about such encounters, they may begin to cultivate a certain kind of "vocational reserve,"[23] in which they can take a moment to consider their own purpose and identity—the full range of their beliefs and commitments—before all their assumptions become set in concrete. Indeed, every such encounter with difference provides us with an astounding opportunity to consider the various strands of our vocations, and to come to a more nuanced understanding of who we are.

Receptivity to advice from outside one's tradition

Of all the stories about the life of Jesus that are recorded in the New Testament, one speaks with particular directness to interfaith encounter, because Jesus seems to allow his perspective to be changed by someone of another faith. The first several chapters of the Gospel of Mark describe Jesus as understanding his mission as directed toward his fellow Jews; his preaching and teaching is described as something of a reform movement within Judaism. But after his visit to the region of Tyre and his encounter with a non-Jew who sees things differently, his mission becomes broader: it is aimed at Gentiles as well as Jews.

> From there he set out and went away to the region of Tyre. He entered a house and did not want anyone to know he was there. Yet he could not escape notice, but a woman whose little daughter had an unclean spirit immediately heard about him, and she came and bowed down at his feet. Now the woman was a Gentile, of Syrophoenician origin. She begged him to cast the demon out of her daughter. He said to her, "Let the children be fed first, for it is not fair to take the children's food and throw it to the dogs." But she answered him, "Sir, even the dogs under the table eat the children's crumbs." Then he said to her, "For saying that, you may go—the demon has left your daughter." So she went home, found the child lying on the bed, and the demon gone. Then he returned from the region of Tyre, and went by way of Sidon towards the Sea of Galilee, in the region of the Decapolis. (Mark 7:24–31)

---

23. For a description of this concept, see David S. Cunningham, "'Who's There?': The Dramatic Role of the 'Caller' in Vocational Discernment," in Cunningham, ed., *At This Time*, 148–64; here, 162–64.

The reference to "the children" points to the Jews (as the "children of Israel"), and the woman's embrace of the word *dogs* functions a reference to negative attitudes toward those who live their lives at the margins of social acceptance. The woman argues that the outsiders should be allowed to gather up the scraps that are tossed aside by the insiders; in doing so, she apparently changes the direction of Jesus's mission. Not only does he heal her daughter (which he had seemed at first unwilling to do); in addition, at this point in Mark's narrative, his mission is increasingly directed to a wider audience, starting with his travels into the Gentile region of the Decapolis.[24]

For our present context, we should begin by noting that Jesus is willing to enter into the house of a person of another faith (she is a Gentile; he is a Jew). In antiquity, this kind of encounter was perhaps more common; today, at least in many contexts, it is much less so, given that we tend to live and work and socialize with people very much like ourselves. This reminds us of the importance of breaking down the residential, social, and cultural barriers that separate us from one another—and of the ways in which the undergraduate context can serve as an important laboratory for doing so. Here, students often live in much closer proximity to people who are not like themselves, compared to what will likely be the case for much of their future lives. They therefore have extraordinary opportunities to encounter difference and to allow it to shape and change their own perspectives. Such encounters can create anxiety for parents, friends, and the students themselves, who often fear that they will be changed by such encounters. They will be changed, of course, but not necessarily in the sense that is often most feared; they are not likely to become exactly like the other person. But these encounters may well reshape the students' understanding of *their own* lifestance, just as it did for Jesus. He did not become a Gentile and take up residence in Tyre; however, he did seem to recognize that he was called to include such persons, and others like them. Many undergraduate students likewise discover that their own vocations are shaped, broadened, and sharpened by their encounter with people from different traditions.

24. This shift in mission is also marked by the two feeding stories that bracket this vignette. Many commentators have noted that not only the geography of those stories, but also their numerology, demonstrate a shift from a Jewish context to a Gentile one. That Jesus himself considers the numbers significant is demonstrated immediately after the second feeding story, in which he reiterates them to his disciples and asks, in apparent exasperation, "Do you still not understand?" (Mark 8:21). Neither, it seems, do many of us who read this text! See, for example, Dennis E. Nineham, *The Gospel of St. Mark* (London: Penguin, 1963).

Failing in, but still called to, gracious reception

I want to be the first to acknowledge that actual Christian practice has rarely lived up to the high calling of encountering difference in a mode of gracious reception. Throughout much of its history, Christianity's response has instead been dismissive, reactive, argumentative, or condemnatory. Often, it allied itself with the empire or the state in order to be much worse: destructive, annihilating, even genocidal. In their encounters with difference, Christians have a great deal of very troubling history on their consciences.

But as I have tried to demonstrate here, the Christian faith also has the resources to develop a very different perspective: Christians are called to a stance of gracious reception. This might be embodied in their general attitude toward the rest of the world (as embodied in Rilke's metaphor of catching a ball thrown by an eternal partner), in their understanding of giving and receiving (as instantiated in the practice of the Eucharist), or in their interpretations of Jesus's own encounters with difference. But in all these cases, the overall message remains the same: difference should be encountered in a mode of receptivity and with the assumption that the presence of others is first of all a gift, not a threat.

Indeed, Christianity's stories of its own origins demonstrate the importance of this claim, both negatively and positively, near the beginnings of each of the Gospels. In the narrative account of the birth of Jesus, his nativity is received with grace and gratitude, both by common folk (the shepherds, in Luke) and by the elite (the wise men, in Matthew). The Gospel of John reminds us that, on the other hand, even some of those who were close to him did not appreciate his presence. And Mark's account tells us that, in spite of the fact that many were indifferent or negatively disposed to Jesus, there was at least one person who lived during his time, "a voice crying in the wilderness," who was willing to receive the difference that Jesus embodied. May those of us who live in the present era, and who claim to be his followers, learn to do the same.

Response

Matthew R. Sayers

David makes an audacious choice in discussing the story of the Syrophoenician woman (Mark 7:24–31): it is explicitly Christian, its interpretations vary (is it a test, or does Jesus change his mind?), it raises questions of racism and gender (Jesus likens an ethnically different woman to a dog), and it takes place within a complex society. In focusing on this story, David addresses a number of concerns that I had when I was first invited into an interfaith conversation about vocation.

I harbored concerns about students seeking their *true* vocation and the anxiety-producing uncertainty of searching. Similarly, interfaith interaction often runs ashore on questions of truth or blithely ignores conflicts around truth claims. Truth, for religion at least, is that which accords with reality; unfortunately, people disagree on reality. In discerning among differing calls to vocation or differing religious claims to truth, we often vainly seek certainty.

The alternative to certainty, I suggest, is authenticity—when what one does accords with who one claims to be. Whereas truth remains uncertain, we can often tell if someone is being authentic by comparing their deeds to their words. We cannot know with any certainty that we are living our true vocation; nevertheless, if we are honest, we can know whether we are living out our vocations authentically—and so can others. Religions share no single truth to serve as the genesis of interfaith cooperation; in its absence, we are left with the fact of religious plurality, of encounter itself. But a call to authenticity can make both vocational discernment and interfaith encounter truthful and productive. David's audacious choice demonstrates this.

By foregrounding an unambiguously Christian story, he models authentic religious expression. In choosing to offer a complex and ambiguous story, he challenges us to reject simplistic understandings and facile solutions for vocational discernment and interfaith encounters. Indeed, he owns up to the fact that, in this realm, Christians have some "very troubling history on their consciences." In the end, the story David cites is not so much about the woman as it is about Jesus's overcoming the "human, all-too-human" reaction to difference. Although it first appears as though Jesus will take a different path, he eventually models humility in the face of difference—not changing who he is, but graciously receiving the woman and honoring her request. He calls Christians to live with authenticity and to receive others with humility. To a cynical non-Christian living in a Christian society, this call is heartening and personally instructive.

6

Renunciation of *Vocation and Renunciation* within *Vocation*

CONTRIBUTIONS FROM THE *BHAGAVADGITA*

Anantanand Rambachan

WHEN FACED WITH a deep and often unprecedented life crisis, we may be tempted to turn away, to withdraw, and to renounce responsibilities. A difficult situation overwhelms us—psychologically, emotionally, and even physically. Instead of engaging the problems that we are facing, we walk away or retreat into silence. A life crisis, however, may also be a profound opportunity for examining our assumptions and reconsidering the categories of thought that we have uncritically inherited. It can be the occasion for new discoveries about vocation and about the meaning of our work in the world.

In this chapter, we will meet Arjuna, the young warrior and protagonist of the Bhagavadgita. Faced with the moral crisis of having to stand against relatives, friends, and teachers who are supporting an unjust cause, Arjuna is ready to walk away from life's battlefield and to disengage from the world. Fortunately for Arjuna, his wise friend and teacher, Krishna, serving as his charioteer, invites him into dialogue about the choices before him—helping him to think in radically new ways about work, renunciation, and the good life. Arjuna discovers that his choices are not just the dualistic ones of renunciation or engagement in the world, but that there is a third way of enriching work by infusing it with the *spirit* of renunciation. To discover this third way, Arjuna has to be open to new ways of thinking. By focusing in a special way on this ancient dialogue, we are invited to think anew about the meaning and practice of our vocations.

Why renounce one's vocation?

To consider how renunciation might be a useful resource for thinking about vocation, we first need to understand its role as a particular stage in the context of Hindu life. In this section, I will describe the four goals of life and the four stages that are understood as a means of pursuing these goals, discussing the final stage—that of "renunciation"—in greater detail. I will then introduce a key passage from the *Bhagavadgita* that offers a possible reinterpretation of renunciation—one that may be useful for us in thinking about vocation.

Hindu life: four goals, four stages

The Hindu tradition has identified four goals that constitute a full human life.[1] These are *artha* (wealth, power, success, social prestige), *kama* (pleasure), *dharma* (duty, virtue) and *moksha* (liberation). As should be clear from the first two goals, the Hindu tradition is neither antimaterialistic nor otherworldly; it recognizes the importance of access to material necessities that enable one to live with dignity and to fulfill family and social obligations. The legitimatizing of pleasure (*kama*) reminds us, further, that the tradition is not life-negating.

Nevertheless, wealth and pleasure are to be sought in a manner that attends to the demands of *dharma*. This third goal emphasizes the social and relational context in which we live our lives, as well as the need to regulate our pursuit of wealth and pleasure in the interests of the well-being of others. Wealth and pleasure that are attained by inflicting pain and suffering on others, or by denying them the freedom to pursue these same ends, would be opposed to *dharma*. And yet, while the Hindu tradition ascribes great value to the practice of *dharma*, this is not the ultimate goal of human existence. Hinduism's highest and most valued goal is *moksha*. *Moksha* means freedom, and, if we keep in mind the diversity of Hinduism, it is not inaccurate to say that this freedom is primarily freedom from ignorance (*avidya*). It is a common view in the Hindu tradition that ignorance about the true nature of the human self (*atman*) and its relationship with the infinite absolute (*brahman*) is the fundamental human problem and the underlying cause of suffering. Freedom or liberation cannot be obtained without right knowledge of reality—and a reorientation of life based on a radically different understanding of self.

1. For a brief discussion see Huston Smith, *The World's Religions* (New York: Harper Collins, 1991), 13–19.

For the progressive attainment of these four goals, Hinduism recommends that the human life be organized into four stages. Each stage is referred to, in Sanskrit, as an *ashrama*; each of these has its own objectives (as well as duties and responsibilities). The first is the student stage, devoted to study and acquiring skills and dispositions necessary for carrying out one's vocation. The second stage is that of the householder, where the focus is on the goals of wealth, pleasure (through marriage and family satisfaction), and duty (*dharma*) through community involvement. The third is the stage of the forest dweller, conceived as a semi-retired stage devoted to contemplation, religious inquiry, and social service. Finally, the fourth stage—renunciation (*samnyasa*)—is devoted strictly to the pursuit of liberation (*moksha).*

In general, males belonging to the upper castes who entered the fourth stage did so after completing the first three stages; the traditional path is one of study, marriage, retirement, and, finally, renunciation. However, for a person who experiences intensely the *limits* of wealth and pleasure (and who wishes to pursue liberation), the stage of renunciation can be entered at any time. As the Jabala Upanishad puts it, "One may renounce directly from Vedic studentship, or from home or from the forest. Let him renounce on the very day that he becomes detached, regardless of whether he has taken the vow or not, whether he has graduated or not, and whether he has kindled the sacred fire or is without a fire."[2] (The sacred fire, mentioned here, is kept in the home of the householder for the purpose of making religious offerings.) Given the four goals of Hindu life and the progressive ordering of life in four stages for their attainment, what consequences for vocation are implied by the path of renunciation?

Renunciation *of* vocation

In the Vedic tradition, ritual worship is obligatory until death.[3] Many of these rituals are to be performed daily (e.g., worship at dawn and dusk) or on special occasions (e.g., rituals performed on the occasions of birth, death, or annually for the benefit of departed ancestors). The only exception is the renouncer, who

2. Cited in Patrick Olivelle, *Saṃnyasa Upanishads: Hindu Scriptures on Asceticism and Renunciation* (New York: Oxford University Press, 2006), 75. This is an excellent study of the tradition of renunciation in Hinduism; I rely on it for my description of this stage.

3. By the Vedic tradition, I mean the practices and beliefs derived from and connected with the four Vedas (*Rg, Sama, Yajur,* and *Atharva*). The earliest of these, the *Rg* Veda, is dated ca. 1500–1200 BCE. The four Vedas are widely acknowledged by Hindus to be revealed sources; acceptance of the authority of the Vedas is commonly regarded as necessary for Hindu orthodoxy, even though such acceptance may be merely formal and nominal.

enters a state of existence comparable to one who has died. The identity of the renouncer is no longer connected with family or community; this is signified by the assumption of a new name. One of the consequences of renunciation is social death; at this point, one's responsibility for the fulfillment of mutual obligations with family and community comes to an end. The renouncer is exempt from having to perform traditional rituals—especially those centered on daily offerings into the fire (*agnihotra*). Entering into the fourth stage of life also frees the renouncer from having to fulfill obligations that are associated with what we regard as responsibilities of vocation.[4] The absence of work obligations eliminates all moral dilemmas connected with choosing and performing one's work. *Samnyasa*, the fourth stage, may be properly described as the renunciation *of* vocation for the sake of pursuing only the goal of liberation (*moksha*).

Freedom from ritual and professional obligations becomes possible because the consequences that ensue from renunciation are similar to those that follow the death of an individual. As Olivelle notes, renunciation results in the dissolution of marriage, freedom from contractual debts, and the distribution of property among heirs.[5] There is a close resemblance between the rituals of death and those that are performed to enter the fourth stage. For example, those who renounce include themselves in the traditional oblation made to departed ancestors. In addition, their ritual implements are disposed of in a manner similar to those of a dead person at the time of cremation. The status of the renouncer is an ambiguous one, occupying, as Olivelle describes it, a "liminal" status between life and death.

This understanding of the nature and significance of renunciation sets the context for an important dialogue in the *Bhagavadgita*. Most important, for our purposes here, is the assumption that renunciation is the only way to liberation (*moksha*) and the fullest living out of the religious life. This seems to diminish the significance of all that is done in those stages of life (student, householder, and forest dweller) that typically precede the fourth stage. These stages become merely preparatory; indeed, according to this approach, one's whole life is merely preparation for renunciation. The difficulties of this position will become clearer as we turn to a specific passage in the text of the *Bhagavadgita*, in which Arjuna considers the possibility of renunciation.

---

4. Although the term *vocation* is not limited in meaning to work that is performed for monetary reward, in this chapter I am focusing particularly on the duties that we usually associate with professional obligations. The term used in the *Bhagavadgita* is *svadharma*.

5. Olivelle, *Saṃnyasa Upanishads*, 90.

Arjuna's predicament

The *Bhagavadgita* recounts the struggle between two sets of cousins, the Pandavas and Kauravas, for a kingdom in North India. The Kaurava leader, Duryodhana, is power hungry and unwilling to do justice to his cousins. All efforts to make peace prove futile and war is inevitable. On the day of the battle, the Pandava leader, Arjuna, instructs Krishna, who has volunteered to be his charioteer, to drive his chariot between the two armies so that he can survey the opposing forces.

Arjuna is overwhelmed by what he sees. Friends, relatives, and teachers stand ready to do battle against him, in support of Duryodhana and the Kauravas. The prospect of having to fight against friends and family throws him into a moral crisis and drains him mentally and physically.

> My limbs sink down, my mouth dries up, my body trembles, and my hair stands on end.
>
> Gandiva [the bow] falls from my hand, my skin burns, I am unable to stand and my mind is whirling. (1:29–30)[6]

Arjuna knows well that the only option that will free him from his obligations as a warrior is entry into the fourth stage of Hindu life, the life of the renunciant. Faced with the dilemma of having to engage relatives in battle, he expresses a preference for renunciation and entry into the life of the monk. His reference to living on alms is to the way of the renouncer:

> Indeed, instead of slaying these noble gurus it would be preferable to live on alms here on earth; having slain the gurus, with desire for worldly gain, I would enjoy here on earth delights smeared with blood. (2:5)

Arjuna also knows that the only justification for entry into the fourth stage is the pursuit of liberation (*moksha*), the highest goal of the Hindu tradition. His understanding is that renunciation alone frees him from his obligations as a warrior and is the only direct path to liberation. What are Arjuna's assumptions in framing his choices in this manner? What is his understanding of renunciation and its relationship to his vocation in the world? Is there any way of attaining liberation without forsaking all participation in action?

---

6. Shri *Bhagavadgita*, trans. Winthrop Sargeant (Albany: State University of New York Press, 1993). The text is dated around 150 BCE–250 CE. Translation modified.

As a first gesture toward a possible answer to this last question, let us consider the argument of Shankara, perhaps the most influential monastic commentator on the *Bhagavadgita*.[7] For Shankara, action in the world is justified on the part of the person seeking liberation only because he is not qualified yet for renunciation. Commenting on 3:3–4, Shankara writes that "Devotion to action is a means to the end, not directly, but only as leading to devotion to knowledge; whereas the latter, which is attainable by means of devotion to action, leads to the goal directly, without extraneous help."[8] Performed with the right attitude, without attachment to the results, everything that one does in the world helps to purify and prepare one for renunciation and for the attainment of liberation.

In this context, the *Bhagavadgita* offers us a different way of thinking about the meaning of renunciation, as well as a description of an authentic religious life that is based on this different viewpoint. Here, I will characterize this different view as *renunciation within vocation*. The *Bhagavadgita* does not *denounce* renunciation; rather, it *redefines* its meaning in a manner that affirms the value of vocation. In the absence of the interpretation offered in the *Bhagavadgita* it is difficult to articulate a Hindu theology of vocation, and especially one that makes possible the attainment of liberation while fulfilling professional, family, and community obligations and responsibilities. I now turn to the *Bhagavadgita*'s characterization of the relationship of renunciation and action; this will, in turn, have significant implications for our understanding of vocation.[9]

Renunciation and the critique of action

The path of renunciation raises questions about the value of action, since it associates action with desire and ignorance (*avidya*). Action is understood in negative terms because it generates results (*karma*); this in turn necessitates rebirth in order for one to experience the results of one's actions. Actions contribute, therefore, to the perpetuation of the cycle of birth, death, and rebirth, rather than to genuine liberation. (Most Hindu traditions equate liberation with freedom from this cycle.[10]) Renunciation, on the other hand, aims for minimization of action for the purpose of limiting these negative consequences.

7. Shankara was active in the eighth century CE. He held that renunciation is necessary for true knowledge.

8. Alladi Mahadeva Sastry, trans., *The Bhagavadgita with the Commentary of Sri Sankaracharya* (Madras: Samata Books, 1979), 93.

9. For another approach to these issues that draws on the rich resources of the *Bhagavadgita* in a different way, see the work of Matthew R. Sayers in chapter 8 of this volume.

10. For a different understanding of liberation, see Anantanand Rambachan, *A Hindu Theology of Liberation: Not-Two is Not One* (Albany: State University of New York Press, 2015), chapter 4.

Knowledge and action together

In the second chapter of the *Bhagavadgita*, Krishna speaks extensively about knowledge of the true self (*atman*) and the necessity of right understanding of self for liberation. He speaks of the self as free from birth and death, eternally existing, and all pervasive. It is not to be limited by the physical body.

> As, after casting away worn out garments, a person later takes new ones, so, after casting away worn out bodies, the embodied Self encounters other, new ones. (2:22)
>
> Weapons do not pierce this, fire does not burn this, water does not wet this, nor does the wind cause it to wither. (2:23)[11]

While instructing Arjuna about the nature of the self, Krishna continues to urge him to fight the battle and fulfill his responsibilities as a warrior.

> Now, if you will not undertake this righteous war, thereupon, having avoided your own duty, you shall incur evil. (2:33)
>
> Holding pleasure and pain to be alike, likewise gain and loss, victory and defeat, then engage in battle. Thus you shall not incur evil. (2:38)

Krishna's emphasis on both knowledge and action confuses Arjuna—and this for a very important reason. Knowledge of the self is associated with renunciation and is sought by the renouncer. Arjuna is rightly puzzled; how could his teacher commend both liberating wisdom (which Arjuna understands to require renunciation) and action in the world (which Arjuna understands to be anathema to renunciation)? In Arjuna's understanding, these two are not compatible. If he became a renouncer, he would give up his vocation as a warrior; he would be justified in walking away from the battlefield.

At the beginning of the third chapter of the *Bhagavadgita*, Arjuna expresses his confusion in a question to Krishna (3:1–2):

> If it is your conviction that knowledge is better than action, Krishna, then why do you urge me to engage in this terrible action? (3:1)
>
> With speech that seems equivocal, you confuse my intelligence. Tell me surely this one thing: how should I attain the highest good? (3:2)

---

11. Translation modified.

Why is Krishna, wonders Arjuna, not giving his approval to the desire for renunciation?

Krishna's response to Arjuna's question offers us a different interpretation of the meaning and value of a life of action in the world; it opens the possibility of attaining life's highest goal without traditional renunciation.

Questioning the necessity of renunciation

Krishna begins by querying any natural connection between renunciation and the attainment of life's highest goal (2:4). Liberation, he teaches, is not the outcome of mere renunciation. It is wrong, Krishna says, for Arjuna to think that renunciation secures liberation simply because it frees him from performing action in the world. Action here includes both traditional ritualistic worship and the fulfillment of professional and other roles and responsibilities. Krishna immediately reminds Arjuna that no one can be free from performing actions; without actions, life becomes impossible:

> Indeed, no one, even in the twinkling of an eye, ever exists without performing action; everyone is forced to perform action by the qualities of nature. (3.5)[12]

Those who renounce do not enter into a literal state of freedom from action that might distinguish them from, or grant them superiority over, those who are engaged in the world. Everyone, renouncer and nonrenouncer, is engaged in action of one kind or another. The maintenance of life in the body is impossible without action (3:8). There are also many, says Krishna (3:6), who take vows of renunciation and who spend a great deal of time brooding and longing for what they have left behind. Such persons are deluded and hypocritical. Superior are those who, with self-control and detachment, engage in action and continue to fulfill their vocations and their other responsibilities in the world. What we see here in Krishna's initial argument is an incisive reframing of the issue: there is no simple distinction between those who perform actions (by choosing not to renounce) and those who try to escape from all action (by renouncing). Since action is common to both, Krishna moves on to emphasize the significance of motivation and aim—the key in distinguishing desirable and undesirable actions. We turn now to this distinction.

12. Translation modified.

Giving and receiving: action as *yajna*

To understand the nature of Krishna's argument, we need to keep in mind why renunciation is commonly pitted against action. Action is typically seen as the less desirable path, because it (1) originates from self-centered desires; (2) creates results; and (3) perpetuates the cycle of birth, death, and rebirth. But Krishna commends a way of acting in the world that is *not motivated by greed*—and is therefore compatible with, and indeed conducive to, liberation. In 3:7, he describes as superior the person "who undertakes the control of the senses by the mind," and who, "without attachment, engages the organs of action in the yoga of action."[13]

Krishna agrees that actions perpetuate ignorance and ensnare us when these are motivated by greed. One should not assume, however, that greed is the only reason for acting. In contrast to greed, Krishna commends actions that are performed for the sake of *yajna*—an ancient mode of worship in the Vedas, which is used here by Krishna as a metaphor for right action in the world. In this worship ceremony, a special altar is constructed, and upon this altar, a fire is lit. The fire symbolizes the divine reality; the worshippers, sitting at the fire, make offerings while reciting Veda verses (*mantras*). At the end of the ritual, food—some of which was offered into the fire—is distributed among the participants. Thus, although food is received, this occurs only after it is worshipfully offered to the various cosmic beings (*devas*) that sustain life. This implies that food may rightly be enjoyed, but only after it is shared. Later patterns of Hindu worship—*puja* in the home and temple, for example—reflect a similar practice of giving and receiving. When Hindus visit temples, they often bring items of food that are first offered to God before being shared with others as God's gift (*prasadam*).[14]

Thus, in the *Bhagavadgita*, Krishna commends this approach:

> Aside from action for the purpose of *yajna*, this world is bound by action. Perform action for the purpose of *yajna*, Arjuna, free from attachment. (3.9)

He commends those who eat what is left after the practice of *yajna*, while condemning those who eat only for themselves:

> The virtuous who eat what is left after *yajna* are free from impurities; but the unrighteous, who cook only for their own sake, eat their own impurity. (3:13)

13. In commending the yoga of action, Krishna is not speaking of postural yoga or the physical exercises that we associate with the term. Here, yoga is a more comprehensive way of performing action in the world; it refers to the performance of all action as religious discipline.

14. On the complexities of giving and receiving, see the discussion by David Cunningham in chapter 5 of this volume.

Indeed, ritual worship is offered by Krishna as a model for all actions. As we make offerings into the sacred fire or take offerings to the temple, we offer our work as worship, for the well-being of others—receiving in turn that which we need for our own sustenance. The thief, says Krishna (3:12), is the person who enjoys the gifts of the world and does not offer anything in return.

The *yajna* mode of acting in the world is deeply informed by an appreciation of the interdependent nature of existence. The universe functions best only when we are both givers and receivers—and when we contribute to the sustenance of the whole. The interdependent universe is likened to a wheel with spokes that has been set in motion; it is both dynamic and interrelated. We live in delusion and vanity if our lives are not attuned with the universe and if we fail to move in its direction (3:16). A self-centered life is one that vainly sets itself against the revolving ethical wheel of the universe.

The *yajna* mode of being is what Krishna commends for human prosperity. It is the way ordained by God for human flourishing. "By this may you prosper; may this be your wish-fulfilling cow" (3:10). The mythological cow referred to in this verse is believed to fulfill the wishes of the person who owns it. The *Bhagavadgita* uses the *yajna* metaphor to teach that our flourishing is inseparable from the flourishing of all. This implies that our vocations, and the way we carry them out in the world, ought to be informed by an understanding of our interdependence with others. Vocations have cosmic significance and must reflect gratitude for the gifts that we receive from others, as well as generous self-giving that enables others to prosper and flourish. To truly flourish, we cannot be concerned only with our own flourishing.

This interdependence is well illustrated by a popular story that is told about the occasion when the Creator of the universe invited the divine beings (*devas*) and the demonic beings (*asuras*) to a grand banquet. The *devas* sat in parallel rows facing each other and so did the *asuras*. Tasty dishes of every imaginable variety were served before them and everyone was anxious to begin the feast. The Creator, however, stood up and explained the procedure: no elbows may be bent! The *asuras* were enraged and started hurling abuses at the Creator for making eating an impossible task. They stormed out of the banquet hall. The *devas* consulted quietly and found a way to enjoy the dinner: seated facing each other, they stretched out their hands and fed one another.

Work that expresses a concern for the well-being of all, as well as one's own well-being, is what Krishna calls nonattached action (*asaktah karma*) or *karmayoga* (action as religious discipline). Unlike attached action (*saktah karma*), which is promoted solely by self-concern and greed, nonattached action springs from a wish for the flourishing of the interrelated whole. The renunciation of attachment is not the same as indifference or lack of care for others; on the contrary, it requires enlarging of the field of one's concern to include all beings. Krishna equates the renunciation of attachment with having a regard for all life. Thus, nonattachment is, somewhat ironically, not a negative attitude at all; it is an expansive love for all of creation. It is the understanding that enables one to be free from the narrow concerns of one's self and to act for the good of others. Arjuna thought that he needed to renounce his vocation as a warrior for the sake of the religious life; Krishna asked him not to renounce his vocation, but to undertake a different form of renunciation *within* his vocation. He was asked to renounce his self-centeredness and expand his understanding of self to embrace all.

To convince Arjuna that there is no need to give up his vocational obligations, Krishna reminded him of renowned and wise political leaders, like the legendary King Janaka (3:20), who never renounced the duties of their profession and still attained life's highest end. Krishna describes him as acting from a concern for the well-being of all—and urges Arjuna to do the same. Krishna even uses himself as an example of one who is motivated by a concern for world well-being and makes explicit the connection between nonattachment and a commitment to the universal common good (*lokasamgraha*): "As the unwise act from attachment to action, so should the wise act without attachment, desiring the well-being of all" (3:25).[15] Ignorance is equated with acting from attachment (*saktah*), whereas wisdom means acting with nonattachment (*asaktah*). Nonattachment is a positive regard for the flourishing of all.

It is important to emphasize that nonattached action, in the teaching of the *Bhagavadgita*, does not mean the absence of consideration for one's own good. Admittedly, the search for harmony between self-interest and the common good is not always a matter of easy discernment! Still, a healthy regard for one's own well-being is certainly not excluded by the two characteristics of nonattached action: concern for the flourishing of all and the understanding of interdependence. In fact, the metaphor used by Krishna, discussed earlier ("the unrighteous who cook only for their own sake, eat their own impurity," 3:13), speaks directly to this issue. Food is shared as God's gift by first offering it to God. The text does not condemn the person who cooks and eats, but rather, those who cook only for themselves. If we understand cooking as a self-interested act, it is given spiritual significance when food is shared with others. One cooks for oneself *and* for others, honoring the obligation to consider the common good. This metaphor (of cooking for oneself and for others) gains further meaning from the fact that the traditional renouncer did no cooking. Having given up fire, one is unable to cook and is thus required to beg from others for

15. Translation modified.

food.[16] Sharing food in the Hindu tradition is one of the important ways of expressing hospitality to others.

While the term *kama* (desire/greed) is generally used in a negative sense in the *Bhagavadgita*, the text does not condemn forms of desire that are consistent with one's own good and the common good. Indeed, in an important text, Krishna identifies himself with desires that are not opposed to one's well-being and the common good: "I am desire in beings that is not opposed to virtue" (7:11). Krishna's redefining of renunciation enables him to offer a different description of the renunciant.

Redefining the renunciant

The *Bhagavadgita*'s description of renunciation—equating it with nonattached action—has important implications for our understanding of vocation and a spirituality of action in the world. Thus far, I have identified two important dimensions of this approach. First, nonattachment is a way of acting that is profoundly cognizant of the interdependence of existence and of the need to act generously. It is a mode of acting in which one is both a receiver and giver. Second, nonattached action involves consideration of the universal common good (*lokasamgraha*) in all that we do.

Lokasamgraha, which I translate here as "universal common good," is a far-reaching category. It includes not only all human beings but also the world of nature. Those who are concerned about the universal common good value and respect all beings. They are devoted to the flourishing of all. They do not privilege unjustly the interests of a particular race, religion, nation, or gender; they strive earnestly to be attentive to the well-being of the fabric of existence. Contemplating the implications of their work for the flourishing of all being is a normative and guiding concern.

By reinterpreting renunciation as nonattached action that is devoted to the common good, the text suggests an alternative understanding of those who renounce. As noted previously, entry into the fourth stage entails the renunciation of the performance of traditional rituals—especially those that involve the making of offerings into the fire. The renouncer is a person without a ritual fire—literally so, in Olivelle's terminology: "a fireless man."

In this light, it is significant that Krishna, in *Bhagavadgita* 5:1, describes the "eternal renouncer (*nityasamnyasi*)" as the one who is free, not from fire, but from hate and greed. Indeed, throughout the text, greed and anger are paired

16. Olivelle, *Samnyasa Upanishads*, 103–4.

and problematized; the writer seems far more concerned with overcoming these than with conventional renunciation as entry into the fourth stage of life. First, greed, whatever its object—wealth, power, or fame—is insatiable. One can never have enough and one lives in a state of perpetual anxiety and insecurity. It leads to the perception of other human beings as competitors and rivals. Second, greed finds expression in greed-filled actions that hurt others and are not conducive to the common good. It also gives rise to oppressive and violent structures and institutions. Third, actions impelled by greed generate anger when outcomes are frustrated. Such intense anger is generally destructive of others and ultimately of self. Ignorance, greed, and anger are associated also in the *Bhagavadgita* with self-centeredness, violence, arrogance, and hate (16:18).

Note that Krishna speaks of the "eternal" renouncer; this suggests that he is speaking of renunciation as a state of being. Here and elsewhere, he places more emphasis on the inward qualities, rather than on exterior changes. Krishna seems to be suggesting that renunciation is best understood as a certain disposition to the world; it can be cultivated by those who are actively engaged in work, and who continue to fulfill religious, family, and community obligations.[17]

At the beginning of the sixth chapter, he becomes even more explicit: "He who performs that action which is his duty, while renouncing the fruit of action, is a renunciant and a yogin; not he who is without fire and without rituals" (6:1).[18] If the redefinition of the renunciant as someone free from hate and greed internalizes the description, here Krishna adds the fulfillment of obligatory responsibilities to the definition along with *freedom from attachment to the fruits of one's actions*. This is a central element of the *Bhagavadgita*'s insights on renunciation within vocation; the next section is devoted to exploring its implications.

Affirming vocation yet renouncing its fruits

The idea of *renouncing the fruit of one's actions* is heavily emphasized in the *Bhagavadgita*. It is first mentioned in the second chapter (2:47), in which Arjuna was urged to stay active, but without the motivation for the results of action. (In contrast, those who are motivated by a desire for such results are described as pitiable, 2:49). Although urging Arjuna to a life of action in the world, Krishna's

17. Some commentators argue otherwise; for example, Shankara equates the terms more narrowly with the person who has undergone the ritual of entry into the fourth stage. See Sastry, *The Bhagavadgita*, 183. However, this approach overlooks Krishna's challenge to think more deeply about the nature and purpose of renunciation.

18. Translation modified.

emphasis on the need to renounce the fruits of one's actions reminds us that our motivation and mode of engagement are as important as the action itself. Detachment from the fruits of one's action is a further elaboration of his re-envisioning of renunciation.

The most detailed discussion of this idea occurs in response to a question from Arjuna for clarification about the difference between *samnyasa* and *tyaga*. In his response Krishna defines *samnyasa* in the more traditional sense of the renunciation of vocation (i.e., the fourth stage of life) and defines *tyaga* as detachment from the fruits of one's action.[19]

Let us begin by clarifying what is *not* the case with regard to the renunciation of the fruits of action. It should not be confused with a kind of indifference toward one's actions, in which one takes action without the expectation of, or concern about, the result. Moreover, it does not signify action without any desire or purpose; according to the understanding of action that is at work here, such action would be meaningless and perhaps not even possible, since human beings initiate action with a specific result in mind. What, then, are the characteristics of a willingness to detach from the fruits of one's actions? Here, I will describe six aspects of this approach, all of which have implications for our understanding of vocational reflection and discernment.

First, nonattachment to the fruits of action helps to remind us that outcomes cannot always be guaranteed. The *Bhagavadgita* (2:47) observes that while we enjoy a right to the performance of action, we do not enjoy a right to the results of our actions. We cannot ensure a particular result. For the commentator Swami Dayananda Saraswati (1930–2015), this reflects our natural human limitations, since there are so many potential intervening factors between action and outcome. "What the result will be," he writes,

> depends on so many unknown factors that it is always a question mark. Whether what you want from a particular *karma* will happen as you expected is anyone's guess. Since you do not have a complete choice over the results of action, you had better recognize this limitation. Limitation here is not helplessness. Helplessness is felt only when you do not accept the limitation and, therefore, it has a negative connotation, whereas acknowledging the limitation is being objective.[20]

19. A good argument may be made, on the basis of this chapter of the text, that the redefinition of renunciation offered by Krishna is better described as *tyaga* and the renunciant as a *tyagi*.

20. Swami Dayananda Saraswati, *Bhagavadgita*, 9 vols. (Chennai: Arsha Vidya Research and Publication Trust, 2011), 2:247.

Recognition of this limitation disposes one to mental and emotional "evenness." The *Bhagavadgita* commends and speaks of this emotional disposition as balance (*samatvam*) in success and failure. In commending a specific attitude to the outcomes of actions, Krishna is suggesting that actions may be less stressful if one is prepared for the nonrealization of an outcome—or even for an outcome different from one for which a person had hoped. He equates this realism with nonattachment and mental and emotional balance. In 18:11, he returns to a point made earlier in the third chapter: no human being can completely desist from action, but one can *renounce the fruits of action*.

Realism about outcomes may be a very useful insight for teachers and students. Acknowledging this fact is an anxiety-relieving approach that prepares us well for coping with uncertainty and unanticipated outcomes.[21] It helps us to direct our energies and efforts where we do exercise more control—namely, the actions that we take in the present moment. Too often, we seek control where it is impossible to exercise it. Detachment from the fruits of one's actions is a shifting of energies from the future to the present, giving more meaning to the quality of our actions in the here and now.

Second, by not being attached to the results of our actions, we are able to focus more on the means and less on the end. Since the end cannot be guaranteed, anxiety about results makes us less attentive to the needs of the present. The joy of action is not limited to the anticipation of a future outcome; it may also be realized in the present moment. Detachment from results is a positive affirmation and reminder of the possibility of intrinsic value and satisfaction in performing actions. The joy of learning, for example, should not depend primarily on the grade awarded at the end of a semester, or the degree awarded at the end of several years, or whether it qualifies a person for a particular job. For both student and teacher, the journey of learning can be infused with meaning and even delight in all stages. As teachers and students, we learn so that we may live more fully in the present. We ought not to exist continuously in a preparatory mode of being.

The Hindu Vaishnava tradition (centered on the worship of God as Vishnu and, in a special way, on God's incarnation as Krishna) employs the term *lila* (play) to describe the activities of Krishna. Krishna's play is its own end; it is action that expresses joy, a way of being that we recognize especially in the play of a child. As

21. See the related comments about how de-emphasizing "choice" can reduce anxiety about vocation in William T. Cavanaugh, "Actually, You *Can't* Be Anything You Want (And It's a Good Thing, Too)," in *At This Time and In This Place: Vocation and Higher Education*, ed. David S. Cunningham (New York: Oxford University Press, 2016), 25–46.

adults, we lose the joy of activity as play when all that we do is oriented toward goals or outcomes, and subject to assessment. The call to renounce the fruits of our action is a reminder that meaningful and fulfilling actions are not limited to those that have specific goals, and that freedom from obsession about results can enhance our enjoyment of vocation as *lila.* The work that we do together, as teachers and students, can be seen as a celebration in the present.[22]

Third, detachment from the results of action is an empowering teaching that liberates us from the fear of failure that is so often a deterrent to engaging in action (or even in reflection and discernment). Uncertainty about attaining success or accomplishing a specific outcome must not paralyze us into inaction. Worry about failure—particularly when it becomes so severe that it deters our ability to act—is another form of attachment to results. Hence, the *Bhagavadgita* also cautions us about "attachment to inaction" (2:47).[23] Detachment from results may be seen in this context as empowering us to take risks in the face of uncertainties. Discerning our vocation is a risk-taking activity from which we should not withdraw because of fear of failure. In some contexts, this may mean overcoming the fear of change, as when students discover that they are overly attached to a particular vocation that does not suit them. Such risks may even involve the possibility of suffering, mentioned specifically in the *Bhagavadgita* (18:8) as something that may come of certain choices that we make. Sometimes the successful and best outcomes of our actions are not immediately obvious—we only come to recognize them long after the actions have been taken; sometimes we never know.

Fourth, by becoming less attached to the results of our actions, we make room for greater attention to the role of powers outside ourselves. In the *Bhagavadgita,* Arjuna is urged to renounce all actions in God:

> Mentally renouncing all actions in Me [Krishna],
> devoted to Me as the Supreme, taking refuge in the yoga of intelligence,
> constantly think of Me. (18:57)[24]

These verses, and others like it, are important in their equation of renunciation (*samnyasa*) with offering actions to God.[25] While outcomes are not irrelevant,

---

22. For further reflections on vocation and vocational discernment as a kind of "play," see the comments of David Cunningham in chapter 5 of this volume.

23. See the related comments in Jerome M. Organ, "Of Doing and Being: Broadening Our Understanding of Vocation," in *Vocation across the Academy: A New Vocabulary for Higher Education* (New York: Oxford University Press, 2017), 225–43.

24. Translation modified.

25. See 3:30 and 9:27.

the meaning of the action is found primarily in the fact that it is done as an expression of love for God, to whom one entrusts also the results of the action. One of the well-known descriptions of God in the Hindu tradition is *karma-phala-data* (the giver of the results of action). Actions, when done for the love of God, become worship and gain deeper significance from that fact. Such actions have the character of being ends in themselves; their significance is not based on an outcome that we engineer. In the *Bhagavadgita,* the idea that our actions can serve as a worshipful offering is advanced as a preferred alternative to the renunciation of action. In a broader sense, we may speak of nonattached actions as those that are done *for the sake of love of another*. This insight invites us to consider the nature and significance of love as the motivation for our own vocational reflection, as well as the ways in which love may be manifested in how we seek to fulfill our callings.

Fifth, there are some actions worth doing because of the very nature of these actions. These are the actions referred to in the Hindu tradition as *niyatam karma* or obligatory responsibilities. These include practices of worship, but also duties associated with one's stage in life and those connected with our professional responsibilities. Such actions should be done for no other reason than the simple fact that "it is to be done" (18:9). Krishna includes religious ritual, acts of generosity, and religious discipline as falling into this category (18:5). Others might include my obligations to my wife as a husband, my responsibilities to my children as a father, and my duties to my students as a teacher. When I reflect on such roles and responsibilities, I am not thinking of or motivated by a desire for results and outcomes. My reflections express the very meaning of what it means to be human in particular relationships; they have more to do with notions of obligation or duty (*dharma*) and faithfulness than with a particular calculation about the results of my actions. The value of such actions is realized even as the actions are being performed; their value is not dependent on future outcomes.

Finally, detachment from results reminds us that actions also express who we are; thus, such actions are worth performing even when results are not assured. One of my favorite childhood stories is about a saintly Hindu teacher who entered a sacred river for his daily bath. He noticed a scorpion struggling in the fast-moving water and gently took it in his palm and moved toward the bank of the river. As soon as the scorpion recovered, it immediately stung the teacher. The pain was sharp and searing, but the teacher did not drop the scorpion into the raging water. He was stung again but continued moving with the scorpion on his palm. His disciple, standing on the riverbank, shouted repeatedly to his teacher to drop the scorpion. After reaching and placing the scorpion on the sand, the teacher turned to his student and said, "I heard you, but the scorpion's nature is to sting and it was being faithful to its nature. It could not do otherwise. It is the nature of a virtuous person to protect and to save lives. I was being faithful to my nature."[26]

Obviously, the point of the story is not to stir debate on self-endangerment (or on alternative ways of saving a scorpion!). Rather, it calls attention to commitment and the spontaneity of moral action that flows from one's being—action that does not merely calculate costs and outcomes. The *Bhagavadgita* on two occasions speaks of the wise person as one who delights in the good of all beings (5:25; 12:4). This acknowledges an intrinsic motivation that flows from a vision of life's unity, spontaneously expressing itself in generosity and compassion. If we practice detachment from the results of our actions, we can be more faithful to who we truly are.

The teaching on the value of detachment from the results of our actions is a fine example of the many ways in which our understanding and practice of vocation may be enriched by a form of renunciation.

Renunciation within *vocation and life* in *the world*

The *Bhagavadgita*'s teaching on renunciation *within* vocation is a meaningful alternative to traditional monasticism and renunciation *of* vocation. It embraces life in the world while, at the same time, commending a way of being that is oriented toward—and indeed expresses—an ultimate reality that is both transcendent and immanent. Knowledge of this reality, and attuning one's life with its nature, is both a pathway and a goal. It is a form of liberation (*moksha*) that infuses vocation with new meaning.

The complete renunciation *of* vocation, to which we might sometimes be tempted, would be a rejection of the significance of life in the world. It is typically based on the assumption that pursuing one's vocation is fundamentally incompatible with the pursuit of liberation—the highest goal of the religious life. Such a view is born of the notion that family relationships, community involvement, paid or unpaid employment, and other aspects of our vocations are necessarily in conflict with one another, or that they demand attachment and desire (which become impediments to true freedom). On the other hand, the ideal of renunciation *within* vocation allows these important relationships, involvement, and work to be affirmed as an important aspect of our life in the world.

In commending the alternative ideal of renunciation within vocation, Krishna offers himself as an example (3:22–24). He explains that even though he has no

26. See Harish Johari, *The Monkeys and the Mango Tree* (Rochester, NY: Inner Traditions, 1998), 7–60. Adapted.

personal goal to accomplish, he continues to stay engaged in action for the well-being of the world. In a similar way, we should all act with a wish for the care of the world (3:25). The world and its flourishing are important; within it, we can attain and celebrate life's highest purpose. Our vocations are among the important ways in which we contribute to the world's well-being and participate in this celebration.

This suggests, in turn, that our vocations will be more fulfilling when we bring to them an understanding of life's interdependence, and when our work expresses gratitude for our continuous receiving from others and for the gifts from God. Renunciation within vocation is the renunciation of greed and hate as motivation for action. It is the embrace of a concern for the flourishing of all. Renunciation within vocation is the expansion of one's heart and not its contraction. By putting the emphasis on the inward transformation—away from greed and hate, and toward caring for all— this form of renunciation becomes possible within a wide variety of vocations. It allows us to reap many of the benefits sought by those who would renounce their vocations altogether and either live the life of a monk or live as though one's work is nothing more than a job.

Concern for the universal common good, however, does not exhaust the meaning of renunciation within vocation. We must learn to renounce attachment to the fruits of our actions and cultivate a healthy relationship with our vocations. While the expectation of a certain outcome is assumed in most of the work we undertake, no outcome can be guaranteed. By placing less emphasis on the fruits of our labors, we can begin to develop a degree of comfort for uncertainty—and even a calm acceptance and humility about our limits as human beings. By renouncing our attachment to results, we gain a degree of freedom from anxiety, which, in turn, liberates us to shift attention from the future to the present, enhancing the meaning of our work in the here and now. Free from the fear of failure, we may be emboldened to take risks that we might not otherwise take—or even seek out and discern new vocations when current ones are no longer intrinsically meaningful.

In a culture driven by consumerism and an economy that legitimizes greed, renunciation appears to be an alien idea (or a negative one at best). Because it is usually understood as renunciation *of* vocation, it tends to be equated with indifference, withdrawal, or uncaring disregard for self, world, and others. Renunciation *within* vocation, on the contrary, is a mode of engagement in vocation and in the world that emphasizes concern for the common good, generosity, and the cultivation of a healthy relationship with our work—deepening its meaning by focusing joyfully on the present. The meaning of work is enhanced when we renounce greed and hate. As paradoxical or countercultural as it seems, this form of renunciation is the way to a deeper delight in vocation.

Response

Rahuldeep Gill

A core problem faced by human beings is the problem of the self. What does it mean, exactly, to be a human person, with an awareness of oneself, one's decisions, one's actions? Facing this problem requires not a rejection of self, but an expansion of the notion of self; it requires a kind of curiosity into otherness. Self-centeredness is at the core of our own dallying in the face of certain death, as well as our personal hope for liberation. This is true whether as an interpretation of Guru Nanak's Sikh perspective or as Anant's insightful reading of the *Gita*.

As Anant points out, no one is free from action, just as no one is free from death. It must be confronted. We are thrown into a world where we do not make the rules, and yet we are expected to engage in that world. The inescapability of such questions provided a driving force for my own chapter, and it was because of Anant's help that I was able to clarify these matters in successive drafts of my own writing.

Working on this book was a particularly lovely experience for me because of the time I was able to spend with Anant. I learned much about the very different stages of life and career that we each inhabit. One of the most valuable things that I gained at his side in the process of working on this book was the opportunity to learn from someone who continually sees fresh questions through ancient lenses. Indeed, this is the best part of hearing vocation differently, across traditions and across disciplines: it requires us to continually be checking and questioning what we think we know, while always engaging with the question of how to live a meaningful life. From this work, there is no break and there is no escape. But we are accompanied by millennia-old wisdom from all continents—and by one another.

PART THREE

Restor(y)ing Our Lives

Narrative as a Vocational Catalyst

As the words *vocation* and *calling* have re-entered the public conversation over the past several decades, they have often been accompanied by another important pair of words: *story* and *narrative*. Vocation, it seems, is integrally related to the stories that we tell—not only the particular stories of our own lives, but also the large-scale narratives that help to ground the religious communities, political structures, and broad cultural assumptions within which we live. These stories have a profound impact on the context within which vocational reflection and discernment take place; they also serve as a catalyst for that work. Our stories urge us to contemplate larger questions of meaning and purpose, to examine the relationship between our personal stories and the broader narratives that shape our world, and to consider the directions that our lives might take as we become a part of those larger stories.

In addition, stories provide a framework within which the work of vocational reflection and discernment can be encapsulated and shared with others. As we consider large questions of meaning and purpose, we are often guided by vocational narratives—which may include stories about how people are called, complex accounts of vocational journeys (which often follow winding paths and lead down a number of blind alleys), and stories that help us see how one person's call might be related to those of others—and to the larger communities of which they are a part.

The three chapters in this part of the book are designed to help us think about how vocational reflection can support, and be supported by, attention to narrative theory and to the practices of storytelling. Woven throughout these chapters, readers will find considerations of questions such as these:

- Which narratives are currently shaping and guiding undergraduate education, particularly those aspects that touch on the two broadest concerns of this book: vocational discernment and the increasingly multi-faith environment of higher education? Which stories help us better understand the complex intersections among vocation, lifestance, and higher education?

- Have the philosophical and cultural assumptions of the modern era changed the way that we look at stories and their relevance? Does the gradual loss of focus on a single, guiding story—what one twentieth-century philosopher described as our "incredulity toward metanarratives"—create new challenges to vocational reflection, interreligious dialogue, and other significant concerns of the present moment?
- Where do our stories originate? Are they something that we mostly receive from others, or are we the creators of our own narratives? In either case, is the word *story* fully adequate to describe the ways that our lives are narrated, particularly when addressing deep questions of meaning, purpose, and identity? Do we need new language, the language of *myth* and *metanarrative*, to understand the ways that these stories shape our lives and our future direction in life?
- To what extent do our stories—whether those that we tell about ourselves or those we have incorporated into our lives from ancient and modern sources—create a moral and imaginative world within which we can dwell? And, in turn, how does such a story-shaped moral universe set the context for vocational reflection and discernment?
- Given the enormous range of narratives that operate in our lives—as well as the various communities of commitment from which they arise—our stories seem unlikely to fit together perfectly. How do we negotiate their potential conflicts in ways that acknowledge our allegiances to the various communities in which we participate? What additional challenges does this create for college students, for whom these conflicts often seem especially salient, and who often feel pressure to "perform" their various religious and cultural commitments in a public way?
- How are the endeavors of vocational reflection and interfaith encounter shaped by the narratives that undergird our contemporary context? What strategies are needed for this work to flourish—despite the challenges of cultural conflict, high levels of anxiety among undergraduates, the diffusion of traditional religious perspectives, and the ever-evolving range of lifestances that students will encounter?

A serious engagement with narrative can be an important catalyst to the work of vocational reflection and discernment. Particularly in the undergraduate years, students must navigate a wide range of intellectual, developmental, and relational challenges; often, they have to concentrate so hard on specific demands that they lose the threads that weave their lives into a whole. By providing space for vocational reflection, colleges and universities can encourage students to discover and rediscover the narratives that sustain them. In the process of "restorying" their lives, students may be able to find their center again—and thereby discover new ways of navigating the pressures and challenges of the undergraduate years.

7

Called by Our Conflicting Allegiances

VOCATION AS AN INTERFAITH ENDEAVOR / INTERFAITH COOPERATION AS A VOCATION

Noah J. Silverman

WHEN I WAS 17 YEARS old, it seemed as though the only thing that I knew with absolute certainty was that my parents knew very little—certainly very little that was useful or relevant to my life. I had been raised in a peculiar and erudite neighborhood on Chicago's South Side known as Hyde Park. I had had many wonderful experiences, both at the private secular school I attended and in the Jewish congregation where my family were members. Nevertheless, by the time I became a senior in high school, the culture of intellectual elitism and the intense pressure to "succeed" that pervaded these institutions had made it all start to feel very claustrophobic.

One night I sat my parents down in our living room and required them to listen, without interruption, to the song "Father & Son" by Cat Stevens. I was especially taken by the line sung by the "son": "from the moment I could talk, I was ordered to listen." Apparently, I felt that such histrionic behavior on my part was the only way to communicate my burning existential desire to define myself as something other than "student," and to experience life somewhere other than in a college neighborhood. The result of this conversation was that in August of 1999 I found myself on a plane to Israel—not in fulfillment of some grand Zionist dream, but rather because I had found a program that fulfilled everyone's objectives. I would finally experience a part of the world that was neither Hyde Park nor a college campus—and my parents would be assured that, if I wasn't going to college, at least I would be doing something useful and structured with my time.

I had not paid a tremendous amount of attention to the nature of this program, however. It therefore came as a surprise to me when, after a few months living on a *kibbutz* in the Galilee, I found myself overcome for the first time with a sense of Jewish peoplehood. Until then, Judaism had been, for me, something of a guiding moral framework; however, its communal obligations did not extend beyond my immediate family. But now, for the first time, I was entirely surrounded not just by other Jews, but by Jews for whom that identity carried both obligations and benefits. I studied Hebrew intensively and observed Shabbat regularly for the first time. I read Leon Uris's *Exodus* and, like one of the characters in the novel, I fantasized about changing my last name to *Ben Ami*—"son of my people"—and making *aliyah* (moving permanently to Israel).

Although I now realize that this "transformation" was deliberately orchestrated by the Zionist program in which I was participating, it felt very authentic to me at the time. What the program directors had not counted on, however, was that after my stint on *kibbutz* ended and I moved to Jerusalem, events conspired to disrupt the convenient fallacy that Israel was populated solely by Jews. Despite the best efforts of the program staff to keep me sequestered near the campus of Hebrew University, the most attractive part of Jerusalem for any 18-year-old was the Old City. So, naturally, I spent most of my time there—and quickly encountered, to my shock, people other than Jews. In retrospect, my discovery of Palestine was as equally wide-eyed as my embrace of Zionism had been. I remember discovering another people, language, culture, and *narrative*—all living in this country that I thought I had come to know. I began immersing myself in Palestinian culture, picking up as much Arabic as I could, and befriending any shopkeeper in the Arab market who was patient enough to entertain me. Not yet old enough to believe that the standard rules of society applied to me, I soon not only wanted to be Israeli; I wanted to be Palestinian as well.

After a few months, I had developed enough trust with my new Palestinian friends—and simultaneously garnered enough attention from my program's staff—for both groups to deliver similar messages to me at about the same time: "Noah, what are you really doing? You say you want to be a part of our community, yet you spend half your time with *them*. Don't you know they hate us and want to push us out of this land entirely? Which is it—are you with us or with *them*?" Their reaction was understandable; among Israelis and Palestinians who were born and raised in the midst of the conflict, the question of aligning with one side or the other is a natural one. It is a matter of membership in, or estrangement from, family and nation. I, on the other hand, was in a much more privileged position; with an American passport in my pocket and none of my immediate family living in Israel/Palestine at the time, I had (and still have) the ability to come and go as I pleased.

But at that time, I was not aware of my privilege, so the demand to "choose sides" struck me as a profoundly false choice. Why should I be forced to choose between two identities that I had assimilated into my own? Shouldn't it be possible for a young American Jew to feel allegiance to both Israel and Palestine? I felt as though I had encountered two peoples whom I adored and two stories that resonated with my soul. I naïvely believed that if they could coexist lovingly in my heart, there was no reason they could not do so in this narrow piece of land on which they both lived. A whole range of social constraints and pre-determined outcomes, which I had sought to escape by traveling halfway around the world, suddenly caught up with me. Once again, just as I was learning how to speak, I felt I was being ordered to listen.

In the modern world, we all will eventually have experiences where we find ourselves called in conflicting directions by the multiple communities to which we owe allegiance. These experiences raise profound questions about what it means to maintain relationships with communities that do not agree with one another about matters of great significance. Furthermore, although such language would have been entirely foreign to me then, I have come to realize that these experiences are at the same time moments of vocational discernment. Increasingly, we must contend with the intertwined nature of the question of what to do with our lives, on the one hand—and on the other, the question of how to respond faithfully to competing demands from various allegiances, including allegiances to different religious communities. For me and for many others, this realization sets us on a path to discover our own vocation in interfaith cooperation, and/or to think about how interfaith cooperation can itself be an important aspect of our vocation (regardless of our professions and careers). In this chapter, I seek to draw together the worlds of interfaith cooperation and vocational reflection in order to consider their deep interrelationship.

Because this interrelationship is distinctively modern, I begin with a discussion of Peter Berger's theory that modernity demands that we define our identity individually and self-reflexively. I find this theory useful in establishing a conceptual space for better understanding both vocational discernment and interfaith cooperation. Both projects attempt to help us grapple with the pluralization of worldviews and alternative life paths that is a signature characteristic of the modern age. Moreover, both projects share a point of convergence in the burgeoning literature on narrative identity. I want to suggest that, by reflecting on the interfaith relationships within our personal narratives, we can begin to understand our vocations as interfaith endeavors—and, perhaps, interfaith cooperation as a vocation. In the second section, I return to my own narrative, both to elucidate and to illustrate what this vocational path entails, including developing a "theology of interfaith cooperation." In a final section, I identify a set of challenges faced by this attempt to think about vocation as an interfaith endeavor and/or interfaith cooperation as a vocation. This process, I believe, can help us consider how to respond faithfully to the multiple, and often conflicting, callings that we hear from the various communities to which we feel allegiance.

Modernity and the "heretical imperative"

Both of the projects described here—undertaking vocational discernment and maintaining allegiances across multiple religious communities—attempt to respond to the same signature characteristic of the modern age: an irreversible fracturing of holistic systems of meaning-making. As sociologist of religion Peter Berger observed in his landmark book *The Heretical Imperative*, "modernity pluralizes."[1] Where there were once only a few social institutions—for example, in the West, the closely aligned structures of family, the Church, and the state—there are now hundreds and thousands, and they are frequently in tension with one another. Air travel, communication technology, and immigration policy have created, for many (though certainly not for all), a world in which people from different backgrounds can interact as never before. The increased encounter with difference is inescapable, Berger argues, and it is significantly different from the world experienced by our grandparents or even by our parents.[2]

Berger argues that we are now "confronted not only by multiple options of possible courses of action, but also by multiple options of possible ways of thinking about the world."[3] As a result of our intense and frequent interaction with dissimilar people and ideas, institutions and traditions lose their taken-for-granted status. The multiplicity of ways of being human is now manifestly apparent to almost everyone; the idea that one must necessarily follow a preordained path is no longer obvious. Instead, Berger argues, most people in the Global North lead lives characterized by choice—and not just in the practical matters of everyday life. Rather, "this necessity of choosing reaches into the areas of beliefs, values, and worldviews."[4]

---

1. Peter Berger, *The Heretical Imperative: Contemporary Possibilities of Religious Affirmation* (Garden City, NY: Anchor Books, 1979), 14.

2. For more on the encounter with difference more generally, see the work of Rachel Mikva in chapter 1 of this volume.

3. Berger, *The Heretical Imperative*, 15.

4. Berger, *The Heretical Imperative*, 18. On the problems associated with choice, see William T. Cavanaugh, "Actually, You *Can't* Be Anything You Want (And It's a Good Thing, Too)," in *At This Time and In This Place: Vocation and Higher Education*, ed. David S. Cunningham (New York: Oxford University Press, 2015), 25–46.

Clearly, this makes the modern world challenging to negotiate. When we encounter a person with a pattern of life vastly different from our own—someone who doesn't attend church in a town dominated by Christianity, someone who eats pork in a neighborhood of Jews and Muslims—one starts to ask questions: If that family doesn't go to church on Sunday, does that mean that we don't have to do so? If she eats pork, can I? Even though I have been taught that our way is the only way, might I perhaps entertain a different path? Throughout most of human history, these questions did not arise; few people were in a position to step outside of the dominant and socially reinforced systems of meaning-making.

Questions such as these lead to the development of a reflexive self: we construct our identities as we make these decisions.[5] In modernity, self-identity is actively shaped, reflected on, and self-monitored to a far greater extent than has ever been the case. As historical traditions lose their monopoly on authority, that authority has shifted from within familial, religious, and political structures to within the self.[6] Consequently, identity—and for our purposes, its attendant questions of vocation—has moved from being a matter of fate to one of choice.[7]

Needless to say, this should not be seen as a simple binary opposition, wherein premodern people made no choices and modern choices are entirely self-made. Obviously, both social and individual forces have constituted identity throughout history, and the modern condition is not unique in its awareness of alternative worldviews. Indeed, particularly in non-Western societies, there is a long history of plurality and hybridity between and among different cultures, traditions, and perspectives on life. In the modern era, however, the dominant and socially reinforced systems of meaning-making—including religious traditions—become fractured, leading to a wider possibility and plausibility of choice. Berger observes that the English word *heresy* derives from a Greek verb meaning "to choose"; a *hairesis* was simply a choice made against the established dominant position within a wider religious community. Thus, as Berger writes, the etymology of the term reveals a presupposition of the authority of a tradition. "The heretic denied this authority, refused to accept the tradition *in toto*," and instead chose its most interesting or relevant aspects. From these pickings and choosings, says Berger, heretics constructed their own "deviant" opinions.[8] Hence, while the earliest use of the term demonstrates that there has always been the possibility of deviation

5. Berger, *The Heretical Imperative*, 18.

6. See the comments on "Sheila" by Trina Jones in chapter 2 of this volume.

7. Berger, *The Heretical Imperative*, 10; see also Cavanaugh, "Actually, You *Can't*."

8. Berger, *The Heretical Imperative*, 25.

and choice, "modernity creates a new situation in which picking and choosing becomes an imperative."[9] As a result, the work of "arranging oneself in the universe" has become considerably more difficult.[10]

Vocational and interfaith responses to modernity

To the extent that Berger's analysis is correct, it suggests that the contemporary challenge for vocational discernment is the need to respond to this fracturing of holistic systems of meaning-making. Indeed, much of the literature on vocational discernment seems to recognize that modernity carries with it this "heretical imperative"—a need to choose how to endow one's life with meaning. As Hannah Schell observes:

> Undergraduate students live in the midst of multiple and competing narratives. . . . They suddenly find themselves overwhelmed by a number of possible candidates for goals that they could pursue and ends that they could seek to achieve. Often the messages they receive are contradictory.[11]

No longer grounded in the metanarrative of a religious worldview that strives to provide its adherents with at least some degree of order and meaning, and with innumerable life paths available, students often find themselves floundering. Vocational discernment, at least in the contemporary context,[12] is an attempt to help students navigate what James McClendon refers to as the "tournament of narratives,"[13] and to find meaningful work and purpose for their lives.

Modern interfaith cooperation is itself predicated on this pluralization of choice and fracturing of meaning. It attempts to help answer questions such as these: Given the plurality of worldviews in my own neighborhood, how can I be sure of my particular Truth? How do I reconcile the beauty and/or goodness I see in other traditions with the claims of exclusivity in my own? How do I remain

---

9. Berger, *The Heretical Imperative*, 25.

10. Berger, *The Heretical Imperative*, 22.

11. Hannah Schell, "Commitment and Community: The Virtue of Loyalty and Vocational Discernment," in Cunningham, ed., *At This Time*, 235–58; here, 235.

12. On the long history of the word *vocation*, see David S. Cunningham, "Time and Place: Why Vocation is Crucial to Undergraduate Education Today," in Cunningham, ed., *At This Time*, 1–24; here, 7–9.

13. Quoted in Douglas V. Henry, "Vocation and Story: Narrating Self and World," in Cunningham, ed., *At This Time*, 165–92; here, 165.

faithful to my tradition without denigrating others? Eboo Patel defines the word *interfaith* by parsing it into its constituent parts:

> The "inter" in interfaith stands for interaction between people who orient around religion differently. The "faith" in interfaith stands for how people relate to their religious and ethical traditions. Put together, "interfaith" is about how our interactions with those who are different have an impact on the way we relate to our religious and ethical traditions, and how our relationships with our traditions have an impact on our interactions with those who are different from us.[14]

Interfaith cooperation thus presumes that individuals have a tradition with which they relate, be it a religious or nonreligious one.[15] It also reminds us of the inherent tension at the heart of this endeavor: the need to contend with an inherited worldview *and* with a world in which that worldview's metanarratives are not universally accepted, or perhaps not even relevant. As Wilfred Cantwell Smith observed over a half century ago: from now on, religious life, "if it is to be lived at all, will be lived in a context of religious pluralism."[16]

Thus, both projects—the discernment of one's vocation and the development of interfaith cooperation—seek to help individuals contend with their life choices, and the commitments that might undergird them. These projects undertake this work in a world characterized by a dizzying plurality of worldviews, career paths, and lifestyles. The imperative to make these choices, and to develop a self-reflexive identity in the wake of these choices, is a fraught and sometimes alienating process.

Narrative identity and multiple callings

Perhaps unsurprisingly (given their similar concerns), conversations about both vocational discernment and interfaith cooperation draw heavily on the recent resurgence of scholarly interest in the relationship between identity and narrative.

---

14. Eboo Patel, *Interfaith Leadership: A Primer* (Boston: Beacon Press, 2016), 39.

15. Much of the interfaith movement—including Interfaith Youth Core (IFYC), the organization that Patel leads and for which I work—is at pains to create spaces for both the nonreligious and the nonidentified. On the use of the term *lifestance* as embracing all of these perspectives, see the comments of Rachel Mikva in chapter 1 of this volume; on the phenomenon of multiple religious belonging, see the comments of Trina Jones in chapter 2.

16. Wilfred Cantwell Smith, *The Faith of Other Men* (New York: New American Library, 1963), 11.

As many writers have noted, a key element of understanding one's vocation is the ability to narrate a story of how it came to be. As Douglas Henry observes, "vocation has a *narrative* quality."[17] Considerations of hearing and responding to a calling take shape within a framework that comprises characters (ourselves and others) and plots (our struggles to realize life goals). These stories are then told and retold. As Henry writes, we "remember our story in order to make sense of our decisions. We tell stories to make our lives intelligible, and those stories can play a role in whether we are able to hear—and perhaps respond to—a calling."[18]

Similarly, much of the literature on interfaith cooperation draws on storytelling and narrative identity, both as a methodology for interfaith dialogue and as a reflective tool for articulating one's call to interfaith engagement.[19] Not surprisingly, many of the stories that are told in these interfaith spaces give significant attention to the presence of other people—particularly those who orient around religion differently than the storyteller. The story of understanding one's vocation as an interfaith endeavor is almost always a story of encountering and responding positively to religious difference, and doing so in a way that proves to be mutually enriching. Because the narrative threads of our lives are inextricably woven with the threads of others', the presence of other people in our narratives implicitly reminds us that we are formed by, and responsible to, people beyond ourselves.

In the modern era, we all contend with both the intense encounter of difference and the heretical imperative to define ourselves individually in relation to the multiple traditions that form us. As a result, all of our stories of self—our vocational narratives—contain interfaith encounters to degrees more or less pronounced and acknowledged. Moreover, we narrate these stories not solely to ourselves, but also to other people; this, in turn, carries with it a certain ethic.

---

17. Henry, "Vocation and Story," 165.

18. Henry, "Vocation and Story," 165.

19. See, for example, Eboo Patel, April Kunze, and Noah Silverman, "Storytelling as a Key Methodology for Interfaith Youth Work," in *Interfaith Dialogue at the Grass Roots*, ed. Rebecca Kratz Mays (Philadelphia: Ecumenical Press, 2008), 35–46; Eboo Patel, April Kunze, and Noah Silverman, "Action through Service—From Shared Values to Common Action," in *InterActive Faith: The Essential Interreligious Community-Building Handbook*, ed. Bud Heckman and Rori Picker Neiss (Woodstock, VT: Skylight Paths Publishing, 2010), 111–38; Jennifer Peace, Or Rose, and Gregory Mobley, eds., *My Neighbor's Faith: Stories of Interreligious Encounter, Growth and Transformation* (New York: Orbis Books, 2012); Eboo Patel, *Interfaith Leadership: A Primer* (Boston: Beacon Press, 2016), 28–37; Matthew Maruggi and Martha E. Stortz, "Teaching the 'Most Beautiful Stories': Narrative Reflection as a Signature Pedagogy for Interfaith Studies," in *Interreligious/Interfaith Studies: Defining a New Field*, ed. Eboo Patel, Jennifer Howe Peace, and Noah J. Silverman (Boston: Beacon Press, 2018).

Inherent in the act of narrating a story about oneself as someone who can engage difference positively is an implicit promise to the listener that one can do it again. When we narrate our vocational stories as marked by interfaith encounters, "we begin to make promises to the world about who we are and what we can do. We are saying, implicitly at least, 'You can count on us to help people who orient around religion differently get along more positively.'"[20]

Thus, modern vocational discernment and interfaith cooperation are intertwined in their recognition that communities—and, significantly, not just the community from which one emerges—make claims to which one has a responsibility to respond.[21] In this important way, discerning a calling to interfaith cooperation is a particularly powerful example of the more general challenge of vocational discernment: not merely in identifying one's calling among the competing narratives of contemporary society, but in attempting to respond to multiple "callings" simultaneously. To understand one's vocation as an interfaith endeavor is to recognize the necessity of responding to the calling of the multiple (and potentially competing) communities to which one owes allegiance.

As noted in the previous section, both the challenge of vocational discernment and the challenge of fostering interfaith cooperation can be understood as attempts to respond to the fracturing of identity attendant in modernity. But in drawing these two projects together and considering them in tandem, we see how they are intrinsically intertwined: we begin to understand how modern life is *predicated on* encounters with the "other" that are (frequently) profound and generative. Moreover, we begin to recognize that such encounters engender a sense of responsibility to the other, who thus "calls" us to be in relationship. At the same time, this call must be drawn into dialogue with the "call" that one continues to feel from one's own tradition. Obviously, these multiple callings might not lend themselves to being easily reconciled—as my own narrative suggests.

Responding to the calling of multiple communities

In the immediate aftermath of having been presented with the "false choice" of aligning myself with either the Palestinian or Israeli narrative, I fortuitously happened upon the Jerusalem office of Seeds of Peace. This organization was

---

20. Patel, *Interfaith Leadership*, 37.

21. See Florence Amamoto's comments on responsibility in chapter 10 of this volume; see also Margaret E. Mohrmann, "'Vocation Is Responsibility': Broader Scope, Deeper Discernment," in *Vocation across the Academy: A New Vocabulary for Higher Education*, ed. David S. Cunningham (New York: Oxford University Press, 2017), 21–43.

working to bring young people from all sides of the conflict together under the banner "the enemy has a face." By getting to know and working with Israeli and Palestinian peers (all of whom remained committed simultaneously to their respective national narratives and to the friendships they had built), I began to imagine that such dual loyalties were possible. In a complete reversal of my previous intransigence about avoiding college campuses, I suddenly could not wait to return to the United States and to start college so that I could embark on the path of peacemaker—the closest approximation that I had, at the time, to my own future vocation. Looking back, I am made more aware of my youthful naïveté and self-importance by the fact that, as I was concluding my program and beginning my undergraduate career, my chief worry was that the Israeli-Palestinian conflict would be resolved before I got to play my starring role in the process.

Upon my arrival on campus, I set out to organize an event for the community on Israeli-Palestinian peacemaking. However, I did not anticipate the degree of vitriol that I encountered from all sides for even attempting to build bridges between the respective communities. Distraught, I sought out a faculty mentor who assured me that the best indication that I was on the right path was that I was receiving equal doses of recrimination from both the Jewish/Israeli and Arab/Palestinian communities.

In this experience, I discovered something important: that, in the eyes of one's various communities of belonging, one's other loyalties can frequently be seen as a betrayal. This reality has stuck with me throughout my adult career; it crystalizes the unique challenge of being called to multiple communities. In my sophomore year of college, I served as the president of my campus's Hillel chapter and received pressure to run pro-Israel programs. I resisted, knowing that these issues created divisions in the community (to say nothing of the divisions in my own mind). As a result, the community adviser to Hillel called me a "wolf in sheep's clothes" and tried to remove me from my position. Over time, this sense of standing at odds with my original community of belonging led to a sense of estrangement. I too was a heretic—and suddenly I began to feel as though I did not actually belong to any community at all.

This gives rise to a peculiar phenomenon that I have come to recognize in myself, as well as other interfaith leaders from different communities: I am frequently most comfortable being Jewish when I am in interfaith spaces, rather than Jewish ones. When I find myself in structured Jewish spaces, I am acutely aware of my interfaith commitments. I know that, while the community adequately represents the extent of many of its members' loyalties, it does not do so for me. I find myself needing to guard my language when I describe what I do, and frequently bite my tongue when the conversation turns to Israel. By contrast, when I find myself in explicitly interfaith spaces, I am free to own and express the parts of Judaism that have formed me, without expecting to be challenged on them.

This obviously speaks to both the overlap and the tension between interfaith and *intra*faith work. Any individual religious tradition, to the extent that such a designation has any meaning, is in reality an amalgamation of multiple, varied, and sometimes contradictory *traditions*.[22] This internal diversity is obvious in the case of denominations and sects; crucially, however, the implication of Berger's argument about the modern fracturing of socially dominant systems is that, today, *all* religious persons engage in a process of selective reconstruction of the various versions of the tradition from which we draw meaning and purpose. We are all "heretics" in this sense, and are therefore subject to innumerable *intrafaith* arguments about the relative validity and worth of one's tradition—as well as one's interpretation of it, over against others'.

In a certain sense, *interfaith* cooperation thus provides an outlet by which individuals or groups can step away from these internal debates. In interfaith spaces, I frequently get to present and live the version of Judaism that is meaningful and life-giving to me—without needing to contend so urgently with the elements I find more troublesome. But if I feel more comfortable being Jewish in the absence of other Jews, does this sanction the idea that interfaith cooperation is, either explicitly or implicitly, its own separate worldview? If I don't feel at home in my home community, but only with other interfaith leaders who (like me) find themselves semi-exiled from their home community, am I not in essence saying that it is the "interfaith tribe," rather than Judaism, that constitutes my true home? Certainly, for some people involved in interfaith cooperation, this does become the case. The call that issues from specific alternative communities, or from humanity as a whole, overwhelms and supplants the call from one's home community.

But for many others, including myself, the desire to work for interfaith cooperation in society is motivated by the desire to bring the disparate and disjointed parts of our own selves together and to constitute a coherent personal identity. I had a mentor who once pointed out a feature of my personality that had carried over from my youth. He said that I had "all these voices in my head" and that, just as a new part of my self was finding expression, the other aspects of my identity were ordering it to be quiet and listen. His advice was for me to figure out how to get all these voices to come together and "have a respectful and generative conversation." The astuteness and irony of this insight was not lost on

22. See the comments on multiple religious belonging by Trina Jones in chapter 2 of this volume, and on "syncretic selves" by Jeff Carlson in chapter 13.

me, for this is exactly what interfaith cooperation involves—promoting positive connections between and among people and communities in the world. As Walt Whitman wrote:

> Do I contradict myself?
> Very well then I contradict myself.
> (I am large. I contain multitudes.)[23]

The work of bringing those internal multitudes into a coherent self is closely related to the work of bringing the multitudes of humanity into peaceful cooperation across lines of religious difference.

Developing a theology or ethic of interfaith cooperation

While I cannot claim that I have entirely succeeded in achieving this internal harmony, I have come a long way. Despite having spent my entire adult life feeling somewhat alienated in Jewish communities, I am convinced that my sense of responsibility to communities outside Judaism is nonetheless an intrinsically *Jewish* response to these additional callings—albeit an inherently selective one (as all hermeneutics are). My experience of feeling at odds with the Jewish community has motivated me to construct my own personal, distinctly Jewish version of what Patel calls a "theology or ethic of interfaith cooperation." This involves "interpreting the key sources of a tradition in a way that puts forth a coherent narrative and deep logic that calls for positive relationships with people who orient around religion differently."[24] Yes, all modern people are "heretics," in that they pick and choose from the various traditions that form them. Still, by developing a personal theology or ethic of interfaith cooperation, we may come to understand our interfaith allegiances not in opposition to our own traditions, nor as merely ancillary to them, but rather as expressing a central tenet of those traditions.[25]

So, what does my personal Jewish theology of interfaith cooperation look like? For me, one place to start this narrative is with the first century BCE sage and scholar Hillel the Elder. In *Pirkei Avot* (*Ethics of the Fathers*), a compilation of ethical teachings from early rabbinic literature, Hillel famously asks

23. Walt Whitman, *Leaves of Grass* (Philadelphia: David McKay, 1891–92), 78.

24. Patel, *Interfaith Leadership*, 119–20.

25. For further discussion of this experience, see the comments of David S. Cunningham, Florence Amamoto, and Jacqueline Bussie in chapters 5, 10, and 11 of this volume, respectively.

three questions: "If I am not for myself, who will be for me? And if I am only for my own self, what am 'I'? And if not now, when?" I learned this teaching, as many young Jews do, in my earliest Hebrew school classes, and throughout my life, I have found these questions to be animating ones. They have begotten an extensive literature of interpretation, for they do not necessarily seem to refer exclusively to individual identity. Indeed, immediately after my experience of having been faced with the false choice of allegiance either to the Israeli or to the Palestinian people, I quoted Hillel to the director of my program. If we, as Jews or Israelis or Zionists, are only for ourselves, what are we? To which he, of course, responded by reminding me of the first question: "If we are not for ourselves, do you really expect the Palestinians to be for us?"

The questions deliberately establish a rhetorical tension that borders on contradiction, but therein lies their beauty and enduring power. Judaism is a tradition whose adherents often embrace and celebrate contradictory truths, as Whitman did. The Chassidic leader Rabbi Bunim of P'shishkha said that everyone should have two pockets, each containing a slip of paper. On one should be written Abraham's words of abasement when he dared to argue with God—"I am but dust and ashes" (Gen. 18:27). And in the other pocket, on the other slip, are the lines of the Talmud: "the world was created for me and me alone."[26] The traditional telling of this story is that from time to time we must reach into one pocket or the other; the secret of living is knowing when to reach into which one. My former rabbi of blessed memory, Arnold Jacob Wolf, observed that another lesson can be drawn from this story: that of *living in contradiction*. The statements on both slips of paper are both true at all times. Within the vast tradition of Judaism, there are ample resources that support the idea that we must be for ourselves. But Judaism is simultaneously universal—replete with wisdom and concern for the entire human family.

One contemporary rabbi who reads Judaism in this light and whose work has been powerful for me—not only in constructing my theology of interfaith cooperation, but for my theology in general—is the late Harold Schulweis. In a beautiful poem entitled "Between," Rabbi Schulweis writes, "God is not in me / nor in you / but between us."[27] The poem articulates a conception of God not as some supernatural, omnipotent, or omniscient being, but rather as a way to conceive of what is potentially divine in human relationships. Schulweis's notion of

26. Babylonian Talmud, Sanhedrin 37B.

27. Harold M. Schulweis, "Between," in *Hearing the Call across Traditions: Readings on Faith and Service*, ed. Adam Davis (Woodstock, VT: Skylight Paths Publishing, 2009), 107–8.

discovering God through discovering other people has been hugely influential for me. Through the lens of this theology, the liturgy of Judaism is transformed; it is no longer meaningless praise of an imagined fatherly figure, but rather fervent worship of that of which I know humanity to be capable. When I beat my chest on Yom Kippur, it is not to an external being that I confess my sins, but to the community around me that I have failed. The notion of the divine existing in the "betweenness" of human interaction is a theology that I can not only embrace, but also enact. I understand Judaism to call me to approach every human interaction with the awareness that what I put into that space between us—charity or suspicion, apathy or love—has the potential either to create and magnify the divine—or to destroy it.

This recognition that "to know God is to know others" is thus at the heart of interfaith cooperation, insofar as it focuses on the dynamic interplay between our relationship with others and our relationship with our own tradition.[28] If entering into real and profound relationship with other people is a way of knowing God, then this necessarily entails a transformation of how one understands God, and thus one's own commitments and understanding of self. This transformation is not necessarily one that involves the abandonment of fundamental theological precepts, but rather the re-articulation of those precepts in newly discovered relationships. The process of developing a theology of interfaith cooperation might originate in a profound relationship with others, but it also leads to the discovery of other facets of one's self and one's tradition. One would not have discovered these facets were it not for that first "divine" relationship that sparked this process of discovery.

In this way, more often than not, interfaith encounter leads individuals not to abandon, but to reaffirm and strengthen the call they feel from their home tradition. These new facets then form the narrative of one's theology or ethic of interfaith cooperation and lead one to behave and orient differently in the world. Taken in this way, a theology or ethic of interfaith cooperation can form a bridge between the two primary callings at the heart of this work: the calling to strengthen our relationships with our primary traditions and the calling to remain open to the divine encounter with the other.

As Alasdair MacIntyre observed, "I can only answer the question 'What am I to do?' if I can answer the prior question 'Of what story or stories do I find myself a part?' "[29] For me, it was and remains important to locate myself within the

---

28. Patel, *Interfaith Leadership*, 39.

29. Alasdair MacIntyre, *After Virtue: A Study in Moral Theory*, 2nd ed. (Notre Dame, IN: University of Notre Dame Press, 1984), 216.

grand narrative of Judaism as it has been told for millennia. I am reminded of the words of Martin Luther King Jr.: "I am many things to many people, but in the quiet recesses of my heart, I am fundamentally a clergyman, a Baptist preacher. This is my being and my heritage for I am also the son of a preacher, the grandson of a Baptist preacher and the great-grandson of a Baptist preacher."[30] In the quiet recesses of my heart I am a Jew; I am unable to be anything else, nor do I wish to be. The estrangement that I occasionally feel from certain instantiations of the Jewish community today is merely a temporal and sociopolitical one, not an existential one. My theology of interfaith cooperation allows me to reaffirm and narrate that distinction.

I have learned how to approach the task of reconciling, for myself, the parts of my own identity and of my tradition that are tribally Jewish with the parts that are universally human. What remains to be done, and what motivates me to adopt interfaith cooperation as my vocation, is to help the various communities to which I belong to do the same. And this demands that I give attention, first and foremost, to the Jewish community that I claim as my own.

The challenges of conflicting allegiances

In this final section, I offer some preliminary thoughts on a set of challenges that arise when attending to interfaith cooperation and vocational discernment as I have described them here.

Charting new professional paths

Knowing *what* one wants to do with one's life, and knowing *how* to go about doing it—these are two very different things. This is particularly true when one feels called to work that lacks ready models upon which to draw. In my own case, by the time I was a senior in college, I began to grapple with a significant conundrum: while I had a much better sense of what I wanted to do with my life than most of my peers, I had absolutely no idea how to pursue it. Blessed as I was with several faculty mentors, I remember getting coffee with one of them and describing my challenge. The advice I was given was to identify people who were successful in the work that I wanted to do, and then to learn what steps they took to get there. It was sound advice, but I knew of few examples of individuals who

---

30. Quoted in Adam Taylor, "Rejecting Sanitized Celebrations of MLK," http://www.beliefnet.com/columnists/godspolitics/2007/01/adam-taylor-rejecting-sanitize.html (accessed May 26, 2017).

had chosen the work of "faithfully responding to multiple callings" as a vocational path. While modern interfaith cooperation (in the sense that I've described it here) has existed for over a century, it is roughly only in the past two decades that it has become something that one might undertake as a profession.

I am reminded of an idea that I think is best expressed by Bob Dylan, who once gave an interview in which he confessed that he never thought of himself as a songwriter, but rather as a singer. This seems surprising coming from someone who is known more for his lyrical dexterity than vocal talent. But what resonated with me was Dylan's account of why he turned to songwriting: "I had to write what I wanted to sing, because what I wanted to sing, nobody else was writing. I couldn't find that song someplace."[31]

For those who want to spend their lives faithfully responding to the calling of multiple communities *and* to support themselves in a world where those jobs don't yet exist, it helps to also have an entrepreneurial and imaginative spirit. A frequent refrain at the organization at which I work, Interfaith Youth Core (IFYC), is the ridiculous metaphor that "we are building the plane while flying it." But, as Dylan points out, this compounds the challenge of living out one's calling. The challenge of discerning a vocational path is difficult enough without also having to clear the brush and move the boulders to build the trail oneself. While this circumstance affords the freedom to define one's vocation in ways that are most personally resonant, it also makes it incredibly difficult to know whether one is walking the path well—or where, exactly, it might lead.

Personal and professional coherence has its downsides

When one understands one's professional identity to be an external reflection of one's deepest theological or ethical commitments, the mundane successes and failures of professional life can take on even greater significance. While I feel blessed to do work that I understand to be fundamentally holy, this work is also draining. More days than not, I find it difficult to face the eight hours of meetings, backlogged emails, and bureaucratic processes that I expect to encounter. And this thought is immediately followed by the guilt of complaining about doing that which I understand myself to be *called* to do—and knowing that there is always more to do.

---

31. Quoted in Brian Ives, "Radio.Com Minimation: Bob Dylan – 'I Had to Write What I Wanted to Sing,'" http://radio.com/2014/09/12/bob-dylan-minimation-i-had-to-write-what-i-wanted-to-sing/ (accessed May 26, 2017).

In a beautiful reflection penned shortly before his death from cancer, Oliver Sacks recounts his lifelong struggle with his Jewish identity, strained by his mother's early rejection of his homosexuality. Sacks reflects:

> And now, weak, short of breath, my once-firm muscles melted away by cancer, I find my thoughts, increasingly, not on the supernatural or spiritual, but on what is meant by living a good and worthwhile life—achieving a sense of peace within oneself. I find my thoughts drifting to the Sabbath, the day of rest, the seventh day of the week, and perhaps the seventh day of one's life as well, when one can feel that one's work is done, and one may, in good conscience, rest.[32]

I find myself returning to this passage frequently as a reminder to ask the question, "Is my work done? Can I now, in good conscience, rest—at least for a few hours?" When one invests one's work with such personal and theological significance, it can be difficult to give oneself permission to log off, shut down, and treat oneself to more trivial pursuits.

This challenge has taken on new meaning for me as I have entered into parenthood. At what point does my sense of responsibility to the communities to which I feel called need to take a back seat to the (often very loud and incessant) calling of my toddler? How do I negotiate the multiple callings of profession, parenthood, and partnerhood, when they are all understood in such deeply theological and personal ways? Here as well, I try to turn to my tradition for guidance. The Torah teaches that "six days shall you labor and do all your work" (Exodus 20:9); but a rabbinic commentary asks, "Is it then possible for a person to do 'all his work' in six days? The meaning is rather: rest on Shabbat *as if* all your work is done."[33] Much more recently, the great twentieth-century rabbi Abraham Joshua Heschel (who himself maintained deep interfaith allegiances) wrote, "the Sabbath is not for the sake of the weekdays; the weekdays are for the sake of Sabbath."[34] Even though I am blessed that my profession *is* my vocation, Judaism calls me to remember that there is still something deeper and more important. I do not observe Shabbat in traditional ways, but my vocation would be meaningless if I were unable, on a weekly basis, to stop, rest, and enjoy the quotidian beauty of my family.

---

32. Oliver Sacks, "Sabbath," *New York Times*, August 14, 2015, http://www.nytimes.com/2015/08/16/opinion/sunday/oliver-sacks-sabbath.html?_r=0 (accessed May 26, 2017).

33. Mekhilta of Rabbi Ishmael: Tractate Bahodesh, Yitro Parsha 7, Exodus 20:8.

34. Abraham Joshua Heschel, *The Sabbath* (New York: Farrar, Straus and Giroux, 1951), 14.

A limited coherence

A third challenge that bears attention is the realization that maintaining interfaith allegiances requires a person to alternate, in a sense, between two hats. The first hat signifies the commitments and viewpoints one holds as a partisan member of any number of religious, social, or political communities. My sense of calling to other communities does not negate my sense that there is right and wrong; that I prefer some policies and social constructions to others; and that, among the communities to which I feel called, I would judge some positions to be just plain evil. But the second hat signifies that, as an interfaith leader—as someone acutely attuned to these multiple callings—my responsibility is also to create spaces where productive and generative conversation can take place, and where reconciliation can be achieved.

Given this difficulty, I do not wish to idealize interfaith spaces. While I have frequently experienced them as a respite from the internal Jewish fights that I naturally find more personal and contentious, real conflict exists in interfaith work as well. At IFYC, we are fond of saying that "diversity isn't just the differences you *like*." When I come to an interfaith dialogue, I may get to present my own distinctly individual version of Judaism, but I also have to contend with the worldviews of others—views that may very well condemn me or those about whom I care deeply.

The challenge thus becomes knowing when to wear each hat. In what contexts and at what times am I allowed to advocate for the partisan positions that I hold dear, and in what contexts am I called to empathize and try to understand the other side? Harkening back to the notion of discovering the divine in the "betweenness" of human relationships, I try to remind myself of the difference between the moral value of people and the moral value of the social, political, or theological positions they espouse. People are more than the sum of their religious and political positions; they are *b'tzelem Elohim*: human beings created in God's image. Interfaith cooperation calls me to strive to engage those human beings—and to remember that, even if others espouse a particular view that I find reprehensible, they can nonetheless build common cause with me on other issues.

Perhaps ironically, then, even as I find fulfillment and coherence in my vocational work, it remains deeply incomplete. The beauty and the burden of responding to multiple callings is that we are never allowed to feel fully reconciled. By definition, there will always be, within the community I am trying to build, people and positions that I find questionable or even objectionable. Understanding one's vocation as an interfaith endeavor carries with it the recognition that, on some level, one never gets to feel totally integrated. The greatest challenge, I suppose, is learning to find contentment in that which is always fundamentally incomplete.

Vocation and identity

In this chapter, I have sought to unpack what is meant by understanding one's vocation as an interfaith endeavor, as well as understanding interfaith cooperation in vocational terms. The fracturing of holistic and socially dominant systems of meaning-making in the modern era creates an imperative with which we must all contend: a dizzying plurality of options out of which we must self-reflexively build our identity. This can create a tension, wherein we feel called to remain faithful both to our inherited traditions and to the encounter with others (who likewise form us, and to whom we develop a sense of responsibility). The desire to respond to these multiple callings is the essence of understanding vocation as an interfaith endeavor, and of adopting interfaith cooperation as a vocation.

Following such a vocational path can be difficult, of course. It creates, and places its followers into, a liminal state between and among the various communities to which they consider themselves called. This can lead to estrangement and alienation. Nevertheless, developing an individual theology of interfaith cooperation can help one negotiate these competing calls and rejections; in some cases, including my own, it may also lead one back to a deeper engagement with one's home community. While this enables some degree of internal reconciliation and motivates one to build external social harmony, it remains a precarious and tentative path on all levels. Despite everything that I and others have endeavored to do, the conflict in Israel/Palestine rages; sectarian and internecine conflict appears to be on the rise the world over; and I continue to struggle every day to balance the competing demands on my time, my psyche, and my sense of self. The world does not necessarily understand or endorse my path, whether on a philosophical or a purely practical level. But it remains my vocational path, and only by following it am I truly able to make sense of my own identity.

Response

Anantanand Rambachan

Noah's chapter offers a thoughtful exploration of the tensions and challenges of embracing the work of interfaith cooperation as a vocation. In doing so, he calls our attention to the many interpenetrating layers of this kind of work. The political layer, if this term is appropriate, is easier to identify, to describe, and even to justify. Any religious tradition that is concerned about the common good must reach across boundaries to find common ground for cooperation with other traditions. Rabbi Abraham Joshua Heschel formulated the political argument in famous words: "No religion is an island." Our hopes for a just and peaceful world will be realized together—or not at all.

The political need for interfaith work is centered on what Noah describes here as "peacemaking." There is, however, a theological layer as well—one that is not always as explicitly acknowledged by practitioners of interfaith cooperation. It is misleading to think that the theological only follows from the political. Admittedly, our engagement with persons of other traditions has the potential to transform our theological self-understanding, as well as our accounts of the claims made by our traditions about persons of other faiths. The theological element, however, is already present at the beginning of our inquiry—in the dispositions, certainties, and doubts that we bring to our engagement with the other. There is no such thing as theology-neutral interfaith work. A theology of the interfaith endeavor requires deep reflection, and Noah provides precisely this.

Attentiveness to our theologies of interfaith cooperation helps us understand how our perception and engagement with others is shaped, positively or negatively, by various theological lenses. In addition, interfaith engagement has the potential radically to transform our theology. Noah writes of it as requiring "a transformation of how one understands God, and thus one's own commitments and understanding of self." The gravity of such an engagement demands that both the political and the theological, both praxis and reflection, acknowledge explicitly the necessity and value of each other. Both will be better for the gifts of the other.

8

The Story of Me

A MYTH-UNDERSTANDING OF VOCATION

Matthew R. Sayers

MYTHS OFFER US windows into religions, but they are more than a means of *access*; they are central to the *constitution of* a religion. The stories we tell about ourselves are also windows into our lives; these stories too—like myths—are more than mere windows. Each of us constitutes a sense of self through an ongoing process of "myth-making." In this chapter, I reflect upon a range of myths—personal stories from my life, narratives from diverse sources, and academic fictions that animate the discipline of religious studies. All of these provide the source material for constructing my own self-understanding. My goal is to redescribe the endeavor-otherwise-known-as-vocation; this will require crafting a new myth about the creation of a life fulfilled. I offer *myth-making* as an alternative to the semantically rich (but theologically loaded) idea of *vocation*.

An alternative "myth-understanding" of vocational discernment rests on three themes: a dynamic concept of self, a recognition of the retrospective nature of self-construction (which, not ironically, illuminates our future), and a balanced conception of human agency. Taking these each in turn: A dynamic concept of self helps us avoid conceiving of ourselves (and others) as possessed of and defined by an essential character throughout our entire lives. A focus on the retrospective nature of self-construction means rejecting the notion that "vocation" is purely a future-oriented, once-or-twice-in-a-lifetime, carefully orchestrated event. And finally, by embracing a more balanced understanding of agency, we can avoid conceiving of ourselves either as completely independent actors able to shape the world to our will, or as mere flotsam in the irresistible currents of culture and circumstance. Being attentive to these themes can allow us to avoid some common pitfalls and become active, informed agents intent on crafting our sense of self through a dynamic process of myth-making.

To begin, I need to describe my methodology, with particular attention to the terms that I will employ. I will then narrate some of my own myths to provide the "raw material" for my analysis. I will take up my three themes explicitly in the second half of this chapter, when I turn to an examination of the *Bhagavadgita* and its implications for this discussion.

Terminology

As an outsider to the ongoing conversation about vocation—as a non-Christian and a scholar new to the discussion—I have concerns about some terminology. Rather than engaging in a prolonged rationale for rejecting certain conventions, I will briefly outline my concerns with respect to two key terms; I will then introduce the alternative terminology that I employ here.

Beyond *calling* and *discernment*

Terms such as *vocation, calling,* and *the summoned life* all presume an external "caller."[1] I prefer the phrase *a fulfilled life*, which is neutral with respect to the location (internal or external) of the impetus for crafting such a life. In particular, this language has the virtue of serving a wider range of readers—not only those who perceive a divine "caller," but also those who understand any obligation to arise from internal or cultural sources.

Additionally, I am intentional in rejecting language that implies an objective, static reality with respect to the self. The word *discernment*, for example, seems to presuppose that a purposeful self already exists, and that it is merely awaiting "revelation" or "discovery." At the other extreme, however, I also reject language such as "invention of the self," because this alternative fails to recognize that the constitution of self occurs in a historical and cultural context. As such, "self-invention" can imply an independence from context, or possibly that the self arises without preconditions. As an alternative to the language of either *discernment* or *invention*, I prefer that of *construction*. This word implies the existence of "raw material" (with which we create a self), as well as one's own agency (the creator); nevertheless, it remains sensitive to context. I think this strikes the necessary balance between two extremes.

---

1. See David S. Cunningham "'Who's There?': The Dramatic Role of the 'Caller' in Vocational Discernment," in *At This Time and In This Place: Vocation and Undergraduate Education*, ed. David S. Cunningham (New York: Oxford University Press, 2016), 143–64.

Self-construction and myth-making

I use two closely related terms throughout this chapter (not synonyms, but near enough); as a pair, they make clear what is at stake and encourage us to be attentive to the process through which the self is both created and understood. Further, the tension between the two terms helps to illustrate the dynamic nature of the process of defining one's life.

The first term, *self-construction*, provides a convenient shorthand for identifying efforts to answer questions fundamental to a fulfilled life. What do I want to do? Who do I want to be? How do I become the person I aspire to be? Why do the choices I make matter? As makers of meaning, human beings strive to understand and define their lives; this meaning-making is a crucial part of human existence. This, I believe, has been the central aim of conversations about vocation from the beginning.

The second term, *myth-making*, expresses the manner in which we construct our self. "Humans are story tellers by nature."[2] Our stories are communal; they rely on (and indeed, our thinking is conditioned by) identifiable patterns of meaning-making, culturally shared content, and common tropes. But when we use stories to narrate our lives, their content and the processes through which we shape them are quite personal and highly individual.[3] Additionally, Jerome Bruner tells us that we know how to tailor a story to our purpose—"beginning with those sly twists that shift the blame for the spilt milk to a younger sibling"—and we recognize this capacity in others, but "we are not very good at grasping how story explicitly 'transfigures the commonplace.'"[4] That is, we don't always recognize the power of the stories we tell. In this vein, McAdams tells us, "Enduring human truths still reside primarily in myth, as they have done for centuries."[5] In other words, narrative and story rise to the level of *myth* when they speak to things beyond the mundane, to some deeper truth.[6] Jonathan Z. Smith has convinced me that—accepting the risks of using simple language—*myths are the stories with*

---

2. Dan P. McAdams, *The Stories We Live By: Personal Myths and the Making of Self* (New York: William Morrow, 1993), 27.

3. See McAdams, *Stories We Live By*, chapter 9.

4. Jerome Bruner, *Making Stories: Law, Literature, Life* (Cambridge, MA: Harvard University Press, 2002), 3–4.

5. McAdams, *Stories We Live By*, 11.

6. See Charlotte Linde, *Life Stories: The Creation of Coherence* (New York: Oxford University Press, 1993), 98–126.

which we think.[7] They are the narratives we tell in order to think about and understand those things that really matter—and thereby determining that they *do* matter. The point is not to assert that myths are "true" (or to deny their truth), but to show that they *speak to* truth—even if not in literal or direct ways.

I assert that *myth* is central to grasping how we understand ourselves and the processes by which we construct the self. Unfortunately, the word *myth* is often flattened, reduced to one aspect of a complex whole; in popular imagination, a "myth" is simply "a false story." Parallels might be drawn to the flattening of the word *vocation*, which—although it can theoretically speak to all aspects of a fulfilled life—is often restricted to "work" or "profession," thereby devaluing much of what is key to the human condition.[8] Just as *vocation* can encompass more than one's job, myth can refer to more than the urban legends that are proven false in popular programs such as "MythBusters." In trying to recover the semantic richness of myth, we must understand it as both an object of human endeavor and a mode of human action. That is, a myth is a cultural artifact (something we make), and myth-making is a way of expressing our humanity (something we do).

So, we live in a mythologized world, but we are not the authors of most of the myths that animate our lives. We grow into personhood by inhabiting myths created by others. Dan McAdams asserts that personal myths do exist: "What myths traditionally have done on the level of culture, a personal myth can accomplish for a human being."[9] Nevertheless, we are first mythologized by others. Our first myths, communal and personal, are inherited. Only when we draw on, and react to, older myths—and thus begin to demythologize or remythologize them—are we able to become myth-makers.

---

7. Smith's more fulsome expression is: "myth is best conceived not as primordium, but rather a limited collection of elements with fixed range of cultural meanings which are applied, thought with, worked with, experimented with in particular situations." Jonathan Z. Smith, *Map Is Not Territory: Studies in the History of Religions* (Leiden: E. J. Brill, 1978), 308. See also McAdams, *Stories We Live By*, 33–34, and Jo-Ann Episkenew, *Taking Back Our Spirits: Indigenous Literature, Public Policy, and Healing* (Winnipeg: University of Manitoba Press, 2009), 109. We see this idea in fiction as well: "I know now that legends in themselves have no power. The power comes from the uses that the living make of the legend. The legends merely represent the ideal." Michael Moorcock, *The Fortress of the Pearl* (New York: Ace Books, 1990), 183.

8. See Christine M. Fletcher, "Laboring in the Garden: Vocation and the Realities of Work," in *Vocation across the Academy: A New Vocabulary for Higher Education*, ed. David S. Cunningham (New York: Oxford University Press, 2017), 183–203; and Margaret E. Mohrmann, "'Vocation Is Responsibility': Broader Scope, Deeper Discernment," in Cunningham, ed., *Vocation across the Academy*, 21–43; here, 38–41.

9. McAdams, *Stories We Live By*, 34.

Our stories rise to the level of myths when they speak to the truths of who we are and who we are becoming—perhaps even transfiguring the mundane into the sacred. They can do so by culminating in an "act of imagination that is a patterned integration of our remembered past, perceived present, and anticipated future."[10] Similarly, when our stories are "so fraught with meaning that we live and die by them," they become "maps by which [we] navigate through time."[11] When these stories "are applied, thought with, worked with, experimented with"[12] over time, they become myths. This is the opportunity presented by a myth-understanding of vocation: not merely to inhabit the vocational myths of our ancestors, but to craft our own.

My myths

In this section, I model the process by which myth-making helps us to understand ourselves by offering a personal account. My hope is that this may serve (as one set of resources among many) to help those seeking to understand themselves and to craft a fulfilled life. Before I turn to my own myths, however, I need to offer a further reflection on my method.

Pedagogical prolegomena

In my role as a professor of religion, I sometimes bring to the classroom the intent of deconstructing the (what I assume to be) ill-constructed worldviews held by some of my students. Unfortunately, I seldom give them time to *reconstruct* something with the pieces left after this savage act, nor do I regularly model how they might undertake such reconstruction. I see one aspect of my job to be giving them critical tools—to reveal hegemony and oppression, to identify racism and sexism, and to discern lines of power that stretch out from the ideas they cherish. However, I rarely move beyond such deconstruction and have recently begun to liken my pedagogical approach to the work of a mechanic who takes a car apart and—having asked the owners whether they were paying attention—"allows" them to reassemble it themselves.[13] In this chapter, I am attempting to take a small step away from

10. McAdams, *Stories We Live By*, 12.

11. Episkenew, *Taking Back Our Spirits*, 109.

12. Smith, *Map Is Not Territory*, 308.

13. I do not suggest abandoning such open-ended pedagogy entirely. We can understand the decision not to resolve the tensions that arise from a critical engagement with a religious

this approach and to articulate how I put the seemingly disparate pieces of my own life into my own myth of self. I hope that others may find some aspects of my project instructive for understanding their own efforts at self-construction.

I begin with a few of the myths that have animated my own self-understanding. First, an origin story: a personal cosmogonic myth.

An origin myth

My father was a Russian linguist in the Air Force. He was an enlisted man, stationed in Wakkanai, Japan, when I was born. My mother had it rough in Japan—living between the tofu factory, the crematorium, and the fish market for most of her pregnancy. Nevertheless, she found ways—some healthy, some not—to deal with the isolation of a military wife there and in Berlin, my father's next duty station. There my sister was born and I was diagnosed with cancer. After a near-immediate medical evacuation and the removal of a grapefruit-sized, tumor-ravaged kidney from my two-year-old body, the tone was set for the next two decades of my life and that of my family. I was already the number one son to parents longing for the ideal life of the 1950s; after skillful surgery, chemotherapy, and radiation, I was transformed into "the boy who lived," saved by God for a special purpose.

This story qualifies as myth, not because of the mention of God, but because it speaks to the truths of who I am—and does so in the terms suggested by the various commentators cited in the last section. It speaks to my past (the discovery of cancer), present (the relationships with my parents), and future (my "special purpose"). It is fraught with meaning for me, in that it defined my disease as purposeful and proposed a map that I could use to navigate through my life—namely, seeking my divine purpose. Finally, it is a myth in that most of my childhood was understood through this narrative. This myth speaks to truths of who I am, but it is inadequate for understanding who I am: it only tells part of my life (failing to include, for example, that I am one of four siblings), and its relevance diminishes as I get older (as the impact of cancer is overwhelmed by other experiences).

---

tradition—for example, a critical reading of the early church fathers—to "force [students] to accept the truth of the complicated origins of their tradition, in which they still abide" (Jeff Robbins, personal communication). Moreover, if we are convinced that questions are often more important than answers, then providing the tools for undertaking critical inquiry is central to our role as educators (Rachel Mikva, personal communication).

Origin stories are intriguing; they seem to speak to the essence of who we are, but they are limited in scope. This is true of the two creation stories in Genesis (Gen. 1.1–2.4 and Gen. 2.5–3.24), the three (at least[14]) Vedic creations hymns (*RV* 1.32, 10.90, and 10.129), and the four accounts of Jesus in the canonical Gospels.[15] In each case, something fundamental is offered about the nature of humanity, but these accounts only scrape the surface.

The vast majority of knowledge about humanity is told in other myths—and so too with our personal myths. For example, my next myth is a coming-of-age story; it may even rise to the level of etiological myth, explaining how things came to be as they are.

An etiological myth

I grew up Catholic, attending the church found on whichever military base where my father was stationed. But I remember best the large church in Ft. Meade, Maryland, operated by two priests—as unalike in personality and demeanor as any two people I knew then—and several nuns, whose focus, in my nostalgic reflections, was education. It was in confirmation class, with peers from my high school, that I faced my first conscious cognitive dissonance. The idealist view of the world I held—steeped in an absolutist notion of truth—contrasted deeply with my experience at the time, which was that of a crisis of faith. Both of my Sunday School teachers, one a convert and one a cradle Catholic, urged what in retrospect would be called the "fake it till you make it" approach. This offended my underdeveloped notion of truth. "How could I stand before God and affirm, swear to the truth of, the Nicene Creed?" I asked myself. "What could God abhor more than a hypocrite?" In the end, I did all the bookwork and, to the extent I was able, the emotional and spiritual work. But I did not complete the ritual; instead, I sat in the pews silently as my peers were confirmed in their faith. The next day—at least as it is reckoned in mythic time—I began reading Huston Smith's *The Religions of Man*.

The main purpose in sharing this myth is to recognize it as key for making sense of my rejection of religion. Additionally, it illustrates that our myths reflect their time of origin. This myth predates any development of a perspective on my historical context, which only came later. For example, only in retrospect

14. Wendy Doniger includes seven in her translation of selected hymns: *The Rig Veda* (New York: Penguin, 1981).

15. Also in many noncanonical gospels. See Willis Barnstone, ed., *The Other Bible* (New York: HarperSanFrancisco, 2005); Bart Ehrman, *Lost Christianities: The Battle for Scripture and the Faiths We Never Knew* (New York: Oxford University Press, 2005).

did I understand those first two decades to be colored by the race-consciousness of my father (himself a son of Detroit white-flight), as well as my mother, who bore similar conceptions of people of color. In addition, both were products (and carriers) of the gender politics of their generation. Only when I met, dated, and eventually married Margery did that perspective begin to widen.

The myth I share next tells that tale and encompasses the last two decades of my life; it is a myth of fruition and loss.

A marriage myth

Before getting married, Margery and I stumbled through life; we considered options for jobs and, vaguely, careers. We talked about our religious differences—she was a nonpracticing Jew and I a lapsed Catholic with a growing affinity for atheism—but this only seemed important in conversations with our parents. We were conscious of class differences when we compared my military family to hers, which included lawyers, a neurosurgeon, a speech pathologist, and an engineer. Our lives focused primarily on work, thinking mostly about how to make enough money to support our spending habits. My dalliance with atheism led to curious choices in college, especially for a computer science major. Eventually I stumbled through to an Interdisciplinary Studies degree and, emulating a favorite professor, decided to become an academic.

The naïveté of youth, which compelled me to avoid confirmation, presented marriage to me as a simple thing: love the other person and work at it, and everything will turn out fine. And that commitment sustained us into dual "careers" in retail, past the shoals of extended family (upon which some marriages crash), and through the various small forms of stupidity we each inflicted upon the other. We learned and grew together. Two key moments in our lives, each productive of enormous stress, coincided and were overcome: at the moment I had decided to pursue graduate school and to step on the path to being a professor, we discovered my wife was pregnant. We ultimately decided to take on both challenges, fully aware that the weight would not fall evenly on both of us; still, I vowed not to make her a graduate school widow.

For the most part, I managed to enjoy school, marriage, and my son's formative years. My wife followed me first from Baltimore to Tallahassee, then to Austin, and finally to just outside Hershey, Pennsylvania, where I now work as a religion professor. I thought I understood what I asked of her. I thought I told her enough for us to decide what was best *for both of us*. I thought that the partnership we had forged over 16 years was working. I heard frustrations and expressions of loss; I trusted her to tell me what she needed. I understood all of these efforts to be my part in a covenant that made us both stronger. I told myself I did it all for her and for my son. I didn't hear the echoes of my own distant father's voice, a man who missed so much of my life because he was working hard "for us."

For want of space, I resist the urge to analyze this myth too closely. It is sufficient for my purposes here to say two things. First, it complements the last myth, in that it describes my journey from saved child to an atheist religion professor and completes a narrative arc. Second, it is an example of a myth of self that serves as a tool for self-reflection—think here of Smith's "stories we think with"—an analysis of which would lie outside the scope of an academic paper.

A vocation myth

As I wrote this chapter and considered which stories to employ in modeling how to think about vocation, I thought and talked about the stories of the time between my youth and my current life. I was certain, despite conscious choices described thus far, that I had no myth of how I became a professor. The process largely involved emulating mentors and was punctuated by moments of reflection and what might pass for "planning for career aspirations"; for the most part, however, I meandered from one short-term goal to another. I had some general sense of a destination on the horizon, but no sense of the terrain between here and there. I could see Mount Doom and had the Ring, but I had no idea of how to reach my goal, other than walking in that direction. (Readers might notice that I was already "mything" myself, but I hadn't realized it yet.)

When I had strung together elements of my journey—which I understood as stories, not myths—these elements almost inevitably became a myth not of my own making: the myth of the American Dream. This was reinforced by many kind listeners, who would comment on my intelligence or drive, on the hard work that must be involved in working a full-time job while going to school, or on the special gift necessary to achieve a doctorate. Usually, I allowed my story to be inscribed within this national myth. Still, I knew that most of my graduate school colleagues were smarter and more driven than I was, and worked harder than I did. I pursued this direction in life because something in my head told me I had no choice. It was an obligation to use my gift; it was expected of me.

The biggest influences were not those factors over which I had control—effort, dedication, or planning—but rather, those over which I had no control. These included my race, my gender, the support of those around me who saw more in me than I could at the time, the perfectly timed "nudge" from a friend or colleague to do this or that, and a lot of luck—in short, all those factors pressing in upon each of us as we navigate our way through the world. It just happened that most of the currents in the river of life—or at least, the parts in which I swam—pushed me with gentle currents and in good directions. But that doesn't tell a very good story; it has no hero.[16] More important, it reflects a failure to understand or accept my own agency.

McAdams tells us, "We first become self-conscious mythmakers . . . when we confront head-on the problem of identity in human lives."[17] In my own case, I had merely inhabited others' myths, allowing them to inscribe me in the myth of the American Dream. McAdams and Bruner suggest that we are all myth-makers, but this claim misses a key aspect of how myth works: constructing a self through myth-making—that is, becoming a myth-maker—requires moving beyond merely inhabiting the myths of others.

Becoming a myth-maker

At a certain point in my life, I became conscious of my storytelling as a form of myth-making. I realized I hadn't drawn on the Catholic myths of my youth to craft my personal myths; perhaps this is why I initially failed to recognize that it was a form of myth-making. Instead, I had found other sources. McAdams tells us that we draw from more than just religious narratives for our personal myth-making; however, when he turns to specify alternative sources, he focuses on television.[18] I would also include novels, comics, movies, and other popular cultural artifacts, as well as our professions. In my own case, my professional work in the field of world religions provides me with vast reserves of raw material. I can draw upon the "mythologies" of works on method and theory, as well as the mythologies of the various religious perspectives that I have studied. And these are located, not just in "traditional" religious belief, but in corporate structures of entertainment and leisure as well. Reflecting on the role of religion in the modern world, Eric Mazur and Tara Koda argue that

> because contemporary trends in American religion have created a situation in which nonreligious entities and activities are often used for personal religious (or "spiritual") ends, Americans (and others) can find in Disney many elements they once found exclusively in traditional religion.[19]

---

16. McAdams speaks at length about the importance, function, and typology of the "main characters," which he calls imagoes, in our life stories (*Stories We Live By*, 117–32).

17. McAdams, *Stories We Live By*, 36.

18. McAdams, *Stories We Live By*, 13.

19. Eric Michael Mazur and Tara K. Koda, "The Happiest Place on Earth: Disney's America and the Commodification of Religion," in *God in the Details: American Religion in Popular Culture*, ed. Eric Michael Mazur and Kate McCarthy (New York: Routledge, 2001), 313.

For me, being a professor has done something very similar. Academia has become my "religion," and it offers rich resources for mythic inspiration.

The moment of awaking consciously to my own myth-making came in a discussion of one particular religious text, the *Bhagavadgita*. It created a moment of insight that led me to a better understanding of my own myths of self, as well as to the myth-understanding of vocation that I describe in this chapter.

Seeing my own reflection

The *Bhagavadgita* is part of the great Hindu epic, the *Mahabharata*—a text that has long been for me a thought-provoking reflection on the nature of humanity. It is a vast storehouse of Hindu myth and discourse about *dharma* (duty), framed in a narrative about a contest for the throne between two sets of cousins, the Pandavas and the Kauravas. The narrative is an exciting tale of intrigue, treachery, magic, and—ultimately—war. Understanding the *Bhagavadgita* requires recognizing that the *Mahabharata* abounds with not only noble heroes and despicable villains but also honorable villains and heroes who cheat (not surreptitiously or accidently, but intentionally and unabashedly). The epic recognizes and portrays vividly how difficult it is to determine the proper behavior in any situation—that is, how complex it can be to determine the right path to a fulfilling life.

The *Bhagavadgita* comes at the climax of the epic, as the Pandavas face off against the Kauravas; they are about to begin the war that will engulf nearly all of India. Arjuna looks across the battlefield at his cousins, his archery teacher, and others to whom he owes loyalty as members of his family. He is torn between his *kula-dharma*, the duty to one's kin, and *ksatriya-dharma*, his duty as a warrior, which urges him to use force to secure the kingdom that he and his brothers are due. The *Bhagavadgita*'s protagonist is caught on the horns of a dilemma. This epic poem captures the tension we all experience when our conscience pushes us in two different directions that seem equally good—when our hearts urge us toward two opposing goals.[20] This tension arises from our desire for the world to be simple, for moral choices to be clear, for our hearts to be whole. Instead, the *Mahabharata* shows us the world is far from simple; indeed, it is cruel and confusing.

---

20. See Jason A. Mahn, "The Conflicts in Our Callings: The Anguish (and Joy) of Willing Several Things," in Cunningham, ed., *Vocation across the Academy*, 44–66. See also Noah Silverman's reflections on "conflicting allegiances" in chapter 7 of this volume.

Another writer in this volume takes up the significance of the *Bhagavadgita* for questions relating to vocation and to how we define our lives.[21] As we compared our respective interpretations of the text, two revelations arose for me. First, I realized I had been myth-making all along: I was using all the raw materials of my life—academic, fictional (predominately sci-fi and fantasy), and religious—to construct my myth of self. This helped me reframe the manner in which I engage questions of self-construction and understand the porous nature of the various contexts in which I live. Second, it occurred to me that the *Bhagavadgita* was illustrative of the dilemmas inherent in our discussion of vocation.

This key moment in the narrative arc of the *Mahabharata* captures the dynamic nature of our lives, within which we must make decisions. It articulates the complexity of motives and loyalties—both within us and pulling at us from outside—as well as the trouble we face in sorting through the variety of advice coming our way. It conveys the sense of how important those life-altering decisions feel. We can feel the stress of seeing such moments as irreversible.

However, this narrative also forced me to formulate for myself (and affords me the opportunity to articulate here) my perspective on self-construction. I now return to the three themes mentioned at the outset of this chapter: the dynamic, retrospective, and agential aspects of myth-making. Drawing from my own complex pool of mythic influences, I offer my readers an understanding of the dynamic conception of self, the retrospective aspect of self-construction, and the complexity of our agency as a tool for seeking a fulfilled and fulfilling life.

Dynamic selfhood

First, our identities are dynamic.[22] They consist of many different aspects—psychological, emotional, biological, social, cultural—that manifest themselves differently in different contexts; these elements are shaped and nurtured in various ways as we grow and develop. The context influences which aspects of one's self manifest themselves, and whether they do so more or less strongly. I am less professorial when I am with my son; I am less fatherly when I am in the classroom.

---

21. See Anantanand Rambachan's discussion in chapter 6 of this volume. See also his essay "Worship, the Public Good, and Self-Fulfillment," in *Calling in Today's World: Voices from Eight Faith Perspectives*, ed. Kathleen Cahalan and Douglas Schuurman (Grand Rapids, MI: Eerdmans, 2016), 107–32.

22. See the related comments by Trina Jones and Younus Mirza in chapters 2 and 4 of this volume, respectively.

Still, neither of these two elements of my self is entirely absent in either context. Additionally, these aspects, and the context in which they are shaped, change over time. Because of this dynamism of self, self-construction is not an activity we can accomplish at any one moment in our life, let alone the first year of college. We are the sum of too many constantly changing variables to expect to be able to make a single firm plan, or to expect that plan to work.

Arjuna knew well the role assigned to him by society when he completed his training as a warrior. However, after many twists and turns, it was a thoroughly transformed Arjuna who pulled Krishna aside to ask for advice before the big battle. The future envisioned by a young warrior prince was waylaid by vicissitudes of the contest with his cousins for the crown. When he stood poised on the edge of battle, he had to reassess his purpose in life. This strikes me as parallel to the experience of dislocation and confusion that can arise as one's plans are waylaid by life. Each of us needs to take the time to consider the ways in which the ever-changing context may be reshaping us and our plans.

Another implication of this dynamism is that our self is never complete; it is constantly in process. Buddhism offers us resources for understanding this in the terms *paticca samuppada* (interdependent origination) and *anicca* (impermanence). The former indicates that everything is inexorably interconnected and interrelated; I will return to this idea shortly. The latter tells us that all states are transient, that our conventional notions of ourselves are illusions of continuity that conceal perpetual change. This reminder, that our selves are perpetually changing, does not deny the possibility of continuity, but it does reinforce the idea that the only constant is change. As we grow and change, our stories change as well.

We rarely tell a story exactly the same way twice; we revise and edit, generating multiple versions of the tale. These are not necessarily selfishly motivated redactions; they illustrate the impact of context and audience on the telling—and, thereby, on our conception of ourselves. Since no single story can tell the entire tale of who we are, we construct multiple myths of self. Yet we never really tell the entire "story of us," even when we believe that we have offered up the full complement of our myths of self.[23] It is only through the multiplicity of our myths, in two senses—their plurality and their changing nature—that we can hint at the complex reality of who we truly are. The process of myth-making is a lifelong endeavor, because we are still in the process of making the life that our myths will define.

---

23. Linde acknowledges that life stories often feature "temporal discontinuity and structural openness" and remarks that the life story is "a rather odd unit. . . . [A]t any given telling of one of its component parts, it is incomplete" (*Life Stories*, 25–37).

Retrospective self-construction

A second point: self-construction necessarily occurs retrospectively.[24] We walk through life backward, unable to see the future any more clearly than with a quick glance over our shoulder. Walking like this, we are more prone to stumble than we like to admit; the accidents of birth that set us on this path, rather than another, often determine whether we will stumble or not. Other bits of luck, both good and bad, influence our direction and speed. People further ahead can see our paths so much more clearly than we can, but it is hard to hear them (facing the past as we are). While their longer and broader experience makes their voices more valuable, their existential and experiential distance makes it harder to hear their advice and warnings—especially when we are young. As we grow older, the trajectories of our paths are more easily understood—just as it was for those behind us (who are, of course, ahead of us).

One key moment in the epic that includes the *Bhagavadgita* illustrates the retrospective nature of self-construction. The Pandavas, exiled to wander the land in obscurity, were required to remain anonymous in their last year of exile; otherwise, they risked another twelve years of wandering. Adventures during their travels allowed them to accumulate knowledge, weapons, skills, and boons that would ensure their anonymity in that final year. On one such adventure, during a visit to Indra's world, Arjuna met Urvasi, a celestial nymph. He came to look upon her as a mother or a sister, despite her efforts to seduce him. This pricked the pride of this supernatural beauty, and she cursed him to be unrecognizable in the near future. This "curse" eventually enabled Arjuna to remain anonymous for the last year of their exile.

A traditional reading—one that coheres with theistic deployments of "vocational discernment"—sees this turn of events (and others) as destiny, fate, a mechanism of karma, or the hand of God working to support the heroes. But these events take on a different sense if religion is understood as an unfolding process of the *imposition* of meaning on the universe by human beings, rather than as a *revelation* of meaning inherent in the universe.

We are most aware of (and preoccupied with) those aspects of our past that illuminate the present moment. We can look back and see "destiny," or at least meaningful synchronicity, in a coincidental meeting with a person who later comes to be special to us. We hear the same thing when friends observe some event in our lives and endow it with meaning by telling us that "there is no such

24. See the comments of Younus Mirza about "connecting the dots" at the beginning of chapter 4 of this volume. See also William T. Cavanaugh, "Actually, You *Can't* Be Anything You Want (And It's a Good Thing, Too)," in Cunningham, ed., *At This Time*, 25–46.

thing as coincidence." I view these tendencies as an expression of the human bias toward patterns and our predisposition toward meaning-making. Psychologists explain such biases by pointing to cognitive processes like pareidolia (the tendency to perceive meaningful patterns in random or ambiguous stimuli),[25] as well as confirmation bias (the tendency to interpret new data as supporting one's previously held position). Popular fiction offers us a more colloquial understanding in Ambassador G'Kar's response to the question, What is the truth, and what is God?:

> If I take a lamp and shine it toward the wall, a bright spot will appear on the wall. The lamp is our search for truth, for understanding. Too often we assume that the light on the wall is God, but the light is not the goal of the search, it is the result of the search. The more intense the search, the brighter the light on the wall. The brighter the light on the wall, the greater the sense of revelation upon seeing it. Similarly, someone who does not search, who does not bring a lantern with him, sees nothing. What we perceive as God is the by-product of our search for God.[26]

G'Kar does not doubt God's existence; instead, he cautions us concerning our tendency to underestimate the influence of our own biases on our perceptions.

Significantly, for our discussion of self-construction, these same tendencies inform our efforts at myth-making. We selectively invoke events that align with our self-conception and use them in our self-construction; we determine which moments are defining and which are insignificant by ascribing meaning to them. McAdams connects this selection to Mircea Eliade's work on myth when he argues that "by 'selectively reconstructing the past,' as Eliade puts it, we attain the status of 'creator.'"[27]

To return to the example from the *Bhagavadgita*, this process of retrospectively rendering moments meaningful is illustrated at the moment the Pandavas needed to go into exile. They redefined those curses and boons as instrumental in their immediate future; they altered their self-understanding to *make* select events important. So too do we all re-evaluate moments in our lives, reorienting

25. An internet search for images related to *pareidolia* produces some interesting results.

26. "Meditations on the Abyss," Babylon 5: The Complete Fifth Season, written by J. Michael Straczynksi, directed by Mike Vejar, Warner Brothers, 1998, DVD.

27. McAdams, *Stories We Live By*, 91.

our understanding of our past in the light of the present moment, to *make* them significant.[28]

Conversely, we regularly render formerly meaningful moments meaningless. We all have stories we *used to* tell—stories that are no longer relevant to us, that no longer tell the truth of who we are. My cosmogonic myth defined who I was for the first two decades of my life; however, while I am still a cancer survivor, that particular myth is less relevant to how I understand my self (and how I narrate it) today.[29] The other myths I shared have greater impact, not simply because they narrate events closer to the present, but because I deem them more relevant to who I am right now, in the present moment.

The retrospective nature of myth-making explains some of the anxiety inherent in finding meaning in our lives. We don't know if the calling we hear or the instincts we follow are fair or foul.[30] In the moment of choosing, we are blind to the consequences; it is only after the fact that we *may* be able to justify our choices. Arjuna's efforts at determining his purpose is vastly different from ours, in that God himself is telling him what to do. He does not grapple with the uncertainty that we must. Michael Moorcock expresses this idea in a different warrior's tale—that of Elric of Melniboné:

> "Fate is cruel, Oone. It would be better if it provided us with one unaltered path. Instead it forces us to make choices and then never to know if those choices were for the best."
>
> "We are mortals," she said with a shrug. "That is our particular doom."[31]

These pitfalls do not invalidate our myth-making. We may not be able to see the ending or discern well the next few steps on our journey; nevertheless, this does not mean that our stories cannot speak to our goals. It does mean, however, that our stories grow and change, alongside changes in our experiences, knowledge, perspectives, and sense of direction.

---

28. What Bruce Lincoln says about religious actors describes this well: "What we have is a situation of mutual mediation, in which the actor's temporal situation of interest provides the lens through which he consults the canonic, putatively timeless text." See *Holy Terrors: Thinking about Religion after September 11* (Chicago: University of Chicago Press, 2006), 35.

29. Ancient religious texts, for example, Genesis and the *Ṛg* veda, are not significant because they survived; they survived because people continue to make them significant.

30. In chapter 12 of this volume, Tracy Sadd addresses this point, which is also present in Frederick Buechner's pithy expression: "The problem is to find out which is the voice of God rather than of Society, say, or the Superego, or Self-Interest." *Wishful Thinking: A Seeker's ABC*, revised and expanded edition (New York: HarperSanFrancisco, 1993), 118–19.

31. Moorcock, *Fortress*, 192–93.

Agency

Finally, the manner in which we construct our myths of self rests on the idea of agency: the idea that neither are we completely independent actors, nor are all our actions determined by historical precedent or cultural norms. As agents, we engage in myth-making in the space—ever-changing, sometimes narrow, sometimes wide—between cultural determinism and absolute independence. Our conception of how much choice we have is influenced by our social and cultural positions, and by the myths we inhabit as we mature. The level of autonomy we possess is not only contingent upon our context; it is also variable throughout our lives. The only way to grapple with this complex situation is to be aware—of ourselves as actors, of how our context influences our actions, and of the impact our choices have on us, others, and the world—and to be conscientious in those actions we are able to take, and the myths we are able to craft.

The *Bhagavadgita* illustrates this as well. Arjuna is not merely a military automaton trained only for war and ready to slay the enemy when the need arises; he makes choices. His actions are not determined only by the duty to his family (including, as it does, relatives on the opposite front of the impending war). Nor is he absolutely free; he cannot ignore the cultural expectations, socially imposed duties, and personal desires that he feels. He is portrayed as a man caught between the many duties pulling him in opposing directions. So too are we all faced with dilemmas repeatedly. We are never perfectly aware of the context within which we make our decisions, nor of the outcomes of our choices. Nevertheless, we accept that we are capable of choice. Arjuna seeks advice from Krishna, weighs the options available to him (as an agent in a complex social, religious, and cultural environment), and seeks to act responsibly—just as we should.

This sense of responsibility stems from our ability to choose—even if we disagree about the extent of our agency—and extends to the power implied in myth-making as well. No story is innocent; likewise, no myth, "speaking to truth" as it does, is innocent. Myth-making—capable of demythologizing, remythologizing, or rehabilitating myth—defines those whom it mythologizes. Myth-making risks reducing people, ourselves and others, to characters or archetypes. Further, it has the potential to effect real harm in the world.

If our life story is to be a myth, it must speak to truth; it must also speak to our true self. By this, I do not mean to imply "a bedrock to our personalities" or a simplistic "combination of our convictions and abilities";[32] the true self is dynamic,

32. Adam Grant, "Unless You're Oprah, 'Be Yourself' Is Terrible Advice," http://nyti.ms/22Fi3eo (accessed January 31, 2017).

not a static unchanging essence. Our myths of self must be authentic.[33] Adam Grant suggests we "pay attention to how we present ourselves to others, and then strive to be the people we claim to be."[34] We owe it to ourselves to find (create) our true selves and live them.

The myths we tell each other affect those around us as well. This is an example of the Buddhist concept of interdependent origination, the idea that all living beings are inexorably interconnected and interrelated. In essence, this speaks to the fact that all phenomena are both effect and cause—each event is caused by something previous to it and causes something subsequent to it—in short, nothing is independent or permanent. Further, this idea asserts that everything is a part of a complex web of interconnections in a perpetual process of change. Each of us is a part of this web of effects and causes. Just as our lives are interwoven with the lives of others, so are our stories interrelated. For each hero, our myths (must) create an innocent bystander, a villain,[35] and other characters shaped in ways good and bad by the myth. Mainstream white myths about Martin Luther King Jr. and Malcolm X typically reduce the complex humanity of these two individuals by telling us only the good parts and only the bad parts, respectively.[36] These accounts do more than merely shape the ways that whites conceive of, and interact with, people of color; they also constrain the interactions between citizens and the state (in, for example, protests).

On a more personal level, the myth my parents told about me surviving cancer—"the boy who lived"—shaped the way I understood who I was. It contributed to my becoming an egocentric, arrogant teenager, thereby influencing my interaction with the world. Reinforced by dominant gender narratives, that myth was significant for my sister in more traumatizing ways. While that myth plays a lesser role in my current self-conception, the same events—understood differently through my sister's own myths—may or may not be relevant to her today, depending on what she has made meaningful through her own myth-making efforts. If we accept the power of myth and take up the challenge to be

33. See also Hannah Schell, "Commitment and Community: The Virtue of Loyalty and Vocational Discernment," in Cunningham, ed., *At This Time,* 235–54, as well as Mahn, "Conflicts in Our Callings."

34. Grant, "Unless You're Oprah."

35. For an insightful analysis of the political mobilization of *Ramayana* in the divinization of kings and the demonization of his enemies, see Sheldon Pollock, "Rāmāyana and Political Imagination in India," *Journal of Asian Studies* 52, no. 2 (May 1993): 261–97.

36. James H. Cone describes the making of popular images of King and Malcolm X and offers a more complex interpretation of their legacy. See his *Martin & Malcolm & America: A Dream or a Nightmare* (Maryknoll, NY: Orbis Books, 1991).

our own myth-makers, we must remember that with great power comes great responsibility.

Myth-making to empower and ennoble

I believe any successful effort at self-construction—or if you prefer, vocational discernment—must recognize three factors that are inherent in the development of our self-understanding through myth-making. First, our myths are dynamic, because they describe and constitute a self that is dynamic—ever-changing, yet marked by certain continuities. Second, we craft these stories in retrospect, as we walk backward through time, gaining more perspective and thereby better understanding who we are (and the world around us). Third, in crafting these myths, we occupy the (perpetually variable) space between cultural or historical determinism and complete free will. That agency allows us some say in who we are, but it also lays upon us great responsibility. If we are attentive to the power of myth and accept the responsibility it imposes upon us, it can serve us in two ways. First, when we are able to recognize the risk inherent in myth and to remain wary of its destructive potential, we can employ myth not to subjugate others, but to empower them. Second, because each new retelling of an authentic myth of self better *reflects* who we are and better *informs* us of who we are, our myths can empower and ennoble us.

Response

Florence Amamoto

As the chapters in this book make clear, stories—those we read and those we create—can be important vehicles for reflecting on values, identity, and vocation. Matt's chapter, while providing us with examples of some of those stories, also challenges us to think more deeply and to be more intentional about what students will learn from the process of reading and creating their own stories and myths.

Matt's chapter points mostly to personal myths; these are certainly important, but he also mentions the cultural myths that also influence our students. Some of these seem especially pressing today: the value placed on individualism, the myth of competition, and the assumption that wealth and status are the best measures of success. Learning to see these as myths, particularly when also being introduced to multicultural or multi-faith perspectives, can perhaps help to loosen the grip of these cultural assumptions. Students may thereby be challenged to move beyond a focus only on the self, and to develop conceptions of the "good life" that include the *common* good.

The current generation of college students faces record levels of anxiety and depression. To them, Matt's emphasis on their own agency may not seem like good news, especially as they are simultaneously being urged to consider the world's great problems and to see the complexities of every situation. Arjuna's hesitations in the face of his conflicting responsibilities and desires would not be strange to today's college students. Perhaps it can also remind them that, yes, life is messy: there is no perfect solution, and sometimes you have to make a choice and carry on.

I remain committed to trying to challenge my students to see more deeply and broadly, and with more complexity, in order to make them better citizens of the world. But Arjuna's desire for guidance—and indeed Matt's chapter as a whole—have also challenged me to think more deeply and to be more intentional about the language I use and the lessons I teach. Matt's account has urged me to think about what I can do as a teacher, adviser, and mentor to encourage students to grow into the more thoughtful, aware, and purposeful selves that we would like them to be.

9

Attentiveness and Humor

VOCATION AS AWAKENING TO SELF

Homayra Ziad

IN HER TIMELY ethnographic study of Muslim American undergraduate women on US college campuses post-9/11, Shabana Mir raises questions about the ideal of pluralism in campus life.[1] She argues that the "stereotyping, double consciousness, self-surveillance, and essentialism,"[2] which is imposed on Muslim Americans in the broader American political and cultural landscape, also deeply marks the experience of Muslim students on college campuses:

> Though identity options on U.S. campuses are becoming almost cliché in their multiplicity, . . . these options are not freely available to all. Nor are these "options" chosen lightly: for Muslims, whose background and lifestyles span a dizzying range, identity choices can be explosive. For minoritized people in a racist social order, these are not really choices at all.[3]

Mir contends that students' identities are fashioned and performed in response to a majority Orientalist gaze that reduces them to a caricature of a Muslim and not much else. Identities are also formed in response to campus cultures that accept diversity, but only as long as it is interesting and fun—not bold or

1. Shabana Mir, *Muslim American Women on Campus: Undergraduate Social Life and Identity* (Chapel Hill: University of North Carolina Press, 2016).

2. Mir, *Muslim American Women*, 15.

3. Mir, *Muslim American Women*, 3.

noticeable.[4] The students she interviewed also experience another form of reductive scrutiny from some fellow Muslims (peers, family, religious leaders, and other community members), who peddle an ideal of the imagined homogenous Muslim community—"good, devout Muslims united on religious doctrine and practice," presenting a unified voice in the public square.[5] And finally, the long arm of the War on Terror has led to public fixations on "security" with respect to Muslim-American identities, as well as the erosion of Muslim civil rights and the targeting of communities by political figures, law enforcement, and the security apparatus. These have all become an indelible presence in the lives of each of the students that Mir met. "This was the community I was investigating," writes Mir: "tense, tired, and under several layers of surveillance."[6]

What does this have to do with vocation? While the women Mir interviewed "sought a third space of uncertainty, flexibility, agency and pluralism," their efforts to cross borders were met with suspicion in both mainstream campus culture and the cultural spaces associated with their religious tradition.[7] Responding to simplistic constructs of who they ought to be or are expected to be, these students often chose either to make their religious identities invisible or to embrace them assertively. In both cases, however, religion functions as an identity marker—a badge to be ripped off or to be worn with stubborn tenacity. In his classic analysis of being black in America, W. E. B. Du Bois articulated the burden of double-consciousness—always seeing oneself through the eyes of another—"as a crisis of identity that threatened to tear the self asunder."[8] How does a student under duress, whose identity is performed in response to public scrutiny, discern purpose and meaning in her life? In performing her religious identity for the sake of others, what space is left for a student to establish a living connection with God and discern her own spiritual needs? How may she know the difference between performing and being?

Among students for whom publicly performing their religion is a daily ordeal, a recentering of self through vocational inquiry can be a lifeline. It can provide a way to live religion as the transformative, life-giving, dynamic presence

4. Mir, *Muslim American Women*, 175.

5. Mir, *Muslim American Women*, 5.

6. Mir, *Muslim American Women*, 8.

7. Mir, *Muslim American Women*, 125.

8. Rachel Mikva, "Brer Rabbit and the Destruction of the Temple in Jerusalem: The Double Voice in Literatures of Exile," *Comparative Literature Studies* 53, no. 1 (2016): 3.

of God, rather than an identity "framed by the majority gaze."[9] In this chapter, I introduce a number of resources from Islamic spiritual traditions that support vocational discernment and self-care, with an emphasis on the long tradition of Islamic virtue ethics, or the shaping of character.

The first section offers a brief description of three concepts that will arise throughout the chapter: vocation, spirituality, and character formation. It then turns to the tradition of Islamic spirituality (the Sufi tradition), describing how it interrelates and integrates these three elements. This provides the background for a more detailed discussion, in the following two sections, of two important habits of character: attentiveness and humor. The section on attentiveness draws from the hagiographical tradition of Islamic spirituality. Its protagonists come from a wide range of backgrounds and professions, and they experience—whether through a gradual process or a dramatic shift—an awakening to a more mindful life. These stories commend the cultivation of a keen attentiveness, recognizing that God is ever-present and will speak to the seeker in unexpected ways. The final section offers a reflection on humor as a tool on the vocational journey. Here too, many of the sources are narrative in form, and they commend the development of a certain kind of character through spiritual practice. The chapter concludes with a brief reflection on how cultivating these character traits can help students with the challenges they face today. In particular, attentiveness and humor may give students a better sense of the difference between performing and being—a very important distinction for the work of vocational discernment.

While I am particularly concerned with the vocational journeys of young people who are asked on a daily basis to perform their religion for others (within their communities and in the public square), these resources are likely to be of interest across a variety of religious and philosophical perspectives and lifestances. To the students who find themselves entwined in religious communities, I would stress that each individual has a different and unique journey with God, with its own rhythms, certainties, questions, and doubts—an ever-evolving and endless source of insight. And to all students, I would emphasize that the journey of self-inquiry must be the greatest commitment we ever make.

Islamic spirituality, vocation, and the shaping of character

I understand vocational inquiry as a spiritual journey, an awakening to the fullness of self in dialogue with the merciful presence of God. This definition resonates

9. Mir, *Muslim American Women*, 175.

with the broader idea of vocation as "calling," in that it moves the concept beyond a search for an appropriate occupation or career and toward a larger inquiry into individual meaning and purpose.[10] This understanding of vocational discernment implies a commitment to personal growth; it also means that, at least for some students, vocation will be integrally related to spirituality.

Drawing from Wayne Teasdale, I understand spirituality as "a contemplative attitude, a disposition to a life of depth, and the search for ultimate meaning, direction and belonging. The spiritual person is committed to growth as an essential ongoing life goal."[11] Teasdale's definition is taken up by Arthur Chickering, Jon Dalton, and Liesa Stamm, as they consider the role of spirituality in higher education. This definition provides a clue as to why, particularly for college-age students, spirituality is likely to be connected to larger questions of meaning, purpose, and identity:

> Spirituality is a way of life that affects and includes every moment of existence. It is at once a contemplative attitude, a disposition to a life of depth, and the search for ultimate meaning, direction and belonging. The spiritual person is committed to growth as an essential ongoing life goal. To be spiritual requires us to stand on our own two feet while being nurtured and supported by our tradition, if we are fortunate enough to have one.[12]

Hence, spirituality is closely related to the category of religion, but it is not identical:

> Being religious connotes belonging to and practicing a religious tradition. Being spiritual suggests a personal commitment to a process of inner development that engages us in our totality. Religion, of course, is one way many people are spiritual. Often, when authentic faith embodies an individual's spirituality the religious and the spiritual will coincide.[13]

---

10. For a history of the term and the parameters of the vocational conversation on college campuses, see David S. Cunningham, "Time and Place: Why Vocation is Essential to Undergraduate Education Today," introduction to *At This Time and In This Place: Vocation and Higher Education* (New York: Oxford University Press, 2017), 1–19; here, 8–9.

11. Wayne Teasdale, *The Mystic Heart: Discovering a Universal Spirituality in the World's Religions* (Novato, CA: New World Library, 1999), 17–18. Teasdale's definition is adopted in Arthur W. Chickering, Jon C. Dalton, and Liesa Stamm, *Encouraging Authenticity and Spirituality in Higher Education* (San Francisco: Wiley, Jossey–Bass, 2006).

12. Chickering, Dalton, and Stamm, *Encouraging Authenticity*, 7.

13. Chickering, Dalton, and Stamm, *Encouraging Authenticity*, 7.

This suggests that not only religious traditions but also spiritual traditions may be particularly important to some students, as they wrestle with the questions of meaning and identity that are closely bound up with vocation.

In turn, the particular spiritual and religious traditions that we practice make an indelible imprint on our character. Drawing on the age-old tradition of virtue ethics, educator Mark Schwehn makes a compelling case for making character formation central to conversations on vocation. Indeed, he sees this task as a fundamental responsibility of educators:

> To teach is to enable others to learn, and their learning depends not only on cognitive skills and abilities (qualities of mind), but also on habits and settled dispositions (qualities of character). These qualities include not only good judgment and intellectual clarity, but also patience, courage, perseverance, diligence, and even charity. They are the same qualities—known since antiquity as virtues—that constitute more generally a good and flourishing human life.[14]

This broader conversation has become a felt need on college campuses, leading to the growth of vocational discernment programs, both theological and secular in nature.[15]

I ground my own understanding of vocation in qur'anic anthropology, with reference to the long tradition of Islamic virtue ethics, the shaping of character.[16] For over a thousand years, Islamic spirituality (*tasawwuf*, or the Sufi tradition) has been a dynamic space for character formation. It is founded in the *shahadah*: there is no God but God, and Muhammad is the Messenger of God. This phrase serves as a reminder that there is no reality but God, and that the Prophet Muhammad provides a model for the moral life.

Sufi spirituality is not an alternative theological or legal school. Often called "the medicine of the soul," it is a devotional approach interwoven through mainstream Sunni schools of orthodox theology and law. It is a deeper integration of belief and practice, forging the intimate human-divine relationship that brought forth the Qur'an and that was experienced by the Prophet Muhammad on the

14. Mark R. Schwehn, "Good Teaching: Character Formation and Vocational Discernment," in *Vocation across the Academy: A New Vocabulary for Higher Education*, ed. David S. Cunningham (New York: Oxford University Press, 2017), 294–315; here, 295.

15. Cunningham, "Time and Place," 14.

16. al-Ghazzali, *Alchemy of Happiness*, trans. Jay R. Crook (Great Books of the Islamic World series) (Chicago: Kazi Publications, 2005), xliv.

night of spiritual ascension (*mi'raj*).[17] Islamic spirituality has often been named by its key practices: "cleansing the heart" or "purifying the ego-self" (*tasfiyat al-qalb, tazkiyat al-nafs*). The goal of this practice is *ihsan*: manifesting God's Beauty through the self into the world. The goal is perfection of character through a self-knowledge that connects us more deeply with the divine presence.

The primordial covenant

In *Alchemy of Happiness*, a guide to character formation, the pre-eminent medieval scholar and systematic theologian al-Ghazali tells us:

> Know that the key to the knowledge of God, may He be honored and glorified, is knowledge of one's own self. For this it has been said: He who knows himself knows his Lord. And it is for this that the Creator Most High said: *We shall show them the signs on the horizons and within themselves so that it will become evident to them that it is the Truth.* (Q 41:53)[18]

The Qur'an speaks of a moment in which every soul that would ever live was gathered before God and came face to face with its ultimate source of being:

> And mention when your Lord took from the children of Adam—from their generative organs—their offspring and called to them to witness of themselves: Am I not your Lord; they said: Yea! We bore witness
>
> So that you say not on the Day of Resurrection: Truly we had been ones who had been heedless of this.[19]

Islamic spirituality calls this event the "primordial covenant," in which each human soul bore witness that God is, indeed, the Sustainer (*Rabb*). To unearth the innate knowledge of who we are requires the development of self-consciousness—a trust given only to human beings: "We [God] offered the trust to the heavens and

17. Around the year 620, the Prophet Muhammad is said to have experienced the Night Journey and Ascension (*isra'* and *mi'raj*). According to accounts in the Qur'an and *hadith*, the angel Gabriel took the Prophet to Jerusalem, ascended with him through the heavens (where he was welcomed by earlier prophets), and brought him into the divine presence. This spiritual experience established Muhammad in the line of Abraham and is also considered the origin of the five daily prayers. The Ascension became a metaphor and template for spiritual experience.

18. al-Ghazzali, *Alchemy of Happiness*, lix.

19. Qur'an 7:172.

the earth and the mountains, but they refused to carry it and were afraid of it, and the human being carried it."[20]

As part of this covenant, every single human being is a *khalifah*, a steward and trustee of God on Earth.[21] This trust has both outer and inner dimensions; a *khalifah* stewards the world around her, but is also charged with cultivating self-awareness and articulating a moral voice. The inner dimension of stewardship is brought to fullness when our very presence in this world becomes an *ayah*, a Sign or living reflection of God's perfection. The relationship between God and humanity is articulated in the well-known teachings of the Prophet Muhammad, "God created Adam in God's image (*'ala suratihi*)" and "the offspring of Adam was created in the image of the Most Merciful." These verses have traditionally been understood to mean that the human being was created with the same attributes that God has used to describe Godself.

God is described by many Names in the Qur'an. Each Name is an attribute of God, and an expression of relationship. The Names include the creator, the sustainer, the loving, the giver of peace, the one who exalts and the one who brings low, the one who hears and the one who sees, the one who hides faults and the one who calls to account, the one who forgives and the one who avenges. Theological traditions are deeply aware of a delicious tension in the Qur'an between God's immanence and God's transcendence—God as intimately connected to, and yet utterly dissimilar from, the creation. Hence, God's attributes have been divided by theologians into those that emphasize immanence and those that emphasize transcendence: the former are the "Names of mercy" or "Names of intimacy," and the latter are the "Names of awe" or "Names of majesty." However, the two Names repeated far more than any other in the Qur'an are *al-Rahman* and *al-Rahim*, the Compassionate and the Merciful. Both Names are linguistically connected to the word *rahm*, the womb, where life is nourished and held close. The spiritual tradition emphasizes the immanent, merciful God, the God that is "closer than the jugular vein."[22] Divine mercy is the lens through which every Name is refracted.

The multiple Names of the divine in the Qur'an are reflected by the multiple attributes of the individual self. A harmonious self gives space to the healthy, balanced expression of each attribute, but honors mercy above all else. If mercy is the lens through which each divine Name is refracted, in the long tradition known as *imitatio dei* (the imitation of God), we are asked to refract and temper each of our

---

20. Qur'an 33:72.

21. al-Ghazzali, *Alchemy of Happiness*, lxii.

22. Qur'an 50:16.

impulses through mercy and so walk gently, but firmly, on this earth.[23] In Islamic spirituality, the Prophet Muhammad is the perfect human being and embodies in balance every divine attribute of mercy and majesty.

Cultivating character

The cultivation of a balance of positive attributes, refracted through mercy, is not a simple task. It requires following a discipline, which includes practices of detachment from material concerns, daily self-accounting, remembrance of God, and service to family and community. In this journey, the seeker becomes keenly aware of the deceptive nature of the ego-self (*nafs*), which leans toward a self-centered hubris. Spiritual discipline allows the seeker to rein in the ego-self while connecting with and activating the spirit (*ruh*). The spirit is the breath of God that resides, figuratively, in the spiritual heart (the seat of emotional intelligence, wisdom, and self-knowledge). The spirit is the breath of life that God breathed into Adam, the primordial human.[24] In this journey of ego-transformation, the seeker slowly but surely begins to cultivate positive character traits, while learning to identify and interrupt the destructive impulses of the ego-self.[25]

A key element in contemplative practice is the spiritual guide. If Sufi spirituality is the medicine of the soul, then the guide is the physician. Sufi theology and practice flow from the transcendent experience of God in the lives of beloved teachers (friends of God: *awliya allah*, Qur'an 10:62). These experiences shape students of Islamic spirituality through direct discipleship or through the study of hagiographical narratives that share stories of beloved teachers and their journeys of self-transformation. The tradition grounds the importance of the teacher in qur'anic theology and narratives of discipleship, such as the parable of Moses and the mysterious prophet-guide Khidr in the chapter *al-Kahf* (The Cave).

Having explored some of the interrelationships among Islamic spirituality, character formation, and vocation, I now turn to two specific dispositions that contribute to good character. Through the cultivation of these two habits of

---

23. Qur'an 25:63.

24. "I have fashioned him [Adam], and breathed into him of my spirit [*ruh*]" (Qur'an 15:29). For a note about the gender of *adam*, see Rachel Mikva's comments in chapter 1 of this volume.

25. It may be useful to compare this process to the cultivation of the virtues in both secular and religious traditions, which in turn has been closely aligned with the work of vocational reflection and discernment. For a brief list of relevant texts, see footnote 3 in Paul J. Wadell, "An Itinerary of Hope: Called to a Magnanimous Way of Life," in Cunningham, ed., *At This Time*, 193–215; here, 195. Part 3 of that volume is titled "Vocation and Virtue"; all three of its chapters provide an excellent discussion of the relationship between these two concepts.

mind and body, college students may find themselves better able to wrestle with the tensions and challenges described at the beginning of this chapter.

Attentiveness in the narrative tradition

Islamic narratives of call can often be found in the Sufi hagiographical tradition. These tales are cast as first-person accounts or third-person narratives of conversion to a more self-conscious and God-conscious life; they recount an experience of gradual awakening or dramatic turnaround. The protagonists in these stories range from perfume merchants and brigands to scholars and kings; that is, the call can come to anyone at any time. These tales often emphasize, first, the cultivation of a keen attentiveness to the Signs of God—recognizing that God may speak to us in the most unexpected of ways. (As the Qur'an teaches, "Wherever you turn, there is the Face of God.") These stories also emphasize the greater struggle (*jihad al-akbar*) against the self-absorption of the ego.[26] To illustrate the work of these narratives, I turn to a particularly rich example of the tradition.

The tale of Ibrahim ibn Adham

One of the most beloved spiritual narratives of self-discovery is the call story of Ibrahim ibn Adham. He was the sultan of Balkh, a cultural and economic center on the Silk Road in present-day Afghanistan, but he gave up his throne for a life of service in another key. His father was a poor dervish who lived in a cave; his mother was the princess of Balkh. They fell deeply in love after one glance from afar; they then endured a series of ordeals before they could finally be together as husband and wife.

Thus, on his mother's side, Ibrahim was descended from a lineage of rulers, and on his father's side, from a lineage of dervishes and spiritual seekers. His life journey was a struggle to integrate these two sides of himself—the public figure who enjoys the trappings of power and splendor, and the dervish who leads a life of solitude, service, and remembrance of God.[27] Among the many threads that are woven through the spiritual journey of this king-turned-mendicant is Ibrahim's increasing attentiveness to the Signs of God at work in the world. In the narratives that I will offer here, Ibrahim is party to a series of bizarre

26. John Renard, *Friends of God: Islamic Images of Piety, Commitment and Servanthood* (Berkeley: UCLA Press, 2008), 43–65.

27. Robert Frager, *Sufi Talks: Teachings of an American Sufi Sheikh* (Wheaton, IL: Theosophical Publishing House, 2012), 101–17.

conversations that cut like lightning bolts through his otherwise ordinary days. He is sharply rebuked on the absurdity of his condition by a stranger on the roof of his palace; he becomes aware of God's ever-responsive presence by a man tied to a tree; and he is reminded of the transient nature of wealth (and life itself) by a caravan guide.

> One day, Ibrahim was lying in bed, resting after his morning prayers. He thought about how he wanted God more than anything else. Just then, he heard a noise on the roof over his head. He went out on his balcony and saw a man walking on the roof of the palace. He asked, "What are you doing up there?"
>
> The man replied, "I'm looking for my camel."
>
> Ibrahim said in amazement, "Are you crazy? How can you find a camel up there on the roof of the palace?"
>
> The man answered, "it is just as likely that I can find a camel on the roof of your palace as you can find God lying in your fancy sultan's bed."[28]

> One day [Ibrahim] went out hunting with a group of companions. As they were eating lunch, a bird swooped down and grabbed a piece of bread from Ibrahim's plate. Ibrahim realized something strange was going on and he followed the bird. He came to a clearing and saw the bird drop the bread into the mouth of a man who was tied to a tree.
>
> The man asked, "Would you please untie me? I've been here for days, hoping someone might come along and rescue me."
>
> "What happened to you? How did you survive tied up for so long?"
>
> "I was robbed by bandits, and they left me tied up here. Birds have brought food to me every day, and each day a few rain clouds came overhead and I opened my mouth and got some water."[29]

> One day a caravan entered the palace grounds. The caravan guide led everyone inside the palace gate and told the caravan to set up their tents and make camp. Ibrahim exclaimed, "What are you doing?"
>
> "We are setting up our tents so we can spend the night here."
>
> "This isn't an inn. This is the palace, not a caravansary for transients."
>
> "Really? Who are you?"
>
> "I am the sultan. I live here."

28. Frager, *Sufi Talks*, 103.

29. Frager, *Sufi Talks*, 105.

"Who lived here before you?"
"My grandfather and grandmother."
"And who before them?"
"My great-grandparents."
"And before them?"
"My great-great grandparents."
"So what is the difference between this place and an inn? One comes and goes, another comes and goes. Same thing."[30]

The story continues thus: the man suddenly departs and Ibrahim races after him, wanting to continue the conversation. Finally the stranger reveals that he is in fact Khidr, the prophet-guide who opened to Moses the secrets of the spiritual path—and who is, in many narratives, the agent of spiritual initiation. Later Ibrahim saddles his mount and in a state of agitation goes hunting in the desert:

> In a daze, he loses track of his retinue and finds himself alone, hearing voices trying to wake him up. Suddenly a gazelle confronts the hunter and speaks, challenging him to consider whether he might have a higher purpose than hunting a defenseless creature for sport. . . . Ibrahim is suddenly swept into an experience of ecstasy. Coming across a shepherd, the king changes places with him. . . . He embarks on a long journey of spiritual discovery, his own pilgrimage to Mecca.[31]

These stories offer a powerful message about the importance of developing habits of attentiveness.

Cultivating attentiveness

Because of the very ordinary nature of his activities—lying in bed, sitting in the palace grounds—the import of these incidents may well have passed Ibrahim by. But he had been cultivating attentiveness. In the first story, he had just spent time in prayer and contemplation. And as he lay in his silken sheets (other versions of this story have him sitting on his throne), he yearned for a vocation that resonated more deeply with his internal hunger. In his case, he sought a life of quiet contemplation and service, a life largely opposed to the duties and obligations of the ruler of a prosperous city. He gave voice to his desire in prayer, the prayer itself being

30. Frager, *Sufi Talks*, 104.

31. Renard, *Friends of God*, 49.

an act of humility that undercut the ego and brought with it a sudden clarity of direction.

In the second story, Ibrahim may well have ignored a bird stealing food from his plate. By cultivating attentiveness, however, he was primed to recognize the Signs offered by God. Something was triggered; he followed the bird and found a stranger tied to a tree, a stranger who offered him a stark reminder of God's ever-present provision. In the third story, Ibrahim's conversation with the caravan guide awakened a knowledge half-remembered. Recognizing that there is more to discover, he ran after the guide. Only then did the guide reveal his true self and propel Ibrahim into his final act of renunciation.

Each of these stories commends the cultivation of attentiveness—a readiness to recognize that God is present to us at every turn in our journey, if we would only open our eyes. In a state of attentiveness, Ibrahim was more attuned to the myriad ways in which God reveals Godself in the world and moves us one step closer to spiritual happiness. Attentiveness propelled him on a journey of self-discovery, to recover his finest self.

Attentiveness is enhanced by daily practices of remembrance. The goal of the seeker is to reignite, in *this* life, the clarity of the primordial covenant—when each soul stood in the presence of God. The soul's yearning to remember what it once beheld is the imaginative foundation of the spiritual practice of *dhikr* (literally, "remembrance"). The goal of this practice is to be alive to the presence of God at every moment. *Dhikr* includes deepening focus and purpose in the ritual prayer (*salat*) and additional devotional exercises that include, at their most basic, a meditative recitation of the qur'anic Names of God and central qur'anic prayers. The practice is founded on the idea that the words of God are immeasurably powerful and that every act of recitation of the words in the Qur'an resonates in the human body—spiritually, psychologically, and physically. We are dyed in the hue of the words we recite. *Dhikr* is also founded on a basic insight of cognitive behavioral therapy: that there are links among cognition, emotion, and behavior. More specifically, "our thoughts determine our feelings and our behavior."[32] The meditative remembrance of God and God's attributes shifts the content of our awareness, helping us to determine who we are and how we act. It silences the chatter of the ego.

The importance of attentiveness

Attentiveness makes everyday life a sacred space. The Islamic spiritual tradition recognizes that the sound and fury of daily existence can hide the presence of

32. Saul McLeod, "Cognitive Behavioral Therapy," 2008, revised 2015, https://www.simplypsychology.org/cognitive-therapy.html (accessed February 22, 2018).

God in our lives. Conversely, when life is lived with attentiveness, everything around us may serve as a Sign (*ayah*) of God's nearness. The choice lies with each of us. The consistent practice of remembrance allows an ordinary day to be infused with sacred import, with the possibility of offering the seeker a glimpse of God's nearness.

> For Sufis, everything done, everything said and everything felt can be meditation, on condition that it leads them to remember God and stay awake and aware. . . .
>
> If I am with you, my daily work is prayer.
> And without you, my prayer is merely work.[33]

Behind the practices of attentiveness are the central theological ideas of God's guidance, grace, and favor (*fadal*) being available to all who seek it.[34] A *hadith* beloved in the spiritual tradition speaks in the voice of God:

> My servant comes ever closer to me through works of devotion. When anyone comes towards me a hand's breadth, I approach a forearm's length; if anyone comes toward me a forearm's length, I approach by the space of outstretched arms; if anyone comes towards me walking, I will come running. Then I love that person so that I become the eyes with which he sees, the ears with which he hears, the hands with which he takes hold. And should that person bring to me sins the size of the earth, my forgiveness will be a match for them.[35]

Attentiveness brought God into Ibrahim's life in more intimate and direct ways than he could have imagined. A fourth story exemplifies the perfection of this relationship:

> Some years later, Ibrahim met a drunk who was lying unconscious in the street. His breath reeked of alcohol. Ibrahim thought to himself, "This man's mouth must have recited prayers. This mouth must have called out God's Names. It should be cleansed." Ibrahim immediately brought fresh

---

33. Scott Kugle, ed., *Sufi Meditation and Contemplation: Timeless Wisdom from Mughal India*, trans. Scott Kugle and Carl Ernst (New Lebanon: Suluk Press, 2012), 38.

34. al-Ghazzali, *Alchemy of Happiness*, lxiii.

35. John Renard, *Islamic Theological Themes: A Primary Source Reader* (Berkeley: University of California Press, 2014), 22–3.

> water from a nearby well and washed the man's mouth. That night a voice came to Ibrahim in a dream, "You have cleansed a mouth for My sake, and I have cleansed your heart."[36]

In this story, Ibrahim had been traveling on the spiritual path for some years. When he came across a man who had clearly committed a sin (public drunkenness), his first response was an act of compassion. It was not a compassion born of pity, which still assumes a hierarchical relationship between self and other, but rather one born of humility. In a stance of attentiveness, Ibrahim saw the man as a beloved creation of God and acted accordingly. His actions served to honor the presence of God in the man before him. Teachers of spirituality understand that the shaping of character can be most effectively accomplished in the context of community life and service.

Historically, the Sufi tradition not only provided moral and spiritual direction; it also supported various forms of relational infrastructure around the Islamic world that could be likened to privatized social welfare (serving the impoverished, sick, and homeless). Such institutions, as well as the ubiquitous presence of spiritual teachers, made the Sufi tradition a dynamic force in Islamic social life. These stories of Ibrahim also illustrate a living, life-giving relationship with God—a conscience so finely honed that Ibrahim receives almost instant affirmation that his actions were indeed sincere.

While attentiveness provides one element of spiritual practice that is important for those embarking on the work of vocational exploration and discernment, it may lead some to take themselves a bit too seriously. It can usefully be balanced by attention to a very different practice: the cultivation of humor and laughter.

Vocation, humor, and laughter

The Islamic spiritual tradition offers another critical tool for self-inquiry: the art of humor. The most beloved teaching tales feature the ubiquitous figure of the holy fool, whose wise, often subtle humor sheds light on individual and communal injustice. The cultivation of humor and the power of laughter are critical tools for individuals who seek vocational fullness in the context of double-consciousness. For those who are attempting to sort out the relationship between performing and being (as described in the introduction to this chapter), these tools are indispensable.

36. Frager, *Sufi Talks*, 109.

Unsettled by the contradictions that lie within us and the injustices that take place around us, we may find some comfort in binary thinking, the "us against them" approach. But, as Jacqueline Bussie points out in *The Laughter of the Oppressed*, "a theology of laughter recognizes that dichotomous thought is usually sin—a grasping after power and placement of ourselves on the 'righteous' side of the dichotomy."[37] While the quest for God-awareness is utterly serious—indeed, it is a matter of life and death—the protagonists are human. The sweet space of humor allows us to honor the interplay of comic and tragic that is the subtext of much of our lives, and to live a life of dignity by embracing the undignified. Humor helps us contend with, perhaps even celebrate, the flaws and contradictions that abound in every aspect of being human and of living in community with others. Another contemporary voice, scholar of religion and humor Conrad Hyers, speaks of the

> importance of understanding . . . the dialectic of the sacred and the comic. . . . There is a plane of spiritual and theological freedom, liberality and humanness, as well as personal maturity, that is not to be achieved apart from a refined sense of humor and sensitivity to the comic perspective.[38]

Without this relationship with ourselves and with each other, Hyers warns that even the sacred is "subject to distortions of far-reaching consequence."[39]

The *hadith* literature shows us that the Prophet Muhammad created significant space in his life and ministry for humor, laughter, and play. In fact, canonical *hadith* collections have enshrined these traits in chapters titled "on smiling and laughing" and "on being cheerful with people." In a wonderful article titled "The Merry Men of Medina," Ze'ev Maghen brings together many of the *hadith* narratives on the Prophet's sense of humor. The Prophet was, in the words of a disciple Anas ibn Malik, "among the merriest of men,"[40] often laughing so hard that his back teeth could be seen. Another disciple, Jarir b. Abd Allah, tells us that he "never encountered Allah's Apostle . . . except that he was

---

37. Jacqueline Bussie, *The Laughter of the Oppressed: Ethical and Theological Resistance in Wiesel, Morrison, and Endo* (New York: T & T Clark, 2007), 187.

38. M. Conrad Hyers, "The Comic Profanation of the Sacred," in *Holy Laughter: Essays on Religion in the Comic Perspective*, ed. M. Conrad Hyers (New York: Seabury Press, 1969), 9–27; here, 10–11.

39. Hyers, "Introduction," in Hyers, ed., *Holy Laughter*, 1–7; here, 3–4.

40. Ze'ev Maghen, "The Merry Men of Medina: Comedy and Humanity in the early days of Islam," *Der Islam* 83 (2008): 298.

laughing."[41] A third disciple declared: "I never saw anyone who smiled as often as the Prophet."[42]

The disciple Abu al-Darda al-Ansari apparently smiled so much that his wife was concerned: "I am afraid people will think you are an idiot!" He answered: "[But] I never saw the Messenger of God speak without smiling."[43] Some close disciples once complained about another disciple who they thought joked too much. "You may be surprised to know," the Prophet replied, "that he will laugh all the way to heaven." The Prophet knew well the power of humor to ease communal relationships. He would often joke and banter with his disciples, drawing them close in love and affection for him and for each other. He removed formalities; he would sit with ease among them, joke with them, and tease them. Other *hadith* show us a Prophet who loved practical jokes: In one instance, a disciple (a prankster) secretly loosened the Prophet's saddle. When the Prophet climbed on his camel, he almost fell off—and dissolved in appreciative laughter![44]

The Prophet saw humor as a school for humility. He adored children and had no compunction about coming down to their level. He smeared their faces with food, stuck his tongue out at them, splashed them with bathwater, and kissed their tummies.[45] Muslims know well the story of the Prophet down on his hands and knees with his two precious grandsons, pretending to be a camel as they bounced on his back with glee!

The Prophet also saw humor as a form of mercy. Maghen shares the *hadith* narrative of a man who came to the Prophet during the month of Ramadan and said: "I am ruined, O Messenger of God!" "And what is it that has ruined you?" asked the Prophet. The man replied that he had deliberately broken his fast. The Prophet asked if he was financially able to free an enslaved person as expiation. The man said no. "Are you able to feed sixty impoverished people?" Again, "No." The Prophet then gave him a basketful of dates and said, "Give these in charity." But the man exclaimed, "There is no household in Medina that is poorer than ours!" The Prophet laughed heartily and said, "Go then and feed your own family with these dates!"[46]

---

41. Maghen, "Merry Men," 295.

42. Maghen, "Merry Men," 295.

43. Maghen, "Merry Men," 295.

44. Maghen, "Merry Men," 326.

45. Maghen, "Merry Men," 319.

46. Maghen, "Merry Men," 328.

The importance of cultivating humor

Humor creates a magical space where the limitations of the human condition are met with mercy. This is how humor itself becomes sacred, essential to the restoration of individual and communal health. A self without humor runs the risk of idolatry in the truest sense—taking refuge in the arrogance of binary thinking. Unable to forgive ourselves, we are quick to judge others. Unable to laugh at ourselves, we cannot show mercy to other human beings.

But humor also serves another purpose. The Prophet and his disciples were engaged in an enterprise of the utmost gravity, translating a revelation into an intentional community and a new social order. In the early years of the ministry in Mecca, they suffered unspeakable horrors at the hands of a powerful socioeconomic elite terrified of losing their privilege. The Prophet and his followers lost brothers, sisters, mothers and fathers, and children to murder, torture, starvation, and fear. Even in Medina, they were faced with implacable enemies, often engaged in mortal combat, always fearful for their lives and livelihood. When language fails, as it often does, to capture the paradox of holding both these narratives within oneself at every moment in time, laughter restores and offers hope.

Thus, in the midst of pain, the Prophet laughed. As Jacqueline Bussie points out:

> The person of faith who encounters radical evil experiences a terrible collision of narratives. Those who suffer deeply and also love a God who they believe acts in history experience their faith as deeply rooted in paradoxical and competing truth claims. . . . In plain language, God is good, and life is often horror. God is love, yet horrible things happen to innocent people.[47]

Laughing in a situation that does not conventionally appear to call for laughter is an expression and restoration of hope in a world of suffering; and as Bussie has so beautifully articulated in her work, to laugh is also to resist.[48] It is a way to render powerless those systems of oppression that rely for their existence on the internalization of fear in those who are oppressed. Despite the repeated attempts of individuals and structures to destroy the human spirit, the spirit breaks free,

---

47. Jacqueline Bussie, "Laughter as Ethical and Theological Resistance: Leymah Gbowee, Sarah, and the Hidden Transcript," *Interpretation: A Journal of Bible and Theology* 69, no. 2 (2015): 169–82; here, 177–8.

48. Bussie, "Laughter as Resistance," 179.

calling attention through laughter to the paradox of beauty and pain that marks the human condition, and calling attention to the absurdity of evil in a life marked by faith. For communities under duress, the cultivation of humor and the power of laughter are critical tools in the journey of vocational inquiry.

Vocation as awakening to self

The spiritual, character-forming practices described in this chapter—attentiveness and humor—are important tools for vocational reflection and discernment. But given the contemporary context of undergraduate education, their importance is magnified many times over. At the outset of this chapter, I quoted Shabana Mir's description of today's students as "tense, tired, and under several layers of surveillance." Such circumstances are certainly not ideal for vocational discernment, but their long-term consequences are still more significant: they leave students feeling exhausted and dispirited. If young people are to discern meaning and purpose in life, they will need to develop a range of spiritual practices that can provide some protection from the corrosive effects of a culture which demands that they perform their identities in response to an invasive and suspicious gaze. These practices, along with others advocated in this book, may help students awaken to their truest selves—and help them forge a path of integrity through the thickets of this political and cultural landscape.

Response

Tracy Wenger Sadd

My own interfaith work, in both the curriculum and the co-curriculum, is based on the key foundation of shared values and seeks to build social capital. In Homayra's chapter, I found a plethora of shared values—particularly between her discussion of the Sufi tradition of Islamic spirituality and my own Church of the Brethren tradition. These include attending to the inner life, finding third spaces, committing to self-care, and facilitating openness to new spiritual illumination and inspiration. Especially powerful to me is our shared understanding of spirituality primarily as a lived experience; it is a transformative engagement with the presence of God, and it takes place at moments and in ways that transcend external political, economic, and social structures.

Thanks to Homayra, I learned of beloved teachers of the Sufi tradition—teachers whose personal narratives, journeys of self-transformation, humor, and vulnerability provide guidance and mentoring. I appreciate the ways that

Homayra has lifted up Sufi narratives and the Islamic spiritual tradition as having particular significance and relevance for Muslim women on our campuses today. For these young Muslim women, "a recentering of self through vocational inquiry can be a lifeline."

Moreover, I experience in Homayra's chapter a third space in which I am able to reaffirm parts of my own tradition and to acknowledge my own hopes, fears, and growing edges. My roots in Anabaptism call me to behaviors and outer forms of life that *reflect* grace. At the same time, the lesser-known Radical Pietism of my heritage calls me to *feel* that grace—an experience that may even perhaps include mystical encounter. Homayra's call to humility and humor, as well as her description of the significance of holy fools, challenges me to claim more fully each day the Radical Pietist ideas of my own tradition. I am also reminded that the true Church is invisible and universal, with members found in all communions.

PART FOUR

Reimagining Our Campuses

The Practice(s) of Hearing Vocation Differently

Higher education often seems to resemble a giant pendulum—swinging back and forth between the intensely theoretical and the imminently practical. Its specialized fields of knowledge and the intense level of expertise among faculty members can result in academic pronouncements that appear esoteric to the point of ridicule. And yet, on actual college campuses, practical matters often prevail—due to the day-to-day demands of educating students, encouraging their personal development, and providing for their various physical, emotional, and spiritual needs. While the first three parts of this book have regularly mentioned implications for actual practice, they have necessarily focused most of their attention on the theoretical questions at stake.

In this fourth part, our authors have sought to swing the pendulum back toward matters of concrete practice. They continue to provide a theoretical underpinning for their claims, but their contributions focus more intentionally on what happens in classrooms, at faculty meetings, among administrators (from student life personnel to development officers), and within various co-curricular spaces at the institution. These four authors describe the actual steps that colleges and universities have taken as they have sought to implement programs of vocational reflection and discernment and to make their campuses more welcoming to students, faculty, and staff of diverse lifestances. Within these chapters, readers will find descriptions of a variety of interfaith encounters—certainly among teachers and students, but also within faculty conversations, across administrative decision-making channels, and in offices of religious life, college advancement, and career services.

The overall effect of these chapters, we hope, will be to allow readers to reimagine their own campuses—an enterprise that will, admittedly, require a great deal of time, organization, and patience. Regardless of the number of students that they enroll, colleges and universities are massive enterprises with long histories and complex constituencies; as a result, they are not, and cannot be, particularly agile or quick in reacting to deep societal change. Higher education is only just beginning to respond to the two impulses described in this volume (namely, the turn toward vocational reflection and the increasingly multi-faith context in which this occurs). The importance of these endeavors might be compared to the light that comes from very distant stars; it is powerful and valuable, but it takes a long time to arrive. The four institutions described in the chapters that follow have been employing a variety of telescopes and scanners to detect some of that light, and to allow it to illuminate their campuses in various ways. Consequently, the authors of these chapters raise a number of intriguing questions, including these:

- What difference does it make when an academic institution, while espousing a particular faith tradition, employs faculty members who do not adhere to that tradition? What effects does this have on the institution, on its students, and on its faculty members (including those who align themselves with the institution's religious perspective, as well as those who do not)?
- Has the increasing religious diversity of our colleges and universities been given adequate attention, particularly with regard to current practices of advising, mentoring, and formulating general education requirements? How might the language of *vocation* and *calling* provide new insights into these important educational practices at a time of great cultural change?
- How should a college's various constituencies understand its *institutional vocation*? Should a college's mission, vision, and goals be marked by deep continuity, regardless of cultural change? Or should these elements be more readily adapted to new realities? Might an institution possibly find the means to achieve both these ends?
- To what degree do the pedagogical practices of higher education encourage (or discourage) the kinds of changes that are needed, as institutions become more sensitive to the increasingly multi-faith context of the wider society? How might these practices address the needs of students to reflect on and discern their callings within that society?
- What kinds of interdisciplinary work are needed to respond well to the increasingly diverse range of students who arrive on campus each year? How might colleges and universities facilitate conversations within and among academic disciplines and applied fields, such that the best insights of these specialties can contribute more fully to an improved educational experience for all?

- Do academic institutions need to do a better job of describing their own understandings of the good, and of what counts as a good life, in order to provide the kind of education needed by students today? Does diversity sometimes become an excuse for evading this kind of highly demanding moral reflection, and if so, how might it be recovered, while still affirming the importance of diversity?
- Are colleges and universities in danger of slipping into a merely instrumental relationship with undergraduates, in which students pay a certain fee and expect to graduate into lucrative employment? Or are these institutions being called to develop a viable alternative to this model, in which their disposition toward students is more explicitly marked by mindfulness and care, by mentoring and encouragement, and perhaps even by *love*?

No book, nor even an entire series of books, can hope to answer all of these questions. But in the four chapters that follow, our authors have presented a number of concrete instances in which these questions have been recognized as significant, diligently considered, and given some form of response—even if only a partial one. Of course, the institutional models that are described in these pages will not automatically transfer to every campus setting; nevertheless, they provide some very nourishing food for thought. We hope that these reflections will encourage other colleges and universities to find their own ways of addressing these same challenges—and many others that are likely to arise in the years ahead.

10

Response-ability in Practice

DISCERNING VOCATION THROUGH CAMPUS RELATIONSHIPS

Florence D. Amamoto

OVER THE PAST several decades, the language of vocational discernment has gained a greater foothold and a broader applicability across higher education. Nevertheless, the word *vocation* itself is still too often used to focus narrowly on a person's career. This tendency persists, despite a different perspective that has been around for at least 500 years. Sixteenth-century theologian Martin Luther observed that we are called into many roles—child, parent, neighbor, and citizen, as well as worker—and that we are called to fulfill each as responsibly and thoughtfully as we can. Similarly, the word *discernment* has a broader range of meanings than our usual usage reflects; it means to see deeply, and especially to perceive what is hidden (as well as to separate by sifting). So while vocational discernment may include our efforts to consider our future career paths, this element certainly does not exhaust its significance.

In my own case, vocational discernment (in the broadest possible sense) has helped me to deepen my understanding of what I do and to sharpen my practice. This reflection has been aided by being carried out in a multi-faith context. In fact, for more than 25 years, I have *lived* in the world that this book is attempting to imagine: a world of "hearing vocation differently." As a Buddhist at a Swedish Lutheran college, I have been deeply involved with vocational exploration and reflection in a multi-faith context at both the personal and institutional levels. In this chapter, I want to consider how our relationships can shape our vocation, if we listen responsibly to others and use our abilities to respond to them.

Although American popular culture celebrates individuality, all of us have been shaped by our relationships—from visible influences, such as parents, to less obvious influences, such as our environments. My own tradition, Buddhism, emphasizes that we are all part of an interdependent web that encompasses both other people and the whole universe; what we do matters well beyond its impact on each of us individually. So discerning a vocation involves not just looking into ourselves and identifying our gifts and desires, but also thinking about how we want to respond to the place and time in which we find ourselves. Our human condition calls us to responsibility—and response-ability.[1]

In the first section of the chapter, I narrate my own vocational and spiritual journeys, showing how they have deepened my concern with issues of diversity and institutional vocation and identity. The second section turns to the important educational practice of advising, showing how a similar kind of "response-ability" can inform and enliven this practice. (Despite its importance, advising too often becomes a merely instrumental or even trivial part of the college experience.) A third major section examines a particular course that is designed to help students undertake the work of vocational reflection and discernment. A brief concluding reflection considers the importance of creating and maintaining a multi-faith context in which vocational reflection can take place.

Growing response-ability: A Buddhist in Lutherland

I never had questions about my future career; I have wanted to be a teacher since I was in the first grade. But the specific shape of my educational practice has been influenced by the fact that I was a first-generation college student, and that I attended college in the late 1960s. In addition, I have been shaped by my reading of educational theorists like Paolo Freire and participating in discussions about educational goals, practices, and experiments at an alternative school where I taught during my master's program in teaching. But the most significant influence on my teaching career has been the place where I have spent most of that career: at a small church-related liberal arts college.

Although I had gone to large research universities for all of my own schooling, teaching at Gustavus Adolphus has been my dream job. I have loved the sense

1. Thanks to Rachel Mikva for pointing out that responsibility is made up of "response" and "ability." See also Margaret E. Mohrmann, "'Vocation Is Responsibility': Broader Scope, Deeper Discernment," in *Vocation across the Academy: A New Vocabulary for Higher Education*, ed. David S. Cunningham (New York: Oxford University Press, 2017), 21–43.

of community, the ability to get to know my students, and the opportunity to nurture the development of the whole person—intellectual and personal. I have appreciated that the college's church-relatedness meant it supported students' exploration of values. What I had not anticipated was how much being at Gustavus would encourage my own exploration of my particular faith—as well as supporting my involvement in initiatives on church-relatedness and on vocation at both the collegiate and national levels. I was often the only Buddhist (indeed, the only non-Christian) in these groups—and I learned that my participation could make a difference. All of these experiences have only reinforced for me the value of church-related colleges *and* of diversity.

When I started teaching at Gustavus in the early 1990s, many church-related institutions were struggling with issues of identity in the face of various challenges. These included a decrease in traditional student constituencies, economic shortfalls, and increased pressure for more diversity in both the faculty and student body. Midwestern Lutheran colleges like Gustavus were still overwhelmingly white and Christian. In such a context, I felt I needed to make the argument for the importance of diversity. I believed then (as I believe now) that, in an increasingly interconnected world, any institution claiming educational excellence must enable students to understand people of many backgrounds and faiths. In the intervening decades, these issues have only become more acute—but at the same time, they have also increased my appreciation for the college's Lutheran identity.

Multi-faith contexts and religious development

As the granddaughter of poor Japanese farmers who immigrated to California early in the twentieth century, I was raised a Jodo Shin Shu Buddhist, going to Sunday School at the Buddhist temple a half mile from my home. In Sunday School, we learned the basic precepts of Buddhism; in our high school years, these "classes" were actually discussion groups, which helped foster my interest in theological issues. However, in college and beyond, what little thinking I did about religion consisted mainly of reading a little Thomas Merton and David Steindl-Rast, with an eye to the ways that Buddhism and Christianity overlapped.

I then found myself teaching at a Lutheran college in a rural area in Minnesota, seventy miles from a Buddhist temple of any kind. (In fact, the closest temple in my own Jodo Shin Shu tradition is hundreds of miles away in Chicago.) Friends often ask me whether, under these circumstances, I can really *practice* my religion. However, Buddhist practice is not primarily focused on following a particular liturgical rite or participation in a communal gathering; rather, it is concerned with all aspects of how one lives one's life. In many ways, being at Gustavus has allowed me to *live* my religion more than I might have otherwise. Buddhism reminds us that we are too often either distracted or mentally asleep; it calls us to be more mindful.[2] Being at Gustavus has encouraged me to practice such mindfulness, as well as reigniting my interest in exploring my own faith and expanding my ideas about the value of multi-faith contexts.

The first impetus was Gustavus's chapel program. When Christ Chapel—a big, beautiful building in the center of campus—was built in the mid-1960s, the then president of the college told the new chaplain that its program was to be modeled on the Swedish folk church. This meant that it was to be *the church of the community*, rather than narrowly denominational. To this day, homilies are given by faculty, staff, and senior students from a wide variety of religious and philosophical traditions and lifestances. The chapel program sees itself as part of the educational mission of the college; it embodies the fact that intellectual and religious development are enriched by the support of diversity, and that people of all faiths and backgrounds should feel equally valued as vital members of the community with something important to say to all of us.

When I started at Gustavus, the usual practice was to give homilists the lectionary text of the day, although they had the option of choosing another text if they so desired. I always saw it as part of my challenge to give a "Buddhist" reflection on that biblical passage. I hoped this would shed some helpful light on the text, as well as increasing the congregation's understanding of Buddhism. My goal was to help my hearers recognize the ways Buddhist and Lutheran beliefs overlapped, and to appreciate the fruitfulness of seeing their differences.

This reflection was enriched as I found myself increasingly involved in multi-faith conversations. Over the years, I was part of two informal faculty groups: a multi-faith "spirituality group" (in which we shared our spiritual and personal journeys, beliefs, issues, and questions) and a multi-faith group that studied Buddhism more specifically. That group was especially important in my development as a Buddhist. The Buddha told his followers not to take anything on authority (not even his own teachings), instructing them to test everything against their own experiences. Questions from the ex-Jesuit in our group made me see that I had done this only in the most superficial way—at best, intellectualized; at worst, rote. Without my Christian friend's prodding, I might not have gone beyond the "Sunday School" teachings of my childhood, to test them against my life. More recently, I have been asked to be part of multi-faith panels discussing

2. For more on mindfulness, see Homayra Ziad's reflections on the related idea of *attentiveness* in chapter 9 of this volume.

concepts of vocation. All of these venues have pushed me to delve more deeply into Buddhist teachings and to consider how those teachings relate to life. I have been able to give Buddhist concepts flesh, and to do so in ways that have been more helpful to my students.

Lest I make Gustavus sound too idyllic, I want to point out that Buddhist-Lutheran interaction is much less fraught than many other multi-faith situations. In fact, my own Jodo Shin Shu form of Buddhism is remarkably similar, theologically speaking, to Lutheranism. Both emphasize the importance of faith and the situation of human beings as "simultaneously sinful and saved." Interest in Buddhism among faculty and especially students has only increased over the years, and meditation has gone mainstream. This is not to say that there have not been alumni who have objected to a Buddhist preaching in chapel; moreover, my participation in the chapel program and in vocation initiatives has been dependent on having chaplains and administrators who value diversity. I know my experience would have been different at other church-related colleges; I also know Hindu and Muslim faculty who have felt much less embraced than I have, including at other Lutheran colleges. Nevertheless, the theological groundwork is in place for a multi-faith approach to conversations about a wide range of important issues, including vocation. And of course, college politics always helps me remember the truth of the Buddhist lessons I'd learned—particularly about the importance of egolessness, and about doing my best to work for the common good while letting go of the results!

Diversity matters

As a number of observers have commented, Lutheranism is particularly welcoming of other perspectives, teaching that no one has direct access to all truth and that dialogue is important.[3] However, this does not necessarily solve the problem of identity and diversity, even at Lutheran colleges. At a conference on the Vocation of a Lutheran College, one suggestion for maintaining denominational identity was a "host-guest" model. Although this was explained in terms of "guests" being necessary to the identity of a "host," it still suggested to me that those who found their religious identity outside Lutheranism were being labeled

3. Despite Luther's own anti-Semitism, the theological ideas he promulgated have provided a foundation for Lutheran colleges' openness to interfaith dialogue. See Richard T. Hughes, "Introduction," *Models for Christian Higher Education: Strategies for Success in the 21st Century* (Grand Rapids, MI: Eerdmans, 1997), 6–7. See also Eboo Patel, "What It Means to Build the Bridge: Identity and Diversity at ELCA Colleges," *Intersections*, no. 40 (Fall 2014): 17–25; here, 23; http://digitalcommons.augustana.edu/intersections/vol2014/iss40/6 (accessed January 18, 2018).

as outsiders. Given how much I identified with the mission of my institution, I found this approach troubling; I was happy that this model had not been the norm at Gustavus.

Discussions with people of different religious backgrounds have only reinforced my belief that there are important commonalities among all religions—including the call to spiritual development and an ethical life and the responsibility to extend love and service to others. Just as importantly, differences of practice and emphasis can deepen our understanding of the world and human nature—and of ourselves. Some differences may be irreconcilable, but this only means that we are called to reach a deeper understanding of one another, unburdened by the labels of *insider* and *outsider*. In an increasingly globalized world, it is only becoming more important to encourage our students to think more deeply and widely about themselves and others, and about their interconnection with the world—and to increase their appreciation of and skills in engaging with people from different faiths and cultures.

In fact, our students are now demanding this global perspective. For example, as a result of student campaigns (which included student lobbying at both faculty and board of trustee meetings), Gustavus now has a beautiful new multi-faith space. On a campus where a beautiful chapel sits at its center, it was important to have an equally inviting space for other religious groups and practices. It is now the home for the Gustavus Meditation group, the Muslim Student Organization, the Multifaith Leadership Council, the Interfaith Advisory Board (which organizes discussions across faith traditions), and alternate worship and wellness practices during "chapel time," drawing on non-Christian traditions. The college had hosted a Buddhist meditation group for more than 10 years (and other religious groups and activities more sporadically), but the beautiful new space and programming testify to a greater commitment to multi-faith and interfaith efforts.

In addition, a new initiative has received external support to strengthen academic programs in "Interfaith Cooperation in Professional and Civic Life." Its leadership team is both multi-faith as well as multi-disciplinary; the faculty leaders are specialists in Buddhism, Lutheranism, and Management, respectively. This project aims to strengthen the three courses that these faculty leaders already teach: World Religions, Interfaith Understanding, and Organizational Behavior. A second aim is to build partnerships between the Religion Department and pre-professional programs, starting with the Department of Economics and Management, but then reaching out to Education and Nursing. The initiative seeks to strengthen religious literacy, to cultivate interfaith awareness, to explore interfaith relationships in professional and civic life, and to encourage students to reflect on their own religious, philosophical, and ethical convictions.

Those who do not share the institution's denominational assumptions can sometimes become great advocates. Learning early of Gustavus's liberal tradition made me feel welcome; my commitment to education of the whole person for the common good has helped me to recognize Gustavus's as a vital part of its identity, which I have long defended. Discussions prompted by Gustavus's participation in the initiative of Programs for the Theological Exploration of Vocation helped me develop a deeper knowledge of, and appreciation for, the specifically *Lutheran* understanding of vocation. However, having non-Lutherans on that committee also pushed the Lutheran members to explore their own tradition's idea of vocation more deeply and to develop more inclusive language—and indeed, more inclusive ideas—based on Lutheran theology. Those discussions were seminal in allowing us to create language and programs that would attract students regardless of religious affiliation or lifestance; they also helped us articulate more clearly how a commitment to vocational exploration, inclusiveness, and lives of leadership and service is deeply rooted in the college's Lutheran heritage.

For good ethical, financial, and demographic reasons, many colleges are becoming increasingly diverse, both in the composition of their faculty and in the student body. This has enriched our educational offerings immeasurably and has energized class discussions. It is important that our students learn *with* (and not just about) people from a wide range of backgrounds; this has the potential not only to broaden their understanding of themselves and the world, but also to bring them into conversations that hone their skills at bridging differences while deepening their commitment to working together for the common good. Notably, however, this kind of focus on diversity need not entail any decrease in an institution's own denominational identity; indeed, it can strengthen it.

Identity matters

Lutheranism was founded by college professor monks; it supports free intellectual inquiry and emphasizes the importance of large questions of meaning and purpose. This combination, to me, is one of Lutheran colleges' contributions to society. As one example among many: Gustavus Adolphus College was founded by a Lutheran pastor who also opened an orphanage, which eventually evolved into Lutheran Social Services. Many of the problems facing the world today are enormous—global climate change, inequalities of all kinds—and will not be solved easily or quickly. It will take many people with a variety of talents many years to move the needle. Change will often be glacially slow and therefore potentially discouraging; hence, we need people of all kinds with a perseverance that is born of vision, commitment, and a deep-seated moral compass. The desire to nurture students with these qualities is certainly not exclusive to Lutheran or church-related colleges, but such institutions may have an easier time seeing such matters as part of their DNA.[4]

Thus, even as they focus on greater religious diversity, church-related colleges should make sure that their sense of identity is not lost. Over the last 15 years, the faculty at Gustavus has turned over enormously. The new faculty has become increasingly diverse (a good thing), but these newer members of the community have received less of an introduction to Gustavus's distinctive Swedish Lutheran heritage than I did. In the past, for instance, at summer faculty vocation workshops, a panel of non-Lutheran faculty spoke about their experiences at Gustavus and about the understanding of vocation in their own faith traditions. These conversations have been tremendously helpful in assuring non-Christian faculty that Lutheranism supports their values of free intellectual exchange and academic excellence and regards them as equal members of the community. The importance of these efforts was underlined when a new Chinese faculty member said to me after that panel, "Now I feel I can belong here."

My institution has recently seen renewed efforts to educate incoming faculty. The provost now hosts a dinner for new tenure-track faculty, at which current faculty members talk about their sense of vocation and various aspects of the college's identity—including its Swedish and Lutheran heritages, its liberal arts tradition, and its support for diversity. A professor has edited a book of short essays, written by over 30 faculty members, covering a range of subjects related to the college's heritage, identity, and practice; this book can now be given to incoming faculty and staff.[5] Gustavus sends a healthy contingent of continuing and new faculty members and administrators to the annual Vocation of a Lutheran College conference and to Network for Vocation in Undergraduate Education (NetVUE) conferences. Such efforts can inspire new and especially non-Lutheran members of the community to enter into this more "vocational" view of the institution and to see they belong.[6]

---

4. In fact, it may make sense to speak of an institution's *vocation* in this regard. See David S. Cunningham, "Colleges Have Callings, Too: Vocational Reflection at the Institutional Level," in Cunningham, ed., *Vocation across the Academy*, 249–71, as well as Jacqueline Bussie's discussion in chapter 11 of the present volume.

5. Marcia J. Bunge, ed., *Rooted in Heritage, Open to the World: Reflections on the Distinctive Character of Gustavus Adolphus College* (Minneapolis: Lutheran University Press, 2017).

6. Needless to say, the success of such efforts depends on making sure that a wide range of college constituencies (including senior administrators) are committed to the project. See Tim Clydesdale, *The Purposeful Graduate: Why Colleges Must Talk to Students about Vocation* (Chicago: University of Chicago Press, 2015), 181–82, 213.

Compassion and response-ability: a Buddhist notion of calling

Working at a Lutheran institution has prompted me to think more about vocation and calling. Perhaps because Jodo Shin Shu Buddhism was founded in the thirteenth century for poor, illiterate Japanese peasants and brought to America by poor Japanese immigrants, my own theological "training" focused mainly on living a life of faith and gratitude. But through my experiences in "Lutherland," I came to see that there might be a notion of "calling" in Buddhism.

Buddha is a title that means "awakened one." Thus, becoming a Buddha is an ideal: the goal is enlightenment, but this is always defined as the gaining of both wisdom *and* compassion. These are always paired because true wisdom—an understanding of reality—recognizes both our deep interconnectedness to everything and the suffering that surrounds us, inevitably evoking our compassion. Thus, enlightenment is not, in and of itself, the final goal. Buddhism is calling us not only to the deepest understanding of reality that we are able to achieve, but also to be the best conduits of compassion that we can be—responding as helpfully as possible to the situations we encounter. If the concept of vocation requires the idea of a "caller," I would argue that, for Buddhists, we are called by *the world and the needs that exist all around us.*[7]

Given this formulation of vocation, it is perhaps not surprising that I resonate so strongly with Dietrich Bonhoeffer's assertion that "Vocation is responsibility, and responsibility is a total response of the whole human being to the whole of reality."[8] In Bonhoeffer's and in Buddhism's understanding of vocation, we are called to develop our ability to respond, our response-ability, to its fullest.[9] This insight has significantly influenced my advising and teaching, as will be explored in the next two sections of this chapter.

---

7. For more on the nature and identity of the "caller" in vocation, see David S. Cunningham, "'Who's There?': The Dramatic Role of the 'Caller' in Vocational Discernment," in *At This Time and In This Place: Vocation and Higher Education*, ed. David S. Cunningham (New York: Oxford University Press, 2015), 143–64.

8. Dietrich Bonhoeffer, *Ethics*, ed. Eberhard Bethge, trans. N. H. Smith (London: Macmillan, 1955), 258, translation slightly altered. See the reflections on this quotation in Mohrmann, "'Vocation Is Responsibility,'" 21.

9. For another discussion of vocation and Buddhism, see Mark Unno, "The Calling of No-Calling: Vocation in Nikaya and Mahayana Buddhism," in *Calling in Today's World: Voices from Eight Faith Perspectives*, ed. Kathleen Cahalan and Douglas Schuurman (Grand Rapids, MI: Eerdmans, 2016), 133–60.

Discernment and advising

Although many educators decry their students' tendencies to see graduation requirements as boxes to check off, few advisers can fully escape the temptation to do the same, given the press of myriad duties. This may be especially true with respect to advising nonmajors, especially first- and second-year students. Yet this is precisely the time when students are most open to influence as to how they will think about their college careers and beyond. Given the cost of college, students and their parents are, not surprisingly, concerned with careers; still, they are also concerned with the student's happiness. The traditional purposes of higher education, particularly liberal arts education, have included widening students' horizons and preparing them for responsible citizenship. At church-related colleges, the shaping of character and an exploration of what gives life meaning have been potential "value added" elements.[10] Many academic institutions use surveys such as the Strong Interest Inventory to point students toward possible careers, but colleges can also help students think beyond matters of employment by using instruments such as Strength Finders or Values Cards, which identify character traits and values. Students need to be encouraged to discern their gifts; however, they also need to think about their relation to the world. Here, it can be helpful to remind ourselves once again of Frederick Buechner's popular definition of vocation: "The place God calls you is the place where your deep gladness and the world's deep hunger meet."[11] Importantly, Buechner's phrase points in two directions at once: it emphasizes the need not just to explore the self, but also to move beyond the self and to understand the world.

Advising in community

As John Donne noted, "No man is an island"; and as the Buddha recognized, everything is interconnected. Students should be encouraged to take classes and participate in activities that expand their horizons and increase their awareness of their interrelatedness with the rest of the world, connecting what they are learning with life. Sharon Parks has noted that people who have become civic leaders have often had meaningful experiences with people they would consider "other."[12]

10. See the observations of Mark R. Schwehn, "Good Teaching: Character Formation and Vocational Discernment," in Cunningham, ed., *Vocation across the Academy*, 294–314.

11. Frederick Buechner, *Wishful Thinking: A Theological ABC* (New York: Harper and Row, 1973), 95.

12. Laurent A. Parks Daloz, Cheryl H. Keen, James P. Keen, and Sharon Daloz Parks, *Common Fire: Leading Lives of Commitment in a Complex World* (Boston: Beacon Press, 1996), 55–79.

Study abroad, community service projects, and service learning all are avenues for such encounters. Such experiences, however, need to be supplemented by guidance that encourages students to reflect on these experiences. Community service, for example, has become such a normalized part of high school and college experiences that, like any normalized activity, its implications and lessons are often taken for granted. For students, these experiences can become merely instrumental: a means of getting into a better college or to show a prospective employer that one is a "good person" and team player. Many members of the current generation of college students have been programmed to schedule themselves up to their eyeballs; for them, such activities can become just one more experience, the meaning of which is easily missed. Students need guidance in learning to explore their experiences—to discern what these experiences have to teach them about themselves and their relationship to the world they live in.[13]

Advisers also need to develop their own discernment skills—what Buddhists would call deep listening and deep seeing. As Buddhism reminds us, we need to listen and see, with all that we are, to all that our students are. We need to listen for what is not being said, to read their body language, to learn to ask questions that will help them explore themselves and their options, and to give them ways to build skills such as perseverance and resilience. We need to learn "skillful means"—a Buddhist concept that recognizes that one size does not fit all, and that we need to discern what will be most helpful to that particular individual sitting right in front of us.[14]

Those who have taught for any length of time can proudly point to students whom they encouraged—and who have admitted that they would never have stayed in the major or considered graduate school without that encouragement. But those who advise first- and second-year students may also recall many pre-med advisees who—after disastrous experiences in biology or chemistry—are suddenly looking for a new major and a new career. These students, as well as those who are simply unsure of their career path, often feel like failures; they may also feel guilty about the tuition bills. Advisers need to help them see such experiences as an opportunity to examine their stories and to think more deeply

13. See Darby Ray, "Self, World, and the Space Between: Community Engagement as Vocational Discernment," in Cunningham, ed., *At This Time*, 301–20.

14. This is closely related to the concepts of prudence and practical wisdom; the implications of these terms for vocational reflection are explored at length in Thomas Albert Howard, "Seeing with All Three Eyes: The Virtue of Prudence and Undergraduate Education," in Cunningham, ed., *At This Time*, 216–34, and Celia Deane-Drummond, "The Art and Science of Vocation: Wisdom and Conscience as Companions on a Way," in Cunningham, ed., *Vocation across the Academy*, 156–77.

about their talents, values, and passions—to consider what gives meaning to their lives.

As an English professor, I am often asked what one can do with a major in my department. Advisers can widen our students' vision of their options. Many English majors have gone into librarianship or law, into writing, editing, or publishing. But I often tell English majors that their analytic and communication skills are highly transferable and that, rather than thinking in terms of particular positions, they might think about their interests or the kinds of organizations where they would like to work. One recent graduate from my institution is a writer for *Outside* magazine; one got a job in the public relations division of Minnesota's professional hockey team; one is a political consultant; another started a software company. Alumni/ae/a have reassured our students that, even though it may be easier for accounting majors to get their first job, English majors are likely to be propelled up the corporate ladder faster because of their communication skills. Students of this generation may need to be more entrepreneurial in crafting the work to which they are called,[15] but they can be helped by advisers who foster a strong sense of self and purpose.

Providing resources for advising

Few members of a college's faculty or staff are trained as advisers, much less as vocational advisers, so it is important to develop materials that can help them. To answer that need, Gustavus formed a committee to develop a series of units to strengthen the advising component of the first-year seminar program. The series included a unit on values clarification, in which students were asked to complete sentences such as these:

- My interests include . . .
- I enjoy participating in . . .
- My skills include . . .
- I enjoy classes or subjects such as . . .
- I value . . .
- My long-term dreams/goals are . . .
- In my free time I enjoy . . .

15. For more on entrepreneurship as an element of vocational discernment, see Noah Silverman's reflections in chapter 7 of this volume.

Exercises like this can give advisers a concrete place to start in helping students to explore possible majors and career directions. They also encourage both the student and the adviser to think more broadly about the process of finding a further direction in life.

The college is also currently piloting training for a small group of interested faculty and staff in "appreciative advising," which provides a structure to build more effective advising relationships. This approach draws on research in positive psychology, appreciative inquiry, reality therapy, and choice theory. It recognizes that a teacher or adviser's perception of a student can have a powerful effect on that person, and that students are more likely to respond positively to someone who shows a genuine interest in them.[16] Jennifer Bloom and her coauthors define appreciative advising as

> a social-constructivist advising philosophy that provides a framework for optimizing advisor interactions with students. . . . Advisors intentionally use positive, active, and attentive listening and questioning strategies to build trust and rapport with students; uncover students' strengths and skills based on their past successes; encourage and be inspired by students' stories and dreams; co-construct action plans with students to make their goals a reality; support students as they carry out their plans; and challenge both themselves and their students to do and become even better.[17]

Although these attitudes and practices—listening, discerning, responding, and supporting—may be familiar to good advisers everywhere, Bloom has provided a robust theoretical framework and workbooks with language and questions. All of these tools can help make positive practices more widespread and intentional.

The college years are a time of exploration for students, often setting their lives' trajectories. Advising can play an important part in deepening how students think about their goals and the meaning of their lives, but faculty and staff often have little training in how to help them do so. Colleges need concrete programming to help faculty and staff better educate our students to live the "lives of leadership and service" that are described as goals in so many of our mission statements.

---

16. For a related argument, see Jeffrey Carlson's reflections in chapter 13 of this volume.

17. Jennifer L. Bloom, Bryant L. Hutson, and Ye He, *The Appreciative Advising Revolution* (Champaign, IL: Stipes Publishing, 2008), 11. See also Jennifer L. Bloom, Bryant L. Hutson, Ye He, and Erin Konkle, *The Appreciative Advising Revolution Training Workbook: Translating Theory to Practice* (Champaign, IL: Stipes Publishing, 2014).

Lessons from a course on vocation

For more than 15 years I have had the privilege of teaching a course that supports students' vocational exploration. The Three Crowns program, Gustavus's alternative general education program, offers an integrated sequence of courses, covering various ways of knowing. It focuses on three themes: the development of the Western tradition with global comparisons, an examination of values, and the relationship of the individual and community. Sixty students go through the four-year program as a learning cohort. The first day of their senior seminar, students are given a copy of a paper that they wrote as first-year students, in which they were asked to provide their definition of "the good life." Reading this work again, several years later, allows them to see how their ideas have changed—or not—over the course of their college career. It also raises the question that will echo throughout the course: how do I want to live?

A reading list to encourage vocational reflection

The beginning of the course asks students to look inward. When I teach it, I begin with bell hooks's *Bone Black*,[18] which focuses on the many factors that shaped her development into a black feminist writer/activist. Although we discuss obvious influences like parents, students are also asked to reflect on the ways that their values, behaviors, and aspirations have been shaped by their race and ethnicity, gender, class, and socioeconomic circumstances, and the social, cultural, and political pressures and assumptions of their time. Gail Tsukiyama's novel *The Samurai's Garden*[19] asks students to examine issues related to love and friendship, loyalty and betrayal, and various ways of coping with loss and disappointment—as well as cultural differences made salient by the book's Chinese protagonist and 1930s Japan setting. A book on Eastern religion[20] is used to ask students to reflect on their worldview; for the last several years, I have also asked students to consider the pros and cons of being part of the digital generation and being

---

18. bell hooks, *Bone Black: Memories of Girlhood* (New York: Henry Holt, 1996).

19. Gail Tsukiyama, *The Samurai's Garden* (New York: St. Martin's Press, 1994).

20. I have often used books on Shin Buddhism: Taitetsu Unno, *River of Fire, River of Water* (New York: Doubleday, 1998) or *Shin Buddhism: Bits of Rubble Turn into Gold* (New York: Doubleday, 2002). Other books suitable as general introductions to Buddhism include Zen teacher Steve Haugen's *Buddhism Plain and Simple* (North Clarendon, VT: Tuttle, 1997, 2013) and the many books by Thich Nhat Hanh and the Dalai Lama. I have also used a non-Buddhist book, Jiddu Krishnamurti, *Think on These Things*, ed. Desikacharya Rajagopal (New York: Harper and Row, 1964).

millennials. The middle part of the course encourages students to think about how they see their place in the world, raising ethical issues in contemporary life. This section includes units on ethical issues in science,[21] on the relationship of the United States to developing nations, and—closer to home—on community service, the environment and lifestyle choices, and immigration or race relations. The final book in the course is Toni Morrison's *Song of Solomon*,[22] which ties together these themes of identity, values, and community responsibilities with the idea of life as a journey or quest. This prepares the students for their final assignment: a vocational autobiography, in which they identify some of their primary values, consider the origins of those values, and reflect on how they are shaping their current vision of "the good life" and their hopes for their own lives beyond college.[23]

Vocational insights through encounters with difference

As Tim Clydesdale argues in *The Purposeful Graduate*, one would hope that students might be introduced to reflecting on vocation early in their college careers.[24] Nevertheless, even as they are about to graduate, students still appreciate the opportunity to engage in wide-ranging reflection on who they are and their relation to the world. In the senior seminar, they are forced to think more deeply—at this critical juncture in their lives—about what they value, as well as what they hope for in the future. In the midst of a culture that values productivity and busyness, they are grateful for the opportunity to pause and reflect. Moreover, this seminar includes an oral presentation, and I have witnessed the power of their sharing their stories with their peers—even when those stories have not been so easy. Many have called the class, and particularly this assignment, the highlight of their college experience. The students' responses serve as a reminder of the importance that students attach to being able to explore and share their stories, as well as their experience of feeling known and having their life lessons valued. This

21. Every year, leading internationally recognized scientific leaders are invited to campus for a two-day Nobel conference, Gustavus Adolphus College's signature academic event. Recent topics have included Addiction; The Universe at Its Limits; and Heating Up: The Energy Debate. A distinguishing characteristic of this conference is its intentional inclusion of consideration of ethical issues raised by the topic.

22. Toni Morrison, *Song of Solomon* (New York: Alfred A. Knopf, 1977).

23. For more classroom assignments to foster vocational reflection, see Tracy Sadd's discussion in chapter 12 of this volume. See also Matthew Sayers's discussion of the value of students creating their life stories in chapter 8 of this volume.

24. Clydesdale, *The Purposeful Graduate*, 2.

assignment gives students a new perspective on their experiences and can reinforce their development of resilience.

But at the same time, the course made clear to me how hard it is for some students to see beyond societal and cultural norms. Therefore, when I teach the course, I include a unit on Buddhism.[25] All schools of Buddhism grow out of the historical Buddha's insight that life is suffering because of our ignorance, desires, and ego. The way to end that suffering is to understand the foundational truths of reality (including the fact that life is change), to end our desires, and to empty ourselves of our ego. One way of doing this is by understanding that we are interconnected and not independent; in fact, we do not have stable selves, insofar as we are constantly being affected by everything around us. An image for this is Indra's net, which extends infinitely in every direction; at every intersecting node, there is a multifaceted jewel, which reflects the colors of the other jewels in the net. Each person is one of those jewels as is everything else in the universe.[26] This interconnectedness helps to explain why wisdom is always connected with compassion.

Indra's net provides a clue as to why Buddhists talk of "no self," which can be a difficult concept for students to grasp. Still, this emphasis on the interconnectedness of all things resonates with some students' understanding of environmentalism, while its emphasis on compassion and love resonates with other students' understanding of their own religious traditions. At the same time, however, Buddhism challenges students' ideas about the importance of the ego and ambition. Americans have been taught to equate the ego with the self and thus with personality; they assume that if one becomes egoless and rejects ambition and attachment, one would lose one's personality and become passive and uncaring. However, Buddhism teaches that, in fact, becoming egoless allows one to become most fully oneself. I ask students to think about when they were most themselves: was it at their first college mixer, or when they were with their best friends? Buddhism also teaches that the ego gets in the way of our truly seeing and responding well to the needs of the situations in front of us, because it keeps us focused on ourselves; it hinders our response-ability. Eastern religions in general, I think, are more likely to think in terms of responding to the situation rather

25. Some of the texts that the students read in this unit are listed in footnote 20.

26. The image of Indra's net comes from the third-century Avatamsaka Sutra. For a translation of the passage, see Francis H. Cook, *Hua-Yen Buddhism: The Jewel Net of Indra* (University Park: Pennsylvania State University Press, 1977). For a discussion of this image, see Kenneth K. Tanaka, *Ocean: An Introduction to Jodo-Shinshu Buddhism in America* (Berkeley, CA: WisdomOcean Publications, 1997), 17, 27.

than acting strictly on some principle.[27] Ambition, attachment, and ego can also prompt us to give up when the going gets rough, because we are looking for a certain outcome or seeking recognition. Many of our most important problems are also the most intractable—the ones needing the long view and persistence in the face of glacial change. Buddhism's emphasis on nonattachment to outcomes and egolessness is useful, in the sense that one must use the most "skillful means" one knows to accomplish these goals; in addition, however, one must be able to let go of the results to continue to work toward the greater good.[28]

The unit on Buddhism fills only a small part of the semester, but the purpose of the course as a whole is to complicate students' assumptions. For example, in the unit on international relations, students read a chapter from *Chinnagounder's Challenge*, which examines the nexus of development, gender, religion, and the environment.[29] It also critiques Western philosophical assumptions about its own universality, using India's very different cultural beliefs (and undoubtedly undergirded by the author's own lifelong practice of Zen meditation).

The process of "complicating one's assumptions" need not rely exclusively on the reading of texts. For example, the college's Community Service Office director, who spent several years with the Peace Corps, tells the story of his group's service learning project with the Mapucha, a poor, marginalized indigenous group in Chile. He had felt that the project was a failure, but then an elder gave a moving speech about what he considered the project's great success. The greatest service that students had done, said the elder, was not helping them glean a field (which indeed the indigenous people could have done faster alone), but asking their youth about their traditions and ways of life, making them proud to be Mapucha.

Of course, students who have studied abroad often come back with their own stories. Even 10 years later I still remember the biology major who admitted that when she saw a fisherman walking up a beach in Madagascar with a turtle, she was about to lecture him about their protected status, but her words died on her

---

27. There is a famous Zen story about two monks meeting a beautiful young woman by the side of a swift river. She asks for help to get across. The two monks look at each other because they have taken a vow not to touch women. However, the older monk picks her up, carries her across the river, and then puts her down; the monks then continue on their way. The junior monk is upset but says nothing until he can contain himself no longer and cries, "We are monks and are not permitted women. How could you carry that woman on your shoulders?" The older monk replies: "I left the woman long ago on the bank; however, you seem to be carrying her still."

28. See Anantanand Rambachan's comments on "renunciation of the fruits of one's actions" in chapter 6 of this volume.

29. Deane Curtin, *Chinnagounder's Challenge: The Question of Ecological Citizenship* (Bloomington: Indiana University Press, 1999), 3–33, 185–92.

lips when he proudly held up the turtle and announced, "Today I can feed my children!" Many of our students want to make the world a better place; it is important that we challenge them to think beyond their desires to help. We need to give them the knowledge, skills, and wisdom to hone their response-ability.

At the same time, teaching this course also helped me to see the dangers in tying vocation too closely to Buechner's emphasis on the needs of the world and with the college's emphasis on service. Students have tended to interpret our current motto ("Make your life count!") rather narrowly, feeling that if they are not activists, they are not living up to this expectation. Introverts, artists, and students interested in scientific research often feel as though the institution's general focus doesn't really apply to them. I remind these students that there are many ways to make the world a better place. As Henry David Thoreau argued in *Walden*: "If a man does not keep pace with his companions, perhaps it is because he hears a different drummer. Let him step to the music which he hears, however measured or far away."[30] When Thoreau died, his mentor Emerson lamented in his eulogy that he felt Thoreau had never fulfilled his promise, content to be "the captain of huckleberry [gathering] parties"—little realizing that, in reflecting on the fruits of his nature explorations, Thoreau had indeed produced something that would inspire through the ages. Thoreau both discerned his true vocation and responded to his world—a world he saw as too conformist and commercial. In doing so, he fulfilled his responsibility to both his talents and the world; he died content, despite his lack of recognition in his own time. And later generations have profited greatly from his wisdom.

Last thoughts

As a Buddhist teaching at a Lutheran college, I have developed relationships that have reinforced my sense of teaching as a vocation. These relationships have also strengthened my belief that the calling of the undergraduate educator goes well beyond teaching students in the specific areas of knowledge that are governed by our disciplines. College is a place for educating the whole person; this includes supporting students' intellectual progress, but also their emotional, moral, and civic development. American society continues to emphasize individualism and economic success, but our students today—perhaps driven by issues such as global climate change, racial conflict, income inequality, and increasing diversity—seem especially open to the call to make the world a better place. Even among those

30. Henry David Thoreau, *Walden; or, Life in the Woods*, in *Walden*, ed. Stephen Fender (Oxford: Oxford University Press, 1997), 290.

who have been disillusioned by particular religious claims to authority, most continue to hunger for lives of meaning and purpose.

Thinking about these vocational issues can be immeasurably enriched by a multi-faith context. Religious, spiritual, and philosophical exploration asks the most fundamental questions: How should I live in the world? What makes for a good life? How would I define a good person? A multi-faith context can encourage us to see more possibilities, to examine our own beliefs more deeply, and to enter into real relationships with those who are different from us. The great majority of undergraduate students want to reflect on their own callings, but they are also calling their teachers and mentors to a deeper understanding of their roles within a broader network of relationships. They are calling us, as the world calls us, to develop not only *our students'* discernment and response-ability —but also our own.

Response

Younus Y. Mirza

Florence's chapter touched me in a number of ways, especially in that she, as a non-Christian teaching at a Christian-affiliated school, was able to explore, develop, and complicate her own faith. Her experience led me to reflect on my own time at Georgetown University, the nation's first Catholic and Jesuit institution. I was attracted to Georgetown partly because it welcomed faith as part of a holistic education and as an integral part of identity formation. The university had hired its first university Muslim chaplain two years before I arrived; it also allowed the Muslim community to build a beautiful prayer room in one of the historic buildings on campus. Every student was required to take two theology classes, but they could pick the classes from any tradition. I began to take classes from the Center for Christian–Muslim Understanding, which would later influence me to pursue a PhD in Islamic studies.

Within my doctoral work, I began to explore the Qur'an's relationship with the Bible. I remember being surprised to learn how medieval Muslim scholars read the Arabic Bible to better understand qur'anic allusions. Toward the end of my undergraduate career, the Office of Mission and Ministry launched a campaign to educate the faculty and student body about Georgetown's "spirit of values." Among them was the idea of educating the "whole person," which included "the development of the spiritual, intellectual, artistic, and physical aspects of each person." The phrase was posted on banners throughout the campus, making it clear that faith and spirituality were essential to Georgetown's mission.

My experience at a Catholic and Jesuit school helped me to develop and complicate my own understanding of Islam and to appreciate the ways in which Muslims and Christians have interacted and learned from one another. In this way it parallels Florence's experience of coming to a greater understanding of her own Buddhist tradition through her work at a Christian institution.

11

The Vocation of Church-Related Colleges in a Multi-Faith World

EDUCATING FOR RELIGIOUS PLURALISM

Jacqueline A. Bussie

IN *NO LONGER Invisible: Religion in University Education*, Douglas and Rhonda Jacobsen observe: "All institutions of higher learning need to address interfaith issues, because everyone now lives in an interfaith world."[1] Indeed, the United States is one of the most religiously diverse nations in the world, and that diversity increases with every passing year.[2] In parts of the country that were once largely homogenous and Christian, today it is commonplace for people of diverse religions and cultures to live and work side by side.[3] Consider the city of Fargo–Moorhead (Fargo, North Dakota, and Moorhead, Minnesota), where I teach at Concordia College, a liberal arts institution of the Evangelical Lutheran Church of America (ELCA). Not so long ago, nearly everyone in Fargo–Moorhead was indigenous or Lutheran; today, the city is an interfaith home to 6,000 Muslims,

---

1. Douglas and Rhonda Hustedt Jacobsen, *No Longer Invisible: Religion in University Education* (New York: Oxford University Press, 2012), 79.

2. For a detailed examination of this claim, see Diana Eck, *A New Religious America: How a "Christian Country" Has Become the World's Most Religiously Diverse Nation* (New York: HarperSanFrancisco, 2002).

3. For detailed statistics regarding the declining number of Christians and the rapidly changing US religious demographics, see the Pew Research Center's study from May 2015: http://www.pewforum.org/2015/05/12/americas-changing-religious-landscape/ (accessed November 13, 2017).

three Jewish synagogues, and flourishing secular, Buddhist, Hindu, and Baha'i communities.

While the presence of this religious diversity undoubtedly enriches our lives and strengthens our communities and nation as a whole, such diversity—especially when manipulated for political ends—also has the dreadful potential to generate intense conflict. As our national news headlines make abundantly clear, in cities like Orlando and Boston, gunmen perpetrate terrorist attacks on innocent victims in the name of the so-called Islamic state (ISIS/ISL). In tandem, although largely ignored by the American media,[4] in 2015 hate crimes committed against American Muslims rose an astonishing 78 percent, reaching their highest levels since the days immediately following the 9/11 attacks.[5] To name only two examples, in April 2016 in New York City, three attackers shouting "ISIS" beat a Muslim man. In June 2016 in Minneapolis, a man screaming obscenities about Islam shot two Muslim men.

For higher education and its educators, increasing religious diversity and its civic repercussions raise urgent questions about our institutional and personal vocations or callings. Foremost among them is: what is a church-related college's vocation in a world of ever-increasing religious diversity?[6] I will argue that, in today's multi-faith world, a church-related college's vocation is to educate intentionally for religious pluralism, with the word *pluralism* here denoting constructive engagement with religious diversity and the search for genuine understanding across difference.[7] The chapter offers three concrete recommendations as to how church-related colleges might successfully educate for religious pluralism and thus constructively re-envision their vocation(s) in the twenty-first century. Along the way, I will also consider the vocation(s) of *educators* in a multi-faith society.

---

4. For a thorough study of the biased way the American media portrays Muslims almost exclusively as perpetrators of violence, see Peter Gottschalk and Gabriel Greenberg, *Islamophobia: Making Muslims the Enemy* (Lanham, MD: Rowman & Littlefield, 2008).

5. Eric Lichtblau, "Hate Crimes against American Muslims Most Since Post-9/11 Era," *New York Times*, September 17, 2016, http://www.nytimes.com/2016/09/18/us/politics/hate-crimes-american-muslims-rise.html?_r=0 (accessed September 27, 2016).

6. See David S. Cunningham, "Colleges Have Callings, Too: Vocational Reflection at the Institutional Level," in *Vocation across the Academy: A New Vocabulary for Higher Education*, ed. David S. Cunningham (New York: Oxford University Press, 2017), 249–71.

7. See Harvard University's Pluralism Project at http://pluralism.org/what-is-pluralism/ (accessed January 29, 2017). Although the meaning of pluralism is often contested, throughout this chapter, I use the term solely in the constructive sense defined here.

Identifying the problem

I earned my PhD in religious studies in 2003 from a very well-respected state institution. My training was exclusively in the academic study of religion. Abstraction and detachment pervaded my graduate school education—an inheritance undoubtedly rooted in religious studies' difficult history of fighting for academic credibility in a world where *faith* is all too often synonymous with fundamentalism and fanaticism. As academics in training, my fellow graduate students and I were socialized to teach and discuss religion objectively, ignoring the fact that nearly everyone else in the world engages religion subjectively—that is, as something practiced and personal, as well as public. My experience is not the exception but the norm:

> Even today, graduate education (especially at the doctoral level) encourages students to bracket any personal feelings or values they might have about the subject they are studying. For individuals nurtured into the academy by way of this regimen, the reappearance of religion in higher education can seem like a bizarre intrusion into a world where, to them, it simply has no place.[8]

This traditional mode of teaching and learning about religion has negative repercussions. My graduate education—though excellent in so many other ways—arguably did not prepare me for the real world (or even for a real classroom). Never once in graduate school did we discuss the practical skills, competencies, or interfaith literacy that we would need in order to navigate—or teach our future students to navigate—the religious diversity that surrounds us all. I had never even heard the word *Islamophobia* used in a classroom, but in my first year of teaching, both the word and the reality were ubiquitous. In my first semester of teaching, a Christian student in my class raised his hand and adamantly announced to everyone present, "Islam is a religion of hate. Unlike Christianity, it understands nothing about forgiveness." Nothing in graduate school had prepared me, pedagogically or theologically, for that moment—nor for the hundreds like it that would follow, both inside and outside the classroom. Yet wasn't it my responsibility not only to address the reality of Islamophobia but to teach my students how to address it as well?

These classroom experiences brought to the fore a nagging question: In a world roiling with rancor and prejudice, how are educators called to responsibly

8. Jacobsen and Jacobsen, *No Longer Invisible*, 33.

guide our students? Are traditional teaching methodologies adequate to meet the challenges of today's multi-faith world and classrooms, or do we need to learn new ones? As a theologian, I originally sought to become a professor of religion because I wanted to teach my students to love theology. I still want this; but after 14 years in the trenches, I've revised my primary goal to one more practical and pressing: I teach religion in order to help stop hate and build peace. Academic institutions need to revise their pedagogical and curricular goals to be more in line with meeting the world's most urgent and practical needs. If we fail to do so, the general public will continue to perceive the education we offer as more and more irrelevant—a perception that some research indicates is already burgeoning at an alarming rate.[9] Academics may resist the practical aspect of higher education, but the public yearns for it and needs it. Responding to this summons to practicality can help rescue us from the perception of irrelevance.

Teaching interreligious literacy

The first way church-related colleges can fulfill their vocation to educate for religious pluralism is by teaching interreligious literacy as a crucial component of twenty-first century intercultural competence and global citizenship. At the moment, higher education tends to focus only on diversity in race, gender, class, and sexuality; responsible educators, however, must add religion to this list. Institutions must require their graduates to acquire basic knowledge of the world's major religions.

Virtually every higher education institution in America prioritizes intercultural competence. But all too often, those very same institutions fail to recognize religion as a crucial, inextricable component of culture; for example, many colleges and universities do not require students to take a single course in religion. Consider the example of Harvard University, where, in 2007, a faculty task force proposed a general education requirement in religion. Faculty backlash against the requirement was swift and powerful, with professors such as Steven Pinker arguing that the university should not waste students' time on what he called the "ignorance and irrationality of religion."[10]

---

9. The American public's faith in the value of college continues to plummet. According to a recent survey, today only 42 percent of Americans believe a college degree is necessary, down from 55 percent in 2009. Ruth McCambridge, "Public Losing Faith in Higher Education as a Jumpstart for Work Lives," *Nonprofit Quarterly*, September 16, 2016, https://nonprofitquarterly.org/2016/09/16/public-losing-faith-higher-education-jumpstart-work-lives/ (accessed November 13, 2017).

10. Jacobsen and Jacobsen, *No Longer Invisible*, 9.

Unfortunately, such academic narrow-mindedness, along with a ferocious public bias against the academic study of religion, is pervasive. Indeed, these are among the primary reasons for the widespread religious illiteracy in America today.[11] As Stephen Prothero argues:

> In today's world it is irresponsible to use the word "educated" to describe high school or college graduates who are ignorant of the ancient stories that continue to motivate the beliefs and behaviors of the overwhelming majority of the world's population. In a world as robustly religious as ours, it is foolish to imagine that such graduates are equipped to participate fully in the politics of the nation or the affairs of the world.[12]

At my own institution, the mission statement explicitly claims that our graduates will "influence the affairs of the world"; many other church-related institutions make similar claims. Because these institutions are already deeply involved in conversations about religion and are boldly willing to engage it as a critical component of world affairs, they are uniquely poised to take up Prothero's charge to educate religiously literate graduates. Most of the nation's church-related colleges still have religion requirements within the core curriculum. Arguably, in today's religiously diverse world, this requirement is not an artifact, but an advantage. It provides institutions with a unique opportunity to teach students the interreligious literacy they will so desperately need for their professional, personal, and civic lives.

Interreligious literacy is important, regardless of future career, as the burgeoning interdisciplinary field of interfaith studies demonstrates. In 2016, Concordia–Moorhead became one of only a dozen schools in the nation to offer such a degree program. Concordia's new interfaith minor includes courses and faculty from eleven different disciplines and supplements any major by providing graduates with the core skills, competencies, and literacy needed to constructively engage religious diversity in the workplace and civic sphere. In today's competitive education marketplace, flagship programs such as these—at Concordia and elsewhere—possess the exciting potential to redouble an institution's relevance.

---

11. The Pew Research Center's 2010 U.S. Religious Knowledge Survey executive summary reports that Americans correctly answer only 16 out of 32 questions about the core teachings, history, and leading figures of the world's major religions. This is 50 percent, a grade of "F." See http://www.pewforum.org/2010/09/28/u-s-religious-knowledge-survey/ (accessed November 13, 2017).

12. Stephen Prothero, *Religious Literacy: What Every American Should Know—and Doesn't* (New York: HarperOne, 2007), 182.

In order to better assess the need and relevance of interreligious literacy for our graduates' future careers, Concordia's student Interfaith Scholars and I received a grant from Interfaith Youth Core and the James S. Kemper Foundation to research religious diversity in local professional settings. We conducted one-on-one interviews at various nonprofit and for-profit corporate businesses in the Fargo–Moorhead area, and queried hiring managers and employees about the knowledge and skills they found necessary to engage religious diversity in the workplace. Though we expected interreligious literacy to be important, we were shocked by how critical our interviewees testified that it actually was. Our research unearthed many concrete examples wherein a lack of interreligious literacy cost an organization valuable time and resources—losses that could have been avoided if basic interreligious literacy had been part of the employees' education.

Consider this example, from one of the regional libraries where we conducted our research. The library had received a grant to design a fiscal literacy education brochure for New Americans in our area, in order to provide them with financial advice on opening a bank account, saving money for their children's education, and the like. In designing the brochure, the librarians emulated a national financial education campaign called Feed the Pig (feedthepig.org). The brochure's cover pictured a piggy-bank head on a man's upper body, underneath the words "FEED THE PIG." However, the majority of Fargo–Moorhead's New Americans—the target audience for the brochure—were Muslims; they took one look at the brochure and were horrified. Pigs symbolize impurity and uncleanness within most Muslim cultures; moreover, the consumption of pork is explicitly forbidden in the Qur'an. Once the designers discovered their error, they were forced to redesign their campaign from scratch. Clearly, even a minimal degree of interreligious literacy could have prevented this entire situation and saved the organization money, time, effort, and embarrassment.

Our research revealed a lamentable gap between the complete lack of religious diversity training (whether in employees' previous education or on the job) and the nearly universal desire, at all levels of seniority, to participate in such training if offered. It unveiled that teaching interreligious literacy, skills, and core competencies to our graduates is a vital means through which institutions can fulfill their calling to educate students for the twenty-first century. In the report to the foundation that helped fund this research, we wrote:

> Colleges, especially church-related colleges and universities with core religion requirements and interfaith studies degrees, are in a unique position to educate exactly the kind of graduates that every hiring manager we encountered said that their organization actually needs—men and

women who can effectively and constructively engage religious and cultural diversity on the job.[13]

In fulfilling our institutional vocation to educate for religious pluralism, we may very well help our students to better fulfill their own callings.

Honoring religious heritage while addressing Christian privilege

A second way church-related colleges can fulfill their vocation to educate for religious pluralism involves the sensitive issue of Christian privilege. I believe that faith-based institutions are called to decenter Christian privilege, yet simultaneously honor—and not jettison—their institution's religious heritage. Here, note that I am *not* at all calling for a decentering or devaluing of an institution's Christian roots or heritage, but instead only for a decentering of Christian *privilege*—meaning a (conscious or unconscious) inequitable prioritization and favoring of the needs, perspectives, and education of Christian students to the detriment or marginalization of the needs of those who do not self-identify as Christian.[14] Stated more positively, the goal is to attend to the needs, perspectives, experiences, and voices of the students on campus who often go unheard and unrecognized, moving these voices from the margins to a shared center stage. These students may be Buddhist, Hindu, Jewish, Native American, nonreligious, atheists, agnostics, or any other lifestance that has been marginalized. To construct a helpful analogy, imagine the difference between listening to a soloist recital and a cappella choir; while both are lovely, what is heard on our campuses should sound like the latter, not the former.

An authentic grappling with difficult issues of privilege requires the transformation of many institutional cultures—a slow and ongoing process which, though it may perhaps never be fully realized, remains a *telos* toward which we are being drawn. I recognize that my own institution has not done this perfectly and that there is no one-size-fits-all way for every church-related institution to achieve this. Nevertheless, I want to describe how this process has taken place at Concordia, in the hope that it might catalyze shared reflection on how church-related colleges and universities can both transform and fulfill their vocations in a multi-faith world.

---

13. The grant report to the Kemper Foundation is currently under review for publication. Available from the author upon request.

14. For more on Christian privilege, see the introduction to this volume, in the section titled "The expansion and diversification of higher education."

Once upon a time, Concordia College–Moorhead consisted of Lutheran professors, who worked alongside a Lutheran staff and administration, educating Lutheran students in a Lutheran town. Today, both the college and the community surrounding it are considerably more diverse. Concordia–Moorhead no longer requires its faculty and staff to be Lutheran; indeed, among our college's faculty and students, one will find Jews, Christians, Pagans, Muslims, atheists, agnostics, Native Americans, and Buddhists, among many others. About 43 percent of our current students are Lutheran, and nearly 18 percent fall into the category of "nones," claiming no religious affiliation at all. Still, the majority of our college's students and faculty self-identify as Christian, and many non-Christian residents in the region continue to assume that the institution is "only for Christians."

Concordia's current strategic plan includes a robust diversity initiative. At the same time, the college remains firmly rooted in its Lutheran heritage, which is a source of great solace and pride to many of our alumni/ae/a. In short, while our traditional Christian heritage attracts and appeals to some, it alienates others. Needless to say, Concordia is not alone in this story of transition and tension; these very issues have caused identity crises at many church-related colleges across the nation.

The vastly divergent ways that church-related institutions have handled this crisis form a continuum. On one end, there are those colleges and universities that respond to growing religious diversity by doubling down on their sectarian identity and taking strong measures to sustain it, such as having all campus constituencies confess allegiance to a particular statement of faith. At the other extreme, there are those institutions that choose to jettison their church affiliation in favor of a more secular approach. Additionally, at nearly every institution, there are people on either side of this argument who spend a lot of time squabbling with one another. To those in the first camp, I can only say that keeping our students in a sectarian bubble does them no favors. Our graduates will inevitably work and live in a religiously diverse world, and if we fail to prepare them for that real world, we disadvantage them. To those in the second camp, I can only say that choosing to stand somewhere and claim a tradition does not necessarily make one exclusivist or un-embracing of folks from other religions.

What I am proposing—and what I believe Concordia–Moorhead and many other ELCA institutions are trying to incarnate—is a *via media*, a middle way or "third way."[15] This third way aims to discern and reconcile the well-meaning

15. The term *third way* comes from the theologian Walter Wink. See *Jesus and Nonviolence: A Third Way* (Minneapolis: Fortress, 2003). ELCA theologian Darrell Jodock also uses a similar term; see https://gustavus.edu/faith/pdf/Third_Path_Article.pdf (accessed July 9, 2017).

intention in both contradictory positions—a desire to remain loyal and proud of one's heritage, on the one hand, and a desire to be universally open and embracing, on the other. The steps I will describe in this section have worked for Concordia to traverse this both/and reconciliation, but I encourage each institution to find its own best path.

On Concordia–Moorhead's campus, the complex issue of our church affiliation has raised institutional vocation questions. What does it mean to be a Christian college in a multi-faith society and community? Must the college eschew its sectarian heritage in order to serve multi-religious constituents effectively? How does a church-related school best serve its diverse student body and honor the multiple religious identities of its students, faculty, and staff? How can the college attract more religiously diverse students? In short, how can a church-related college embrace interfaith engagement, while still sustaining a commitment to its own faith tradition? As Rabbi Abraham Joshua Heschel has observed, "The problem to be faced is: how to combine loyalty to one's own tradition with reverence for different traditions."[16] Though these wise words originally described a problem faced by individuals, we can apply them equally well to institutions.

How indeed does a faith-based institution remain loyal to its historical religious tradition yet also embrace the diverse traditions of its contemporary constituents? Seven years ago, a critical mass of Concordia faculty, students, and administrators discerned that the institution was being called to transform itself vocationally into an institution dedicated to interfaith engagement, cooperation, service, dialogue, and peace-building. More specifically, we felt ourselves called by the college's Lutheran heritage, and by the diversifying community that surrounded the institution, to become a place where faith and learning could relate to one another—not as academic enemies, but as intellectual sisters. A spirit of free inquiry has long been a hallmark of Lutheran higher education; Martin Luther's own life and work strongly exemplified that no subject was off limits for learning or interrogation (including faith itself).[17]

The reasoning behind Concordia's dedication to an interfaith approach was therefore theological and pedagogical, as well as strategic. Theologically, Lutheranism provides strong resources for the rejection of dichotomous either/or thinking and an embrace of both/and thinking. For example, Martin Luther famously stated that all Christians are *simul justus et peccator*—simultaneously

16. Abraham Joshua Heschel, *Moral Grandeur and Spiritual Audacity: Essays* (New York: Farrar, Straus & Giroux, 1996), 242.

17. See the similar conclusions about Luther drawn by Florence Amamoto in chapter 10 of this volume.

saved and sinful; Luther also dismantled the usual dichotomy of faith and doubt, embracing doubt as a component of a vibrant faith.[18] In my view, because the Lutheran tradition accepts paradox as the tough truth about the world, Lutheran higher education institutions are theologically empowered to answer Heschel's both/and call for loyalty to one's own tradition and reverence for others' traditions. Lutheran higher education is set free to educate for pluralism rather than privilege.

Pedagogically, religion and faith had always mattered at Concordia; the institution had always encouraged its students to bring their whole selves—messy spiritual lives and all—to their educational pursuits. The college had never shied away from those hard and often uncomfortable faith-based conversations that much of the larger academy eschewed as "unacademic" and therefore anathema. We had always had a general education religion requirement and, for the past decade, had required a course of all graduates on religious diversity. Given this history, the next step was simply a logical extension. The college would continue to be a place where faith mattered—not only the institution's original faith heritage, but *all* faiths. In 2011, the president of Concordia College stated in the college's strategic plan that interfaith dialogue, service, and cooperation would be priorities of the college as it moved forward. This was not a top-down proclamation, but rather a reflection of the powerful grassroots movement already occurring across the campus.

In order for Concordia to become a place where all faiths (and nonfaiths) mattered, many felt that the Christian privilege that had flavored the school since 1891 needed to be recognized and addressed (though without jettisoning the institution's identity and heritage). As a community, we intentionally brought folks from traditions other than Christianity from the margins to the center; they were invited to the table and heard, and their advice valued and heeded. Of course, this road was long and paved with difficulty, occasional conflict, and detractors (often in the form of alumni who expressed concern that the college was abandoning its roots). I do not want to idealize this process, or make it seem smooth, easy, or without mistakes. But in the end, we succeeded, and two years ago Concordia was recognized by Interfaith Youth Core as a vanguard interfaith institution.[19] We became living proof that a faithful transformation of institutional vocation is possible. How did we find our way?

---

18. Martin Luther, *Lectures on Romans*, trans. Wilhelm Pauck (Philadelphia: Westminster Press, 1961), xliv–xlv.

19. See Eboo Patel, Katie Bringman Baxter, and Noah Silverman, "Leadership Practices for Interfaith Excellence in Higher Education," *Liberal Education* 101, nos. 1–2 (Winter/Spring 2015): 48–53, https://www.aacu.org/liberaleducation/2015/winter-spring/patel (accessed

First, in 2011 the institution founded an interfaith center on campus, the Forum on Faith and Life. This office's mission is to "create opportunities for genuine encounter with the interfaith neighbor," as well as to "foster a deeper and more compassionate understanding of one another across traditional boundaries." The Forum's work ensures that Concordia consistently offers both co-curricular and curricular opportunities for students to acquire and enhance their interreligious literacy. The Forum on Faith and Life regularly organizes events that expose students to diverse interfaith voices, such as "Ask an Atheist" panels, "Meet Your Muslim Neighbor" events, and a signature speaker series that has brought to campus interfaith activists such as Interfaith Youth Core president Eboo Patel, acclaimed Muslim playwright Rohina Malik, and Nobel Peace Prize winner Leymah Gbowee.

When Eboo Patel spoke at Concordia in 2012, he was our school's first Muslim convocation speaker. The morning after his visit, I received an email from a Muslim colleague that I have saved to this day. My Muslim friend had taught at the college for 15 years, and she wrote, "All I can say is last night I felt my love for Concordia multiplied 10 times. Last night at last I felt like I belonged to this place. Thank you from the depth of my soul."[20] One can only imagine that our college's Muslim students felt much the same way. In order for any church-related college to send this strong message of belonging and respect to everyone on campus, co-curricular campus programming must foreground underrepresented religious and nonreligious voices.

Second, Concordia students formed a student organization, the Better Together Interfaith Alliance, which regularly brings together students of different faiths and lifestances to do service projects for the common good. With their weekly "Common Grounds" meetings, these students created a robust co-curricular space on campus for students to come together and share their perspectives. Every institution claims to prioritize empowering its students. Wonderfully, many of these very students are already deeply committed to pluralism, and simply need to be provided the resources and encouragement necessary to galvanize their peers.

Third, Concordia established an Interfaith Scholars program, which provides paid internships for students to conduct original interfaith studies research, serve as community liaisons to Fargo–Moorhead's diverse religious communities, and

---

March 18, 2017). Concordia's interfaith statement is explicitly mentioned in this article as an exemplary means of establishing a college's public identity as an institution committed to interfaith work.

20. Personal email correspondence from Dr. M. Ibrahim, August 31, 2012.

coordinate educational interfaith events. This scholarship program trains students to become the interfaith leaders for which the world so desperately longs. All college graduates will inevitably end up working alongside or managing interfaith coworkers, as well as serving a religiously diverse clientele; our institutions need to do their very best to prepare them for this reality. To do so successfully—and to avoid the aforementioned feed-the-pig-type gaffes, as well as major conflicts such as the recent Cargill firing of 150 Muslim workers whose prayer needs were not accommodated on the job—twenty-first-century graduates absolutely will need basic interreligious literacy.[21] As Eboo Patel has written, "An interfaith leader is someone who can create the spaces, organize the social processes, and craft the conversations such that people who orient around religion differently can have a common life together."[22]

Fourth and of utmost importance, Concordia in 2012 established a President's Interfaith Advisory Council (PIAC) that consists of nonreligious and religiously diverse students, faculty, staff, and administration, who advise the president and the board of regents on matters of religious diversity. This is one of the only committees on our campus that brings together voices from all segments of the campus, including admissions, advancement, the faculty senate, the dean's office, the business school, the religion department, and student government, among others. This group has been helpful in providing feedback to the college from diverse voices who express what they find valuable about the school's Lutheran heritage, even though they do not themselves identify as Lutheran.

The rewards of the PIAC have been financial as well. It has helped connect faculty and students to advancement officers, who come to understand more deeply the how, why, and what of the college's interfaith activities, and are thus better enabled to take those stories out to donors interested in funding the interfaith initiatives in which faculty and students are engaged. Admittedly, a few donors (inaccurately) perceive Concordia's interfaith work as a rejection of its Lutheran heritage and have threatened to withdraw their financial support. This is a sad reality and it must be acknowledged as a possible consequence, if a church-related college or university is courageous enough to transform its vocation to one of educating for pluralism. Interestingly, however, Concordia's advancement office reports that it doesn't know of any actual instances in which a gift was withdrawn.[23]

---

21. See http://www.cnn.com/2016/01/02/us/colorado-muslim-workers-fired-prayer-dispute/ (accessed March 18, 2017).

22. Eboo Patel, *Interfaith Leadership: A Primer* (Boston: Beacon Press, 2016), 11.

23. Trina Hall, personal email correspondence, March 29, 2017.

But it is equally important to note that Concordia's new interfaith work has also brought new donors out of the woodwork—especially alumni who themselves are not Christian or Lutheran, and who previously felt too little resonance with the institution's culture or mission to desire to give back. Trina Hall, PIAC member and Concordia's innovative director of development, regularly introduces students and professors to interested donors and has successfully brought in numerous gifts to fund student interfaith leadership training. Other gifts have followed. For example, this summer, I visited with a potential donor who had never given a gift to Concordia; he gave a generous gift that doubled the budget of the Forum on Faith and Life for two years. It is not unreasonable to expect similar positive responses among the alumni base at other institutions. Hall observes:

> Most alumni I encounter express a deep sense of joy and hopefulness when they hear how students are fostering peaceful dialogue and service to the neighbor through interfaith cooperation. In several instances, alumni were drawn back to supporting and engaging with the college *because of* the interfaith momentum and the hope it inspires.[24]

But even if this financial windfall were not the case, should financial considerations trump an institution's principles? If a church-related institution professes a commitment to diversity, shouldn't it stand firm in its commitment, even when it comes to religious diversity? Should market considerations outweigh foundational values? History has painted with a heroic brush those educational institutions that stood up for racial diversity and integration during the civil rights movement. These institutions perceived their commitment to racial justice and equality as essential to their mission and vocation, even though to many such a move was wildly unpopular.

As this historical example suggests, the real gains of an interfaith advisory council soar far beyond the financial. Concordia's PIAC has facilitated continued community conversations about what it means to be a Lutheran institution in today's ever-changing educational and societal landscape. Our PIAC's greatest contribution to date has been the creation of an institutional interfaith cooperation statement, which was intended to supplement (rather than replace) our college mission statement. This official statement helped to establish our public identity as a faith-based institution committed to cultivating interreligious literacy and promoting interfaith engagement. Institutions should seek to tie their

24. Hall, personal email correspondence, March 29, 2017.

interfaith commitments to the institution's mission, values, and identity—a move that Interfaith Youth Core has identified as a best practice.[25]

Concordia's current mission statement, last revised in 1956, has a specifically Christian focus. It reads: "The purpose of Concordia College is to influence the affairs of the world by sending into society thoughtful and informed men and women dedicated to the Christian life." Over the course of one year, the PIAC facilitated rich campus-wide conversations about the college's mission and brought together diverse constituents from across the campus to formulate a supplemental statement. In the classroom, students engaged in peer-led discussions about what interfaith work is (and isn't), as well as how our original mission statement is heard by students in a multi-faith environment. Members of the college community learned to discuss issues of Christian privilege and contributed to the formation of a broad consensus on interfaith understanding. In 2014, the following statement was unanimously approved by both the faculty senate and student government organizations: "Concordia College practices interfaith cooperation because of its Lutheran dedication to prepare thoughtful and informed global citizens who foster wholeness and hope, build peace through understanding, and serve the world together."[26]

As one might imagine, the subordinate clause describing the college's "Lutheran dedication" provided a challenge to the wordsmiths, but perhaps not in the way one might think. Several Lutheran (and other Christian) advocates wanted the statement to affirm that Concordia practiced interfaith cooperation that was *guided by* its Lutheran dedication to certain principles. But an atheist student and a Muslim professor insisted instead that the language declare unequivocally that we practice interfaith cooperation *because of* our Lutheran dedication. When asked to say more about their perspective, the Muslim professor replied, "I want to know that there will *always* be a place for me here . . . that I belong here [precisely] *because* this place is Lutheran, not because some folks might possibly be 'guided' to create a space for me . . . or not." This was a reminder that our dedication to pluralism and interfaith peace-building comes not *in spite of* our Lutheran heritage, but precisely *because of* it.[27]

Why "because of," many might ask? As Concordia's statement suggests, service to the neighbor and love of one's neighbor are paramount principles in the

25. See Patel, Bringman Baxter, and Silverman, "Leadership Practices."

26. See https://www.concordiacollege.edu/studentlife/spiritual-life/ (accessed July 10, 2017).

27. This thinking is in keeping with the work of Eboo Patel, who consistently encourages institutions to plumb their own heritage for resources to nurture interfaith engagement. See Patel, Baxter, and Silverman, "Leadership Practices."

Lutheran tradition, and this should logically extend to the interfaith neighbor. In theological support of this view, as a public theologian of the Lutheran church, I have long taught and preached that, unbeknownst to most contemporary readers, the Good Samaritan parable is a story of interfaith instruction.[28] In the parable, which Jesus presumably tells to a Jewish audience, several upstanding Jewish folks walk by a beat-up Jewish man in a ditch and do not stop to help. A Samaritan, however, stops and shows radical love for the man, including staying with him all night and paying for his medical care. Jesus concludes the parable by saying that if we want to be a good neighbor, we should all go and behave like the Samaritan.

Contemporary Christian audiences who do not understand Jesus's original context miss the deep meaning and shock of this story. In Jesus's day, the Samaritans and Jews were enemies. Why? *Because they practiced different religions.* Virtually all of Jesus's Jewish community believed the Samaritans practiced a false faith. In the fourth century BCE, the Samaritans scandalously built on Mt. Gezirim the only temple which ever rivaled the Jerusalem temple, creating a deep schism between the faiths. The thrust of Jesus's parable, then, is that a man of a different religion—a religion his audience was taught to fear and hate—was the only one who stopped to help the man in a ditch. (The shock that this must have had on Jesus's original listeners can perhaps best be recaptured in our day if we substitute "Muslim" for Samaritan.) Jesus's message? We should not only cherish our interfaith neighbors and treat them with radical love; we should also learn from them. In other words, the Good Samaritan parable is Jesus's direct summons to interfaith friendship, cooperation, care, and mercy. As Jesus is a reconciler, so we Christians are called to "a ministry of reconciliation."[29]

Taking the Good Samaritan parable's message to heart, Concordia College–Moorhead chose to embrace interfaith cooperation and construct its interfaith statement. Rather than renounce the college's religious heritage as an embarrassing parochial artifact from a bygone era—a move made by many church-related colleges—Concordia instead decided to harness the tradition's resources and use them to guide the institution through the process of re-imagining its vocation in a multi-faith world. We did this because we believe that genuine pluralism entails empowering everyone to cherish their identities and traditions and to bring their whole undiluted self to the table—and that this includes Christians, no less than people of other lifestances. Constructing our interfaith

---

28. Luke 10:25–37. The interpretation that follows comes from my book, *Love Without Limits: Jesus' Radical Vision for Love with No Exceptions* (Minneapolis: Fortress, 2018).

29. This phrase comes from 2 Corinthians 5:18.

statement allowed Concordia to understand its institutional identity, likewise, as a source not of shame, but instead of pride and joy. As I noted earlier, educating for pluralism at a church-related institution involves destabilizing Christian privilege, *not* abandoning Christian principles and all they potentially have to offer the world—especially the principle of radical love toward the neighbor.

Those of us who helped draft Concordia's statement, therefore, feel that it was a crucial step toward creating spaces for people of every religious tradition on our campus. Yet, at the same time, we honored and plumbed our college's rich Lutheran tradition in order to do so. After all, peace-building, loving and serving the neighbor, and cultivating hope and integrity are all deeply Lutheran values, but not exclusively Lutheran. Fortunately, these are values that so many people of good will share and can support, whether they are humanist, Buddhist, Muslim, Sikh, Jewish, Christian, or indigenous.

Finally, with respect to specifically Lutheran concerns, our statement connects us to a long-upheld value of our sponsoring denomination, namely, that of "reconciled diversity." In a 1991 social statement on ecumenism, the ELCA explained its relationship to other Christian traditions this way: "It is a communion where diversities contribute to fullness and are no longer barriers to unity. . . . [T]he diversities are reconciled and transformed into a legitimate and indispensable multiformity."[30] I believe this principle can be used to apply to interfaith relations as well. As a church, we advocate for harmony within heterogeneity—not unity through uniformity. The ELCA believes that God calls the church body to embrace diversity, rather than to erase it. The problem is never diversity itself, but instead the tragic fact that we have let our diversity divide us. The ELCA therefore considers one of its vocations to be the reconciling of diversity in a broken world. Concordia College–Moorhead likewise understands the creation of its interfaith cooperation statement to have brought us one small step closer to fulfilling our twenty-first-century vocations of educating for pluralism and reconciling our diversity.

Creating pedagogical space for interfaith exploration

A third and final way that institutions can fulfill their vocations is to ensure that their classrooms are multivocal, student-centered spaces where all participants

30. ELCA, *The Vision of the Evangelical Lutheran Church in America*, http://download.elca.org/ELCA%20Resource%20Repository/The_Vision_Of_The_ELCA.pdf?_ga=1.156510136.20878209.1334002044 (accessed September 29, 2016).

are exposed to, and in dialogue with, religiously diverse voices. In this section, I will explore issues of pedagogy, and in particular address the questions: How specifically do we *teach* for pluralism? How do we not only honor religious diversity in a classroom setting but also harness it as a teaching tool? How can professors step back and allow their religiously diverse community members and students to teach one another?

Sadly, our nation's colleges and universities are failing our students in this regard; in fact, with regard to students' religious or spiritual journeys or related questions of meaning and purpose, they are too rarely allowed to speak at all. Drawing on a report from the Higher Education Research Institute, Larry Braskamp observes that

> if there is one thing that stands out with regard to the curriculum, however, it is the dearth of support students find for their own spiritual or religious journeys in classes, coursework, and conversations with faculty. A recent UCLA poll indicated that juniors at forty-six diverse institutions expressed a strong desire to become more engaged in their religious/spiritual journeys, but few students receive any guidance or direction related to this concern in their classes or from their professors. Over half of college students report that their professors never offered them any opportunities to discuss the meaning and purpose of life, and nearly half are dissatisfied because the college experience did not provide them with any "opportunities for religious and spiritual reflection."[31]

A recent study on general education religion classes yielded similar results. Barbara Woolvord's research discovered a "great divide" between faculty and student learning goals: while most religion professors want their religion course to teach critical thinking, most college students enrolled in the course want an opportunity to explore their own personal faith and/or spirituality.[32] Creating space in our classrooms for student reflection on their own religious/spiritual journeys is a crucial component of our pedagogical vocation in today's multi-faith world.

As Paolo Freire pointed out, far too many instructors practice a "banking model" of education, in which students are mere empty vessels waiting to be filled with the waters of knowledge that professors pour into their heads. Freire argued

---

31. Larry A. Braskamp, "The Religious and Spiritual Journeys of College Students," in *The American University in a Postsecular Age*, ed. Douglas Jacobsen and Rhonda Hustedt Jacobsen (New York: Oxford University Press, 2008), 117–34; here, 130–31.

32. Barbara Walvoord, *Teaching and Learning in College Introductory Religion Courses* (Oxford: Blackwell, 2008), 13–56.

that this teacher-centered pedagogy reflects a colonial and oppressive mindset, and should be replaced with a student-centered model:

> Through dialogue, the teacher-of-the-students and the students-of-the-teacher cease to exist and a new term emerges: teacher-student with students-teachers. The teacher is no longer merely the-one-who-teaches, but the one who is herself taught in dialogue with the students, who in turn while being taught also teach. The students become jointly responsible for a process in which all grow.[33]

This sentence from Freire appears on all my course syllabi; it helps students understand why I expect them to speak every day in class and why the chairs in my classroom are arranged in a circle rather than in rows facing me.

If only the professor's voice is heard, interfaith dialogue is unlikely to occur, and religiously diverse perspectives are unlikely to be offered. A student-centered classroom is of paramount importance in conversations about religion:

> Learning is maximized when students bring themselves wholeheartedly into the learning experience, and for many students, religion is a part of who they are. . . . student-centered learning contains an implicit receptivity to religion, because respecting the autonomy of students as learners necessarily entails some degree of respect for the religious identities and the spiritual quest of the students.[34]

Educators need to step back from their role as a mere source of information, instead letting students learn from one another—and, ideally, from community members as well. Instructors can bring in numerous practitioners of diverse religions for dialogue; some classes can travel to local mosques, synagogues, and temples, further de-centering the focus on instructor and classroom. In several of my service-learning courses, my students befriend local New American families of various religious traditions, visiting with them weekly. So many times, this has led

---

33. Paolo Freire, *Pedagogy of the Oppressed* (New York: Continuum, 1986), 80. For more on the significance of Freire for vocation, see Rachel Mikva's comments in chapter 1 of this volume, as well as Caryn Riswold, "Vocational Discernment: A Pedagogy of Humanization," in *At This Time and In This Place: Vocation and Higher Education*, ed. David S. Cunningham (New York: Oxford University Press, 2016), 72–95; and Jeff R. Brown, "Unplugging the GPS: Rethinking Undergraduate Professional Degree Programs," in Cunningham, ed., *Vocation across the Academy*, 204–24; here, 214–16.

34. Jacobsen and Jacobsen, *No Longer Invisible*, 29.

to lasting friendships—what Brian McLaren terms transgressive friendships—across traditional boundaries that we have been taught not to cross.[35] Service learning and community-based learning are essential to educating for pluralism; they inherently create a pluralistic situation in which students have not just one teacher, but many. Moreover, when people are allowed to actually get to know one another, stereotypes and biases are challenged, and at times even crumble.

Scientific evidence supports the claim that transgressive friendships dismantle prejudice. In particular, regard for an entire religious community improves among those who develop a positive meaningful relationship with even one member of that group.[36] This provides yet another warrant for educators to reject banking-style pedagogies and embrace student-centered models that allow for genuine encounter and transformative relationships.

No pedagogical advice has ever transformed my own teaching of religion as much as these courageous words from feminist activist and educator bell hooks:

> When education is the practice of freedom, students are not the only ones asked to share, to confess. . . . Empowerment cannot happen if we refuse to be vulnerable while encouraging students to take risks. . . . In my classrooms, I do not expect students to take any risks that I would not take, to share in any way that I would not share. . . . It is often productive if professors take the first risk, linking confessional narratives to academic discussions so as to show how experience can illuminate and enhance our understanding of academic material.[37]

Following hooks's lead, I see vulnerability as part of my vocation. I do not hide my religious or justice-related commitments from my students, nor do I expect them to hide theirs. Of course, this means I always run the risk of unintentionally dominating the classroom with my viewpoint and further silencing already-marginalized voices. This is a delicate balancing act, and no doubt I often make mistakes and fail.

Nonetheless, I strongly agree with those who claim that "a professor who makes believe that his or her convictions have no salience for the classroom is

35. Brian McLaren, *Why Did Jesus, Moses, the Buddha, and Mohammed Cross the Road? Christian Identity in a Multi-Faith World* (New York: Jericho, 2012), 228.

36. Robert D. Putnam and David E. Campbell, *American Grace: How Religion Divides and Unites Us* (New York: Simon & Schuster, 2010).

37. bell hooks, *Teaching to Transgress: Education as the Practice of Freedom* (New York: Routledge, 1994), 21.

living a fantasy."[38] Therefore, I want my students to understand that I am a person who is deeply committed to (and critical of) my own Lutheran tradition, and I am also a person who is just as deeply committed to valuing, learning from, and acting for the common good alongside the traditions of my atheist, Buddhist, Jewish, Hindu, Sikh, Baha'i, Muslim, and indigenous brothers and sisters. If we educators continue to hide our own religious/spiritual commitments and loyalties from our students, how can we ever model for them a simultaneous loyalty to our own tradition and reverence for others' traditions? Most of what the public hears about religion involves the examples of extremists whose loyalties inculcate hate.[39] Educators need to offer a counterexample: living proof that, yes, it is indeed possible to live as people who cherish their own tradition, as well as those of others.

Academic discourse should be willing to move from theory to praxis, addressing real-world solutions in the classrooms and in scholarship. This will sometimes require writing in a more colloquial, accessible style, and/or a more practical format such as a blog, letter to the editor, or mainstream trade book. Many academics are far too eager to assert that such practical and accessible efforts are "not real scholarship," as evidenced by the fact that such activities often "do not count" toward tenure or promotion. As Gerald Graff argues, if academics today hope to be effective writers and teachers, we must become bilingual—that is, able to convey thoughts *both* in academic discourse *and* in more accessible styles. Rather than dismissing any popular style of writing as a form of dumbing down for ignorant nonspecialists, we should challenge ourselves to speak and write in more accessible language—at the very least, as a "self-checking device to ensure that we are actually saying something."[40]

In light of Graff's and hooks's insights, church-related colleges and their faculty should take up the vocation of fostering an institutional culture that rejects academic elitism and rewards scholar-activism. Only in this way will we faculty move beyond mere intellectualism and model for our students the necessity and beauty of a life committed to pluralism. If we are honest with ourselves, we must acknowledge that achieving such a goal will require activism in addition to knowledge. The multivocal classroom should create a space for the

---

38. Jacobsen and Jacobsen, *No Longer Invisible*, 134.

39. See Mark U. Edwards Jr., "Religion, Reluctance, and Conversations about Vocation," in Cunningham, ed., *Vocation across the Academy*, 272–93.

40. Gerald Graff, *Clueless in Academe: How Schooling Obscures the Life of the Mind* (New Haven, CT: Yale University Press, 2004), 142.

professor's own views and commitments and—even more important—the views and commitments of the students.

In my own teaching, I have sought to create a space in which my students' whole selves are welcome—and where conversations about vocation, purpose, and one's spiritual journey occur on a regular basis. I have found several effective ways of doing this: students write six-word memoirs (always a class favorite), develop a five-page religious/spiritual autobiography (graded, but not on content), and engage in an identity-mapping assignment in class. Once students have grasped the content of the assigned reading, I ask questions that solicit personal reflection. For example, when we read Elie Wiesel's *Night*, I asked students whether they too had ever had an experience in which they asked, "Where is God now?" In my experience, asking such questions confirms what research has proven: because these questions are precisely the kind students are longing to answer and to discuss, they energize the classroom. They make room for a capacious education of the whole person.

I hope that the approaches described here will help our church-related institutions and their professors rediscover and re-imagine their contemporary callings in a multi-faith world. As professors, our callings are deeply both/and. We are called to listen and speak, to teach and learn, to reflect and act, and to model both loyalty and reverence. And above all, our vocation is to help students discover theirs.

Response

Jeffrey Carlson

Jacqueline's notion of decentering Christian privilege at a Christian institution is brilliant and exemplary. It means inviting those from diverse religious traditions to move "from the margins to a shared center stage," while fostering many forms of respectful interfaith engagement. Decentering Christian privilege, in my view, entails avoiding not only overtly exclusionary practices but also the more subtle and pervasive (and thus actually more insidious) forms of assimilationist "inclusion." These can easily distort the beliefs and practices of religious minorities so that they (seem to) fit into dominant Christian categories. Our colleges and universities should conduct audits in which they identify, and move to eliminate, such practices of pseudo-inclusion.

As Jacqueline notes, institutions can still make room for a distinctive role for their own traditions (Lutheran at Concordia; Catholic at my own institution, Dominican University). Three examples among many: First, while *all* perspectives can never be fully "at the table" in any encounter, it is reasonable to expect that, more often than not, one of the "voices at the table" when engaging religious diversity should be a distinctively Lutheran (at Concordia) or Catholic (at Dominican) perspective. Second, all students should study some aspects of the school's founding tradition. Third, students should have opportunities to study that tradition at a depth that is not likely to be available, to quite the same extent, for many other traditions. I would not call any of this Christian "privilege," however, so long as the founding tradition is not construed as the normative lens through which all others are viewed.

Finally, Jacqueline observes that Concordia's interfaith commitment is in some sense grounded in its Lutheran heritage. Of course, as I suspect the author would agree, this typically requires a selective appropriation of carefully chosen aspects of that heritage—in this case, those that support pluralism and interfaith peace-building. Meanwhile, some other aspects of that heritage have to be deliberately de-emphasized. As a further step, we should seek to acknowledge the reality of this sort of selection process more explicitly, and perhaps even to identify some of the elements that are being deliberately de-emphasized—and why. This would signal something important to those from other traditions; it would demonstrate that the selective reconstruction of one's own tradition is an act of humility, hope, and often contrition. Jacqueline's essay, it seems to me, tacitly encourages us to take this next step.

12

Vocational Exploration as Transformative Pedagogy

RETRIEVING THE AFFECTIVE, EDUCATING FOR DIFFERENCE

Tracy Wenger Sadd

DECADES AGO, SHARON Daloz Parks suggested that faculty and staff in the academy need to be able to mentor, teach, and guide college and university students as they pursue "big questions and worthy dreams."[1] She pointed out that, for most students, college encompasses a unique developmental period. During this time, young people are moving in and out of dependence and independence, celebrating freedom from authority, and emerging as adults. Parks called the academy to accountability, asking it to respect the whole of its mission and identity:

> The academy's commitment to truth requires engagement with the whole of truth, the full scope of reality. . . . A critical appraisal of the epistemological assumptions of the academy itself points toward a new reordering of the relationship among the academy, the young adult's search for faith, and the relationship between the academy and society.[2]

1. Sharon Daloz Parks, *Big Questions, Worthy Dreams: Mentoring Young Adults in Their Search for Meaning, Purpose, and Faith* (San Francisco: Jossey–Bass, 2000). The tenth anniversary edition (2011) is a revised version; the editions will be cited by year of publication.

2. Parks, *Big Questions, Worthy Dreams* (2000), 163. Unfortunately, this quotation is not in the 2011 edition.

Parks has discussed "enriched epistemologies,"[3] which understand the role of higher education to include not only scholarship that discovers objective reality but also engagements with the personal experiences, passion, emotion, imagination, intuition, values, and big questions of the observing knower. Nevertheless, as Nancy J. Evans and others have noted, few in the academy have fully implemented Parks's call in practice, and what little has been done has largely occurred outside the classroom.[4]

In some sense, Parks is asking us to think through the question that Western culture has been pondering since the days of Tertullian, who asked, centuries ago, "What indeed has Athens to do with Jerusalem?"[5] In his era, Athens, the birthplace of secular learning, and Jerusalem, the originating city of Jewish and Christian thought and practice, were geographical centers; today, they remain symbolic markers of the division between academy and religion, philosophy and theology, reason and revelation. What is the appropriate relationship between Athens and Jerusalem? In a secular democratic nation—one which, even in the twenty-first century, remains majority Christian—we wrestle again and again with this question as we educate students for vocation in multi-faith contexts.

Tertullian's question comes quickly to mind when exploring the results of a seven-year study on the spiritual development of college and university students. It found that more than two-thirds of students describe as "essential" or "very important" the search for personal meaning through self-understanding and developing personal values. About half attach similar importance to a college's encouragement of their personal spirituality.[6] The study also discussed the role of faculty in encouraging and influencing students' spiritual growth; 81 percent of the faculty considered themselves to be "spiritual," and 64 percent indicated that they were "religious." However, in a follow-up study, only 19 percent of college juniors indicated that faculty had frequently encouraged them to explore spiritual or religious matters, and 58 percent of juniors said that their faculty *never* had done so.[7]

---

3. Parks, *Big Questions, Worthy Dreams* (2011), 204–10.

4. Nancy J. Evans, Deanna S. Forney, Florence M. Guido, Lori D. Patton, and Kristen A. Renn, *Student Development in College: Theory, Research, and Practice,* 2nd ed. (San Francisco: Jossey–Bass, 2009), 208.

5. Tertullian, *Prescription against Heretics*, 7, trans. Peter Holmes (Savage, MN: Lighthouse Christian Publishing, 2015), 13.

6. Alexander W. Astin, Helen S. Astin, and Jennifer A. Lindholm, *Cultivating the Spirit: How College Can Enhance Students' Inner Lives* (San Francisco: Jossey–Bass, 2011).

7. Astin, Astin, and Lindholm, *Cultivating the Spirit*, 7. Similar evidence is cited by Jacqueline Bussie in chapter 11 of this volume.

How can we explain the disconnect between the importance placed on religious and spiritual questions ("Jerusalem") among students, and the relative neglect of the same issues in pedagogical settings that focus primarily on other matters ("Athens")? Many of the reasons for this divide are explored elsewhere in this volume: a commitment to questionable pedagogical models,[8] a failure to embrace the moral imperatives of teaching,[9] a distrust of the mixed and multiple "personal theologies"[10] that students bring to college.[11] In any event, spiritual and religious elements deeply affect the lives of many students, and will continue to do so once they have left college. Moreover, their personal theologies and philosophical worldviews affect the way that students think and learn—not only about religion, but also about physics, social work, history, or any other subject.

I begin this chapter by exploring the importance of spiritual and affective learning for forms of education that take vocational reflection seriously, as well as some suggestions as to how it might be allowed into the college classroom (regardless of the department in which it is taught or the diversity of faith traditions among its students). The second and third sections then turn to more practical matters: pedagogical techniques and matters of assessment. I hope that these offerings will inspire at least some readers to give it a try: to educate for vocation in the context of the multi-faith classroom.

Broadening our understanding of the educational process

Transformative educators Alan Mandell and Lee Herman have observed that college faculty often have a limited view of "the lifeworld," compared to the views of their students. While the lifeworld for academics is primarily the world of scholarship, the lifeworld for students and nonacademics is "myriad instances and contexts in which we have to make decisions and accomplish things in order to get along and thrive."[12] This difference is exacerbated by the rise and prevalence

8. See the reflections on this matter by Jacqueline Bussie in chapter 11 of this volume.

9. See the comments on this concern by Rahuldeep Gill, Noah Silverman, and Jeffrey Carlson in chapters 3, 7, and 13 of this volume, respectively.

10. See David Gortner's extensive research on young adult views on this topic in *Varieties of Personal Theology: Charting the Beliefs and Values of Young Adults* (Burlington, VT: Ashgate, 2013).

11. See the comments of Trina Jones in chapter 2 of this volume.

12. Alan Mandell and Lee Herman, "Mentoring: When Learners Make the Learning," in Jack Mezirow, Edward Taylor, and Associates, *Transformative Learning in Practice: Insights from Community, Workplace, and Higher Education* (San Francisco: Jossey-Bass, 2009), 81.

of the modern research university and its pursuit of objective, systematic, methodological research at the expense of questions of values, meaning, purpose, and other existential concerns.[13] Anthony Kronman suggests that a number of developments have eclipsed the role of higher education in shaping the souls and spirits of students: the rise of secular humanism, the academy's focus on research, and the dominance of the scientific method. Questions about the meaning of life, about what really matters, involve our ultimate commitments; they can never be exhaustively answered through empirical science or even the objective moral reasoning of philosophy.[14] These questions often create anxiety; moreover, they remain with us throughout our lifespan, at certain times with more urgency than others.[15]

Although students vary widely in cognitive ability and academic training, they all bring affective concerns to college. They are driven by questions that are central to their lives and their pursuits: Who am I? To whom shall I relate? Whom should I love? According to Erik Erikson's psychosocial model, students are working to resolve the tensions between the categories of *ego identity* and *role confusion*, and between *intimacy* and *isolation*.[16] During the college years, they are constructing narratives, philosophies, and theologies for life.[17]

The pedagogy of vocation and purposeful life work is one way to engage students developmentally, dealing with questions of identity and intimacy. Such engagement allows students to ask questions that are relevant and interesting to them—big questions of life, meaning, and purpose. It also gives them space to think about their relationships with themselves, with their beliefs, with their various communities, and with the world. This approach resonates with Parks's alternative and enriched epistemologies, which honor knowledge itself, the personal experience of each knower, the multiplicity of perspectives, and the inner authority of each student and instructor.[18] According to Parks,

---

13. Anthony Kronman, *Education's End: Why Colleges and Universities Have Given Up on the Meaning of Life* (New Haven, CT: Yale University Press, 2007), 7–8.

14. Kronman, *Education's End*, especially chapter 3, "The Research Ideal," and chapter 5, "Spirit in an Age of Science," 91–136 and 205–59, respectively.

15. On the power of what is not taught or what is left out of the curriculum, see David J. Flinders, Nel Noddings, and Stephen J. Thornton, "The Null Curriculum: Its Theoretical Basis and Practical Implications," *Curriculum Inquiry* 16, no. 1 (Autumn 1986): 33–42.

16. Erik H. Erikson, "Eight Ages of Man," chapter 7 of *Childhood and Society*, reissue edition (New York: W. W. Norton, 1993), 247–74.

17. For an in-depth story of the journey of a young adult to a vocation as an interfaith leader, see Noah Silverman's narrative in chapter 7 of this book.

18. Parks, *Big Questions, Worthy Dreams* (2011), 204–10.

"an educator-professor is one who leads out toward truth by professing his or her intuitions, apprehensions, and convictions of truth *in a manner that encourages dialogue with the emerging inner authority of the student.*"[19] In Parks's view, what emerges from this honoring of the multiplicity of voices and perspectives may become a community of imagination and courage; such a community can make headway on the difficult problems of our world today.

Exploring specific pedagogical approaches

I have taught vocation and interfaith approaches in both core and elective courses; my students had academic majors ranging from the humanities to the natural sciences to pre-professional tracks. They have represented worldviews ranging from active Christians, to angry and/or disenfranchised Christians, to Shinto, Muslim, Hindu, Buddhist, Jewish, Wiccan, atheist, and humanist perspectives. Teaching in the midst of such diversity requires an interdisciplinary and multi-faith approach. The combination of disciplines and methods will differ from one person to another; my own have drawn on religious studies for a focus on vocation and narrative theology, on the student development literature for self-authorship theory, on philosophy for ethics and judgment, and on positive psychology for the concepts of flow and *eudaimonia*. Here, I will mention four aspects of my own approach to teaching that have helped me to educate for vocation in a multi-faith context: broadening the idea of the cognitive, freeing up our thinking processes, creating a sanctuary classroom, and validating the importance of contemplation.

The modern academy tends to regard affective and personal knowledge as less significant than the cognitive and the objective. Indeed, critics have argued that faith, introspection, affect, worldviews, and contemplation cannot and should not be explored in the classroom, on the grounds that they are too value laden, too open to bias, not academic, or not cognitive intellectual work. But other experts argue that ignoring these issues tends to marginalize important concerns of students, including questions about spiritual and religious life. In the end, there is no such thing "as 'pure' cognition that can be considered in isolation from affect; on the contrary, it would appear that our thoughts and our reasoning are almost always taking place in some kind of affective 'bed' or context."[20]

Higher education should develop the integrity of the whole student. Unfortunately, the structure of the university often militates against this;

---

19. Parks, *Big Questions, Worthy Dreams* (2011), 214.

20. Astin, Astin, and Lindholm, *Cultivating the Spirit*, 7.

Parks observes that, for example, the division of labor between faculty and student affairs professionals has been "polarized and their separation reified at the expense of students as whole persons."[21] The recent turn to the language of vocation and calling suggests a greater awareness that the affective and cognitive are interwoven, and that educators should pay attention to the whole student in their classrooms—and not just leave the affective realm to the student life staff.

In order to bring out both the affective and cognitive elements of learning, we need to expand our definition of "thinking." Elizabeth Kamarck Minnich describes the importance of creating assignments in "free thinking," which include internal conversation and conscience, in addition to what we traditionally call "knowledge."[22] In her classes, Minnich gives assignments which require a level of conversation with classmates, as well as contemplation and internal conversation for each student. This can create deep vulnerability in the classroom; Minnich says that it has, for example, resulted in a student crying when she read one of her "thinking papers" to the other students.[23] The criteria that Minnich has used in grading her students' work include freedom of mind, inclusiveness, rhetoric, beauty, play, emotion, originality, reflexivity, revelation, and making connections.

Minnich notes that the work that students undertake in these contexts is unique to each student. Given that vocational reflection requires this kind of specific attention to the particularities of each student, her approach seems particularly appropriate for such work—as well as for developing personal theologies in interfaith contexts, and for educating for a strong democracy. Indeed, one of Minnich's students suggests that three related elements—thinking for oneself, thinking in the place of others, and thinking out loud together—help to form the basis for a democratic life.[24] Any productive form of life together requires the capacity of each individual to honor self, empathize with others, and commit to discerning truth together.

---

21. Parks, *Big Questions, Worthy Dreams* (2011), 205.

22. Elizabeth Kamarck Minnich, "Teaching Thinking: Moral and Political Considerations," *Change* 35, no. 5 (September/October 2003): 19–24. Minnich differentiates thinking from calculative reasoning, instrumental reasoning, deduction, induction, rational deliberation, or any cognitive rules or conventions that can be used coercively as proof.

23. Minnich, "Teaching Thinking," 24. The footnote to the article names the student as Valeri Jones.

24. Minnich, "Teaching Thinking," 23. The footnote to the article names the student as Cole Campbell.

To undertake this kind of work, instructors often find it important to establish classroom spaces conducive to doing this work. Elizabeth Lange explains the "learning sanctuary" concept in this way:

> A sanctuary is a special place set aside as a refuge of protection and shelter, enabling growth. Thus, to be transformative, adult education ought to provide a protective sanctuary for a deep encounter with self (mind, spirit, and body), social relationships, habits of thinking and living, and the conjoined individual and social myths that constrain human freedom and justice. This becomes a container for the dialectics between a pedagogy of critique and a pedagogy of hope.[25]

Many instructors may resonate with, and even find comfort in, Lange's observations—particularly when she notes that the process of creating learning sanctuaries in our classrooms cannot be defined too precisely or systematically:

> Perhaps in naming elements of transformation, we disenchant the process or ignore the fruits of transformation. . . . This is what I hope to convey through the concept of learning sanctuary: a protective space held open for bidden but unseen processes.[26]

To think of one's classroom as a learning sanctuary means to give attention not only to the subjective, the affective, and the experiential, but also to the mystical—which suggests a range of notions, from the mysterious, inexplicable, and ineffable, to the esoteric, spiritual, and symbolic.

Educating for vocation and purposeful life work is also closely aligned with contemplative practices and introspective pedagogies. Contemplation means "to gaze attentively," which means creating or reserving a space for observing. Introspection is focusing on what is happening within.[27] The field of

---

25. Elizabeth Lange, "Fostering a Learning Sanctuary for Transformation in Sustainability Education," in Jack Mezirow, Edward Taylor, and Associates, *Transformative Learning in Practice: Insights from Community, Workplace, and Higher Education* (San Francisco: Jossey–Bass, 2009), 193–204. See also Vincenzo Giorgino, "Contemplative Methods Meet Social Sciences: Back to Human Experience It Is," *Journal for the Theory of Social Behaviour* 45, no. 4 (December 2015): 461–83.

26. Lange, "Learning Sanctuary," 203.

27. Daniel Barbezat and Mirabai Bush, *Contemplative Practices in Higher Education: Powerful Methods to Transform Teaching and Learning* (San Francisco, CA: Jossey–Bass, 2014), 11.

contemplative pedagogies in higher education continues to grow. Arthur Zajonc summarizes the issues quite well:

> The university is well-practiced at educating the mind for critical reasoning, critical writing and critical speaking as well as for scientific and quantitative analysis. But is this sufficient? In a world beset with conflicts, internal as well as external, isn't it of equal if not greater importance to balance the sharpening of our intellects with the systematic cultivation of our hearts?[28]

This kind of cultivation can be a natural part of conversations about vocation and calling.

A number of different interdisciplinary approaches can provide a means to address questions of vocation, meaning, purpose, and lifestance. Questions about these matters play a significant role in the lives of most people in the world (including undergraduate students); the impact of these matters on individual lives has ranged from thoroughly empowering to extraordinarily painful. In the end, questions about religion and spirituality, about the affective and emotional aspects of our lives (and about larger questions of meaning and purpose) will not vanish, no matter how ardently we refuse to talk about them in the public square or in the college classroom. I am not ready to give up on the loftiest goals of higher education; as such, I feel compelled to engage my students in these ways in the classroom.

The benefits of retrieving the affective

The practices described here can help create an inviting atmosphere for conversations about vocation, spirituality, and purposeful life work in multi-faith contexts. Doing so has a number of important benefits; first among these, this work is good for the students. Students make gains, psychologically and spiritually, by having a dream and a purpose—whether understood as a single calling or many callings.

Moreover, these aspects of an undergraduate education help to reduce the pressure that many students feel to treat college primarily as a means to increase their material wealth. In fact, the fields of positive psychology and behavioral economics have corroborated some of what the world's religions have claimed for thousands of years: namely, that there is a "happiness paradox," or a point of

---

28. Barbezat and Bush, *Contemplative Practices*, xii.

diminishing return, in the relationship between material possessions and happiness (or what Aristotle called *eudaimonia*).[29] Beyond a very low threshold, increased income is not automatically correlated with increased happiness. In fact, the happiest people are those who pay little attention to becoming happy; they have a larger purpose outside themselves. Faculty and staff lament the instrumental view of education held by so many students, who seem to value education primarily as a credential to being very well off financially.[30] Working with students to explore vocation may help renew student engagement in education for less instrumental reasons, including constructing philosophies and theologies of life, developing civic virtues, and contemplating the joy of being an educated person.

Rethinking education along these lines would also have benefits for the entire enterprise of higher education, as well as our individual institutions. Institutions themselves have vocations—specific strengths, personalities, missions, and purposes. Discerning the integrity and relevance of these institutional narratives on a regular basis can impact institutional effectiveness and employee morale, including the range of faculty and staff that these institutions can attract and retain.[31]

Finally, educating for vocation in multi-faith contexts is good for our nation and the world.[32] By helping students to find a sense of vocation and by developing their inner lives, we take an important step toward cultivating the kind of civic and public habits we would like to see in a democracy. Moving

29. Happiness in this context is not an emotion; it denotes human welfare, flourishing, abundant living, and comprehensive well-being. For a historical view of happiness, see Darrin M. McMahon, *Happiness: A History* (New York: Atlantic Monthly Press, 2006). For the connection between happiness and Christian theology and ethics, see Miroslav Volf and Justin E. Crisp, *Joy and Human Flourishing: Essays on Theology, Culture and the Good Life* (Minneapolis: Fortress Press, 2015) and David S. Cunningham, *Christian Ethics: The End of the Law* (New York: Routledge, 2008). For the research literature on happiness in positive psychology, see Sonja Lyubomirsky, *The How of Happiness* (New York: Penguin Press, 2008).

30. See also Dan Berrett, "The Day the Purpose of College Changed," *Chronicle of Higher Education*, January 26, 2015, http://www.chronicle.com/article/The-Day-the-Purpose-of-College/151359 (accessed October 2, 2017). Data on the shift is available at Freshman Survey, Higher Education Research Institute at the University of California, Los Angeles.

31. See the reflections on institutional vocation and multi-faith campus culture by Florence Amamoto, Jacqueline Bussie, and Jeffrey Carlson in chapters 10, 11, and 13 of this book, respectively. On institutional vocation, see David S. Cunningham, "Colleges Have Callings, Too: Vocational Reflection at the Institutional Level," in *Vocation across the Academy: A New Vocabulary for Higher Education*, ed. David S. Cunningham (New York: Oxford University Press, 2017), 249–71.

32. Martha C. Nussbaum, "Education for Profit, Education for Freedom," *Liberal Education* 11, no. 3 (Summer 2009): 6–13.

students toward bridge-building behaviors across race, ethnicity, religion, and social and economic class cannot be done in a deep and lasting way without engaging students' personal theologies and epistemologies.[33] Many civic models of education seem to assume that most students have a strong religious identity, an articulate personal theology or other lifestance, and a clear commitment to specific civic practices and citizenship practices. Often, however, students do not arrive at college with these traits, nor are they given much of a chance to develop them. By educating for vocation in a multi-faith context, we offer this opportunity; our students can build upon their developing sense of identity to think through questions of civic engagement and the creation of a more just society.

Given the many benefits of rethinking education along the lines that I have described here, I now want to offer some concrete examples of this work. These activities are particularly well suited for helping students to explore vocation in a multi-faith context.

Sample mini-modules and assignments

The examples given here have all been developed and employed repeatedly in the college classroom. Some are best inserted into introductory courses of any kind, while other exercises might be adapted for upper-level students in various academic disciplines. Later in this chapter, I will discuss the problem of assessing this kind of academic work, offering a rubric for the evaluation of student learning related to vocational exploration in multi-faith contexts.

Sorting: too many voices calling

I have used the following exercise for years in a class of about 35 students; the course participants come from nearly all of our academic majors and all academic years. I begin by giving each student or pair of students a handout with the following questions, allowing them about 15 minutes to jot down some notes in response to each question:

1. What messages is society giving you about what will make your life meaningful or purposeful or happy?

---

33. Potential dangers of the approaches in this chapter include their use coercively in service to extremist ideologies on any part of the religious, social, or political spectrum.

2. What are the voices of your *family* telling you about what will make your life meaningful or happy?
3. What about the voices of others (friends, coaches, professors, religious leaders, or others who are in a position to influence you)?
4. To what extent might there be too many voices and callings in our lives?

Individuals or pairs can then be invited to share items as they are willing; in my experience, they are quite willing to do so, and enjoy unpacking the plethora of voices and calls. They are especially interested in thinking about the voices of society (and exactly how its messages are conveyed). Often students bring to the surface narratives of their families of origins, lifestances, and other communities; some of these conflict with prevailing messages of the larger society.

I conclude this exercise with a quotation from Frederick Buechner—not his oft-cited definition of vocation, but his comment on the importance of sorting out our various calls: "There are all different kinds of voices calling you to all different kinds of work, and the problem is to find out which is the voice of God rather than of Society, say, or the Superego, or Self-Interest."[34] I invite students to write a reflection on one of the following: What is my voice trying to say? To whom should I listen more and to whom should I listen less?

Receiving the call of community: the vocations of cultures and religions

This activity begins with an invitation for students to consider the idea that groups not only have callings of their own; they can also issue calls. These groups, which include corporations, colleges, religions, cultures, nations, and families, call out to us—sometimes in vague ways, sometimes in very specific ones—to do something or to be something. Class members are then encouraged to discuss, with one or two others in the class, the following questions:

- In American society, to what extent are the messages and callings different for men than for women?
- Compare and contrast differences in the highest callings and priorities, or by the following:
  - Women and men
  - Young and old

34. Frederick Buechner, "Vocation," in *Wishful Thinking: A Seeker's ABC*, revised and expanded (New York: HarperSanFrancisco, 1993), 118–19.

    - US citizens and another national culture known to the class
    - Communal cultures and individualistic cultures
- List what each of these groups might believe about the world and think is most valuable.

There are many ways to close the session. I have found that students especially appreciate the opportunity to get up and talk with each other. I use a grid handout to facilitate this; it has two sections, with columns headed as follows:

Sharing Commonalities:
Beliefs and Values in Common with Others

Things my culture, religious, or nonreligious worldview believes and values	Name of another person in the class who also has this belief or value	What do we *like* about this belief or value?	How might this activity be part of a larger calling or noble purpose?

Appreciating Difference:
Diverse Beliefs and Values

Beliefs and values from a culture or lifestance that I don't share	Name of a person who has this belief or value	What do they say are the positives of this belief or value?	How might this belief or value be part of a larger calling or noble purpose?

In the end, students are usually happy to share the cultural and religious differences in purpose that they have seen in their own extended families and communities. Many report a renewed connection or respect for part of their own familial, religious, or cultural story they previously ignored or discounted.

Narrating: many ways to tell my life story

Many have lamented the loss of metanarratives in postmodernity; at the same time, our own individual and particular narratives remain a powerful force in our culture and in our personal lives. The expansive literature on the importance of narrative makes it a rich resource for thinking about vocation in a multi-faith context; it has significant confluences with the fields of philosophy and theology, as well as specific perspectives such as self-authorship theory.

I have incorporated these insights into the classroom through an exercise that begins by asking students to read Mary Catherine Bateson's essay "Composing a Life Story."[35] I use this exercise to challenge students to realize their role in choosing how to narrate their own stories—that is, to give them an increased vision of self-authorship. I distribute a list of questions, giving students 30 minutes to write quick words and phrases (or draw doodles and sketches) for any new insights provoked by each particular question. Questions may include:

- How would I tell my life story as a comedy?
- What points would I emphasize in telling my life story as the script of an adventure film?
- How would I tell my life story in music?
- What if I told my story as an intersection with the stories of other people, places, times, books, religions, or philosophies?
- If I told my story in a long book, what would be the outline of the chapter titles?
- How would I share my life story in a comic book or superhero tale?

To encourage deeper contemplation of vocation, one might assign a creative art, music, drawing, or writing project to the students based on one of these questions.

On my campus, I find that many students have never been asked to tell their stories. Even when I am not using this specific exercise, I try in most classes to create space for students to narrate their lives. I find students quite receptive to and empowered by the idea of choosing the frame for their own stories. They respond with surprise ("no one ever told me I had any strengths before") or with appreciation for a new sense of freedom ("I like how the professor never tells us that we are wrong"). Instructors who use journals and narrative work must be willing to engage the full reality of the details of students' stories.[36]

Seeing: vocation as dream

John Neafsey reminds us that vocation and calling can take the form of vision and dream.[37] An obvious example of this is the practice of the Ojibwa and other

35. Included in Mark R. Schwehn and Dorothy C. Bass, eds., *Leading Lives That Matter: What We Should Do and Who We Should Be* (Grand Rapids, MI: Eerdmans, 2006), 459–66.

36. In the United States, instructors need to be aware of current laws related to mandatory reporting including, but not limited to, Title IX and the Clery Act.

37. John Neafsey, *A Sacred Voice Is Calling: Personal Vocation and Social Conscience* (Maryknoll, NY: Orbis Books, 2006), 89–108.

Native American tribes of the vision quest.[38] But any form of vocational discernment may be a quest for a worthy dream—whether a dream with a capital "D," a venture of the imagination, a prophecy, or just your ordinary, everyday (every night) dream.

An entry-level activity would include providing magazines of all sorts to students and asking them to create a vocation and imagination box or a vision or dream board. Either of these items involves students collecting things that they imagine or dream for the future (e.g., words, quotes, pictures, doodles, sketches, poems, or magazine cutouts) and then either putting them in a box or pasting them on a board. One student in a class where these exercises were used said that "it put a lot of things in perspective," and another student said it "made me examine myself more than any other class; it helped me look at my future and find a path that may be right for me."

Feeling: vocation as dream interrupted or ended

In today's politically charged and divided society, many people have experienced vocational dreams that have been deferred, interrupted, obstructed, or ended. This presents a very important opportunity to understand the nature of vocation and calling, particularly as it might be seen differently in different cultural contexts. One can build a class session or mini-module around dreams—deferred, interrupted, or ended. Langston Hughes's poem "Harlem" can be helpful and accessible to undergraduate students.[39] Here is one possible approach to working with the concept of deferred or blocked vocational dreams:

- Ask students to create a timeline of their lives, making special note of times when a vision or dream for the future became clear or was accomplished, and when setbacks occurred on the journey to making a vision or dream a reality, or a dream was put off, interrupted, given up, ended, or replaced.
- Read "Harlem" (or, alternatively, read the narrative experiences of Muslim young women as told by writers such as Shabana Mir[40]), and discuss both

38. This is a ritual for some Native American traditions, such as the Ojibwa; it is often a rite of passage in which a young person goes away from the community to receive a vision, to be given an animal spirit, or to simply contemplate the meaning and purpose of his or her life.

39. A copy of Langston Hughes, "Harlem," reprinted with permission, can be found at the website of the Poetry Foundation, https://www.poetryfoundation.org/poems-and-poets/poems/detail/46548 (accessed May 1, 2017).

40. See the references to Mir's work that are cited by Homayra Ziad in chapter 9 of this volume. Shabana Mir, *Muslim American Women on Campus: Undergraduate Social Life and Identity* (Chapel Hill: University of North Carolina Press, 2016).

personal, emotional responses and critical and analytical responses to these texts (social, communal, national).

- Invite students to share two items from their timelines, as they are willing.
- Close by asking them to write on an index card one thing they could do in the next 48 hours to take positive steps moving forward to help prevent any feelings of impotence, paralysis, or hopelessness.

I have had students say how helpful it was to remember previous setbacks that had been turned into positive growth and development. I frequently read in students' journals, contemplative in-class writings, and reading reflections how surprised they are to discover that others have "been there" or experienced this kind of obstacle.

Healing: vocation as compassionate action

Ideas about sickness, disease, health, well-being, and healing often are deeply rooted in religious and cultural mythology, beliefs, and lifestances. This makes the work of vocational discernment particularly important for students who are contemplating careers that intersect with these concerns. Effective caregiving requires greater cultural sensitivity in all aspects of healthcare; my students have especially appreciated the account of Black Elk's call to become a medicine man or shaman.[41] The following items could be used individually for one or two specific class sessions, or they could be used together to constitute a multiple-class-period module.

- Read *Black Elk Speaks* or another relevant text.[42]
- Invite students to do deep listening in pairs about the origins of their own calling to a healing profession. Ask them to listen for positive themes to affirm, and also to note contradictions.
- Assign students the task of creating a diagram of connections between their religious beliefs or nonreligious worldviews and their beliefs and values about healing, sickness, physical disease, or mental illness.
- Ask students to create a personal action plan related to the vocation or calling to care for oneself.

---

41. Nicholas Black Elk and John G. Neihardt, *Black Elk Speaks: Being the Life Story of a Holy Man of the Oglala Sioux* (Lincoln: University of Nebraska Press, 2005).

42. Another option would be Henri M. Nouwen, *The Wounded Healer: Ministry in Contemporary Society* (New York: Doubleday Image Books, 1979).

- Assign a brief research project on illness and healing in at least two other lifestances or cultures.
- Draft a theology or philosophy of healing as a calling or noble purpose.

While I have found this exercise to work with all students, I originally developed it for students and faculty in the field of occupational therapy. These colleagues have consistently connected the ideas of vocation and purpose with their own work of helping others pursue the wide variety of "occupations" involved in living a meaningful and abundant life.

Studying real-world cases: vocation and noble purpose in any class

This assignment could be used in an upper-level course in any major. The instructor begins by asking students to read a case study in the disciplinary field of the course. Before class lecture, discussion, or debate begins, students are given a personal reflection handout, in which they are asked questions about how they relate to the case study. Questions could include:

- Who made the decisions in the case study? What do you think they valued most? Least?
- Do you think the decision-makers in the case were religious or not? Why or why not?
- Whose perspectives, beliefs, values, and voices were ignored in the case?
- In what way do your personal religious beliefs or nonreligious worldview, sacred texts that you read, or commandments you follow tell you what to do in this case?
- What do you believe most strongly or value most in life that would affect how you might act in this case?

At the end of class, students can be invited to reflect briefly on the different beliefs, worldviews, lifestances, and ethical codes they heard described during class.

With the exercises in this section, I have tried to keep my descriptions general so that they are infinitely adaptable to particular instructional settings. I also have endeavored to provide enough details so that both affective skeptics and vocation novices will have a good chance of success in providing students a chance to reflect on the questions that concern them most—thus opening the way to a deeper conversation about vocation, faith commitments, and lifestances.

Student learning outcomes for vocation in multi-faith contexts

If education is to be holistic, and if it can include more than a cognitive activity or gains in skills, how might we formulate learning goals and measure gains related to other types of development? Clearly, such work is challenging. In educating students in matters such as vocational discernment, awareness of the increasingly multi-faith context in which they live, and interfaith leadership and service, we are attempting to make room where the academy currently has few categories.[43] In the literature on student learning outcomes, I have found few explicit categories for thinking about areas such as vocational reflection, inner life, passion, and purpose. This lack is all the more striking when we seek to measure these outcomes in a multi-faith context. The Association of American Colleges and Universities has promulgated VALUE rubrics (Valid Assessment of Learning in Undergraduate Education), developed by teams of faculty, which are designed to assess student learning related to a plethora of areas of liberal education—including civic engagement, creative thinking, ethical reasoning, global learning, integrative learning, intercultural knowledge, and many others.[44] A rubric developed by Interfaith Youth Core, Elon University, and Wofford College provides a way of formulating student learning outcomes related to worldview and interfaith action for civic purposes.[45] Its categories include knowledge of own worldview, knowledge of other worldviews, attitudes toward pluralism, interpersonal engagement, and interfaith action and reflection.[46]

These rubrics are valuable, but none of them maps directly onto learning about vocation, calling, passion, purpose, or meaningful life work. Moreover,

---

43. For some reasons as to why this is so, see Kronman, *Education's End.*

44. Terrel L. Rhodes, ed., *Assessing Outcomes and Improving Achievement: Tips and Tools for Using Rubrics* (Washington, DC: Association of American Colleges and Universities, 2010). All rubrics can be viewed and downloaded for free from the Association of American Colleges and Universities at https://www.aacu.org/value-rubrics (accessed October 1, 2017).

45. This resource is available for free from Interfaith Youth Core at http://www.ifyc.org/sites/default/files/u4/PluralismWorldviewEngagementRubric2.pdf (accessed October 1, 2017).

46. In some sense, this rubric is a modification of the Association of American Colleges and Universities' rubric called Intercultural Knowledge and Competence replacing the language of "culture" with that of "worldview." Through its use of language such as "appreciative understanding" and similar constructions, the creators of that rubric have moved beyond purely cognitive learning, and have utilized some verbs related to affective learning outcomes. On the other hand, its focus on shaping students for public life as citizens in a democracy means that it does not cover the full range of outcomes and benefits to be derived from a focus on beliefs, values, lifestances, vocation, and purposeful life work.

the roles of spirituality, personal theology, philosophy of life, or lifestance are largely ignored—even in the rubrics on ethical reasoning, global learning, intercultural knowledge, worldview knowledge, and interfaith action. These rubrics have only limited language related to moral formation, character dispositions, or affective learning. Yet these considerations are often highly important for undergraduate learning across a wide range of academic disciplines and applied fields.

At my own institution, the IDEA course evaluation forms have provided an entry point for my coursework related to vocation and purposeful life work. They allow faculty to choose, as a primary course learning objective, the following statement: "Students gain a clearer commitment to, or sense of, personal values." Values often are connected to religious and spiritual beliefs, philosophical worldviews, emotion, passion, preferences, purpose, personal theologies, and personal narratives—the stuff of which vocation is made. At the same time, vocation is far broader than "values," and as we think more deliberatively about student learning related to vocational reflection in multi-faith contexts, we may find it helpful to frame student learning in ways that include and use Krathwohl's Taxonomy of the Affective Domain, which includes the concepts of affect, valuing, and internalizing in ways that influence behavior.[47]

In my own efforts both to educate and to advise for vocation and purposeful life work, I focus my attention on my students' vocational identities—on their ability to articulate and to act upon what really matters most, for self and world. In a multi-faith context, this means not forcing one particular religion (or religion in general) on students, but making space for them to think about and appreciatively understand a variety of personal and organized communal theologies, philosophies, and lifestances. In order to set student learning goals related to vocation, passion, and purposeful life work in such contexts, it can be helpful to use multiple languages: the traditional language of vocation, the wisdom languages of the world's religions, the language of introspective practices and contemplative pedagogies, and the language and research of positive psychology.[48] In appendix A, I have drafted a working rubric for assessing student learning related to vocation, passion, and noble purpose. (This rubric may be copied freely.) I look forward to future conversations about assessing student

47. David Krathwohl and Benjamin Bloom, *Taxonomy of Educational Objectives, Book 2: Affective Domain* (Upper Saddle River, NJ: Longman Publishing Group, 1999).

48. See David S. Cunningham, "Vocabularies of Vocation: Language for a Complex Educational Landscape," epilogue to Cunningham, ed., *Vocation across the Academy*, 315–25.

learning for vocation in multi-faith contexts in ways that honor both affective and cognitive learning.

Vocation, multi-faith contexts, and the affective realm

Educating for vocation, purposeful life work, and civic participation in a multi-faith democracy—these are value-laden endeavors that carry risks along with rewards. If I am successful in creating a true learning sanctuary in my classes, then "restorative learning" can occur; individuals can be reconnected to childhood dreams, awakening submerged passions, or latent knowledge. The goals of such education include examining, deconstructing, and reconstructing worldviews (even our own); improving literacy; and creating new ways of being and acting in the world. We cannot always predict what will happen, and we may even feel uncomfortable about what happens in our own classrooms. Focusing on vocation and purposeful life work and related activities and pedagogies takes valuable "class time," and we still have to deliver disciplinary content. Students still need instrumental knowledge and skills to find well-paying jobs and to honor the sacrifices their families have made for them to go to college.[49] But many students express a strong desire to be educated for vocation and purposeful life work, and this kind of work is good for their well-being. It also may advance their capacity to be engaged learners and good citizens.

In the end, significant progress will be made—with respect to students' inner lives and their interfaith understanding and engagement—only when we have begun to heal what Sharon Daloz Parks has summarized so well as "the epistemological wound":[50] the gap noted by students between what they desire—cognition that includes affective (even personal and subjective) knowledge—and the (supposedly) purely cognitive knowledge they often receive in our classrooms. If we hope to overcome the Jerusalem-Athens divide, then we will need a more integrated approach to these matters—in our individual academic courses, in the entire academy, and in ourselves.

49. For more on this see Monica A. Coleman, "Transforming to Teach: Teaching Religion to Today's Black College Student," *Teaching Theology and Religion* 10, no. 2 (April 2007): 95–100.

50. Sharon Daloz Parks, "Privileged Presence: Faithful Imagination at the Crossroads, the Edge . . . in the Gap," *College Chaplaincy in the 21st Century Conference*, Princeton Theological Seminary, November 8, 2013.

Response

Noah J. Silverman

Unlike my co-contributors, my primary vocational setting is not in the academy proper. I work at a mission-driven nonprofit organization, where we have the great privilege of hiring many recent college graduates, most of whom are former students at stellar liberal arts programs across the country. These new hires usually arrive flush with excitement to demonstrate the critical analysis and deconstruction in which they were academically trained. They typically spend their first months at their new job explaining to their superiors precisely what is wrong with everything that the organization is doing. They are frequently baffled when their amused new colleagues explain, patiently, that they were hired for what they could contribute, not what they could critique.

This pattern, which I assume repeats itself at many other institutions around the country, is one of many natural outgrowths of the phenomenon that Tracy diagnoses so well in this chapter. In particular, she laments the anemic attention that affective and constructive pedagogy receives in contemporary higher education. When the academy abdicates educating whole persons in favor of purely cognitive development, the results should not surprise us. Even those students who remain vocationally driven—and who elect to take on underpaid work at civic institutions or nonprofits—still know mostly how to deconstruct, rather than to build or to solve.

When the cognitive reigns supreme, we tend to fall into the fallacy that change occurs only when we think our way into new patterns of action. But as those of us immersed in the rough-and-tumble of civic life often learn the hard way, people are actually more inclined to *act* their way into new patterns of thinking. I particularly appreciate the way that Tracy not only offers manifold examples of new pedagogical practices that we can enact, but also pushes us to reconceptualize just what is meant by "thinking" in the first place. Only when we pay attention to the larger life worlds and lifestances of students can we expect them to do the same—especially as they re-enter the world at large and seek to contribute to it.

Tracy argues compellingly that "educating for vocation in multi-faith contexts is good for our nation and the world." The paradigm shift that she describes would surely have at least one direct and immediate implication: a strengthening of our country's civic institutions and nonprofit organizations.

Appendix A

Rubric for Evaluating Vocation and Purposeful Life Work in Multi-Faith Contexts

	Beginning 1	**Developing** 2	**Advanced** 3
Becoming Interdependent	• Unable to name beliefs and values with clarity • Dependent completely on the authority of others' ideas, wholesale and uncritiqued • Cannot name a tradition, community, or cause that is a vocational, spiritual, philosophical, or activist "home base" • Articulates beliefs and values only in reactionary, oppositional, or deconstructive ways; no constructive theology or lifestance	• Names beliefs and values with some degree of clarity • Draws on beliefs and values of other individuals or traditions, but includes reflection and critique • Describes at least one tradition, community, or cause as a vocational, spiritual, philosophical, or activist "home base" • Articulates beliefs and values as an emerging authentic, integrated, constructive theology or lifestance	• Names beliefs and values with a high degree of clarity and some maturity • Begins to sound like wisdom, with true interdependence between self and other people or traditions, with significant reflection and critique • Describes multiple traditions, communities, or causes as vocational, spiritual, philosophical, or activist "home bases" • Articulates beliefs and values in an authentic, integrated, constructive theology or lifestance which may serve as a foundation for resilience

(*Continued*)

<table>
<tr><th></th><th>Beginning
1</th><th>Developing
2</th><th>Advanced
3</th></tr>
<tr><td>Discerning</td><td>• Unable to listen accurately to voices of self and other, including sources of human or divine authority as relevant to the student’s lifestance
• Refuses to hear certain voices (the oppressed, the poor, the authoritative, those not in the in-group)
• Expresses perpetual feelings of being overwhelmed, stressed, and confused from too many “voices” calling (people, activities, work, commitments)
• No method or structure for discerning (telling this from that, making confident decisions, hearing the most important callings)</td><td>• Tries to listen with some accuracy to voices of self and other, including sources of human or divine authority as relevant to the student’s lifestance
• Hears many calls of different voices, and still misses some significant or important calls
• Attempts strategies to balance focus and limit attention to the many “voices” calling (people, activities, work, commitments)
• Explores or uses rudimentary methods or structures for discerning (telling this from that, making confident decisions, hearing the most important callings)</td><td>• Listens quite accurately to voices of self and other, including sources of human or divine authority as relevant to the student’s lifestance
• Willing to hear many calls of different voices (the oppressed, the poor, the authoritative, those not in the in-group) and prioritizes responses
• Achieves a significant degree of balance in focus and limitation on attention to the many “voices” calling (people, activities, work, commitments)
• Uses one or more methods or structures for discerning effectively (telling this from that, making confident decisions, hearing the most important callings)</td></tr>
</table>

Valuing Vocation and Purposeful Life Work	• States with some detail how an academic major or career is a vocation or part of a purposeful lifestance • Sketches general career future related to personal needs, goals, and ambitions (or those of nuclear family) • Realizes from a service or volunteer experience how lucky student is and wants to "give back" • Applies heuristics or slogans for motivation in service and life work • Focuses career goals solely on the self, and socioeconomic success	• Frames nascent scholarly and/or spiritual understandings of vocation, lifestance, or purposeful life work • Makes some connection between personal vocation and lifestance to academic major or future career • States clearly how service experience relates to, confirms, or challenges vocation, lifestance, academic major, or career path • Names motivations for service and life work with some nuance and complexity • Focuses career goals on making a difference and a unique contribution	• States scholarly working definitions of vocation, life philosophy, lifestance, or purposeful life work • Connects clearly academic major and future career to personal spiritual beliefs, ethical commitments, personal interests, skills, abilities, and life work choices • Discusses service experiences as part of spiritual or ethical commitment to humanity, divine calling, or the common good • Names motivations for service and life work as both personal passions and the world's needs • Articulates vocation as more than career, related to the good life lived for the common good of larger society

(*Continued*)

	Beginning 1	Developing 2	Advanced 3
Acting on Dreams and Imagination	• Unaware of or does not believe in own unique talents and strengths • Cannot name hopes, aspirations, or dreams • Articulates a dream but cannot see any way to take even the first step to make it reality • Does not connect dream to passion or sense of purpose	• Aware of some unique talents and strengths • Names some hopes, aspirations, or dreams • Articulates a dream and sees ways to take several steps to make it reality • Connects parts of dream to passion or sense of purpose	• Names how one has utilized unique talents and strengths in pursuing passions and dreams • Names hopes, aspirations, or dreams with great clarity and nuance • Articulates multiple passions and dreams, and has taken several steps to make them reality • Connects dream and action to passion or sense of purpose
Making Meaning in Narrative	• Narrative is unclear, illogical, or difficult to follow • Articulates little or no sense of self-authorship • Discusses personal dreams and fulfillment focused mostly on personal preferences and external demands, pushes, or pulls • Narrative indicates no real curiosity or quest for meaning, little resilience, and no openness to change, surprise, and wonder	• Narrative is clear and coherent • Articulates some sense of self-authorship • Discusses dreams and fulfillment with some personal authority • Narrative indicates nascent quest for meaning, some resilience, and some openness to change, surprise, and wonder	• Narrative includes connections between personal spiritual beliefs, ethical commitments, personal interests, skills, and life work choices • Articulates high degree of self-authorship • Discusses the excitement and challenge of balancing self-authorship with the claims of others on our lives • Narrative indicates quest for meaning, resilience, and openness to change, surprise, and wonder

Planning for Eudaimonia and Noble Purpose	• Actions in and out of the classroom inconsistent with student's beliefs and values • Exhibits no conscious work toward personal well-being • Unable to articulate plans or a general pathway for student's own eudaimonia and a better world	• Actions in and out of the classroom somewhat consistent with student's beliefs and values and the needs of a diverse society • Exhibits some conscious work toward personal well-being • Begins to articulate plans or a general pathway for student's own eudaimonia and a better world	• Actions in and out of the classroom show compassionate service, civic action, purposeful activism, or ethical leadership • Exhibits conscious work toward personal well-being • Articulates plans or a general pathway for student's own eudaimonia and a better world

13

Do You Love Us?

HIGHER EDUCATION AS AN INTERFAITH CONVERSATION ABOUT THE GOOD LIFE

Jeffrey Carlson

FOR STUDENTS, COLLEGE is many things: an education, certainly, but also a springboard into the job market or further education, an opportunity to discover who they are, a culture shock and a wake-up call. Still, when most people look back on their entire undergraduate experience, they tend to think about their relationships with specific members of a college's faculty and staff—the educators who opened their minds to new possibilities. These individuals often seek to bring undergraduates into conversation with their own ideas, discoveries, and convictions, as well as those of others. Through such conversations, all of us—teachers and students alike—seek to shape a life that is right, that is good.

In this chapter, I argue that higher education should be construed as a courageous and loving interfaith dialogue about the good life for all. The goal of this process is to educate one student at a time, in the company of others, so that diverse insights coalesce and inform each student's distinct educational trajectory. Colleges and universities should be sites where students are inspired to discern a big picture and to name their place within it—to stand somewhere and to stand for something, conscientiously positioned, in an ongoing relationship to an ever-changing world. Educators who work in the undergraduate context must demand more of themselves, even though they may not see positive results of their work easily or immediately. I fundamentally trust that this work is good, and that it is the educator's primary vocation: to foster interfaith dialogue about vocation, and about the meaning and purpose of the good life.

Teachers and students: called into conversation

I have been blessed to have known wonderful educators. As a college student at DePaul University, I met Frank Keenan, an adjunct religious studies instructor, "just passing through,"[1] who taught my first college world religions course. This course introduced me to kindred spirits who were asking my questions and inviting, or imposing, new ones. Also at DePaul, Dominic Crossan opened a vision of a parabolic Jesus and an aniconic, unimaginable God—a compelling and radical vision for what religion could be (as well as a critique of what it should never be, but too often is).[2]

In my final year of college, I was asking: what does a first-generation college student now majoring in religious studies, a Catholic boy whose Catholicism has been altered dramatically, who is enamored and captivated by a dizzying array of compelling questions—what does he "do" with such a degree? He teaches in a Catholic high school, it seemed. And so, I took education courses, and spent time in three different Chicago high schools during my senior year. But I was miserable. The high school classrooms I observed, at that time and in that place, could not compete with my exhilarating college experiences. And while I did and do admire those who teach religion in high schools, it was not right for me. I met with my academic adviser, Jack Leahy, and told him that I hated my life. I was about to graduate and I did not want to do the work for which I had been preparing. "So don't," he said. "Since you love the university so much, you should go to graduate school." The thought had, quite literally, never occurred to me—but in an instant, I knew it was right. "It would be right up your alley," Jack concluded.

Over the years, since that conversation with my adviser, I occasionally find myself saying to a student that something "would be right up your alley." When I say it, the words take on as much resonance, for me, as any liturgical formulation I have ever heard or spoken. In such infrequent moments, the past becomes present; I am hoping to be a catalyst, to create conditions for the possibility of an insight for this student, as my adviser had done for me. Years later, I would be chair of that same religious studies department, working with some of my inspiring undergraduate teachers, including Jack. One spring, our department was relocating offices and I found an old box of advising files in storage. I opened the box and my student folder was there. I brought it to Jack and we had a moment; it

---

1. I say this because, years later—when I became chair of that department and asked about Frank—none of the faculty remembered him.

2. See John Dominic Crossan, *The Dark Interval: Towards a Theology of Story* (Niles, IL: Argus Communications, 1975).

is with me still (both the moment and the folder). Educators, and indeed even educational institutions, ought to create conditions for the possibility of students' own discernment of what is right for them, what fascinates them, what is "right up their alley."

After that meeting, all of my religious studies teachers were telling me the same thing: I should go to graduate school at the University of Chicago. That summer, I read Chicago professor David Tracy's *Blessed Rage for Order*.[3] It introduced the concept of a fundamental trust in the significance of our lives, best construed as a kind of "faith" that is shared by secular and religious persons. The book also described how some religious dimensions of human experience are disclosed through the *limits* on our ordinary experience, which evoke overarching limits of our lives. Christian texts and human experiences were brought into mutually critical correlations; both had questions and answers to offer.

Later, I sat in a room in Hyde Park, with Professor Tracy reading passages from a typed manuscript, followed by a wonderful discussion filled with questions, comments, and suggestions. That manuscript became *The Analogical Imagination*, which included an exploration of the permanence and excess of meaning disclosed in religious classics—never exhausted, always open to new experiences and expressions. Tracy emphasized radical plurality *within* the Christian tradition and thus a "hermeneutics of suspicion upon any and all claims that christology can *only* be expressed in some one manner."[4]

Years later, as a faculty member at DePaul, I drafted a proposal for an interdisciplinary "Focal Point Seminar" program for first-year students. It was, for me, a direct application and translation of Tracy's ideas into an undergraduate curriculum—asking students and professors to spend an entire term problematizing and exploring, through multiple lenses, the surplus and excess of meaning evoked by some very particular person, place, text, object, or event. The idea was to create a practice session for how college-educated students should think critically, and to do so from multiple perspectives. Eventually, as my colleagues and I worked to develop the proposal, it became part of the university's required general education program.[5]

3. David Tracy, *Blessed Rage for Order: The New Pluralism in Theology* (New York: Seabury Press, 1979).

4. David Tracy, *The Analogical Imagination: Christian Theology and the Culture of Pluralism* (New York: Crossroad, 1981), 320.

5. Jeffrey Carlson, "'The Symbol Gives Rise . . .': Problematizing Superficial Readings through a 'Focal Point Seminar,'" *Council of Societies for the Study of Religion Bulletin* 30 (2001): 38–40.

Tracy's 1987 book *Plurality and Ambiguity* offered a study of interpretation itself—especially those transformative interpretations that are true *conversations* with classic texts, symbols, events, persons, or rituals. Authentic conversation, Tracy wrote, is

> a game with some hard rules: say only what you mean; say it as accurately as you can; listen to and respect what the other says, however different or other; be willing to correct or defend your opinions if challenged by the conversation partner; be willing to argue if necessary, to confront if demanded, to endure necessary conflict, to change your mind if the evidence suggests it.[6]

I have included Tracy's statement, or a paraphrase of it, in practically all syllabi I have created since then. I have alluded to its intent in talks to students and families, in vision statements and planning documents, and in curricular goals and designs. And in my current administrative role, the quote is displayed in a large glass case outside of my office.

Through my experiences as both a student and an educator, I have come to believe that in our universities, students and professors should create opportunities to contemplate enduring questions and to invite compelling texts, written and otherwise, to interrogate us—as we compare notes, share our different lenses, incorporate learning from elsewhere, and combine our insights.[7] Together, with our different interests, varied lives, and always-multiple perspectives, we can experience a richer, fuller, deeper sense of the truth we pursue.

When educators do this, courses and curricula do in fact become "practice sessions"—not only for college, but for the rest of students' lives, as they prepare to think and live in relation to the crucial issues they will face. They will practice how they might reflect and act, not merely as well-trained specialists in this or that specific area, but as liberally educated persons. They will develop essential knowledge and skills in reading complex texts, in critical and integrative thinking, and in written, oral, and visual communication. They will graduate with an increased capacity for collaboration and for addressing grand, complex problems—intellectual work for which no single discipline will suffice.

---

6. David Tracy, *Plurality and Ambiguity: Hermeneutics, Religion, Hope* (San Francisco: Harper and Row, 1987), 19.

7. See David Cunningham's reflections on Hans-Georg Gadamer's discussion of this approach to textual interpretation in chapter 5 of this volume.

Obstacles to education as conversation

Of course, the kind of conversational model described here is not easy to achieve, particularly in the contemporary context of higher education. Students and teachers alike face a number of obstacles that make it far easier to turn this rich, complex learning environment into an instrumental process, the goals and methods of which are overly simplified and sometimes even mundane. Overcoming these obstacles can provide a key step toward understanding the entire educational process—teaching and learning, research and advising—as a vocational endeavor.

Disengaged (or silenced) students

One-third of first-year college students in the United States report spending zero hours reading for pleasure during a typical week in their last year of high school, and another 25 percent report spending less than one hour doing so.[8] I find compelling and persuasive bell hooks's observation that, in the United States, children are educated for conformity and obedience and are told that thinking is dangerous. As a result, college students have come to dread thinking; their task, they assume, is merely to consume information and regurgitate it at appropriate moments.[9]

In addition, hooks goes on to argue that today, students lack basic skills of communication because they are passive consumers of information; they feel they have nothing worthy to say. A model of education as conversation, rightly understood, presupposes that, on the contrary, they have much to say.[10] Educators need to encourage them to find their voices and also need to render themselves teachable—which can be done if we cultivate a capacity to listen, if we have ears to hear. Conversations like these can heal students' spirits, fostering a sense of wonder.[11]

Sometimes, our conversation partners inspire us to become educators, or provide us with experiences that clarify what kinds of educators we hope to become. While in high school and college, I worked in a restaurant and a factory.

---

8. Kevin Eagan et al., "The American Freshman: National Norms Fall 2015," (Los Angeles: Higher Education Research Institute, UCLA, 2016), 50. Online at, http://www.heri.ucla.edu/monographs/TheAmericanFreshman2015.pdf (accessed November 27, 2016).

9. bell hooks, *Teaching Critical Thinking: Practical Wisdom* (New York: Routledge, 2009), 8.

10. hooks, *Teaching Critical Thinking*, 45.

11. hooks, *Teaching Critical Thinking*, 188.

I remember a time when one of my coworkers asked if I would do him a favor. His uncle in Zacatecas, Mexico, had sent him a book—*Bulfinch's Mythology*. My friend's English reading skills were not that good and so he asked if I would read some of the book and tell him the stories. "My uncle is a learned man," he kept saying. He wanted to discuss the myths with this uncle he loved, this learned man he so wanted to impress and emulate. (By then I was about to enter graduate school, pretty sure I wanted to be a college professor someday. "If I ever do become a teacher," I thought, "I hope to find students with this desire to learn.") Near the end of the summer, my coworker gave me an Aztec sun stone and told me a couple of his grandmother's stories about Jaguar and Rabbit and what the stone meant to her. None of these stories were in *Bulfinch's* (of course). I promised myself then that I would try to remember my friend, and thus to remember what real students were like, as I entered the hallowed halls of my doctoral program. I would seek out these students, and I would try to emulate my friend's intense "need to know."

How do we engage students who have become disengaged from, or who have been actively discouraged from participating in, genuine conversation? Higher education must create curricula that include pursuit of the "why at all" questions, in and across our disciplines, in ways that speak to our broader lives. The "then what, so what, for what, toward what" questions—arising out of our disciplinary knowledge—should envelop our studies from beginning to end. This should be an ongoing process throughout higher *and toward still higher* education, on a trajectory toward what Karl Rahner called an "ever-receding horizon" of human questioning.[12] We strive and we reach, but not just for the next problem to solve. We have a question, seek the information, analyze the information, and draw conclusions. But every conclusion leads to another question, and in that striving, through that process, along that trajectory, we approach those deep questions that animate our conversations and lure us toward a novel future.

In the health sciences, for example, our focus should not be limited to advanced anatomy. We also need to ask: What does it mean to heal? Why heal at all? In pre-law courses, we teach cases, precedents, and statutes; but we should also ask: What does it mean to be just? Why be just at all? And so it goes with all of our educational pursuits. There are layers upon layers of knowledge, discovery, and application—all necessary, but not sufficient without the depth toward which they point, to which we are drawn, and to which we are even called,

12. See Karl Rahner, *Foundations of Christian Faith: An Introduction to the Idea of Christianity* (New York: Seabury, 1978), especially chapter 1.

as a kind of vocation. We are depth-seekers and depth-finders so that, as Soren Kierkegaard said, we seek "a truth which is truth *for me*, to find *the idea for which I am willing to live and die*."[13] Our calling is to take that next step, to ask that next question, to transcend the given.

Toward what? I encourage students to catch the spirit of Augustine, who wrote that, when he was 19 years old, "all my empty dreams suddenly lost their charm" and that he "burned with longing . . . not simply to admire one or another of the schools of philosophy, but to love wisdom itself, whatever it might be, and to search for it, pursue it, hold it, and embrace it firmly."[14] As educators, we need to know our students well enough to help them engage in this love of wisdom, to find what fascinates them.

Mimetic Desire

Education can become conversation only in spaces of genuineness rather than mere mimicry. Imagine someone brewing a cup of tea, savoring it, and being nourished by it. But then, after this person leaves, someone else comes along and fills the cup again, reusing the old tea leaves—then drinks and departs. People keep coming, and they say (and even think) they're drinking tea; but of course, now it's mostly just water.[15] The upshot: We should not live diluted lives, and we cannot be nourished simply by mimicking someone else's prior choices. We need to think and live and brew for ourselves. And so higher education must relentlessly unmask what René Girard calls "mimetic desire," in which we allow our own needs and wants to be shaped by those that we observe in others.[16] Students' selection of major fields and of careers is too often based on limited options and little genuine discernment—relying instead, uncritically and sometimes nearly exclusively, on parents or friends, or on perceptions about the "hottest" majors and most lucrative jobs.

---

13. *Soren Kierkegaard's Journals and Papers*, vol. 5, ed. and trans. Howard V. Hong and Edna H. Hong (Bloomington: Indiana University Press, 1978), 34.

14. Saint Augustine, *Confessions*, trans. R. S. Pine-Coffin (New York: Penguin, 1977), 59.

15. The origins of the metaphor are in Kierkegaard, who critiqued organized Christianity as "Charming religiousness—just as authentic as tea made from a piece of paper which once lay in a drawer together with another piece of paper in which a few dried tea leaves had been kept, leaves which had already been used three times." *Soren Kierkegaard's Journals and Papers*, vol. 4, ed. and trans. Howard V. Hong and Edna H. Hong (Bloomington: Indiana University Press, 1975), 437.

16. René Girard, *The Scapegoat* (Baltimore: Johns Hopkins, 1986), 133.

By contrast, Kierkegaard writes of the rare but precious authenticity of individual conscience and decision, as opposed to the superficial, uncritical parroting of whatever "the crowd" does. He commented that, when he wrote, he imagined a genuine individual who stands out from the crowd—the person "whom with joy and gratitude I call my reader."[17] I hope that educators think of their students this way—educating them one at a time, but in the company of others in a supportive community.

Inauthentic mimicry, which runs counter to a vision of education as conversation, can also be seen in our own institutions' public self-presentations. The view-books and websites of various colleges and universities tend to be much the same, yet ironically they make repeated and unswerving assertions of their own institution's utter uniqueness! Tim Clydesdale cautions wisely that educators need to transform higher education from within, or else they will end up watching as it is transformed from without as their institutions capitulate to market-driven forces.[18] Universities need to offer students a counternarrative to mimetic desire and should not simply succumb to it.

In our universities, each student should be able to take in a variety of educational experiences, such that they come together in each student's own "blend" and trajectory. Through dialogue with trusted mentors and advisers, students should be creating their own particular and progressively coherent narrative[19]—created from a combination of courses and professors, majors and minors, papers and projects, internships, study abroad, service learning, seminars, undergraduate research, and co-curricular engagement. Alfred North Whitehead, in his felicitous phrase, says, "The many become one and are increased by one."[20] Many experiences become one in the student, and the student enriches a community of strong and independent thinkers, who will participate in the transformation that our society requires.

---

17. Soren Kierkegaard, *Purity of Heart Is to Will One Thing*, trans. Douglas V. Steere (New York: Harper and Row, 1956), 27.

18. Tim Clydesdale, *The Purposeful Graduate: Why Colleges Must Talk to Students about Vocation* (Chicago: University of Chicago Press, 2015), 207.

19. See the discussion of this process by Matt Sayers, as well as the exercises offered to encourage it by Tracy Wenger Sadd, in chapters 8 and 12 of this volume, respectively. See also Shirley Hershey Showalter, "Called to Tell Our Stories: The Narrative Structure of Vocation," in *Vocation across the Academy: A New Vocabulary for Higher Education*, ed. David S. Cunningham (New York: Oxford University Press, 2017), 67–88.

20. Alfred North Whitehead, *A Key to Whitehead's Process and Reality*, ed. Donald Sherburne (Chicago: University of Chicago Press, 1981), 34.

Attainment gaps

A vision of education as conversation would be naïve if it were to assume a "level playing field" or "equal access" to some comfortable, well-fed, seminar-style salon. In reality, massive global and local inequality and suffering keep many impoverished and in peril. We live in and perpetuate a system that keeps many of our most important potential conversation partners out of college altogether, or makes it difficult for them to remain. We know that the gap in degree attainment between students from the highest and lowest quartiles of family income has been increasing, as has the gap in degree attainment across racial and ethnic groups.[21]

On university campuses, do faculty members know the percentage of their students whose family incomes are such that they are eligible for Pell Grants, compared with the percentage nationally and in relation to similar institutions? Do they know the difference in graduation rates between Pell and non-Pell students at their institutions? Do they know the levels of bachelor degree attainment across the family income quartiles or racial/ethnic groups at their institutions? These matters should evoke conversations among faculty members, as active participants in the shared governance of their universities, so that they can champion what is best for students. Only with this kind of intervention will our universities stop perpetuating and exacerbating the disparities being described here. Otherwise, universities will continue to mimic one another's complicity, rather than working actively to close these insidious (and widening) gaps.

Colleges and universities must become what Charles Strain has called "countervailing institutions" in society.[22] They should play a crucial role in social transformation—"working the linkages" among institutions, grassroots communities, and social movements—through such tactics as community-based

---

21. Robert D. Putnam, *Our Kids: The American Dream in Crisis* (New York: Simon and Schuster, 2015), 187. Putnam further argues that a family's socioeconomic status has become even more important than test scores in predicting which eighth graders would graduate from college, noting that "high-scoring poor kids are now slightly less likely (29 percent) to get a college degree than low-scoring rich kids (30 percent)" (190). See also "Step Up and Lead for Equity: What Higher Education Can Do to Reverse Our Deepening Divides," Association of American Colleges and Universities, https://www.aacu.org/publications/step-up-and-lead (accessed July 18, 2017).

22. Charles Strain, *The Prophet and the Bodhisattva: Daniel Berrigan, Thich Nhat Hanh, and the Ethics of Peace and Justice* (Eugene, OR: Wipf and Stock, 2014), 114. Charles Strain was another of my undergraduate teachers; he taught me about rigorous research and modeled, for me, a Catholic who studied deeply in another tradition (Buddhism).

learning and research, social justice efforts, and programs in interfaith studies and related fields.[23] In these and other ways, universities can counter society's "pernicious fictions" that support manifestations of inequity and violence. They can challenge the status quo and coordinate actions in order to effectively promote social transformation.[24]

We must be "professionals with an edge," Strain argues, chipping away at social problems—the way medieval stonemasons worked on cathedrals, knowing that their massive churches would not be finished for many centuries.[25] I love this imagery, because such work demands precision, dedication, skill, and also a nonattachment from the immediate results we might crave.[26] A craving for immediate, full results can cause burnout; on the other hand, a stonemason's approach demands that, while not attached to final results, we remain deeply and irrevocably attached to the work at hand—each and every day. Such work demands our very best selves and our most critical thinking. As educators in "countervailing institutions," we must remain committed to enacting a counter-narrative to the one in which so many of our universities are often inexcusably complicit. We must be equity-minded, analyzing our practices, policies, structures, and culture to discern ways in which they may contribute to inequities; next we must take specific, concrete, measurable steps to change for the better; and then we must keep revisiting this process.[27]

---

23. For examples, see Caryn Riswold, "Vocational Discernment: A Pedagogy of Humanization" and Darby Ray, "Self, World, and the Space Between: Community Engagement as Vocational Discernment," both in *At This Time and In This Place: Vocation and Higher Education*, ed. David S. Cunningham (New York: Oxford University Press, 2015), 72–95 and 301–20, respectively; Catherine Fobes, "Calling over the Life Course: Sociological Insights," in Cunningham, ed., *Vocation across the Academy*; and Jacqueline Bussie's reflections in chapter 11 of this volume.

24. Strain, *Prophet*, 116. Institutions matter, Strain insists, citing many positive examples such as the NAACP during the civil rights era, the Roman Catholic Church in support of Christian base communities in Latin America, the Solidarity movement in Poland, and the divestiture movement among US universities in opposition to transnational corporations doing business in apartheid South Africa (248).

25. Strain, *Prophet*, 250.

26. See the comments by Anantanand Rambachan concerning "nonattachment to the fruit of one's actions" in chapter 6 of this volume.

27. Lindsey Malcom-Piqueux and Estela Mara Bensimon, "Taking Equity-Minded Action to Close Equity Gaps," *Peer Review, a Publication of the Association of American Colleges and Universities* 19, no. 2 (Spring 2017): 5–8.

Facing our flaws, lovingly

At a recent student protest on my campus, a large coalition of students from multiple racial, ethnic, and religious backgrounds rallied in support of an ongoing Black Lives Matter movement, and the first words from one of the black student spokespersons were these: "Do you love us?" And then: "No plans, no action, no peace!" "We want deadlines!" Students called for concrete activities, responsible parties, and specific outcomes around goals such as recruiting, supporting, and retaining a diverse community. They sought an enhancement of the "cultural competency" of administrators, faculty, staff, and students, as well as an increase in the infusion of multiculturalism across the curriculum. They called on the university to amplify and empower the voices and lives of those marginalized by institutional racism, and to promote research that deepens our understanding of diversity, community, the common good, and social justice. But beyond all these practical matters, the initial question remains: "Do you love us?"

To say yes is not enough, of course; we need to say yes with an intention to transcend the given, to aim higher, to take stock, to know ourselves, to change when the evidence suggests it, and then to take action. This is what we are called to do as educators—to perform what we profess. Perhaps the student on my campus felt she could ask this question because we speak so often of our motto: *Caritas et Veritas* ("love and truth"). The Sinsinawa Dominican sisters who founded my institution say that "relationship is at the heart of mission," and it strikes me that this makes for a very particular kind of conversation—one steeped in love. It means we have to care when our students become exhausted from explaining themselves again and again, correcting misunderstandings or countering biases toward them as Muslims, Jews, Hindus, Sikhs, or Mormons, for example.[28] It means caring enough to unearth a host of implicit beliefs leading to biased behaviors, to detect and respond to microinsults and microinvalidations.[29]

I have argued that, through free and open interaction, students can experience genuine learning, transformation, and the discovery of their own best selves and their true vocational trajectory. For these conversations to be genuine, however, our universities must deliberately build a student, faculty, and staff community that is intentionally diverse—racially, socioeconomically, religiously, and in other ways. Doing this with integrity means that we must intend to enter into conversation with precisely those others who may reveal our own gaps and flaws—our

28. Douglas Jacobsen and Rhonda Hustedt Jacobsen, *No Longer Invisible: Religion in University Education* (New York: Oxford University Press, 2012), 79.

29. See Kelly A. Burns, "Minimizing and Managing Microaggressions in the Philosophy Classroom," *Teaching Philosophy* 37 (2014): 131–52.

perhaps unintended and unwitting (but still operative) bigotries, stereotypes, errors, and false assumptions. These others may see and name things about me that I cannot or will not see; they may experience the truth I *perform* as being quite different, in actuality, from the truth I would *profess to believe*.

Conversation should not, as I have argued elsewhere,[30] be merely an act of "inclusion" or assimilation; our conversation partners should not be forced to fit into preconceived categories. Nor should our courageous truth seeking, truth telling, and true listening be mean-spirited, vindictive, or unforgiving; instead, it should be loving. We should love, and teach what we will.

Since stereotypes may persist even when practitioners view themselves as "culturally competent," we also need to move toward a sense of cultural humility. This requires a lifelong commitment to self-evaluation and self-critique, to redressing power imbalances, and to developing mutually beneficial partnerships with communities—again, so that we might perform what we profess. Cultural humility takes into account the fluidity and subjectivity of culture; it challenges both individuals and institutions to address inequalities. It calls for active engagement in a lifelong endeavor, rather than focusing on a discrete endpoint.[31]

Cultural humility is a relationship-based, ongoing process; this is what we should aspire to embody and practice as educators, rather than seeking to exhibit a reified sense of "competence," which is too often viewed as a delimited proficiency that one can achieve once and for all. Catherine Cornille also calls for humility as a key condition for the possibility of interreligious dialogue; she sees it as "an active and dynamic force that drives one beyond oneself to encounter with the other," leading to a "freedom from preoccupation with one's own thoughts and feelings" so that "humility facilitates understanding through love of the other and an enhanced awareness of one's own prideful ignorance."[32]

At my institution, on a given day each September, the university suspends classes and over 1,200 students, faculty, and staff register for and participate in our annual "Caritas Veritas Symposium."[33] At this event, students, faculty, and staff raise

---

30. Jeffrey Carlson, "Against Being Inclusive," *Liberal Education* 101, no. 4 and 102, no. 1 (Fall 2015/Winter 2016): 58–63, https://www.aacu.org/liberaleducation/2015-2016/fall-winter/carlson (accessed July 10, 2018).

31. Marcie Fisher-Borne, Jessie Montana Cain, and Suzanne L. Martin, "From Mastery to Accountability: Cultural Humility as an Alternative to Cultural Competence," *Social Work Education* 34, no. 2 (2015): 165–81.

32. Catherine Cornille, *The im-Possibility of Interreligious Dialogue* (New York: Crossroad, 2008), 24.

33. Dominican University, "Caritas Veritas Symposium," http://www.dom.edu/about/mission/cvsymposium (accessed November 27, 2016).

and address questions about the good life in relation to the university's motto through formal papers, panel presentations, roundtable discussions, workshops, debates, and original creative work.

At a recent symposium, an economist told us we have to "throw our hearts over the bar, and everything else will follow. Commit yourself fully and without reservations. Let that lead you. Like a high-jumper: commit, and leap." At another, a historian urged each of us to "do something we care about enormously, to reflect constantly on what this is, to be sure that it is truly something worth doing. The institution wants to free us from the institution, so that we will pursue truth wherever we are." A mathematician observed his astonishment when he, an Orthodox Jew, joined a Catholic college and discovered that no one questioned his need to take time off for the Jewish holy days that first fall. He felt affirmed and trusted, and he returned that affirmation and trust to others, encouraging us to "Love these students. They're very, very dear. You have to realize that their lives in a certain way are in our hands."

Do you love us?

Interfaith dialogue as conversation about the good life

This chapter has argued for education as conversation and it has sought to raise and address some of the obstacles to that conversation. But it is also, most profoundly, an *interfaith* conversation that we most need to foster on our campuses.

Faculty, staff, and students at our institutions may or may not practice within any historical religious tradition, but surely we all seek a deeper place. We strive and we reach, not just for the next problem to solve, but to approach a mystery that, beyond all finite problems, envelops and animates our curiosity. One may or may not believe in a God, but there is a sense in which we are all people of faith: what Tracy called a fundamental trust in the worthwhileness of being at all.[34] Educators share a fundamental trust in the intelligibility of reality, so that our research, scholarship, and creative investigations strike us as worth pursuing. Activists share a fundamental trust that we can, somehow, do something good; we can translate our own best gifts into effective contributions to a world in need, beyond our parochial selves and our narrow zones of comfort.

This fundamental trust, this primary stance toward the world, will be expressed in vastly varied beliefs, bodies of knowledge, and systems of thought and practice. Given this understanding of faith, then, we need to foster *interfaith*

---

34. Tracy, *Analogical Imagination*, 47.

dialogue on our campuses—dialogue about core commitments (within and across disciplines), about our criteria for holding them, and about what they inspire us to do. Our students may be "orthodox believers," "mainline believers," "spiritual seekers," "spiritual humanists," or "spiritual skeptics"—or they may not identify with any of these categories.[35] Our interfaith dialogue should intend to exclude no one and should seek to engage the multiple and varied "religious, spiritual, and value-based worldviews"[36] represented in our universities, including those who reject religion altogether.[37]

Seeking the good

If higher education is a courageous and loving interfaith dialogue, ultimately its primary subject matter is "the good life." Throughout students' curricular and co-curricular experiences, they should regularly return to touchstones such as these: What does it mean to be good, to lead a good life? How does a person find, or create, a good life? What does it mean for a student, professional, scholar, or educator to be good? How have others' love and truth shaped and transformed one's life? How does one reconcile self-interest with a sense of broader responsibility?[38] Students should be asked to address these kinds of questions regularly—not simply as aspiring chemists, nurses, graphic designers, and accountants, but as liberal learners who can think in integrative ways.

Educators should model for their students the capacity to address these kinds of "why at all" questions, expressing their own core convictions, their own "faith." Moreover, they should tell students their own stories of their journeys toward meaningful work—not so that students can mimic professors' choices and

---

35. Robert J. Nash and DeMethra LaSha Bradley, "The Different Spiritualities of the Students We Teach," in *The American University in a Postsecular Age: Religion in the Academy*, ed. Douglas Jacobsen and Rhonda Hustedt Jacobsen (New York: Oxford University Press, 2008), 138–47.

36. For a description of these categories in relation to interfaith work at Dominican University, see Jeffrey Carlson, "Building and Assessing a Culture of Interfaith Learning," *Diversity & Democracy* 16, no. 2 (Summer 2013): 18–19.

37. I do not wish to offend or exclude atheists with this religious rhetoric. As Paul Tillich said so well, if the word "God" has not much meaning, "translate it, and speak of the depths of your life, of the source of your being, of your ultimate concern, of what you take seriously without any reservation. . . . For you cannot think or say: Life has no depth! Life itself is shallow. Being itself is surface only." Paul Tillich, *The Shaking of the Foundations* (New York: Charles Scribner's Sons, 1948), 57.

38. These themes were explored in Dominican University's 2016 "Caritas Veritas Symposium," http://www.dom.edu/about/mission/cvsymposium/archive/2016 (accessed April 13, 2017).

outcomes, but to demonstrate how a life of purpose and meaning can be pursued, thereby helping students participate in such a process themselves.[39] Through dialogues about such stories, participants may, as Robert Nash and DeMethra LaSha Bradley have suggested, learn to "love and live in the questions of life, and thereby model how to accept and return questions."[40]

At the end of the day, our students must develop the capacity to describe their own journeys, to tell their own stories, to identify their current locations, and to cite and defend the criteria by which they make choices. Only by doing so can they craft a narrative of their lives in which they begin to discern and articulate their own right ways forward. In my university we say that "we educate one student at a time in the company of others" in "a distinctively relationship-centered educational community."[41] Students should think for themselves, but think dialogically; they should think for themselves, but live for and with others. Steeped in that kind of ethos, their studies—exploring foundations, depth, breadth, and integration—can prepare them to be globally aware students, committed to a good life for all.[42]

Genuine dialogue across genuine difference

Today, many people increasingly mistrust higher education; this is part of the fractious context in which we currently operate. In a 2017 Pew Research Center study, a majority of Republicans and Republican-leading independents stated that colleges and universities have a negative effect on the country. As recently as two years earlier, a majority of the same group held a positive view of colleges and universities.[43] Peter Wood views these results as evidence that "public confidence in higher education's basic ability to provide an environment in which ideas can be freely debated" has been shaken.[44]

---

39. For more on faculty modeling, see chapters 4 (by Younus Mirza) and 11 (by Jacqueline Bussie) in this volume.

40. Nash and Bradley, "Different Spiritualities," 150.

41. Dominican University Identity Statement, http://dom.edu/about/mission (accessed November 27, 2016).

42. Dominican University, "Vision for Undergraduate Education," http://www.dom.edu/academics/undergraduate/corecurriculum/vision (accessed November 27, 2016).

43. "Sharp Partisan Divisions in Views of National Institutions," Pew Research Center, http://www.people-press.org/2017/07/10/sharp-partisan-divisions-in-views-of-national-institutions/ (accessed July 20, 2017).

44. Peter Wood, "Colleges Are to Blame for the Contempt in Which They're Held," *Chronicle of Higher Education*, July 12, 2017, http://www.chronicle.com/article/

In response, educators need to ask themselves: How much ideological diversity do we seek to engage, to consider seriously, in our campus conversations? To what extent is the campus a site, in service to society, where rigorous debates on serious issues occur—a site that invites the broader public to participate, where we invite and engage a genuine diversity of thought? In helping students to think about the good life, to reflect on vocation, I would argue that we need to conduct a serious inventory of the texts we assign our students and the viewpoints we consider in our curricula. We need to ask ourselves how diverse we are and want to be—so that we can live up to our highest ideals as a university that would dare to claim to pursue truth.

An honest dialogue with a thoughtfully assembled, truly *diverse range* of *potentially plausible live options* is a condition for the possibility of a genuine pursuit of truth, and this enterprise should shape the context in which our students engage in vocational discernment. I am not suggesting we debate the merits of the Ku Klux Klan, "pro or con," or the existence of gravity, "true or false"; however, educators owe it to their students to select and consider seriously a genuine range of potentially plausible live options. In the film *The Blues Brothers*, Jake and Elwood walk into a bar and ask what kind of music is played there. "We play both kinds," the bartender says. "Country and Western."[45] Education as conversation about vocation, and about the good life for all, must have the courage and the integrity to expand the conversation—rather than simply giving students more of the same from a narrow range of worldviews and lifestances.

This work of conversation is tremendous, and awesome, and not for the faint of heart. We profess to pursue truth; but when we penetrate the appearances and look beneath the surfaces, we may not like what we see. And if we are in a dialogue, we may not recognize (or choose to acknowledge) what others see in us, or how they challenge us to change. Yet if we are in relationship—steeped in an ethos of both active love and courageous truth-seeking—then perhaps we will listen and learn, speak our truths, listen again, and embody a vocation that participates in the creation of a more just and humane world.

Colleges-Are-to-Blame-for-the/240617 (accessed July 14, 2017). For more on the current public perception of higher education, see the remarks of Jacqueline Bussie in chapter 11 of this volume.

45. *The Blues Brothers*, directed by John Landis (1980; Universal City, CA: Universal Studios Home Entertainment, 1998), DVD.

Beyond the homogeneity of Babel

I conclude this section of the chapter with a reflection on a text that has influenced a number of religious and secular traditions. This version of the story comes from the Hebrew Bible:

> "Let us then go down there and confuse their language, so that one will not understand what another says." Thus the Lord scattered them from there all over the earth, and they stopped building the city. That is why it was called Babel, because there the Lord confused the speech of all the world. It was from that place that he scattered them all over the earth. (Genesis 11:8–9)

It seems that the people, speaking one language and building a tower to the sky, had "come together"; but they had done so for themselves, and not in relation to God. They were denying the best of themselves: the part that connects them with God and with the variegated creation. The story suggests that the vast panoply of languages and peoples and cultures is part of God's "very good" creation. Babel's homogeneity constitutes nothing less than a failure to relish God's diverse world. Hence, God scattered the people.

What were they supposed to do out there, scattered and confused? Perhaps they were meant to find each other, and many others, across and through their differences. They were supposed to learn how to love and appreciate the magisterial beauty of the vastly varied creation of God, including in their own pluriform lives, languages, and cultures. They were scattered because the oneness they had constructed was shallow and artificial; it was unworthy of God's richly complex creation and of their own fullest life trajectories.

Today, humanity has not done much better. But we have the opportunity to venture forth, beyond the boundaries of in-group sameness, single-language homogeneity, and single-family ziggurats; we can cross lines of class, race, gender, religion, and nation. In my own tradition, for example, Jesus's life and work and message offer a boundary-crossing itinerant movement of seeking out, quite deliberately and strategically, precisely those who are different.[46]

Yet for all our posturing, we do not really like dealing with those who are significantly different from ourselves—at least if that means having to hear and respond to difference in a way that might require us to change in a more-than-trivial

46. For an examination of some of Jesus's encounters with difference, see David Cunningham's discussion in the last section of chapter 5 of this volume, as well as Jacqueline Bussie's interpretation of Jesus's parable of Good Samaritan in chapter 11.

way. We prefer to surround ourselves with those who "seem" different, but who really are not allowed to "be" different.[47] This turns difference into sameness—and we are back at the original Babel all over again.

Sometimes we "make a name for ourselves," just as the people wanted to do at Babel, and we call that name "diversity" or "multiculturalism." Sometimes we prefer to be thought of as "inclusive," but too often the way we "include" entails granting the other an assigned role in our current, dominant, and unchallenged story. We give others a pre-determined seat at our fixed and stable table, a persona in which others get to be, not themselves, but merely a slightly altered version of what we already know—something with which we are already comfortable.

We do not really want to venture out; we crave the easy sameness of Babel, but with the added post-Babel bonus of appearing to "celebrate diversity," so long as our contrived sameness is not ever concretely or severely threatened. But we are called to something more: called to a deep dialogue—not merely to the fashioning of decorative episodic moments of "diversity" in the curriculum, but rather to a thoroughgoing lifestance of diversity, threaded throughout the curriculum. Such an encounter with difference puts our comfort at risk; it provides for an emergence of, and dialogue among, the "why at all" questions that are evoked by our disciplines.

And so whatever part we play in our educational communities, we have to ask ourselves: Are we constructing a tower of Babel, giving out degrees in Mimetic Studies, seeking the comfortable sameness of who and what we are and know already? Or, alternatively, is our educational vocation truly one of going forth, of submitting ourselves to the disorientation of being scattered away from more of the same, so that we can find each other, out there? When we accept an itinerant and boundary-crossing invitation like the one that Jesus and other religious and spiritual figures have extended, we may have reason to hope that we can truly come together. At least in this song, it is God who gets to sing that last line. We get to hum along, or maybe dance, but God gets to sing it, and it sounds like this: "Come together, right now, over me."[48]

Syncretic and ever-changing selves

As we educate one student at a time in the company of others, and as we help students to find that company, we need to help them to see (as I have argued

47. See also Homayra Ziad's description of this problem in her introductory comments in chapter 9 of this volume.

48. The Beatles, "Come Together," *Abbey Road*, Apple Records, 1969, audiocassette.

elsewhere)[49] that "multiple belonging" is not only possible but actually inevitable. [50] In fact, it may be potentially misleading as a category, if it is construed as erroneously assuming the existence or even possibility of some unmixed, pure tradition in the first place. Such a pristine prior state is a fiction (albeit often a useful one). Unmixed traditions are not to be found. Religious and other deep, value-based worldviews are intrinsically syncretic; each is an inevitably selective reconstruction from an array of possibilities, which become one coherent amalgam that works to provide meaning and purpose. The "tradition" to which one belongs is itself the product of a process of selective reconstruction, achieved by those who came before and inherited now by others. One encounters facets of that body of practices and beliefs and one is presented with an opportunity to interact with it, to selectively appropriate it, and ultimately to contribute to its revision and reconstitution—drawing upon and including practices and beliefs that are in turn drawn from other places and times. There is no permanent, essential core of any religion, or of any deep, value-based worldview; there are only multiple products of ongoing processes of selective reconstruction.

This is good news for our vocationally pressured and often highly anxious students. Hannah Schell is right to note the immense pressure society and educators often put on students to make the perfect vocationally relevant choices. Instead, educators need to support students in an ongoing process of both listening to their own inner voice and looking to others for guidance.[51] The good news for students is this: if I am always-already complex and diverse, if my identity comprises an ever-developing plurality, then the plural "others" seem far less "other," since they too are syncretic selves. Self and community are already plural—never pure, but always mixed and mixing. We all share that formal, structural sameness, that inevitably hybrid status of our identities; hence, there is no "pure other" to be reviled and scapegoated. *Do you love us?*

Students need to be affirmed in their need to stand somewhere and to name a self, but compassionate educators need to help them to appreciate that such naming is not final, but tentative and ongoing. This may provide our students with the confidence they need to continue the conversation—as well as a modicum of relief from the anxiety they face when confronted with the work of

49. Jeffrey Carlson, "'Syncretistic Religiosity': The Significance of this Tautology," *Journal of Ecumenical Studies* 29 (1992): 24–34; "Pretending to Be Buddhist and Christian: Thich Nhat Hanh and the Two Truths of Religious Identity," *Buddhist-Christian Studies* 20 (2000): 115–25.

50. See Trina Jones's reflections on multiple religious belonging in chapter 2 of this volume.

51. Hannah Schell, "Commitment and Community: The Virtue of Loyalty and Vocational Discernment," in Cunningham, ed., *At This Time*, 235–54; here, 238–39, 249.

vocational reflection and discernment.[52] Despite what they may have heard, such work is never the high-stakes, either-or, once-and-for-all process that they fear. It is, rather, a part of the ongoing conversation about the good life—a conversation that, at its best, undergraduate education can encourage and promote.

I think we have reason to hope, even in spite of our all-too-human failings, our distortions and pride, our self-trivialization and our self-deception, our mimicry and our boundary-making. I think we have reason to hope that in our teaching and learning, through a vast array of methods and practices, we can together create conditions for the possibility of the pursuit of truth, of depth, of the "why at all." In our work together, the transmission of current or past knowledge or truth claims will be necessary but not sufficient. There will be more: in our teaching and learning there will be an experience, a marvelous interactive dialogue. It will include, first, our fundamental desire to know and to live a good and ethically responsible life; second, the things and ideas that we study and create; third, our friends—those other teachers and learners, living and dead—who join us in the dialogue; and fourth, our shared world outside the university. That world is filled with knowledge and insight, as well as suffering and injustice. It compels us to ask of ourselves: now, what are we prepared to do?

Response

Katherine (Trina) Janiec Jones

I love the rituals surrounding the beginning of the academic year. At my college, we hold an opening convocation, at which the faculty process in full regalia, the community hears inspiring talks about the meaning of higher education, and we all sing the alma mater. We engage in the rituals of civic religion that have grown up around our college's life, and I walk away feeling renewed in my vocation, excited and hopeful, and ready to go. Usually by the end of the semester, though, I have gotten mightily worn down by the torrent of assignments, the endless to-do lists, and the sheer number of things to which I have needed to attend. My temper has grown short, my voice snarly, my words largely monosyllabic.

Jeff's vision of education as an ongoing, loving conversation reminds me that love and fidelity toward one's vocation can take many outward forms. It reminds

52. For further discussion of the dynamic and ongoing nature of vocation discernment, see David S. Cunningham, "Language that Works: Vocation and the Complexity of Higher Education," in Cunningham, ed., *Vocation across the Academy*, 1–18; here, 11–12.

me that long-term love—like my relationship with my vocation—is not always the Valentine's Day kind of love. Sometimes it is Laundry Day love, or Bill-Paying Day love. Loving our students, our work, and those with whom we work—all of this is both the stuff of the early-year uplifting convocations *and* of the late-year, grumpy, cursory head nods as we pass each other in the halls on the way to get more coffee. This kind of love, the kind that sees education as a conversation, is a marathon rather than a sprint; it requires ongoing care and attention, day after day, year after year. As Jeff says, this kind of love "calls for active engagement in a lifelong endeavor, rather than focusing on a discrete endpoint."

Jeff's chapter is the kind of essay that I need to reread every year, and to share with as many people as I can. Being able to read this kind of text again—each time while encountering a new group of students—is like greeting an old friend (and having the honor of introducing that old friend to new friends). This chapter is a friend with whom I would like to spend considerable time in the future—one whose words of wisdom I would like to absorb deeply into my consciousness.

Epilogue

Hearing in a New Key

VOCATION BEYOND THE LIMITS OF REASON ALONE

David S. Cunningham

AS IS OFTEN noted, the roots of the word *vocation* are found in a Latin verb that means "to call." Hence, descriptions of and conversations about vocation tend to make significant use of metaphors involving the spoken word and other forms of audible communication; similarly, references to receiving a call, or to attending to one's calling, make significant use of aural and auditory metaphors. If we hope to discern our callings in life, we need, first of all, to be willing to listen; second, to attend carefully to what we are hearing; and third, to internalize and acknowledge the importance of what we have heard—even if we are sometimes unwilling or unable to take up a particular call that has come our way. Listening, hearing, thinking, deliberating, and perhaps answering: these are the primary elements of response to a call. And in the contemporary multi-faith context of higher education, this also means listening and hearing differently, thinking and judging differently, and ultimately *acting* differently in response to the many calls and callings that come to us over the course of lives.

Yet as valuable as these metaphors may be, the work that they describe—listening, hearing, internalizing, responding—can make vocational reflection and discernment seem like a wholly rational endeavor, highly dependent on specific forms of linguistic communication. We listen for a particular form of words, hear a summons or an entreaty that is expressed in language, think about what we have heard, evaluate it, and act on it: all of these are primarily activities of the intellect and the will. What space is left for the affects, the intuitive, the experiential? What role is played by those elements of human existence that may not fit the received patterns of rational discourse: the spiritual, the reflective, even the mystical? Does vocation too often become one more deductive enterprise, in which a range of premises are explored and arranged in priority order until the outcome or the solution becomes almost inevitable?

In 1793, Immanuel Kant published *Religion within the Limits of Reason Alone*. He characterized religion as a bare or "naked" reality that had been inappropriately "clothed" by layers of historical accretion: superstition, ritual, and myth. He argued for a stripping down of religion to what he regarded as its "true nature," in which reason reigned supreme. Kant's perspective, deeply embedded in his Enlightenment context, continues to be popular today. Religious perspectives are often criticized as "irrational"; new interpretations of various faith traditions and lifestances often argue for the removal of their "excess layers," in search of the reason-based claims at their core. But as many scholars of religion have observed, this process often resembles the process of peeling an onion; if the cook continues to remove layer after layer, there will eventually be nothing left (though a great many tears will have been shed in the process). As it turns out, the layers *are* the onion. This is not to say that religion is not rational, but it is to say that the attempt to find a purely rational core at the "heart" of religion is a misconceived enterprise. It will always exceed the bounds of mere reason.

Something similar can be said about vocation—and this claim, too, emerges throughout the pages of this book. One might be tempted to reduce vocational discernment to a mere deductive choice, to a straightforward cost-benefit analysis, or simply to finding the right role model to emulate. But vocational reflection always leaves us with an excess of meaning—a depth and breadth that exceeds the narrow frameworks of calculation and analytical assessment. Like religion, vocation transcends the limits of reason alone.

In the brief space that follows, I want to try to sketch five themes that appear regularly throughout this book, and that all resonate with accounts of both religion and vocation that transcend narrow accounts of rationalism and instrumental reason. In each case, I suggest that the contributors to this volume have helped us to move beyond a typically "modern" account of religion and of vocation—one that is heavily beholden to the strictures of "pure reason" that was touted by Kant and his fellow Enlightenment-era thinkers.

Five themes in a new key

To help us understand the sense in which we are asked to move "beyond" our typical assumptions (without necessarily abandoning them entirely), I propose a musical metaphor. The authors of this book urge us to modulate the "key" in which we have typically considered the primary elements of vocational reflection and discernment. Perhaps we are moving a half-step higher or lower, moving from major to minor (or vice versa); the music is still recognizable, but it sounds different to our ears. We have discovered, through the chapters of this book, that "hearing vocation differently" means hearing it in a new key: one which takes full account of the emotional, spiritual, and embodied nature of our commitments to a particular vocational path and to a particular lifestance.

The five religious and vocational themes that we have inherited from the age of Enlightenment, and which these authors ask us to transcend, are: otherness, univocity, rationality, results, and activity. The five themes that this book has opened up—themes that lie beyond "bare reason" and that constitute the new key into which our authors have encouraged us to modulate—are: difference, multiplicity, the affects, process, and integration. As we become more and more attuned to this new music, we develop and cultivate capacities that allow us to hear vocation differently.

Meeting: beyond otherness to difference

When we first confront something that seems strange, foreign, and not like us, our tendency is to categorize it as "other." This is certainly not a surprising reaction; from our earliest days, we learn to differentiate ourselves from that which is not us. But we rarely think about the larger and longer-term effects of this label: when we name those whom we encounter as "other," we automatically and subconsciously rank them as lower than ourselves, inadequate, inferior. Even if these "others" seem demonstrably superior to us in some ways, we will soon be reminding ourselves that we prefer to be ourselves, and that we certainly do not want to be like them. As a number of our authors note, treating those we encounter as "other" tends to create or reinforce claims about who is wiser and who is more foolish, stronger and weaker, better and worse. All these tendencies are redoubled when the "otherness" is about religion: about those matters to which, according to the etymology of the word, we most thoroughly bind ourselves.

These claims of "otherness" are increasingly present on college and university campuses, made manifest by increasing diversity, uncertainty about one's own cultural location, and ever more polarized forms of political and civic discourse. Those who are not like us, and particularly when they are not like the majority population in a particular setting, are labeled "not": non-white, non-Christian, uneducated, uncommitted, unbelieving. We define people over against ourselves, and yet are somehow surprised when this leads to anxiety, defensiveness, and animosity—not only among those who are defined as "not," but also among those who have sought to do the defining.

A number of our authors have therefore employed the language of *difference* rather than that of *otherness*. At first, the distinction may seem an overly fine one; the two words would appear to have roughly the same range of reference. But while otherness is often employed in order to assert the superiority of one perspective over another, the language of difference is somewhat less definitive. It suggests that, while another person is clearly "not like me" in certain respects, this need not necessarily imply a kind of rank-ordering of various perspectives. I can permit, respect, and perhaps even appreciate the perspectives of my coworkers, neighbors, and friends—even though these perspectives may be very different from my own.

Of course, this perspective does not require us to avoid rendering judgments altogether. I may still be convinced of the superiority of, for example, my own religious perspective; after all, such convictions help to explain why I retain that particular perspective, rather than converting to the views of an acquaintance. But the fact that I am persuaded of the truth of my own religious, moral, or philosophical perspective does not necessitate that I denounce all others as wholly untenable. A number of contributors to this volume teach and study at institutions founded on religious claims that differ from their own: a Buddhist teaches at a Lutheran institution, a Jew at a largely Christian seminary, an atheist at a church-related college. If *otherness* were the only category for understanding these circumstances, such persons would be faced with the choice of promoting the institution above their own convictions, or proclaiming the superiority of their own perspective over against that of the institution they serve. A perspective focused on *difference* allows them to remain committed to their own traditions, without setting this in a hierarchical relationship to their institution, their colleagues, and their students.

Hearing: beyond univocity to multiplicity

As noted earlier, the language of vocation makes significant use of auditory metaphors. One result of usage, as noted throughout this book and in the two books that preceded it in this series, is the tendency to think of one's "call" as clear, focused, and definitive. Undergraduates in particular, when asked to describe their own callings, will often describe a dramatic moment of clarity, in which they became convinced that their one true purpose in life was to become a teacher, or a doctor, or a business leader. One voice has called out to me—be it the voice of God (whose authority seems absolute), or of my friends (who don't want me to end up in an uncool career), or of my parents (who are, after all, usually helping to pay the bills). Once an authority has spoken, the matter seems no longer up for debate.

These assumptions carry over into our judgments about the religious and philosophical perspectives that people use to organize their lives: their worldview or lifestance. We tend to assume that there are a relatively limited number of obvious possibilities, as reflected in the "religious preference" checkboxes on many documents, ranging from college interest surveys and passport forms to job applications and the US census. On such documents, one may find a list of "traditional" world religions—typically defined by the standards of the West—alongside (perhaps) options to designate oneself as an atheist or an agnostic. Sometimes, one can "prefer not to say."

But the perspective of the single voice—in vocation, religious belief, or any other major element of a person's identity—is misleading at best, and often illusory. We are, in fact, called by myriad voices, and some of these will at least seem to be at odds with one another. In their undergraduate years, most students will encounter a wide variety of perspectives, not all of which will fall into the predetermined categories that they have brought with them to college. Nor will their religious perspectives fit neatly into the little checkboxes on the forms: they may identify with a particular religious tradition but disagree strongly with some of its precepts; they may have worked out a fairly nuanced perspective on the world, which is not listed as one of the options; increasingly, they will have adopted a perspective that blends elements from a number of lifestances. In fact, a number of our authors suggest that most of us are "blended" adherents; we draw on a variety of traditions and weave them together in ways that differ from one another (even if we check the same box on the form). We are being asked to recognize the multiple perspectives that are part and parcel of our experience of the contemporary world, rather than to imagine that we are shaped only by a single, clearly demarcated voice.

Needless to say, this multiplicity of voices carries over into the work of vocational reflection and discernment. This work only rarely takes the form of a clear and definitive call; most undergraduates will find themselves being drawn in a variety of directions simultaneously, and some of their most important work will be to sort out these various voices, to prioritize them, and to follow some paths while leaving others to another day. When educators become more aware of the multiple and sometimes conflicting callings that their students experience, they are in a better position to help them navigate the undergraduate years.

Learning: beyond the rational to the affective

As we turn to this third theme, we come closest to (and farthest away from) the Enlightenment perspective described at the beginning of this epilogue—to the work of those who sought to set everything under the sway of pure reason. Admittedly, rational thought has led to enormous progress for the human race: scientific discoveries, cures for previously fatal diseases, successful treatment of mental illness, technological advances—all owe something to the setting aside of superstition and fear, allowing the human mind to follow matters through to their logical conclusions. Some people may rail against the excesses of rational thought; in many cases, however, they will do so while using their smartphones, sitting in an airport, and perhaps even having recently been freed of a dreaded disease by the workings of modern medicine. We live as we live today because of the triumph of reason.

Nevertheless, as many of our authors observe, one can be appreciative of what rational thought has accomplished without imagining that it fully sums up the significance of human life. The search for meaning and purpose demands attention to the affective domain: to our emotions and our intuitions, to anger and to laughter, to the ways that we allow our souls to be shaped by our encounter with new ideas, unfamiliar cultures, and different people. In the classroom, educators need to allow students to explore these elements of their experience, even as we help them to think more logically and to analyze matters more critically. In co-curricular activities on campus, leaders need to consider the degree to which students may be motivated by an experience of crass marginalization or of unexpected acceptance, of anger or of love. We cannot set such matters aside as "just a feeling," to which we briefly attend (and then get back to the "real" work of learning the course material). In fact, the affective is usually what motivates the rational: students learn best when they discover a passion for learning.

Many of the most important undergraduate experiences do not appear on any syllabus. In college, young people learn how to concentrate on an idea or an action for far longer, and much more intensely, than they had ever thought possible. They learn the importance of paying attention, and also the importance of allowing oneself to be distracted—temporarily to be sure, but also definitively—by experiences of laughter and lightness and love. The literature that they encounter, the case studies that they examine, the patients whom they observe while doing clinical rounds—all of these may lead students, perhaps for the first time, to take their own mortality seriously. They may come to rethink their assumptions and reorder their priorities through the realization that they will have a limited time on this earth. As Samuel Johnson remarked, such experiences concentrate the mind wonderfully; they motivate true vocational discernment, an exploration of the meaning of life, and an inquiry into one's deepest purpose.

Judging: beyond results to process

We live in a culture that is obsessed with results. Who won the game? How much money did you make? Did those people achieve their goals? What's the bottom line? Within such a culture, it can be very difficult to get people interested in even the most obvious of deeper questions: Yes, that team won the game (the contract, the election); but did they do so fairly? That company made the most money, but are we concerned that their products are used primarily for nefarious purposes? Those people reached their goals (money, popularity, possessions, adulation), but what did they have to give up in the process of doing so? At its worst, undergraduate life sums it all up in one nice, neat package: don't ask me to wonder whether I'm in the right major, or who really wrote my paper, or about the state of my mental health; just tell me my grade!

In the face of such cultural assumptions, it can be incredibly difficult to ask students to pay as much attention to the *process* as to the *result*. They need to learn to be critical thinkers, to express their doubts and uncertainties, and to admit that they are sometimes overwhelmed. But they are surrounded by a pernicious set of demands: go with the flow, exude confidence, never let them see your pain. The work of vocational reflection and discernment can offer an alternative. It acknowledges the likelihood of uncertainty and doubt, assumes that college life will sometimes feel overwhelming, and helps young people to recognize that giving attention to the *process* of discernment is at least as important, and perhaps more important, than is the need to achieve some kind of definitive result.

As the contributors to this volume point out, many of the world's longstanding religious and philosophical traditions have a great many resources to offer in this regard. They provide us with stories of individuals who experience doubt and uncertainty, and who sometimes have to let go of the fruits of their actions. These traditions offer words of wisdom—thought-provoking aphorisms, narrative vignettes, epic poetry—that draw us away, however briefly, from a culture that relies only on results and makes judgments based on speed, efficiency, and value for money. These traditions have known conflict, and have sometimes been threatened with extinction; yet they have endured, and indeed have prospered, because they have helped their adherents to remember that there are more important things than maximizing some hypothetical bottom line. If the wisdom of these traditions can be made more accessible to undergraduates, they will emerge from the college experience with a more profound sense of the meaning and purpose of their lives. They will be concerned not only about the maximization of positive results and the defeat of the competition, but also about the kinds of lives that they will live along the way.

Sending: beyond activity to integration

Where, then, does all this work lead us? What is the hoped-for outcome of the work that we promote in this book: the work of vocational discernment, of interreligious and interfaith dialogue, and of—in all these endeavors—a generous appreciation of difference? At one level, our authors are encouraging a certain kind of action: a change in the way that we educate and are educated, a willingness to engage the world in a different way, a new approach in the college classroom and across the entire campus. We want our students to venture forth, prepared not simply to do well themselves, but also to take action that will make the world a better place for their fellow human beings and for future generations. We want them to act.

But every chapter of this book makes a larger claim as well: the claim that mere activity is not enough. Students can be armed with the right words, the most effective strategies, and the practices that will bring about positive change; but they are not mere instruments, and human beings are more than the strategies they employ and the actions they carry out. Higher education seeks something greater, something larger: integrated human lives, people who face the world with a sense of wholeness and a commitment to personal and relational well-being. Such lives cultivate practices of attentiveness and humor, of solidarity and love. A well-integrated life means being able to tell one's own stories—and to do so authentically, and not just according to the conventions demanded by the wider culture. Students who recognize the importance of such integration are likely to pay attention to more than the new cognitive knowledge they are absorbing from their coursework; they also reflect on how their classes affect them emotionally, spiritually, and even physically. They seek to be exposed to a wide range of religious traditions and philosophical perspectives in which such matters have been the subject of deep reflection. Here, they find words of wisdom for living a life that is not merely successful, but truly fulfilling; not merely productive, but genuinely good.

By encouraging students to take on the work of vocational reflection and discernment, educators set them on a path to an integrated life. That path can be made broader and more rewarding when students are pointed to the full panoply of resources that are available, through centuries of thought and practice, from all over the world. They will stay on the path for much longer if they are reminded that the affective, spiritual, and ethical realms deserve their attention, along with the (also very important) rational and analytical aspects of their work. And they are most likely to pursue the path to its best possible conclusion if—ironically enough—they are able to stop focusing on the end goal, and simply to enjoy the journey. This is the kind of integrated life made possible by attention to the themes that are developed in this book.

Vocation beyond its limits

This book has sought to offer an account of vocation and calling that is not limited by a narrow focus on any one perspective—whether a specific religious tradition, a particular facet of life, or a narrowly defined account of what makes for a life well lived. When vocation is limited in these ways, it cannot achieve its full potential; but when released from these limitations, it can become a kind of pedagogy that helps us to embody the good and to live a fulfilled, fulfilling, and flourishing life. The previous section of this epilogue described five specific limits that can tend to make vocation into a thoroughly instrumental endeavor. In the higher education context, such an account makes vocation into a mere tool with which colleges can move their charges along, comfortably and rationally, from "high school graduate with no clear plan" to "gainfully employed college graduate." In this starkly limited account, the "call" comes from a single, specific, and familiar voice of authority; it asks the hearer to use deductive tools to make a reasonable and logical choice; and it leads inexorably to a single, specific, and measurable result: long-term commitment to a career (or at least to a job).

Most observers would recognize this as a mere parody of the rich and multilayered nature of vocation and calling. But on the other hand, vocation can and often *does* include these elements: the clearly discerned voice of a caller, a step-by-step process of discernment, a good fit in an appropriate career. Indeed, this language has found a foothold in many quarters of higher education precisely because it can boast of real success in helping students to navigate the undergraduate experience. But it would be a shame if vocation were seen as only this, as limited to the kind of instrumental service described here. For this reason, the contributors to this book—as well as the contributors to the two volumes that preceded it—have consistently emphasized that the language of vocation and calling invites us to transcend these limits. It can encourage students to listen to multiple voices (and not just the most familiar ones), to attend to the affective and spiritual dimensions of their lives (and not just its rational and calculative elements), and to consider the directions in which they are being drawn, not just with respect to their future employment, but in *all* facets of their lives.

Of course, the five elements described here are hardly the only limits imposed on the language of vocation. It is still sometimes defined in its medieval form as applying only to those considering a call to some form of ordained ministry. Or, even if the concept is allowed to reach a bit further, it is often considered to be applicable only within a specifically Christian perspective, or only to those who operate within a widely identified and carefully demarcated faith tradition. Moreover, in the undergraduate setting, vocational discernment can sometimes seem to demand a once-and-for-all decision, by means of which students determine the entire course of their lives. And in some quarters, the word *vocation* still retains a residue of its twentieth-century sojourn: "vocational education" as training for a trade.

Still, addressing these truncated accounts of vocation is a complicated matter, because—as was the case for the other limits described here—certain elements of these descriptions *can be true in some cases*. For some students, vocational reflection may indeed lead them to discern a call to ordained ministry. For even more students, it may involve a specifically Christian approach to wrestling with God's claim upon their lives. But for a larger group still, including those who do not operate from a Christian perspective, a calling still comes from outside oneself; its origins lie in a being or a power or a reality that transcends our ability to grasp it fully. For some students, vocational discernment will lead to a clear and long-lasting career path, even though a greater number are likely to encounter many unexpected twists and turns along the way, requiring further reflection on and discernment of one's calling. A few students, even if they complete an undergraduate degree, will in fact enter a trade; but the vast majority will enter some form of professional life, where the language of vocation and calling is of the utmost significance, and where they will encounter others who are discerning their own vocations—others whom they can serve as mentors and guides and fellow-travelers along the way. Moreover, regardless of their career trajectories, all undergraduates are faced with other questions about their futures: the shape of their domestic lives, the contours of their voluntary associations, and the extent of their civic engagement.

In short, while the work of vocational exploration and discernment functions well in some of its more traditional contexts, we have encountered a multitude of good reasons for extending its benefits to all students. Its importance transcends the boundaries erected by religious belief, cultural claims, socioeconomic structures, and political loyalties. It is a practice in which all people can be engaged; and although it can be appropriate at many different stages of life, it has a particular resonance in the undergraduate years, when students are facing deep questions of meaning, purpose, and identity—and when they are graced with the time and space that the work of discernment demands. Moreover, these are the years during which young people can develop habits and patterns of life that will allow them to engage in the ongoing work of vocational reflection that they will need to undertake throughout their lives.

We therefore close this volume with an appreciation for the language of vocation and calling. When freed of inappropriate limitations, and when adequately adapted to the multi-faith academy, it provides an important new element in the vocabulary of higher education. This cultural moment is the right time, and the undergraduate years provide the right place, for this work to occur. Opportunities for vocational reflection and discernment allow students to reflect on questions of deep purpose, to explore the many calls that they hear, and to discern their future directions in life. If higher education can leave its students with such a legacy, the work required to achieve this lofty goal will certainly have been worth it.

Index of Names

Index of Subjects